Employment Protection Legislation in Emerging Economies

Samir Amine
Universite du Quebec en Outaouais, Canada

A volume in the Advances in Finance, Accounting, and Economics (AFAE) Book Series

IGI Global
DISSEMINATOR OF KNOWLEDGE

Published in the United States of America by
IGI Global
Business Science Reference (an imprint of IGI Global)
701 E. Chocolate Avenue
Hershey PA, USA 17033
Tel: 717-533-8845
Fax: 717-533-8661
E-mail: cust@igi-global.com
Web site: http://www.igi-global.com

Library of Congress Cataloging-in-Publication Data

Names: Amine, Samir, editor.
Title: Employment protection legislation in emerging economies / Samir Amine, Editor.
Description: Hershey PA : Business Science Reference, 2018.
Identifiers: LCCN 2017028914| ISBN 9781522541349 (hardcover) | ISBN 9781522541356 (ebook)
Subjects: LCSH: Labor laws and legislation--Economic aspects--Developing countries. | Job security--Developing countries.
Classification: LCC K1705 .E477 2018 | DDC 344/.124012596--dc23 LC record available at https://lccn.loc.gov/2017028914

British Cataloguing in Publication Data
A Cataloguing in Publication record for this book is available from the British Library.

For electronic access to this publication, please contact: eresources@igi-global.com.

Advances in Finance, Accounting, and Economics (AFAE) Book Series

ISSN:2327-5677
EISSN:2327-5685

Editor-in-Chief: Ahmed Driouchi, Al Akhawayn University, Morocco

MISSION

In our changing economic and business environment, it is important to consider the financial changes occurring internationally as well as within individual organizations and business environments. Understanding these changes as well as the factors that influence them is crucial in preparing for our financial future and ensuring economic sustainability and growth.

The **Advances in Finance, Accounting, and Economics (AFAE)** book series aims to publish comprehensive and informative titles in all areas of economics and economic theory, finance, and accounting to assist in advancing the available knowledge and providing for further research development in these dynamic fields.

COVERAGE

- International Economics
- Accounting information systems
- E-finance
- Economics of Agriculture and Biotechnology
- Banking
- Economics of Migration and Spatial Mobility
- Managerial Accounting
- Macroeconomics
- International Trade
- Fiscal Policy

IGI Global is currently accepting manuscripts for publication within this series. To submit a proposal for a volume in this series, please contact our Acquisition Editors at Acquisitions@igi-global.com or visit: http://www.igi-global.com/publish/.

The Advances in Finance, Accounting, and Economics (AFAE) Book Series (ISSN 2327-5677) is published by IGI Global, 701 E. Chocolate Avenue, Hershey, PA 17033-1240, USA, www.igi-global.com. This series is composed of titles available for purchase individually; each title is edited to be contextually exclusive from any other title within the series. For pricing and ordering information please visit http://www.igi-global.com/book-series/advances-finance-accounting-economics/73685. Postmaster: Send all address changes to above address.

Titles in this Series

For a list of additional titles in this series, please visit:
https://www.igi-global.com/book-series/advances-finance-accounting-economics/73685

Economic Reforms for Global Competitiveness
Denis Ushakov (International College Suan Sunandha Rajabhat University, Thailand & Russian Academy of National Economy and Public Administration–South, Russia)
Business Science Reference • ©2018 • 363pp • H/C (ISBN: 9781522538561) • US $235.00

Alternative Decision-Making Models for Financial Portfolio Management Emerging ...
Narela Spaseski (International University of Sarajevo, Bosnia and Herzegovina)
Business Science Reference • ©2018 • 333pp • H/C (ISBN: 9781522532590) • US $175.00

Ranking Economic Performance and Efficiency in the Global Market Emerging Research ...
Benjamen Franklen Gussen (University of Southern Queensland, Australia & Australian Law and Economics Association, Australia)
Business Science Reference • ©2018 • 372pp • H/C (ISBN: 9781522527565) • US $195.00

Financial Entrepreneurship for Economic Growth in Emerging Nations
Atsede Woldie (University of South Wales, UK) and Brychan Thomas (University of South Wales, UK)
Business Science Reference • ©2018 • 304pp • H/C (ISBN: 9781522527008) • US $225.00

Technological Integration as a Catalyst for Industrial Development and Economic Growth
Bryan Christiansen (PryMarke, LLC, USA) and Ülkü Yüksel (The University of Sydney Business School, Australia)
Business Science Reference • ©2017 • 272pp • H/C (ISBN: 9781522523192) • US $185.00

Handbook of Research on Economic, Financial, and Industrial Impacts on Infrastructure ...
Ramesh Chandra Das (Katwa College, India)
Business Science Reference • ©2017 • 466pp • H/C (ISBN: 9781522523611) • US $230.00

For an enitre list of titles in this series, please visit:
https://www.igi-global.com/book-series/advances-finance-accounting-economics/73685

IGI Global
DISSEMINATOR OF KNOWLEDGE

701 East Chocolate Avenue, Hershey, PA 17033, USA
Tel: 717-533-8845 x100 • Fax: 717-533-8661
E-Mail: cust@igi-global.com • www.igi-global.com

Table of Contents

Detailed Table of Contents

This chapter presents an inventory of the employment protection legislation (EPL) in France. As shown by the OECD indicators, legal provisions have met with an overall stability since the 1980s, despite some reforms weighing in favor of flexibility. Simultaneously, France has been faced with a high rate of unemployment, especially long-term unemployment, as well as with a phenomenon of dualization of its job market. Precariousness remains limited to a part of workers whose situation tends, however, to worsen. This twofold observation leads us to the conclusion that current employment protection is relatively powerless, with a bleak future. Therefore, an adaptation to current circumstances is required, such adaptation being coupled with an improvement of the training system. Flexicurity is the direction that seems unavoidable in order to guide future reforms in France.

With emerging economies facing significant lags in the use of information technology to improve their productivity and compete with industrialized economies, the availability of relatively lower-cost labor in the emerging economies is considered a powerful asset that can compensate for their technological disadvantage. However, regulating the labor market often proves to be rather challenging as it is important that a balance be struck between protecting workers and stimulating economic growth. This chapter analyzes the literature on labor market regulations in the emerging economies to observe that the trade-off between employment protection legislation (EPL), job creation, productivity, and innovation often cited in the literature is not conclusive.

Occupational health and safety (OHS) is an important aspect of the labour protection field. This chapter compares OHS legal regimes of China and EU. Comprehensive workplace health and safety legislations of the two systems are described, and the different aspects, including for example, legislative aim, the legislation structure, general obligation, OHS insurance, moral harassment, law enforcement, etc., are detailed. Based on the analysis, conclusions are made and policy recommendations from both legislation aspect and enforcement aspect are provided.

Throughout history, Argentina has undergone a series of profound economic variations, which, as such, have produced a strong impact on labor legislation and social security. The access key in Argentina to labour law protection is the existence of a relationship of dependence. This turns to be an inclusive and exclusive condition because it divides strictly the labour market and the labour force inherent in two different areas, namely, the subordinate workers (who are included in the labour protection system) and the rest of the employees, including among the latest, the ones involved in non-typical forms of employment contracts. For such purposes, it is important to analyze different periods of time, selecting the more significant ones to see the evolution of Argentinean labour legislation. It is also relevant to describe the consequences caused by economic and political variations on collective bargaining in order to understand the composition of the actual labour force in Argentina.

regulate matters such as job-retention and work creation (for example, by activating the work force and through the creation of public works programmes), and if so, does the present statutory and policy framework address this expectation adequately? 3) To what extent is the legislation compliant with international standards and best practices, and are there fresh approaches to address the present malaise, perhaps emanating from regional standards and experiences? 4) Finally, are there any best practices or lessons learned through the South African experience that should influence developments in other emerging economies?

Chapter 8

Happy Siphambe, University of Botswana, Botswana
Mavis Kolobe, University of Botswana, Botswana
Itumeleng Primrose Oageng, University of Botswana, Botswana

Botswana has experienced phenomenon economic growth and structural transformation since independence. Despite the achievement in terms of economic growth, the country has had challenges with unemployment averaging 20% and being quite high for youth. The labour laws have changed over time to conform to international standards. The current changes have, however, not been positive in terms of labour relations with the transition from consultative system to collective bargaining almost forestalled. The labour movement has been quite weak. The labour laws have had mixed impact on employment and the labour market and employment creation. The chapter makes key recommendations on how Botswana's labour environment can be transformed based on international experience. Key recommendations are towards employment creation and improving the social dialogue space, especially for labour as the weaker party. This should go a long way in increasing labour productivity and dealing with the persistent problem of poor work ethic.

Chapter 9

Moses Adesola Adebisi, University of Ilorin, Nigeria

Social protection represents part of the global agenda of the International Labour Organization in its concerted attempt to improve and promote global labour standards, labour rights as human rights, and reduce poverty. The situation of African countries is precarious given the poor state of their economies, poor national incomes, and the widespread state of poverty. In addition, most African countries south of the Sahara have poor databases on vital statistics, security insecurity, mono-cultural economies, and the failure to effectively entrench governance and democratic institutions and

Preface

Although many Western labor market experts believed that a consensus was emerging in the mid-2000s around an effective and efficient remedy (while controlling fiscal deficits and therefore the national debt) against persistent unemployment, a real challenge for, the industrialized countries (and more symptomatically of the European countries) since the end of the glorious thirties (see Figure 1), the current international crisis seems to complicate matters.

Indeed, the remarkable success of the so-called "flexicurity" policies in several northern European countries (the "Danish model" was the most mentioned) seemed to open a new way to reduce unemployment rates, on the one hand, and to avoid creating insecurity and working poor, on the other.

Employment policies developed in northern Europe showed remarkable performances in terms of low unemployment rates between 1993 (end of the 1992-93 monetary crisis) and 2008 (the beginning of the financial and then economic crisis), while continental European countries such as France, Belgium and Germany had high and relatively stable unemployment rates. This, while reducing their public debts for a comparable economic growth (see Figure 1).

Recent developments in unemployment in the western world have led to the concept of flexicurity (which is seen as achieving both the objectives of full employment and quality of employment) which is at the heart of the European strategy for Employment to increase the employment rate by increasing incentives to work. However, the countries that implemented such a "flexi-safe" policy have experienced rising unemployment rates since 2008, alongside high employment rates.

In general, the debate on unemployment and wage inequality leads to the assumption of that job security (even in its weak understanding of flexicurity) and full employment is incompatible. This would lead for the years to come, to the societal and ethical question as to whether it is better for a country to have many poor workers without unemployment or a large number of unemployed people poor workers.

Figure 1. Unemployment in some developed countries, total (% of total labor force) from 1991 to 2016
Source: International Labour Organization, ILOSTAT database.

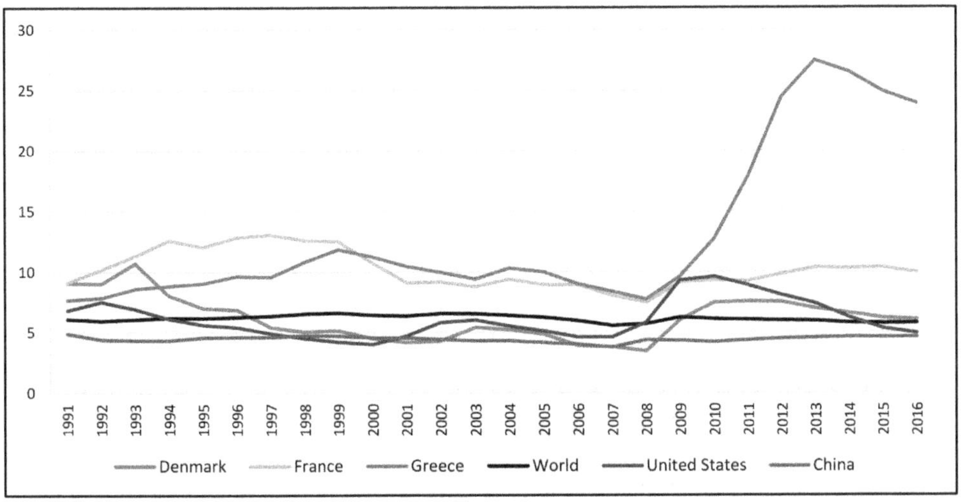

**For a more accurate representation see the electronic version.*

In this perspective, Esping-Andersen (2007) proposes a political, ideological and cultural analysis to highlight a country's poor performance in terms of unemployment. In other words, Esping-Andersen (2007) proposes a relevant typology to characterize the major types of employment policies pursued by industrialized countries in their struggle to fight unemployment. More concretely, the type of employment policy depends strongly on the type of welfare state.

Indeed, according to Esping-Andersen (2007), Liberal-dominated countries classified as "Liberal Welfare State" practice liberal employment policies (i.e., sparingly: we must not intervene too much in markets so as not to create distortions); those whose welfare states are labeled "Conservative Corporatists" practice much more intrusive employment policies in the economy; and finally, Socio-Democrats are trying to find an intermediate path: to intervene heavily in the labor market to help those who are excluded via high, progressive, proportional salary allowances and financed mainly by tax but to leave enough flexibility to prevent the market mechanisms from getting in the way. Thus, drawing on this typology, we can form three groups of countries:

- **Liberal Welfare State:** In this group are three large countries with a strong liberal tradition: the United States, Canada and the United Kingdom. Their "welfare states" are characterized by modest tax-financed transfers. From a policy standpoint, the safety of workers is low (low job protection, low replacement incomes, etc.) and the flexibility of the labor market is high (high mobility of workers, simple and inexpensive lay-off procedures). The development of precariousness is also strong, many "hardworking" workers do not earn enough to make ends meet.

- **Conservative Corporatists:** Group whose employment policies are considered "safe" and social system is based on the social contributions of the workers. By way of example, three countries are included in this group: Germany, France and Italy for their welfare state system, which is predominantly Bismarck; i.e. essentially basing on insurance and impacting wage costs and introducing strong barriers to the free functioning of the labor market that would be responsible for persisting unemployment at a high level.
- **Socio-Democrats:** We chose to place here the Scandinavian countries that are the precursors in flexicurity (with the Netherlands). European studies on employment, quality of life and poverty rates have, in most cases, underscored the remarkable performance of the Scandinavian countries.

Analyzing the labor market in the three groups, the dominant economic theory considers that: rigidities introduced by state intervention measures such as minimum wage, unemployment benefits...create disincentives to work, traps to inactivity and thus generate both high and persistent unemployment rates. However, is unemployment the worst of the plagues of today's societies?

If the flexibilization of the labor market targeted is pursued at the expense of workers' peacefulness, the society is on the brink of becoming more and more anxiogenic to finally produce, in the long run, nocuous effects on the collective wellbeing, and most certainly on economic results, for doubt and uncertainty can disturb market mechanisms more than most public policies, without consideration for social unrests that policies heavily focused on competition and individuals can generate.

We are not there yet, but it is useful to start pondering about the choice of our societies for the future, without necessarily pretending that unemployment is less damaging than "flexiprecarity", at least ask ourselves about the consequences on social welfare and on development of inequalities as we are weakening the welfare states which have been progressively put in place since 1945 with the aim of fighting inequality, poverty and social unrests.

In this context, most of the countries with either relatively high unemployment rates or large cross-sector pay gaps have initiated reform processes aimed at bringing more flexibility to their labor market regulation. Among the laws related to the labor market and that have been reformed, we note the employment protection legislation (EPL).

From this perspective, under the recommendations of the OECD, the World Bank and the IMF, more rigid economies have started a reform process aimed at increasing the flexibility of the labor market and reducing persistent inequalities, so questioning the rigid nature of EPL.

Before discussing the impact of EPL on the performance of the labor market, it is important to recall the OECD definition of EPL which we believe to be the most complete in comparison with other definitions (For example, the ILO approach).

The OECD EPL covers all legislative provisions that impose costs on employers when they wish to make labor adjustments (OECD, 2014). These provisions are grouped into three categories. There is at first, the rules governing the protection of regular workers in the event of individual dismissals. Then, the second component is the regulation of temporary contracts. The latter is divided into two categories: fixed-term contracts and temporary contracts. For this category, OECD estimates, for example, the maximum number of successive fixed-term contracts that can make a firm and the types of jobs that temporary contracts are allowed (OECD, 2014). Finally, the third category represents obligations relating to collective redundancies. To evaluate this component, the OECD based its analysis in particular on the definition of collective redundancy, on the obligations of additional notifications to individual dismissals and on the specific costs for the employer for this type of dismissal (OECD, 2014).

In the literature, several studies examine the effects and the analysis models of EPL (OECD and International Labor Organization). However, few of them seem to emphasize the need for improvement of these models to reflect precisely the legal reality of each country.

Abundant researches have attempted to measure the impact of EPL on various economic indicators such as unemployment, the employment rate, mobility of labor, productivity, innovation, etc.

For example, using an empirical study, Di Tella and McCulloch (2005) show that countries with more flexible labor market have a higher employment rate. In the same way, Blanchard and Wolfers (2000), relying on data from 20 OECD countries, stress that a highly protective EPL may make it difficult adjustment of an economy following a macroeconomic shock. In addition, Boeri and Jimeno (2005) show, by studying the case of Italy, particularly that EPL would reduce hiring but would not affect job growth thereof. Millán et al. (2013) get the same conclusions and show that a strict EPL result in a low-level redundancy, reducing mobility labor that can affect productivity growth. In this direction, Muller and Berger (2013) study the EPL effect on the total labor productivity of an economy. They show that when the rigor on individual dismissals increased by 1 point, total labor productivity increases of 0,22.

Contrary to these studies and books have focused only on developed countries, we are going to focus this book on the emerging economies whose labor market is often characterized by a dualism that makes the efficiency of EPL less obvious. Moreover, the labor market in emerging countries is also experiencing transitions and structural changes in the composition of the workforce. It would then be interesting to analyze how the reforms and laws governing the protection of employment evolve in this context.

As in developed countries, emerging economies also suffer from a relatively high unemployment rates and an increase in inequalities to the detriment of young people and less skilled workers (see Figure 2). Even if the institutional and legislative framework differs from one country to another, we study in this book the protection of employment in countries such as China, Mexico, Argentina, Brazil and South-Africa.

To better contextualize our analysis, we deemed useful to provide the evolution of the unemployment rate from 1991 to 2016 in the countries covered by this study. Figure 2 makes it possible to accompany and to facilitate the reading and the analyze of the chapters.

Generally, this book aims to provide an analytical and critical reading of the state of knowledge on legislation relating to employment protection, in some developing economies, and its impacts on unemployment, jobs creation, productivity and more generally efficiency of the labor market.

Figure 2. Unemployment in the emerging and developing countries studied in this book, total (% of total labor force) from 1991 to 2016
Source: International Labour Organization, ILOSTAT database.

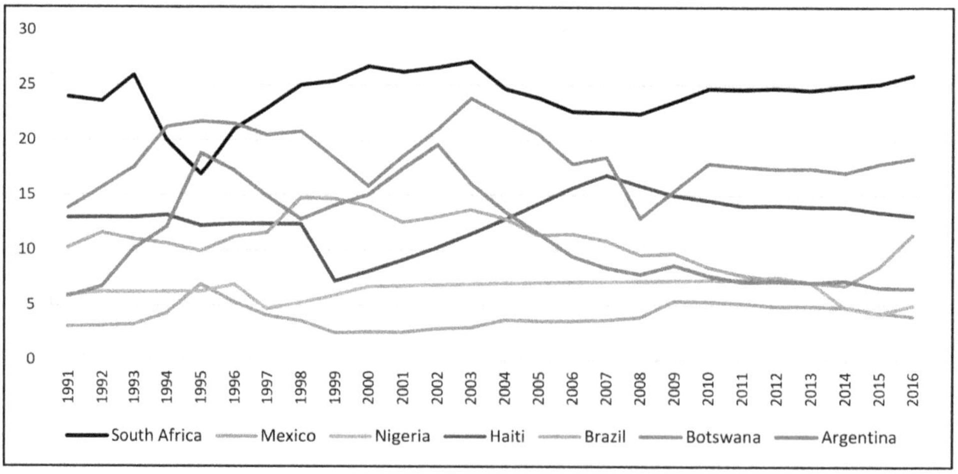

**For a more accurate representation see the electronic version.*

We are very aware that in some cases the analysis may appear incomplete or not very thorough because of a lack of data on EPL in developing countries. Nevertheless, in this case, we consider that even a descriptive approach can be useful to account for the labor market situation in such countries.

Concerning the target audience, it is expected that this book will be a reference book for academics, institutions and organizations concerned with labor market, private sector and non-governmental organizations. This audience will enjoy a rich analysis performed on recent data, assessments and policy proposals in this book.

We begin the book with a first chapter on the case of France. This chapter will help the readers not too accustomed to the topic to understand the mechanisms that govern the protection of workers in a developed economy. The choice of France is not insignificant. This country is considered to be rigid in terms of labor market legislation. The French model has been exported to other countries. The second chapter is devoted to the review of the literature on the effects of EPL in emerging economies. This chapter makes it possible to compare the results obtained in this book with the results already highlighted in the literature. The third chapter of the study focuses on China, while the fourth chapter analyzes the case of Argentina. The Mexican labor market is the subject of the fifth chapter. We then move on to the African continent to study in Chapter 6 the case of South Africa. In the same context, Chapters 7 and 8 present studies on Botswana and Nigeria, respectively. We finish this book with a descriptive study on Haiti in Chapter 9.

In the first chapter, "An Inventory of Employment Protection Legislation in France," the author, Hervé Charmettant, using OECD data, examines employment situation in France along with its evolution since the 1980s. His primary focus are the two main issues that afflict the labor market in France (unemployment and a phenomenon of dualization). Likewise, the author draws reform (flexicurity) directions of employment protection in France in order to meet the current and future diagnosis of the labor market issues in France.

Then we begin our analysis of the emerging economies in the second chapter, "Employment Protection Legislation in Emerging Economies: A Critical Review of the Literature." Samir Amine and Wilner Predelus consider that a well-documented literature on the flexibilization of the labor market in the developed economies must cover three areas where EPL has been the cause for policy concerns: employment, productivity and innovation. In other words, the authors analyze the literature on the effects of labor market regulations in emerging economies (namely China, India, Brazil and sub-Saharan Africa) and find that the trade-off between EPL and employment is not clearly established. They further show that the widespread debate over the effects of EPL on innovation and productivity growth is still ongoing as the findings has, so far, been inconclusive.

The third chapter, "Regulating Occupational Health and Safety in The European Union and China: From a Comparative Law Perspective," compares two systems (Work Safety Law and Occupational Disease Prevention Law) to see how the Chinese system may benefit from the EU one. The aim of the comparison is to investigate whether what convergences and divergences exist between the EU system and the Chinese system. In this framework, Kai Liu shows that the causes of workplace incidents are typically complex and may involve a series of events, which are of varying probabilities. Under the prescriptive approach, to cover as many situations as possible, the regulator must correspondingly write as many rules or standards as possible. However, with the introduction of general obligation, the regulator does not need to provide rules to cover all the situations.

In a bid to understand the composition of the actual labor force in Argentina, Andrea Isabel Franconi analyses the consequences of economic and political variations on collective bargaining. Indeed, the fourth chapter "Economic Variations and Their Impact on Labor Legislation Throughout History in Argentina" shows how unions have acquired a high level of importance in Argentina's working relationship system due to the signing of collective labor agreements. In other words, this chapter analyzes the individual labor law and the collective labor relationships in order to understand the role of economic variations in the creation of Labor Legislation in Argentina.

In the same context, José Ernesto Rangel Delgado and Antonina Ivanova Boncheva explore in the fifth chapter, "Labor Protection in Mexico: Recent Reforms and Future Challenges," the recent developments in the Mexican labor market and the labor protection normativity during the post-crisis period. They discuss the impacts of the crisis on Mexican economy and the policy responses of the country to economic and financial effects. In conclusion, they consider that international labor rights are recognized in Mexican law. However, important legal ambiguities exist about collective bargaining and many rights are not respected in practice.

Ina similar context, the sixth chapter, developed by Roberta Ferme Sivolella, aims to analyze the evolution of the employment regulation in Brazil. The author shows that in the current political, economic and social crisis scenario, the protection system, historically valid and justified by the intense social inequalities is questioned, trying to deal with the urgencies of a big economic downturn, without trust of local and international investors in internal market.

In the seventh chapter, "Employment Protection in South Africa: An Analysis of Recent Labor and Social Security Legislative and Policy Developments," Avinash Govindjee studies the situation of the labor market in South Africa by providing a detailed critique of the applicable legislative and policy framework, including the most recent labor and social security statutory developments (such as the regulation of fixed-term employment contracts and the proposed introduction of return-to-work arrangements). In other words, this chapter juxtaposes the South African legislative approach with the existing realities of poverty, inequality and unemployment.

In the same African context, Happy Siphambe, Mavis Kolobe, and Itumeleng Oageng consider, in the framework of the eighth chapter, "Employment Protection Legislation and Unemployment in Botswana," that the current changes in the labor laws have not been positive in terms of labor relations, with the transition from consultative system to collective bargaining almost forestalled. They make key recommendations on how Botswana's labor environment can be transformed based on international experience.

In the same register, the ninth chapter, developed by Moses Adesola Adebisi, tries to analyze and to understand how social protection and social security policies are faced with the burden of responsibility and sustainability. The author considers that the necessity of reform: governance, legislative, economic diversification, power sector, and the need to meet up with international best practices represent the developmental dilemma before African countries.

The author focuses his analysis on the case of Nigeria.

We conclude this chapter by a descriptive analysis of the case of Haiti. Indeed, the last chapter, "Employment Protection Legislation in Haiti: An Overview," analyzes the provisions of the Haitian Labor Law, as there are related to job security, to observe a flexible structure that rather benefits employers. Samir Amine and Wilner Predelus consider that the situation is even more fragile for workers since the Haitian Labor Legislation is based on the very assumption that employers and workers are on the same footing when it comes to industrial relations, while historic facts do not support such an assumption.

REFERENCES

Blanchard, O., & Wolfers, J. (2000). The Role of Shocks and Institutions in the Rise of European Unemployment: The Aggregate Evidence. *Economic Journal (London)*, *110*(462), 1–33. doi:10.1111/1468-0297.00518

Boeri, T., & Jimeno, J. (2005). The Effects of Employment Protection: Learning from Variable Enforcement. *European Economic Review*, *49*(8), 2057–2077. doi:10.1016/j.euroecorev.2004.09.013

Esping-Andersen, G. (2007). *Les trois mondes de l'Etat-providence; essai sur le capitalisme moderne*. Paris: PUF. doi:10.3917/puf.espin.2007.01

Millán, A., Millán, J. M., Román, C., & Van Stel, A. (2013). How does employment protection legislation influence hiring and firing decisions by the smallest firms? *Economics Letters*, *121*(3), 444–448. doi:10.1016/j.econlet.2013.09.021

Muller, L., & Berger, D. P. (2013). The Impact of a Country's Employment Protection Legislation on its Economic Prosperity. *International Journal of Humanities and Social Science*, *3*(12), 1–13.

OECD. (2014). *Les indicateurs de l'OCDE sur la protection de l'emploi*. Retrieved from http://www.oecd.org/fr/emploi/emp/lesindicateursdelocdesurlaprotectiondelemploi.htm

Chapter 1
An Inventory of Employment Protection Legislation in France:
A Preserved Past Primarily but an Uncertain Future

Hervé Charmettant
Université Grenoble Alpes (UGA), France

ABSTRACT

This chapter presents an inventory of the employment protection legislation (EPL) in France. As shown by the OECD indicators, legal provisions have met with an overall stability since the 1980s, despite some reforms weighing in favor of flexibility. Simultaneously, France has been faced with a high rate of unemployment, especially long-term unemployment, as well as with a phenomenon of dualization of its job market. Precariousness remains limited to a part of workers whose situation tends, however, to worsen. This twofold observation leads us to the conclusion that current employment protection is relatively powerless, with a bleak future. Therefore, an adaptation to current circumstances is required, such adaptation being coupled with an improvement of the training system. Flexicurity is the direction that seems unavoidable in order to guide future reforms in France.

DOI: 10.4018/978-1-5225-4134-9.ch001

INTRODUCTION

The OECD (Organization for Economic Cooperation and Development) has the merit of having contributed to a thorough analysis of the links between employment legal regulation and the employment situation according to countries. The results of its work have resulted in regular publications, which include the famous annual report on "Employment Outlook". This organization is the source of a quantitative indicator of the legal provisions on employment protection since the beginning of the 1980s until today, an indicator known as EPL (Employment Protection Legislation) indicator. Those very instructive data enable to follow the evolution of this regulation since the mid-1980s until today in a large number of countries. The OECD defines employment protection as "the whole set of rules that governs the hiring and above all, the redundancy of employees" (OECD, 2016, p.145). The principles of its construction will be further seen in details.

The World Bank initiated a similar draft for a quantitative measure of regulation at the beginning of the 2000s, with extending such drafts to other areas than the employment protection one. These are the indicators "Doing Business" that deal with areas such as business creation, implementation of contracts etc. (World Bank, 2017). Initially, those plans have delivered a liberal speech that advocated market deregulation, in line with the dominant ideology that has prevailed in major international organizations since the 1980s. Therefore, the OECD put the emphasis on an "employment strategy" that pointed out all the rigidities related to employment protection, as it considered such rigidities as the cause of the low growth of employment as well as the cause of unemployment. It must be recognized that the OECD has widely amended its speech since the mid-2000s. The 2006 report on "Employment Outlook" marks a turning point with a redefinition of this "employment strategy" in a much less liberal way (OECD, 2006).

Today, the analysis carried out by the OECD concludes that there is no clear link between the LPE degree of rigidity and unemployment rate. However, such rigidity would be harmful to flows and to mobility in the labor market, which would put a brake on innovation and on the necessary restructuring of sectoral activities. The EPL configuration, and in particular, the protection gap between permanent contracts and temporary ones, would be involved in the dualization of the labor market, that is to say the separation into two categories of unequally treated workers. As to structural reforms that must be implemented, the OECD warns against the social cost of certain measures aiming to flexibilize employment, with the consequence of making them less efficient to reach the objective of improving the functioning of labor market. Since 2006, as said earlier, this organization has very clearly reassessed its recommendations in favor of flexicurity. It is a model of regulation of labor market that may be initially found in the countries of Northern Europe, the leader figure of which is Denmark. That is clearly meant by the following statements "Authorities who are responsible for public action must imperatively search for the right balance between the need to protect employees and the need to allow an efficient allocation of human resources" (OECD, 2013, p.71). "Security" for workers and "flexibility" for employers are so, the ingredients of a carefully thought out employment protection according to the OECD.

It is from this perspective that we shall examine the French situation. We will wonder where the situation is concerning the EPL and whether its rigidity is blatant in comparison with other countries. We will question too, the sense of its evolution over time. To answer these questions, we will base our arguments on the data provided by the OECD of course, but without being satisfied with those data alone. We will go a little bit into the details of the legal provisions and of their evolution over the last 30 years. It will allow in particular, correcting the often-put forward flaw of this OECD EPL indicator, because such indicator is blind as to the effectiveness of regulations, that is to say their concrete application.

The answers to these initial questions will be linked with a thorough diagnosis of employment situation in France and of its main evolutions over the same period since the 1980s. In particular, we will present the two main ills that afflict labor market in France, these ills being a mass unemployment and a phenomenon of dualization the just evaluation of which we will try to make. We shall see then, whether the suspicions about the negative impacts of the LPE on labor market are valid in the French case. We will try too, to look to the future that is taking shape, through the evolutions of company practices that can be expected and through major economic and social trends. This study will allow us to face the question of how employment protection will be impacted by those mutations.

The last part of this chapter will then draw reform directions of employment protection in France in order to meet the current and future diagnosis of the labor market ills in France. Flexicurity will be the key term by which we will envisage possible reforms, through coming back to some recent reforms that are already exploring this direction.

So, we will have dealt with the whole issue so as to clarify, we hope so, this important issue of the importance of adapting the legal framework of employment protection to circumstances, which is our main object of reflection but also the training system and social protections, a subject we'll talk about more briefly. France has everything to win in such perspective.

BACKGROUND

The issue we will deal with is very up to date with our actuality. Emmanuel Macron, the new president who was elected in 2017, has made the reform of labor law a priority number one in his diary. Such reform should continue the movement that was initiated in 2015 through the law he has himself made as Economy Minister at that time, a law that aimed at "growth, activity and equality of economic opportunity" according to its official title. This "Macron law" was followed in 2016 by the "labor law" said "El Khomri law" named after the Minister of Labor at the time. These two laws, especially the latter one, have led to tussles between the government and most trade unions with the support of the most to the left political parties.

The paradox is that two opposing speeches on this issue of employment regulation are simultaneously made in France. The one that, among others, companies carry through the voice of their union, the Medef (Mouvement des entreprises de France), denounces a France paralyzed by a regulatory straightjacket that would prevent job creation and would block entrepreneurial initiatives. Jean Tirole, the recent French Nobel Prize in Economics develops such a point of view in his latest book (2016) with other eminent economists and lawyers. On the contrary, the protesting unions and many voices of politicians on the left, denounce an excessive regulation of labor market in France, a regulation that would have been influenced by the liberal Anglo-Saxon model. Very authorized voices express themselves in that direction, for example, the renowned French economist, Thomas Piketty (2016), on the side also of equally eminent colleagues and jurists.

This chapter has a modest ambition, although..., the ambition of getting a glimpse of the state of employment protection and of the links that can be reasonably created with the employment situation in France. We are not fooled by the fact that it is impossible to remain neutral in this area and to create a consensus. At the very least, we have made the choice to stick to a pragmatic premise rather than to develop an ideological reading. We do hope that the readers will be sensitive to this intention, even if they do not agree on everything.

THE PROTECTION OF EMPLOYMENT IN FRANCE: ESSENTIAL PRESERVES... UNTIL NOW

Employment Guarantees Largely Maintained, Contrary to the General Trend

The inventory of employment protection in France can be first obtained from the EPL indicators, as the OECD calculates them. Despite the limitations that the OECD itself acknowledges about such indicators and the fact that these limitations have led to new versions of those indicators and to the stopping of the calculation of a global indicator (OECD, 2006), this first approach is highly instructive. Table 1 iterates the figures of the two indicators used in France, the first with respect to permanent jobs (EPRC) and the second concerning temporary jobs (EPT).

A certain degree of stability of both indicators is evident, although it is down slightly for the first and up for the second between 1985 and 2013. Despite this virtual status quo, France, which was initially situated in the middle of a group of twenty countries according to the indicators at our disposal for both dates, has improved its ranking and moved into a top position, indicating that France is one of the countries in which the EPL is the most inflexible. Implicitly, it is the general trend of deregulation in most other countries that emerges from this evolution of the relative position of France. Thus, over the same period, some countries, such as Greece, Spain and Finland, ranked behind France with respect to the severity of the EPL for permanent contracts. This is even more obvious for temporary contracts as France is currently ranked first based on this indicator. The EPT value has, for example, been divided into four segments in Germany. This French peculiarity has an impact on the establishing of jobs in its territory in a harsh international competitive environment. Accordingly, the OECD indicators support the observation of the preservation of the level of employment protection since the 1980s in France. We are going to do it by taking back for the three dimensions the EPL indicator distinguishes, the rules that form its base and the principal evolutions that occurred during this period:

- **Permanent Contracts:** The Labor Code states, in its 2008 rewriting, that the CDI (permanent contract) is "the normal and general form of the work relationship" (art. 1221-2). The termination of the CDI through redundancy conforms to the strict formalism regarding deadlines and employee information procedures. Above all, this termination is determined by the existence of a "real and genuine cause," and it has been this way since the passing of a

Table 1.

	1985		2013	
	Figure	**Rank**	**Figure**	**Rank**
EPRC v1	2.59	9th	2.38	6th
EPT v1	3.06	10th	3.63	1st

Source: OECD.

Note: These indicators are presented in their "version 1" so that comparisons can be made in time.

1973 law. The administrative authorization to which any redundancy is subordinate was applied only between 1975 and 1986. The examination of the real and serious nature of the redundancy is the source of heavy litigation in the labor court, a jurisdiction specializing in the settlement of individual disputes between employees and employers, particularly with respect to redundancies for personal reasons. Heavy fines accompany such litigation if the redundancy is considered abusive. A recent 2015 law, the Macron law, created a fee schedule of the compensation payable in the event of abusive redundancy, the absolute limit of such compensation being an agenda item of the labor reform bills of the present French President, Emmanuel Macron (the Economy Minister when the law was passed).

An economic lay-off, however, generates lower litigation, which can be explained by the fact that it more often accompanies collective lay-offs with particular guarantees (Key: infra). The August 2016 labor law, i.e., the "El Khomri law", has made clear the economic difficulties that companies can induce by linking such difficulties with a turnover decrease, cash issues or a deterioration in operating results, with such observations being conducted over several months. These clarifications aim to avoid the litigation dealing with the reality of the economic reason. Additionally, this law has ratified the "technical changes" as another acceptable relevant document as well as "any company reorganization that is necessary for the safeguarding of its competitiveness" thus widening even further the use of economic justifications.

Among the other protection rules of permanent contracts is the principle of the statuary dismissal compensation, which, while far from exorbitant, can be increased contractually or through collective agreement. Two laws reformed these rules in 2008 in a direction favorable to employees who are victims of a lay-off, specifically, the requiring only one year of service to be entitled to compensation and the doubling of the legal minimum amount. Furthermore, there is a limitation regarding the test period, which varies according to the level of qualification. This test period lasts from two to four months, a period renewed once since 2008. This limitation is considered "reasonable" regarding the number 158 OIT convention. Conversely, a 2006 attempt failed to evade this limitation through special contracts, namely CNE and CPE, aimed to extend the employer's right to dismiss beyond all real and serious reason over a two-year period.

An important innovation was the creation of "contractual termination" by a 2008 law, named "law of modernization of the labor market", as an alternative to redundancy as well as to resignation. The aim of this legal provision is a separation by mutual consent between the employee and his employer, which leads to the same consequences as an economic layoff, i.e., right to dismissal compensation and unemployment benefits. Its approval by the administrative authority significantly reduces potential litigation, thus leaving no doubt that this legal securing of contractual termination is an undeniable asset and a critical part of the success of the law.

- **The Particular Rules of Mass Layoffs:** Special regulations are applied in all developed countries in the case of a layoff of a significant number of employees, given the consequences of such a layoff, particularly at the local level. In France, mass layoffs lead to a formal consultation procedure with staff representatives and to the development of special measures by the employer. These measures aim at reducing the number of layoffs and at reducing the consequences of those layoffs for those affected and for the local economy. These measures form what is called a "job saving plan" (PSE in French), the content of which differs according to the size of the firm.

Since 1993, these new regulations have been enacted with an emphasis on increasing the employer's responsibilities to prevent planned state funded early retirement. These PSEs must establish measures that limit the number of jobs loss, i.e., reorganization and part-time work or partial unemployment, and prevent compulsory redundancies, i.e., internal or external redeployment and assistance towards entrepreneurship. Furthermore, in the case of site closures and large companies, there has been a plan since 2014 to enhance PSE measures in the local economy and seek a new investor. However, the implementation of the measures that constitute the PSE are subject to threatening control.

The social accountability of companies following their decision to lay off a substantial number of employees has increased over time, as evidenced by various debates and notorious cases over time. For example, Michelin, the tire manufacturer, announced in 1999 the cutting of several thousands of jobs while simultaneously announcing record profits. This is a case in which "relevant the stock exchange activities", the layoffs become part of the restructuring of a financially sound company. However, the legal provisions to prevent such consequences put in place have been ineffective. Another media relayed event in 2013 was the closing of the Florange site where several Arcelor-Mittal steelmaker blast furnaces were situated even though aid had been granted to the company. A 2014 law, struck down in part, has compelled employers in similar cases to actively seek a buyer of the site and, in some cases, to repay the state grants received by the company.

A major source of risk, with respect to the outcome of the proceedings, resulted from the judicialization of conflicts following mass layoffs where compliance with the procedure and the content of the PSE was being contested in ordinary courts. The PSE could be canceled for failure to comply with the planned measures, whereby control of a proportion of the means is used to fit the economic size of the company or of the group. Such decisions invalidate the layoffs and incur exceptionally high allowances, the legal minimum being doubled in 2002. The June 2013 law of economic security (LSE) completely changed things, however, by revising the procedures for mass layoffs. This law gives negotiating priority over the employer's unilateral decision, with such a method being possible in the absence of any agreement. Further, the consultation periods were specified and shortened, and the power of control was given to the administrative authority. Thus, in the case of a collective agreement, the administration validates its content, whereas in the case of a plan unilaterally drawn by the employer, the administration approves the content of the PSE through analysis of compliance. This law has significantly framed the implications linked to the judicialization of the mass layoffs and has resulted in a noticeable reduction in litigation.

- **Temporary Contracts:** Temporary contracts are a type of "special" contract, and as such, they must comply with rules of writing or are otherwise requalified in common law contracts, i.e., permanent contract, for the duration of the employment period. There are two types of contracts, the fixed-term contract (CDD) and the temporary contract (CTT), also referred to as temporary work. Both are subject to strict limitations regarding grounds for appeal. Temporary contracts are applicable during temporary increases in activity, when replacing an absent employee, during times of seasonal work and, in addition, waiting periods are established to prevent successive precarious contracts within the workplace. The total duration of a temporary contract, generally, must not exceed 18 months, including its renewals, which are allowed twice after the adoption of the 2015 Rebsamen Law. The cost of temporary contracts is greater than that of permanent contracts as the law provides for equal treatment through the payment of a 10% bonus of precariousness. The 2013 LSE law has also created additional contributions for contracts whose duration is less than three months in an attempt to stem the increase of short duration contracts. This same law has introduced an innovation that provides for a "temporary work CDI" that ensures job guarantees through a job consisting of temporary assignments. It is the duty of the temporary employment agency to ensure the continuity of these missions and to complete them by providing training time, for example, between these missions.

A breach in this legislation has been open since 1982 through the recognition of temporary contracts (CDD) that are customary in a number of industry sectors, named "CDD d'usage". There is a restrictive list of these industry sectors since 1990 that is subject to a decree and includes the hotel-restaurant sector, moving companies, the entertainment sector, etc., seasonal work being assimilated thereto.

This type of CDD does not provide for a precariousness premium, waiting time or initial term. These customary fixed-term contracts constitute a strong vector for the casualization of a specific part of the workforce (Key: infra). Furthermore, a particular type of temporary contract, the "project CDD", was created in 2008 for engineers and executives for the purpose of achieving a definite objective without any initial term limits and for a duration between 18 and 36 months. These new measures have contributed to promoting the use of temporary contracts.

With respect to part-time work, a contract that represents a derogatory form of classic employment which is yet not considered in the EPL indicator of the OECD, it was encouraged in the 1990s with a tax exemption measure. The incentive was called into question in 2001 because of its perverse effect to increase unwanted part-time work. Recently, France's LSE 2013 law adjusted a minimum 24-hour weekly floor, the legal working time being 35 hours, now regarded as the minimal unit unless the employee consents to other terms. However, this modification in minimum hours has not had much effect on part-time work when the duration of the position is significantly short and low wages are the consequence. In most cases, companies successfully obtain the consent of the employees' as these employees realize they must accept the situation.

A powerful factor in the proliferation of derogatory contracts was the public policy for employment as this policy contributed to creating many contractual arrangements aimed at a target audience, namely, young people, seniors, and unskilled laborers, who were to be awarded such contracts for a limited period or for part-time work. These contracts sometimes allowed for training periods. These types of contracts succeeded one another and were perceived as a key measure established by one government and taken over by a successive government. For example, the "jobs for the future" created in 2012 targeted young people who were experiencing integration difficulties. The jobs were generally for a period of 12 to 36 months, and the wages were generally equal to the legal minimum wage.

The regulation of the use of temporary contracts reflects a gap between the rule of law and its application, which the EPL indicators have difficulty measuring accurately. Therefore, while the possibilities for recourse regarding these special contracts are limited on paper, companies broadly use these contracts, as revealed by the development of the precariousness of some employees in the secondary labor market. To complete this regulatory evaluation, it is further noted that the employment protection provisions in France were enacted in the 1970s and 1980s, the time when unemployment became a source of concern in the country. This period was part of a historical movement that gradually resulted in the typical type of employment, permanent contract (CDI), and full-time employment where by the form is testimony of a social compromise between capital and labor. Accordingly, regarding the undefined term of employment contract, we must go back as far as

1890 to find a trace of its emergence, such creation being jointly desired by the working people who sought job security and by the employers who wanted to attract and retain staff (Sauze, 2005). It is these protections that create the legacy of a fully employment society that continues to exist today, albeit one that is at odds with the present context from many perspectives. In particular, self-employment, though increasing and unaffected by definition, does not fall under the rules of employment protection with respect to salaried employment, indicating the inability of such rules to prevent evolutions that are likely to generate insecurity for workers. In any case, it is important to acknowledge that the existing regulations regarding employment protection result from long history, which explains the extreme difficulty involved in reforming the regulations.

Recent intense legislative activity has admittedly remodeled these protections without indicating a one-way evolution given that political change promotes a pendulum swing. Thus, relief measures under employment protection, such as contractual termination (2008), the extension of cases using temporary contracts, etc., are evident during the same time as measures that strengthen this protection, such as the doubling of dismissal compensation and the enforcement of the obligations related to mass layoffs (2014), etc. The main result of this legislative creativity consists of a significant growing complexity of the rule of law on these issues, which many observers have not failed to condemn (Badinter and Lyon-Caen, 2015). This explains why, since the mid-2000s, legislators have sought to increase the legal securing of procedures for employers to reduce the delays and uncertainties resulting from the litigation on breaches of contract. From this, there has emerged a decreased rigidity with respect to some of the provisions offered under employment protection, the scope of which is, nevertheless, extremely limited.

These evolutions are not related to foreign reforms, such as those that occurred in Germany in the early the 2000s through the Hartz Law or in Italy through the adoption of the 2014 Jobs Act. These rather radical reforms have in common the characteristics of having allowed the use of precarious derogation contracts for mini and midi jobs in Germany or the voucher system in Italy and of having reduced the possibility of receiving benefits in the event of unemployment. These reforms and their effects are not relevant to France, a country that continues to differ significantly from countries with low employment protection such as the United States and the United Kingdom. There is no equivalent to the zero hour contracts of the UK, which constitute a form of whistle work (just-in-time work), or the rules concerning layoffs, which are far from the principle of almost total freedom found in the US through the at-will employment concept. The right to employment protection emanates primarily from state laws and regulations, such rights being supplemented by the jurisprudence provided by ordinary courts and labor courts. Many laws in such areas are negotiated laws in the sense that they endorse the results of the negotiations between trade unions of salaried employees and trade unions of employers. Such negotiations result in national inter-professional agreements (ANI), which constitute the legal framework for an employment relationship, and collective agreements, which, in France, have the characteristic of being extended to all concerned companies. However, the recent movement, which is expected to grow, consists of giving a greater part to company agreements. This movement, which began as early as 2004, calls into question the norms of hierarchy, which corresponds to the argument that any disposition taken at a lower level can only be ameliorative. Accordingly, this favorability principle requires that collective branch agreements plan improvements with respect to general rights and, similarly, company agreements.

This movement is illustrated through job retention agreements (AME) as provided by the 2013 LSE law with respect to the context of collective redundancies. These AMEs open the possibility that a collective agreement may be founded upon measures related to working time and wages to limit job cuts. Such agreements, whether they lead to a reduction in work time and, hence, a reduction in remuneration or an increase in work time without an increase in pay, are reached within a framework that includes a necessary two year limit and the mandatory approval of the majority trade unions in the company. It is possible to deviate from the general rules of labor law, a possibility that has been only marginally exploited since 2013. The 2016 El Khomri labor law went further in the reversal of the norms hierarchy that is involved in this type of agreements by opening them only to questions specific to work time. The planned reform as announced by the Executive President Macron in operation since May 2017 aims precisely at extending the scope of the issues likely to be relevant to company agreements accepted to the majority. It is a prospect that can result in the redesigning of the labor law and, more specifically, the redesigning of job protection, the scope of which is subject to conflicting perspectives. Some critics highlight the risk of the degradation of the guarantees granted to employees by placing them into generalized competition as well as the risk regarding the weakening of their negotiating position opposite that of employers. Others, in contrast, consider that this plan offers an opportunity to find arrangements appropriate to the characteristics of every company and arrangements that will therefore better respond to the present problems facing job protection.

In all cases, the debates on the legal rules concerning job protection, which are numerous and virulent in France, must take into account employees' real situations in the labor market. This is what we will see.

A Labor Market Marked by Significant Dualization and High Unemployment

The first point to note as to the labor market conditions in France is the persistence of mass unemployment since the beginning of the 1980s, a trend that, while accompanied by fluctuations related to economic periods, never drops below 7% of the working population, a level reached in 2007. The 2008 crisis resulted in a sharp increase in the unemployment rate, similar to that in all developed countries. Nevertheless, contrary to many other countries, that rate has persisted at approximately 10% until now. Such persistence proves the strong unemployment structural dimension in France, as also demonstrated by the large proportion of long-term unemployment (CLD). Specifically, approximately 44% of the unemployed have been out of work for more than one year, an increase of ten percentage points since 2009 (Eurostat source). These figures further suggest major integration difficulties with respect to working age population, which is confirmed by the relatively low employment rates for the working age generations at the beginning and end of work life (COE, 2014). Table 2 presents quantified data for France and Germany.

Such exclusion from employment of a portion of the population in France must, on the one hand, be connected to the legal framework of the employment relationship and, on the other hand, to the inadequacies of the initial and continuous training system. The dualization of the labor market also reflects these barriers to access employment that the market is expected to bring.

To approach this split between primary and secondary labor markets in France, the resistance of typical employment to economic and social changes that occurred during these last decades must be acknowledged. It is noted that 85% of employees are still in permanent employment (permanent contract = CDI or civil servants) and that less than one in six employees is employed through temporary work (fixed-term contract = CDD, temporary work, assisted jobs or apprenticeship training). Although this share has multiplied by approximately three since the beginning of the 1980s, it has remained limited and stable since the beginning of the 2000s. This resistance to the forms of permanent employment appears, at first sight, to contradict other

Table 2.

	Unemployment Rate			Employment Rate*		Long-term unemployment Rate*	Part-Time Work Rate*
	2005	2010	2015	15-24 Old	55-64 Old		
France	8.9%	9.4%	10.3%	27.8%	60.3%	4.3%	18.3%
Germany	11.2%	7%	4.6%	45.8%	74.8%	1.7%	26.7%

* Figures of 2016 Source: EuroStat

figures concerning the predominance of temporary contracts in the recruiting flow, with only one in ten employees being hired today on a permanent contract. However, while the contradiction is apparent, it can be resolved through the awareness of the durable relegation of a part of labor force to the secondary segment of labor market, this segment being marked by increasing insecurity. Furthermore, surveys indicate that the stability of some employees reflects their anxiety about the possibilities of getting a new job, such stability appearing to be tolerated rather than selected (Flamand, 2016). It is at this level that the job market in France does not allow motilities that are likely to satisfy employees, whether they are compelled to do so by the precarious forms of employment or they are prevented by the uncertainty of finding another job.

These fractures between workers' situations have widened over time, with a part of the labor force being confined to an increasingly more unstable and hopeless precariat. The recent trend is in the increase of the shortest contracts, that is, less than three months and in some cases even less than one month. Thus, the number of individuals given temporary contracts for less than one month has increased 61% since 2000, while the number of individuals given temporary contracts for more than one month has come to a standstill. This increase in insecurity is also evidenced by dividing the average duration of both temporary assignments (CTT) and temporary jobs (CDD) by three since the beginning of the 1980s (Cahuc and Prost, 2015). If precarious workers note that their length of employment is increasingly fragmented, they face increasing difficulties emerging from this situation of a succession of short-term jobs and unemployment or inactivity. Accordingly, the transition rate for transforming fixed-term contracts (CDD) into permanent ones (CDI) after one year has decreased from 50% in 1982 to 20% in 2008, which is a significant sign of their confinement to their current situation (Picard 2011). Temporary contracts are increasingly less a perquisite for obtaining a permanent contract and are more of a trap to draw one into the secondary segment of the job market or unemployment. The risk of becoming unemployed in a one year horizon is six times greater for employees holding a temporary contract (CDD) and ten times greater for temporary agency workers (CTT) than it is for employees holding a permanent contract (CDI). It is further noted that the duration of temporary employment is also decisive, as those with less than one month temporary contracts (CDD) have a risk of unemployment two times greater than those with temporary contracts (CDD) of one or more years (Flamand op. cit.). Moreover, the CDI (permanent contract) is no longer a way to avoid this terminal slide into the precarious part of the workforce in France as more than 36% of the newly signed permanent contracts (CDI) are completed within a year, which is indicative of a rising proportion. This premature termination of permanent contracts is caused in approximately 50% of the cases by resignation and in approximately 33% of the cases by separation during the trial period (Paraire,

2015). These data indicate that in addition to the temporary employment types that companies have recourse to, these types of permanent employment are also applicable in employment management as they allow the company to be flexible, and they are precarious for the employees.

Part-time jobs, which have doubled since the 1980s, are also involved in these fractures in the labor market in France. However, the proportion of part-time jobs remains limited in France (see Table 2) and has not experienced an increase since the beginning of the 2000s. Beyond the contractual forms and work time, there are breaches to the standard of paid employment including staggered work hours (nights or Sundays) and contracting with several employers. Accordingly, employees who are permanently employed in full-time or voluntary part-time jobs with normal work hours and only one employer represent 56% of the total employment in France (63% of all employees in 2011) (Picart, 2014). Abnormal forms of work, according to the standard defined above, correspond to independent work as well, which is currently on the increase and spreading into disparate situations (see infra). Multiple other special situations that appeared over time, such as in-home working, working for a third party, crowd working, etc., could be added to this latter category, i.e., independent work. Such examples reflect the deep changes that have occurred in the workforce (Everaere, 2014).

The differentiated access to primary and secondary segments of the labor market depends, to a large extent, on socio-cultural characteristics, with more disadvantaged situations for seniors, young people, immigrants, people with no diplomas, etc. More specifically, young people are the most affected by the premature termination of temporary contracts (CDI) because approximately 50% of the newly signed CDIs are broken within a year for those in the 15 to 24 age category (Paraire, op. cit.). For seniors over 50, the CDD frequency, although below the total average, quadrupled between the beginning of 1980 and today. The contracts that seniors typically terminate (Picart, op. cit.) are more often short-term contracts, indicating that seniors who no longer benefit from a permanent job are condemned to terminate one short-term contract after another (Picart, op. cit.). These same characteristics are also a determining factor in the risk of unemployment. Thus, the holders of a temporary contract, an interim contract (CTT) or a fixed-term contract (CDD) have more than twice the risk of being unemployed one year later if they are unskilled workers compared to corporate executives. Young people illustrate very well this unequal employment dynamic in France with striking carrier path differences between graduates and employees without diplomas. A survey on the transition of young people from school to work three years after leaving school provides valuable information with regard to this (Céreq, 2014). Table 3 presents some of the characteristics of employees without a diploma and fifth year university graduates. Other factors of inequality are added to this, such as social origin, geographic location, nationality, etc. The

Table 3.

	Characteristics of the 1st Contract			Situation 3 Years After		
	Part-Time Job	**Permanent Contract**	**Median Wage***	**Unemployment Rate**	**Activity Rate**	**Permanent Contract**
Non-graduates	32%	15%	100	50%	80%	33%
Fifth year university graduate	11%	46%	159	10%	97%	76%

* Index Source: Céreq, 2014

difficulties accessing employment, particularly for the young people in France, is focused on a part of this population, i.e., young individuals who have not succeeded in school and those who have accumulated social handicaps.

Nonetheless, the resilience of the French society to these centrifugal changes is quite remarkable. The cohesive strength in France is related to the maintaining of a social safety net that is strong and consolidated even as the employment situation for a segment of its population declines. The spreading of a social minima, as well as the creation of additional income for low activity income, which constitutes the activity premium ("Prime d'activité"), has attempted to meet such degradation. Such measures were recently strengthened in favor of young people through the youth guarantee ("Garantie Jeunes") that, since 2017, has enabled young people without a diploma or with a low-level diploma under the age of 26 to benefit from an allowance as well as from a support towards professional integration. The unemployment compensation system in France is also relatively generous when compared with European systems (Ourliac, 2017), which is why the 2015 13.6% monetary poverty rate has not exploded in the last decade but only slightly increased (+0.6 point) and has even decreased in the last 20 years. Germany, on the contrary, which was at the same level as France 20 years ago, exceeds France today with a 16.7% rate (Eurostat source). The rate of poor workers has, as well, remained low with 7.5% employed in 2015, which is an increase of only 1.4 point in ten years. Here, again, Germany has been far more affected by employment changes, as this same rate has doubled in ten years, reaching 9.6% today. Barriers to the compensation system of unemployment in France still exist, however, as such compensation does not always encourage a return to employment (Cahuc and Prost, op. cit.). The opening to the perception of an earned income as well as unemployment allowance has promoted the preservation of the weak activity of some workers. The perception of additional income in addition to weak earned income presents this same ambivalence by improving the situation of precarious workers while allowing companies to pass on to the state the responsibility of providing sufficiently profitable jobs.

The presentation of the degraded situation of the labor market in France, particularly the high and long-term unemployment and the confinement in the secondary segment of a portion of the workers, even if such degradation has limited social impact, contrasts with the quasi status quo of the legal framework of employment protection. Thus, we are led to question the links between these two points and, even more directly, the ability of the present legal framework to prevent any further deterioration of the labor market.

An Uncertain Future With Rising Perils

The gap between the acknowledgment of the safeguarding of a generally high level of employment protection and the precariousness suffered by a part of employees, this part being admittedly numerically limited, is liable to exponentially increase in the future. This is what justifies the fact that some prospects of reforming employment protection might be presented further, on the basis of a reading of economic and social evolutions that seem to make such reform inevitable.

The background of this conviction is constituted by the profound changes of productive activity that are encompassed within a set of essential changes of economy and society. Of course, this is not the right place here, to complete a thorough analysis of this prospect (France Stratégie, 2016). Our analysis will be limited to point out some key points, without aiming to give an exhaustive list, in direct link with the break with the past labor mobilization practices.

1. At the level of production organization, the "lean manufacturing" aims to make companies responsive to the fluctuations in demand on the market,in both quantity and quality, in variety as well. Consequently, a flexibilization of production processes can be observed.
2. At the level of industrial organization, companies call the integration principle into question through outsourcing some peripheral functions and through subcontracting a part of their production activity. One can then speak about the fragmentation of the value chain.
3. With regard to technology, digital technology induces a profound renewal of activities through creating some new ones, destroying other ones and transforming the production and consumption modes of most of them. We are witnessing a real technological revolution.
4. At the level of the capitalist system, the globalization of production processes and markets and the financialization that has accompanied and reinforced such globalization, destabilize traditional regulations. Such movement can be summarized by its exacerbating effects on the competitive sector.

This set of profound changes upset our economies and societies, without being a guarantee for economic and social progress for everyone, which justifies the urgency of bringing out regulation that should be appropriate for this new context. That is the case in terms of employment relationship, given the unfortunate evolutions a part of French workers suffer, whether it is their exclusion from employment or their relegation on the secondary market. However, employment protection, as it is currently configured, is unable to prevent such evolutions, or even contributes to them. So, the regulation of temporary jobs didn't prevent the increasing use of such contracts in the direction of a greater job insecurity, through the growing frequency of short contracts, even though these latter were overtaxed in 2013. The use of permanent contracts that can be observed today with a high rate of early breaking is another token of this relative powerlessness of the current employment protection to fight this evolution. We can plainly see the current business practices through the numbers of hiring in fixed-terms contracts (CDD) that correspond to rehiring in 70% of cases (Picart, op.cit.). There is, in addition, a concentration of these succession of temporary contracts practices in the sectors that are allowed to use such contracts "in a normal way" with the "CDD d'usage", as hiring in CDD in those sectors represents half of the total. In those sectors, recurrence is a standard, such recurrence that tends to extend to other sectors, which the current regulations still successfully restrict but without totally preventing it (Unédic, 2016).

However, such precariousness has still a limited scope, as we have seen. Of course, this is due to the fact that these regulations contain such precariousness today to a certain extent, with no guarantee as to the future however. Another reason to consider is the fact that there are also forces in favor of the stabilization of workers. The mutations we have rapidly mentioned above create a framework for productive activity, a framework in which the employees' involvement is decisive, in any case for those whose contributions confer a competitive advantage. Creativity that is crucial for innovation, personal commitment such it is required in "lean manufacturing", the essential social skills in service activities and the relational ones, cooperation requirements within firms networks, etc. are certainly strengths that call for the stabilization of workers within work collectives. Companies so, find it advantageous to maintain some employees over time and this, even apart from the employment protection rules. The fact of giving employees the permanent employment advantages is rather a sign of confidence that is given to the employees who can be counted on by companies to develop their competitive advantages. This is how the differential pathways to professional integration of young people can be interpreted, as some of them achieve rather rapidly stable employment while others remain forever in the status of alternating between unemployment and precarious jobs. In the light of this analysis, one might wonder why we couldn't reconsider some provisions of employment protection, as they are relatively unable to counter impoverishment practices of a part of workers, while being of little help to the stabilization of another part of workers!

In the same vein, employment protection that clearly concerns wage earners, is more and more got round by the use of commercial services, either with supplier companies or with freelancers. Since the 2000s, we can observe in France an increase in the number of free-lancers who sell their working performances without owning any physical assets. Such self-employment was encouraged in France by the creation of the status of "self-entrepreneur" in 2009, such status being renamed in 2014 under the name of "micro-entrepreneur". This status opens the possibility of selling working performances with a favorable tax treatment and simplified administrative formalities, on condition that the turnover should not be in excess of a certain amount. Such status has met with great success since micro-entrepreneurs account today for over a quarter of the self-employed. For one-third of them, they combine this status with the employed one. Such observation partly explains the so generated low income-in addition to the rules for access to the status themselves, since one in four of these people receive less than 70 euros (≈78 dollars) and only one in ten more than 1100 euros (≈1220 dollars) per month (ibid.). We can see in this status a deteriorated situation by comparison with other self-employed workers, as their average monthly income is 8 times lower (ibid.). This is the sign of a dualization regarding self-employed workers too, with micro-entrepreneurs who are involved in the secondary segment with other self-employed people whose income is low and who are economically highly dependent on their clients and thereby, who assume all economic risks. This self-employment has been a response to the employment crisis and a form of deregulation of the labor market that has been observed too in other developed countries. However, France remains moderate in such evolution, both in increase and in level: with 11.5% of employment, the part of the self-employed remains low, the UK and the Netherlands being rather above 16% (France Stratégie, op. cit.). However, it is likely that independence is also due to a voluntary choice of status from some people aiming to work independently and to earn revenue directly based on their activity. A recent survey (Alberola *et alii*, 2016) shows that it is a minority choice today as 30% find that the status of self-employed is worth living but it shows too that, among young people, nearly half of them consider that option. Beside a sustained "necessity entrepreneurship", a voluntary "membership entrepreneurship" may exist too that justifies the extension also to the self-employed of the issue of job security, which is hardly the case today in France, since the employment protection provisions can apply only to salaried workers.

In the same way, we must, of course, mention the disruptive perspective the development of "on-demand economy" brings. Digital platforms that put applicants for services in touch with independent suppliers is a mode of organization that may well disrupt the work world. Such mode pushes to the calling into question of the salary system and to the shifting to the paying by task. Employment protection and beyond it, our social model, as they are focused on the salary system, employment uberisation according to the traditional expression, is a real danger for workers.

All these are evolutions that lead us to consider that the objective of protecting all workers from the risks relevant to salary, employment or health, etc. is no longer met by employment protection as this latter exists today in France. What directions can we have to follow to rectify such deficiencies that risk becoming wide open in the future?

The Prospects for "French Style Flexicurity"

The sayings of major international organizations upon job protection have become more nuanced than before. In particular, the OECD did its chief aggiornamento in 2006, through promoting reforms that move toward flexicurity, which is the association of employment flexibility with security for career paths. The OECD's experts are doubtful about the efficiency of liberal deregulation through emphasizing moreover that resultant social costs have an impact on its acceptability by the population and as a consequence, more on its efficiency. For all that, France is still singled out, due to the absence of structural reforms that penalizes it and keeps it away from global movement. We can find recommendations in the same tone in the reports of the OECD (OECD, 2015) or of the European Union (European Commission, 2017). What does the inventory of job protection, such we have drawn it up above, allow us to assert?

In fact, France was comparatively put at a disadvantage with similar countries, with which it is in direct competition, whether it is Germany, the UK, the US, the countries of southern Europe... Reforms directed to the reduction of the job protection regulation have been made in most of them, sometimes focused on temporary contracts as in Germany, sometimes on the whole of the EPL as in Italy, as every country has followed a specific way. One cannot ignore the fact that France is at the top of the OECD rankings as to the EPL rigor (see supra) and that it suffers from such situation as a reputation effect subjectively amplifies the effects of objective comparison. In the rankings relevant to national attractiveness, the foreign investors' sentiment is effectively influenced by such belief in a France the job market of which is still highly regulated and more generally, a country that suffers from a regulatory straightjacket at all levels (Business France, 2016). Such belief exists widely too in the minds of the entrepreneurs who are set up in France, which erodes their trust. It is a first argument for making labor market more flexible, through a reform likely to alleviate appropriately job protection in order to create a "psychological shock" internally and externally. The second argument that moves in this direction is the one essential concerning the current inefficiency of these protections we have described as "sand dams" against the practices of flexibility used by companies. The development of self-employment is a way of circumventing the protections of paid employment that does risk growing in the future. The architecture of the job protection in France seems very involved, furthermore, in the stronger and stronger dualization of its labor market. The rules relevant to temporary work, although protective on paper, are hardly effective in reality (see supra).

A first set of recommendations would consequently aim at reasonably softening the rules relevant to permanent employment through a greater legal securing of its breach in terms of both time and litigation. Complementarily, to fight against the dualization of labor market, such plan implies too that the rules of the protection of labor employment should be made more effective. The analysis conducted above, shows that the uses of this type of contract, although spreading, take a clearly abusive turn only in a few sectors. In particular, the fixed-term contract said "CDD d'usage" is greatly involved in the increase of precarious work the employees suffer in those sectors. An official report (IGAS, 2016) did put the spotlight on the consequences of this derogatory contract that, in this instance, matches a very strong deregulation of the legal framework of the employment relationship, such deregulation seeming admitted since limited to a short list of activities. A revision of the regulation of temporary employment in those sectors does appear necessary. Can be added to those legal orientations, a proposal for recasting the funding for unemployment insurance, in a way more encouraging than it is today. In that sense, the proposal for taking into account the social effects of corporate practices according to the "polluter pays principle", as regard to hiring and termination of the employment contract, must be taken into account. Compelling to more contribute the companies that use their privilege of being allowed to use employment flexibility with a strain on the collective unemployment insurance as a consequence, is a way fraught with difficulties of course, as two promoters of such measure have shown. For example, industrial organization with sub-contracting chains can transfer the flexibility and so, the eventually incurred costs, to the most peripheral businesses. Nevertheless, it is a way to explore because it can lead to weigh on business practices more efficiently than it is the case today with the legal provisions that exist in France.

For all that, the lessons we can draw from the radical reforms carried out in different countries through the opening of very deregulated derogatory contracts, as in Germany or in the UK, or the establishment of a single contract the rules of which are lightened, including permanent employment as in Italy, lead to the conclusion that such measures are inadequate as to France. It is not an answer likely to be adapted to the problems of its labor market as the employment protection and more broadly the labor law, are not the main causes of the evils that are structural unemployment and the dualization of labor market. Besides, such way would call into question the social cohesion that is, so far, preserved in France. Of course, barriers to mobility in labor market are not totally disconnected from the renewal of its productive strengths, the evils French economy structurally suffers from. It is definitely the diagnosis detailed by the OECD (2016) according to which the lack of fluidity in labor markets is the origin of barriers to innovation and to productivity gains. However, flexicurity appears in fact, a much more promising way for France, in parallel to the remediation of the drawbacks of its training system. The awareness of the interest to follow the Scandinavian model with which flexicurity is linked has moreover begun to emerge among politicians and union leaders. Measures aiming at establishing a "French style flexicurity" have gradually been taken, although timidly.

Some of the mentioned above reforms can be so resumed with regard to this orientation. So, the 2013 law, called LSE, opened the way to job maintenance agreements (AME) and promoted too, the use of "partial activity" with state compensation for the partially put out of work employees, in order to allow companies to go through rough times as to their business, without throwing employees in the external job market. There is a real "flexibility" for companies at the level of labor costs and "security" for employees as to employment maintenance. The 2010 unemployment insurance reform, in the sense of rechargeable rights, is a safeguarding of carrier paths too, by ensuring greater rights through the possibility of hiring for any kind of job without damage to their rights. More broadly, the start of the building up of a base of "portable" social rights, which means that they are kept by his holder, whatever his situation, is illustrated by the creation of the "personal activity account" by the 2016 labor law. That account described as "universal" since it is open to employees of public and private sectors, to civil servants and to self-employed workers, collects previously created accounts: the "hardship prevention account" that keeps in mind the work periods the conditions of which were harsh and that entitles to some benefits (calculation of the pension etc.), the "personal training account" provided with legally scheduled hours for accessing to continuous training and still other measures.

The achieving of a high level of employability within the meaning of the ability to remain in employment is in the core of the logics of flexicurity (Gazier and Gautié, 2011). The exclusion from employment and the relegation to the secondary labor market of a part of the population are strongly related to the inability of the French school system to give everyone an initial training that is a diploma-awarding or qualifying one (European Commission, op.cit.). The part of the people without a diploma, around 15% of a generation, remains constant over time and the development of apprenticeship still remains a pious wish, despite the displaying of a political will. The diagnosis too, of the failure of the support towards employment, either the back-to-work and on-the-job support, remains valid (COE, 2016). Similarly, the deficiencies of the organization of professional training in France are clear, with a significant "Matthew Effect" resulting from the fact that it is the most qualified employees who have most access to such training (European Commission, op. cit.). Consequently, remain in France innumerable projects of structural reforms able to better secure professional careers through providing the whole population, young people in particular, with employability assets. That does not mean that nothing has been done during the last decades. For example, the registration in labor law through the May 4th, 2004 law of the obligation for companies to maintain the workers' employability, which could result in condemning the companies found negligent in the implementation of this obligation that falls within their initiative. The creation in 2011 of the "professional security contract" (CSP) that consists in an increased support of the employees who are victims of lay-offs for economic reasons is a success too. The lifelong training rights have been reinforced over time. An" individual right to training" (DIF) was initiated in 2004, then replaced by the "personal training account" (CPF) in 2014, this latter being included in the "personal activity account" (CPA) that was set up in 2016. Training rights were increased at the same time, with additional grants for unqualified employees. A training plan concerning 500.000 long-term unemployed that was initiated in 2016 can be considered as a laudable effort, even if it might seem inspired by short-term electoral prospects. What is probably missing, is a real will of deep long-term changes, these latter being accompanied by a rationalization of funding, as such funding is too sprinkled and often badly coordinated today. It is the condition allowing that the "security" of becoming re-employed might be truly strengthened, while at the same time, the employment "flexibility" increases, a condition allowing too, that we could really talk about a "flexicurity" in France.

At the time of this writing, the newly elected President Emmanuel Macron has announced a reform of the labor law that appears to be inspired by a balanced diagnosis of the employment situation. Some measures, such as the setting of scales for labor court allowances in case of judged abusive dismissal, the extension of unemployment allowance to self-employed workers as well as to resigning employees, the will to reform professional training, all those measures have been announced during the election campaign. They do not seem to testify a radically liberal reform in the direction of deregulation. The will, as well, to promote business negotiations at the level of the company and to carry on the reversal of the hierarchy of norms, beyond the scope of the August 2016 labor law, has been expressed by Emmanuel Macron with the idea of a better matching of the regulation with companies specific situations. Let us wait and see how action will follow such intentions, the reaction of trade unions and the social movements that may arise in response, such consequences representing a potential threat as to the implementation of those reforms. The current status quo that has, as we have seen, preserved the essence of employment protection through accommodating to a heavy unemployment and to a high but targeted at a part of employees job insecurity, such status quo doesn't seem hardly any longer bearable to face the future as this latter looms!

Other Ways of Expressing Workers' Speech

Beyond the reforms that deal with the diagnosed problems of employment protection in France, such reforms being inspired by the flexicurity Scandinavian model, two worth exploring directions can be drawn. The first one is the taking into consideration of the workers' words, not only through the trade-union voice, but within the governance body itself of companies. It is a too often ignored lesson of the economic success of Germany, a country that has, for a long time, experimented" co-management" through the employees' involvement in management boards. So, surveys show that economic and social performances and consequently, the capacity to stabilize and develop a quality employment are linked with the level of the employees' participation (Sigot and Vero, 2014). Our own observation of SCOP, that are self-governed production cooperatives, show their capacity for preserving jobs, thanks to special formula of internal flexibility (Charmettant and alii,2016), which brings us to talk about "secuflexibility" by inverting the words composing flexicurity. The historian of labor law, Jacques Le Goff (2004) has summed up the conquest movement of social rights in an expressive title "From silence to speech". It is that "employees' speech" that must now go through means other than state regulation and the employees' participation in power in companies is a promising prospect that heads in this direction, although such prospect is still nebulous.

The second direction to explore concerns the quality of social dialogue, the importance of which in the improving of competitiveness, the Dublin Foundation's work (Euro found, 2015 and 2016) trends to show. So, it is hoped that the start of reforming social dialogue, through the law on trade-unions representativeness (August 20th 2008 law), through the opening of broader collective negotiation areas at company level (2015 labor law), etc. will enable to better benefit from this evolution in France. Much remains to be done as the Dublin Foundation places us in 25th position within EU, on 28countries, as to the mode of "extensive dialogue"....

In the final analysis, it's a revolution of social relationship in France, a revolution that consists in breaking with an ideological model of the capital-labor conflict and with widespread distrust (Algan and Cahuc, 2007), a revolution we can call for in order to that France might get out of its paradoxical situation.

CONCLUSION

At the end of this inventory, it can be concluded that employment protection in France has little evolved for 30 years and continues providing guarantees in terms of job stability and of break-off compensation, such guarantees being considered as relatively strong for most of them. The justification for a dismissal on "real and serious" causes is the basis for such protection, as the trial period during which there is no imposed justification is of short duration. The main opening was in 2008 the possibility of signing an agreement for termination by mutual agreement through "contractual termination", as this latter provides the same compensation as a classic dismissal (dismissal compensation and unemployment benefit). As to mass layoffs, the employer's accountability has been increased through the obligation of caring about the fate of the dismissed employees and about the place where the effects of this decision have an impact. The 2013 reform aimed particularly to allow staff representatives to be involved in the plan negotiation that implements the measures taken by the company and to have such plan validated by the administration. Through the contractual termination for permanent contracts, as well as through the reform of massive layoffs, the legal securing has been the legislator's main objective. This latter has especially aimed to limit the uncertainty relating to the cost of judgment and to shorten the delays for settling disputes.

As regards temporary contracts, legislation, there too, has been maintained all in all unchanged, about the extra cost in relation to permanent contracts, about too, cases of appeal and waiting periods in their successive actions. The acknowledgment of temporary contracts that may be normally used in some sectors, the "CDD d'usage", has however led to a precariousness of the employees working in those sectors. More broadly, the temporary contracts legislation is not a very effective barrier against companies' practices of resorting to a "reserve" of flexible workers. The impotence of the law may be visible too, through the development of self-employed workers, as the 2009 micro-entrepreneur status has promoted such development.

The result of such evolution has been a dualization of the labor market, with a secondary segment that represents until today only a minority and a part that has remained stable since the 2000s. It is the most "vulnerable" people, young people and senior workers, immigrants, unskilled workers, who find themselves in this secondary segment with fewer and fewer chances of being able to reach the primary segment or to go back to this segment. In addition, they suffer an increase of their precariousness through the reducing of the duration of temporary contracts. Nevertheless, French society demonstrates great resilience, thanks to a social State that has maintained its support and has even extended such support to new categories such as the poor workers or young people.

If it appears that we can say that "the key is preserved", it would nevertheless be dangerous to be satisfied with this status quo for the future. Flexibilization is rooted in company practices and tends to spread through circumventing regulations, including those concerning the permanent contract with more and more early terminations of contract. Self-employment is also an upward trend that makes the EPL more and more powerless as such protection deals only with employees. It should not be forgotten any more that mass unemployment that excludes from employment a part of the French population remains at high and unacceptable levels. France is involved too in an international context that is marked by the radical reforms of employment protection that exist in the countries with which it is in competition. Besides, stable employment is suffered by a part of workers who dread the risks related to mobility. More positively, we can anticipate, too, a willingness of companies to retain, out of interest, an important part of their employees to benefit from their full contribution, without regulation being the main reason for this.

All these elements put together call for a reform of employment protection in France. Such reform, however, must be carefully considered and must not call into question the delicate balance that employment protection represents between efficiency imperative for companies and safety requirements for employees. Flexicurity is the direction that must guide these reforms. The quest for increased flexibility must be accompanied by a securing of the workers' career paths as the simultaneity of both movements is needed to make these reforms accepted and not to come up against trade unions obstructions. The improvement of initial and professional training in a direction of democratization and adequacy to the companies' needs seems quite essential. Finally, the adaptation of regulation to the specific situations of sectors and companies requires a decentralization of the levels of its elaboration with a calling into question of the hierarchy of norms. Such directions have begun to be pursued in France, timidly, over the last decade.

The EPL remains quite often a totem linked to our history and that taboos any reform. It does appear nevertheless that an awareness begins to emerge and that the new power that was elected in 2017 through the election of President Macron is willing to cut down certain totems and overcome taboos. Those taboos have deprived France of an evolution likely to strengthen its economy without preventing the loss of certain securities by a part of the workers. It is necessary therefore to have a position, not a principled one but a pragmatic one, as to the means of making French economy more dynamic, whilst providing effective security for all workers, which will still contribute to this dynamism. The future will tell whether the announced reforms have gone in a direction likely to meet the discomforts of the situation in France.

REFERENCES

Alberola, E., Aldeghi, I., & Hoibian, S. (2016). *Les mutations du travail. L'envie du salariat domine sauf chez les jeunes. Document de recherche*. Paris: Crédoc.

Algan, Y., & Cahuc, P. (2007). *La société de défiance. Comment le modèle social français s'autodétruit*. Paris: Editions Rue d'Ulm.

Badinter, R., & Lyon-Caen, A. (2015). *Le travail et la loi*. Paris: Editions Fayard.

Business France. (2016). *International Rankings. Distinguishing between Perception and Reality, 2016 Edition*. Retrieved June 28, 2017, from http://www.businessfrance.fr/Media/Default/discover/livre_blanc_des_classements_internationaux_en_dave_2016-07-05.pdf

Cahuc, P., & Prost, C. (2015). Améliorer l'assurance chômage pour limiter l'instabilité de l'emploi. *Notes d'analyse économique*, *24*, 1-12.

Céreq. (2014). *Quand l'école est finie. Premiers pas dans la vie active de la génération 2013*. Paris: Céreq.

Charmettant, H., Juban, J.-Y., Magne, N., & Renou, Y. (2016). La "sécuflexibilité": au-delà des tensions entre flexibilité et sécurité de l'emploi, les sociétés coopératives et participatives (Scop). *Formation emploi*, *134*, 107-124.

COE. (2014). *L'évolution des formes d'emploi*. Rapport, 8 April. COE.

COE. (2015). *Labour markets reforms in Europe -Executive summary*. Report, 5th November. COE.

COE. (2016). *Labour markets reforms in Europe -Executive summary*. Report, 5th November. COE.

Eurofound. (2015). *Third European Company Survey - Workplace innovation in European companies*. Luxembourg: Publications Office of the European Union.

Eurofound. (2016). *Win-win arrangements: Innovative measures through social dialogue at company level*. Eurofound report. Luxembourg: Publications Office of the European Union.

European Commission. (2017). *Council Recommendations on the 2017 National Reform Programme of France and delivering a Council opinion on the 2017 Stability Programme of France*. Retrieved June 28, 2017, from https://ec.europa.eu/info/sites/info/files/2017-european-semester-country-specific-recommendations-commission-recommendations-france.pdf

Everaere, C. (2014). *Les emplois atypiques. Quelles réponses au besoin de flexicurité?* Paris: Editions Liaisons sociales, Walters Kluwer.

Flamand, J. (2016). *Les transitions professionnelles, révélatrices d'un marché du travail à deux vitesses.* Paris: France Stratégie.

France Stratégie. (2016). *2017-2027 - Enjeux pour une décennie.* Paris: La Documentation Française.

Gazier, B., & Gautie, J. (2011). The "Transitional Labour Markets" Approach: Theory, History and Future Research Agenda. *Journal of Economic and Social Policy, 14*(1), 6.

IGAS. (2016). *Evaluation du contrat à durée déterminée dit d'usage.* Retrieved June 28, 2017, from http://www.igas.gouv.fr/IMG/pdf/2015 049R_Rapport_CDDU_.pdf

Jolly, C., Prouet, E., & Wisnia-Weill, V. (2016). *2017-2027: Repenser la protection des actifs. Note d'analyse, décembre.* Paris: France Stratégie.

Le Goff, J. (2004). *Du silence à la parole. Une histoire du droit du travail des années 1830 à nos jours. Collection: L'Univers des normes.* Rennes: PUR.

OECD. (2006). *OECD Employment Outlook 2006.* OECD Publishing.

OECD. (2013). *OECD Employment Outlook 2013.* OECD Publishing.

OECD. (2015). *OECD Economic Surveys.* OECD Publishing.

OECD. (2016). *OECD Employment Outlook 2016.* OECD Publishing.

Ourliac, B. (2017). *Comparaisons internationales des régimes d'assurance chômage: quels enseignements? Documents d'études, n°209, mai.* Paris: DARES.

Paraire, X. (2015). Plus d'un tiers des CDI sont rompus avant un an. DARES Analyses, janvier, n°05, DARES.

Picart, C. (2014). Une rotation de la main-d'œuvre presque quintuplée en 30 ans: plus qu'un essor des formes particulières d'emploi, un profond changement de leur usage. In INSEE Références (Ed.), *Emplois et salaires, édition 2014* (pp. 29–46). Paris: INSEE.

Piketty, T. (2016). *Loi travail: un effroyable gâchis.* Retrieved June 28, 2017, from http://piketty.blog.lemonde.fr/2016/06/02/loi-travail-un-effroyable-gachis/

Sauze, D. (2005). Stabilité de l'emploi: conquête sociale ou politiques patronales? *Travail et Emploi, 103*, 113-122.

Sigot, J.-C., & Vero, J. (2014). Politiques d'entreprise et sécurisation des parcours: un lien à explorer. *Bref du Céreq, 318.*

Tirole, J. (2016). *Economie du Bien commun.* Paris: PUF.

Unedic. (2016). La majorité des embauches en contrats courts se font chez un ancien employeur. *Eclairages – Études & Analyses, 14.*

World Bank Group. (2016). *Doing Business 2017: Equal Opportunity for All.* Washington, DC: World Bank.

KEY TERMS AND DEFINITIONS

Dualization: Dualization or segmentation corresponds to fractures between categories of workers who don't access to the same benefits in the labor market. The primary market corresponds to those who benefit from the guarantees included in the permanent contract and from the rights relating to this contract. The second market is the precariousness one, this precariousness being higher or lower.

Employment Protection Legislation (EPL): Quantitative indicator of the level of employment protection, such it has been calculated by the OCDE since the 1980s. It synthesizes 21 criteria that are divided into three items: permanent employment, temporary employment and mass layoff. It goes from 0 (total lack of protection) to 6 (maximum protection).

Flexicurity: This approach is typical of the countries of Northern Europe and aims to simultaneously develop "flexibility" for companies and "security" for employees. It is the securing for career paths that becomes more important than employment security.

Hierarchy of Norms: Hierarchy of norms corresponds to the existence of sources of law that place the State law above sectorial collective agreements, these latter being themselves above company-level agreements. Lower sources can depart from higher sources, only if they improve the workers' situation (favorability principle).

Micro-Entrepreneurs: This self-employed status was created in 2009 in France in order to foster entrepreneurship. It has favorable social and tax provisions and follows simplified administrative formalities on condition of not going above a turnover threshold.

Portable Rights: "Portable rights" are those that are not attached to the status of the worker (salaried worker or self-employed worker) or to the company where we work. Such rights allow to facilitate mobility and changes in status, as they are safe for the already acquired rights.

Chapter 2
Employment Protection Legislation in Emerging Economies:
A Critical Literature Review

Samir Amine
Université du Quebec en Outaouais, Canada

Wilner Predelus
Université du Québec en Ouatouais, Canada

ABSTRACT

With emerging economies facing significant lags in the use of information technology to improve their productivity and compete with industrialized economies, the availability of relatively lower-cost labor in the emerging economies is considered a powerful asset that can compensate for their technological disadvantage. However, regulating the labor market often proves to be rather challenging as it is important that a balance be struck between protecting workers and stimulating economic growth. This chapter analyzes the literature on labor market regulations in the emerging economies to observe that the trade-off between employment protection legislation (EPL), job creation, productivity, and innovation often cited in the literature is not conclusive.

DOI: 10.4018/978-1-5225-4134-9.ch002

INTRODUCTION

In a globalized world where economic survival rests solely on competitiveness and sustainable efficiency; the knowledge-based economy (KBE) has put the emerging economies in a disadvantaged position as they significantly lag the industrialized ones in the use of information technology (IT) to improve their productivity. At the same time, emerging economies find themselves competing with developed economies for highly skilled labor. To avoid an "*erosion*" of their most talented and accomplished people in search of a better life, it is imperative that these emerging economies improve their social well-being rapidly, including developing effective labor protection laws. Therefore, Employment Protection Legislation (EPL), which protects the labor rights, plays an important role in emerging economies in reducing the loss of highly skilled workers to developed countries. However, putting in place the right set of regulations that strike a fair balance between social protections and economic growth in the labor market can prove to be challenging, as a too flexible or a too rigid labor market can affect the firms' competitiveness and productivity (see Besley and Burgess, 2004; Baker et al., 2004 & 2005; Howell at al., 2007; Messina et al., 2007 and Rubery, 2011). In that respect, a well-documented literature on the flexibilization of the labor market in the developed economies identifies three areas where EPL has been the cause for policy concerns: employment, productivity and innovation. While the effects of a rigid labor market on unemployment and productivity are well established (Nunziata and Ochel, 2005, and Griffith et al., 2007); its relationship with innovation is less clear (Akerloff, 1982; Shapiro and Stiglitz, 1984; Saint-Paul, 1996; Boeri and Jimeno, 2005; van Schaik and van de Klundert (2013); and Griffith and Macartney, 2014). This paper analyzes the literature on the effects of labor market regulations in emerging economies (namely China, India, Brazil and sub-Saharan Africa) and finds that the trade-off between EPL and employment is not clearly established. It further observes that the widespread debate over the effects of EPL on innovation and productivity growth is still ongoing as the findings has, so far, been inconclusive.

The rest of the paper is structured as follows. Section 2 analyzes the relationship between EPL and employment. Section 3 looks at the impact of EPL on productivity. Section 4 reviews the effects of EPL on innovation; and finally, a conclusion is made in Section 5.

EPL AND EMPLOYMENT

The recent debate over the relationship between EPL and employment has virtually been reduced to a discussion about the labor market flexibility. Theoretically, it is argued that EPL can be diligently designed to enhance the social protection of workers without distorting the labor market; while the contrarian view suggests that any intervention in the labor market can potentially lead to higher costs of hiring and firing, and consequently increase unemployment[1]. By analyzing the strength of the arguments, it is safe to conclude that the effects of EPL on employment is the most contentious topic relating to labor market policy, especially in emerging economies where the abundance of cheap labor is relied upon to fill the technology gap with their industrialized counterparts.

From an empirical perspective, the results vary from countries or regions within the same country and depending on the methodology used by the researcher.

In China, the recent literature on EPL has heavily been dominated by the impacts of the Labor Contract Law that took effect on January 1, 2008. The new law requires that labor contracts be in writing and be delivered to all workers. In retrospect, labor standards set by the 1994 Labor Law were not cause of concern for employment, and China continued to attract negative attention for its poor labor standards (Chan, 2003). However, even in that precarious labor environment, Li (2008) points out that some local governments either lacked the manpower for labor law enforcement, or deliberately ignored labor law violations in order to attract investment. The new law intends to strengthen the rights of the workers who, in general, have no written contracts and therefore do not have sufficient grounds to file for claims labor disputes arise. Following the coming into effect of the new Labor Contract Law in 2008, its impact on employment has not abundantly been surveyed, although Smith et al. (2006) report that employers were very hostile to the enactment of the law. This issue has been extensively discussed by Cooper et al. (2013) and Yan (2015). Using Chinese firm level data from the Annual Survey of Industrial Production (1998-2007), Cooper et al (2013) have designed an equilibrium model, which shows that, by simulation, severance payment imposed by EPL will eventually lead to larger firm size, bigger firm exit rate, and lower labor participation rate in the long run. Their findings are confirmed by Yan (2015) who, using firm-level data for the period of 1998 to 2008 (i.e. before and after the legislative change), observes that private firms, in comparison to their public counterpart, reduces employment both through lower employment growth at the firm level and through higher firm exit rates. These results contrast with those obtained by Hartwell (2010) for Armenia, a country with relatively stringent labor law, where overall unemployment is found not affected by EPL. Although Yan's coefficients for employment in private firms after the law came into force are negative and highly statistically significant, it is unclear whether these results are attributable to the new law or the Global Financial Crisis (GFC), or both. Yan (2015) admits that there was an abrupt rise in exit firms from 2007 to 2008, which could be either related to GFC or the Labor Contract Law, or both. However, the model does not take GFC into consideration, as the data are limited to 2008, the year during which the new law took effect.

In India, where *de facto* regulations differ across states (Holmes, 1998; Autor et al., 2007; Besley and Burgess, 2004; Ahmad and Pagés, 2007; Amin, 2007a), two different methodological approaches have been used in the literature to analyze the relationship between EPL and employment. In both cases, the conclusions are either rejected as flawed or accepted with caution. In the first group, Fallon and Lucas (1991 and 1993), Bhalotra (1998); Aggwaral (2002) and Dutta Roy (2004), use the 1976, 1982 and 1984 amendments respectively as reference points to examine the effects of EPL on employment, while the second group, which comprises Besley and Burgess (2004), Shyam Sundar (2005); Anant et al. (2006); Sharma (2006); Aghion et al. (2008) and; Ahsan and Pagés (2009), focus on the issue through the lens of the regional variations in the amendments to made to the Industrial Disputes Act of 1947 by the state governments.

Using industry data for the period 1959-81, Fallon and Lucas (1991 & 1993) find no change in the speed of employment adjustment, but a drop in labor demand after 1976, the year following the introduction of job security regulations in India. With estimates significant at 5 percent for 11 out of 35 industries, they raise the level of significance to 25 percent to conclude that job security regulation has a negative effect on labor demand in 25 of 35 industries. Both their methodology and the conclusions are criticized by Bhalotra (1998); Anant et al. (2006); Sharma (2006) and Bhattacharjea (2006 & 2009). Bhalotra (1998), in particular, questions the validity of the conclusions by pointing out that the estimates for labor demand are significant at a very high level of significance for a majority of the sectors, while the estimate for the average drop in employment is based on averaging across statistically insignificant coefficients at conventional level.

For their part, Besley and Burgess (2004) use the regional variations among the amendments made by the state governments to the Industrial Disputes Act of 1947 by the state governments to categorize the labor market into three groups: pro-worker, neutral and pro-employer. From that point, they create an index by attributing the scores 1; 0 and -1 to each group respectively, depending on the level of rigidity of the labor market in any given state, to finally conclude that EPL negatively impacts employment. The labor regulation index, methodology and conclusion of this study are all questioned by Bhattacharjea (2006), who suggests other ways to address the issue.

With the results of the above studies being disputed, other researchers such as Aggwaral (2002), Dutta Roy (2004), D'Souza (2010) applied different econometric techniques to the same datasets but reached the opposite conclusions that EPL has none or limited impact on employment in India.

However, the methodologies of both Fallon and Lucas (1991 & 1993) and Besley and Burgess (2004) do not take into consideration the wide discrepancy between the law of the books and the law in action (see Friedman 1977). In fact, when a law comes into force, the most important thing to consider is not what is on paper, but rather what is in practice, hence the notion of legal culture[2]. The papers cited here, instead of analyzing how the law and its associated regulations are applied, narrowly focus on the formal substantive rules in the statute. For instance, in the absence of enforcement, as acknowledged D'Souza (2010), or in the presence of a lax legal culture, an amendment may well be classified as pro-worker on the book, but end up being pro-employer or neutral on the ground. The gap between the formal law and the law in action may explain why it is so difficult for a state like Kerala, which is classified by Besley and Burgess (2004) as pro-employer, to attract manufacturing activity (D'Souza, 2004). In fact, Dollar et al. (2002) find that small and medium-sized businesses (SMEs) in states like Kerala received twice as many factory inspections in a year as did states like Maharashtra and Gujarat, identified as pro-worker. Therefore, in its current state, one can infer that the debate over the effect of EPL on employment in India is far from reaching a convincing conclusion, as it is the case for another emerging country like Brazil.

In Brazil, where most labor regulations are traditionally enshrined in the constitution, the new Constitution of 1988 considerably affected labor regulations by increasing the degree of workers' protection along the lines of the re-democratization environment (Barros and Corseuil, 2001). In this highly-regulated labor market (Heckman and Pagés-Serra, 2000), which exists alongside an unregulated one, the effect of EPL on employment is as ambiguous as in other emerging countries, as suggested by other relevant studies. For instance, having recourse to a very elaborated methodology, Barros, Corseuil and Gonzaga (1999); Barros, Corseuil and Bahia (1999); and Barros and Corseuil (2015) use monthly data from a longitudinal survey of a stratified sample of approximately 5,000 manufacturing establishments, which employed five or more workers, to investigate the effect of the 1988 constitution on employment. They find no evidence at all that the constitutional change had any effect on labor demand in Brazil. In fact, the findings by Barros and Corseuil (2015) are exceptionally interesting that, contrary to studies, they control for the changes in the macroeconomic environment in their model.

Looking at the two sides of the Brazilian labor market, Hoek (2002) observes that the regulated and unregulated labouor markets in Brazil lie on opposite ends of the restructuring continuum. Using data from the Brazilian Monthly Employment Survey, he finds that the unregulated labor market relies almost exclusively on the separation rate as an adjustment mechanism while the regulated labor market adjusts the hiring rate. These findings are confirmed by Almeida and Caneiro (2007 & 2009) who look at the impact of the enforcement side of labor regulations in Brazil on unemployment. Using the distance between the city where the firm is located and surrounding enforcement offices, they observe that stricter enforcement of labor regulation constrains firm size, thus leading to higher unemployment. Although these findings confirm the notion of legal culture, which is often cited by scholars to explain the gap between formal laws and actual implementation of the laws on the ground, these papers do not take into consideration specific macroeconomic characteristics of the cities to isolate other potential sources of unemployment. It is arguable that the actual unemployment observed may be caused by factors specific to the cities other than the stricter enforcement. As empirical findings have divided researchers on the effect of the 1988 Constitution on the Brazilian labor market for more than two decades, one cannot expect any conclusive closure in a near future. Let us now look at the impact of EPL in Africa.

With its 2008 World Bank's average employment rigidity indicator sitting at 47, sub-Saharan Africa region has been classified as the region with the highest number of employment regulations (Gwatidzo and Moyo, 2014). This situation, coupled with poor economic performance, a high level of unemployment and a rampant poverty, provides incentives for exploration. While some researchers such as Warner (1997); Rodrick (1998) and Elbadawi et al. (2006) blame sub-Saharan Africa's misfortune on its weak infrastructure, armed conflicts and poor governance, Habyarimana (2008); Fox and Oviedo (2013); and Gwatidzo and Moyo (2014) turn to its high labor market regulations for answers. Using firm-level survey data from manufacturing sector in 20 Sub-Saharan African countries and World Bank Doing Business indicators, Fox and Oviedo (2013) find weak evidence for a negative effect of EPL on job growth. They further observe that not only is there no difference between the job growth among the less and the most regulated countries as measured by the World Bank indicator, but firms, in the absence of labor-related restrictions, would also expand instead of reducing their demand for labor. These findings support the observations of Habyarimana (2008) who, in his survey of South Africa, finds that labor regulations rank at the lowest scale of firms' preoccupations. However, with a sample of six African countries, including five in f the pool used by Fox and Oviedo (20013), Gwatidzo and Moyo (2014) come up with quite the opposite results. Using data for 4,700 firms from the World Bank's Investment Climate Survey, they find that more restrictive labor market regulations are detrimental to investment and employment. With firms in the same countries investigated by Gwatidzo and Moyo (2014) ranking labor regulations at the lowest level among a group of eight obstacles proposed in the World Bank's Enterprise Survey (World Bank, 2008c), it is not reasonable to expect a statistically significant negative effect of EPL on employment in those countries. In fact, the legitimate question one can infer in this situation is whether, in the absence of the other seven obstacles, firms would make firing or hiring decisions because of employment regulations. To see whether EPL negatively affects employment in those countries, one needs to control for these variables, which the surveyors failed to do. Regardless of the results for Africa, the fact remains that the effects of EPL on employment in emerging economies is inconclusive.

EPL AND PRODUCTIVITY

After employment, productivity is the second most debatable topic in the literature surrounding the impact of EPL. From a theoretical viewpoint, the prevalent assumption in this area is that EPL has a negative impact on productivity (see, for example, Hopenhayn and Rogerson, 1993; Bertola, 1994; Davis and Henrekson, 1997; Saint Paul, 1997 & 2002; Garibaldi, 1998; Mortensen and Pissarides, 1999; Gust and Marquez, 2004; Boeri and Garibaldi (2005); Ichino and Riphahn, 2005; Cuña and Melitz, 2007; Bassanini et al., 2009; Poshke, 2009). However, Schivardi (2000) and Lisi (2008) propose a different perspective, arguing that EPL positively affects productivity. As the empirical evidence remains largely disputable, it is reasonable to argue that the debate is far from being settled.

Among the most notable studies on this issue in the emerging economies, Besley and Burgess (2004) conclude that Indian states which amended the Industrial Disputes in a pro-worker fashion tend to experience lower output and productivity in registered manufacturing. Though his methodology is widely criticized, Aghion et al. (2006), and Mitra and Ural (2006), Ahsan and Pages (2009), Dougherty (2009), Gupta et al. (2009), Dougherty et al. (2011) and Adhvaryu et al. (2013) confirm his findings with either slightly or radically different methodology. In addition to finding that EPL negatively affect both total factor productivity (TFP) and labor productivity, Dougherty et al. (2011) further observe that firms in labor-intensive industries in more flexible labor markets have a higher TFP than those in the states with more stringent laws. As for firms operating in low labor intensity industries, they find no difference in the productivity across states. Though these conclusions are well known in India, there are not shared by Sofi and Sharma (2015), who call into question the "flexibility thought", which is often invoked by employers to demand for weakening EPL. Using a panel dataset on twenty-eight industrial sectors across thirteen major states of India, they find that not only has EPL no effect on TFP but it also has no significant impact even in highly volatile industries. Although Sofi and Sharma's (2015) findings do not come in surprise as they are well grounded in solid economic theories (for example, see Lisi, 2008), they are not very popular in India. In a two-tier labor market where employers can use either informal or formal employment, different work conditions can play a positive role in the level of effort provided by workers and positively affect TFP and labor productivity. In fact,

Sofi and Sharma (2015) notice that the last two decades have seen a sharp growth in informal employment, which could easily be attributed to the phenomenon of employer's innovative compliance to EPL.

In China, a leading study of the effects of EPL on productivity is conducted by Hsieh and Klenow (2009). With the general view that resources misallocation negatively affects total factor of productivity (TFP) as a starting point, they develop a monopolistic competition model with heterogenous firms to show how the misallocation of capital and labor can lower aggregate TFP. In their empirical assessment model, they use plant-level data survey from the Chinese Industrial Survey (1998-2005), the Indian Annual Survey of Industries (ASI: 1987-1994) and the US Census of Manufacturing for measuring the dispersion in the marginal products of capital and labor within the industrial four-digit manufacturing sectors. Their findings reveal that deteriorating allocative efficiency negatively affect both Chinese and India TFP growth. They conclude that EPL, being a misallocation agent, leads to resource misallocation and therefore affects productivity. Following Hsieh and Klenow (2009); Song et al. (2011), Cooper et al. (2013 & 2013b); and Gon and Hu (2015) use either slightly or radically different models and obtained identical results for China. It is worth pointing out that none of these models, which use pre-2008 Chinese Labor Contract Law data, take into account the growing phenomenon of dispatched labor. Cairns (2015) notices that in the first years following the enactment of the Labor Contract Law, dispatched workers grew from a negligible share of China labor force into a pervasive phenomenon. In fact, this situation was so widespread in China that it led to the 2013 drastic amendments which bar firms from hiring more than ten percent of their workforce as dispatched workers. As observed by Chan, C. K., & Nadvi, K. (2014), China's recent regulatory initiatives to improve employment conditions are a direct response to growing labor unrest. Credible models that try to analyze TFP and labor productivity in the context of the integration of EPL need to include the effects of the improvement in workers' wellbeing improvement due to EPL.

Contrary to the relatively prolific literature existing in India and China on EPL and productivity, the issue does not draw too much attention in Brazil and sub-Saharan Africa. The few studies published that analyzed the Brazilian situation are limited to the aspect enforcement only. In this regard, Almeida and Carneiro (2006 and2009) suggest that increased enforcement can lead to lower labor productivity and lower capital intensity. However, it is unclear what "increased enforcement" is defined, and the authors do not explain the mechanisms by which lower labor productivity is resulted.

EPL AND INNOVATION

Although there is an abundant literature on the effects of EPL on innovation, existing studies from the perspective of an emerging economy are far and between, and none of them analyze from an empirical viewpoint. Theoretically, when it comes to the effects of EPL on firms' innovation, the literature distinguishes between incremental and radical or science-based innovations (Aghion and Howitt, 1998; Griffith and Macartney, 2014). Though more profitable than incremental innovation, radical innovation requires a far higher employment adjustment, as workers with new skills are necessary to derive benefits from the innovation. As a result, Saint-Paul (1997 & 2002), Samaniego (2006), and Cunat and Melitz (2007) suggest that countries with high EPL experience an increase in the cost of innovation, for their costs of firing is higher. With emerging economies often being characterized by weak labor protection, it follows that radical innovation should be more profitable for firms operating in emerging economies than in developed economies.

However, Naghavi (2007) observes that the relocation of firms to developing countries tends to increase the cost of labor in those countries and triggers a competition effect, which leads to lowering ex-post output, and consequently decreasing the potential profit of the relocating firm. However, it is unlikely that the increase in the cost of labor due to relocation would totally or more than offset the benefits of relocation to developing countries, as the wage gap between industrialized and developing economies remains incommensurably high[3]. This might explain the findings of Islam and Nazara (2000), which show the persistence of business profitability in Indonesia between 1985 and 1997 despite a sharp increase in the level of minimum wage during the same period. In this regard, several theoretical and empirical papers see a paradox where multinational firms are more likely to relocate to countries where labor standards are enforced (see Rodrick, 1996; Kucera, 2003 and Naghavi, 2007). However, it seems reasonable to believe that the true motivation of relocation remains the relatively low labor costs in developing countries, but preferably, in countries with a minimum level of legal and political stabilities and where the laws of the land are enforced.

From a different perspective, Berdugo and Hadad (2012) investigate the effects of EPL on innovation through the screening process of employees using a model with imperfect information, where probation periods for identifying incompetent workers are disallowed. It follows that the costs of dismissal of workers would push innovators to embark on medium than high tech projects as the former are more flexible in their labor requirements. It is therefore concluded that EPL distort the pattern of specialization in favour of medium-tech firms at the expense of high-tech firms. However, the main weakness of this model lies in its core hypothesis because there are few countries, if any, that have EPL which is so stringent that labor trial period is disallowed.

Aleksynska and Eberlein (2016) demonstrate that the level of EPL protection in lower-income countries is not a reflection of the proportion of workers covered by these rules. In fact, in many developing countries, sections of the labor market are effectively controlled by dispatched work agencies. As a result, wage employment in developing countries is limited, and only a very small proportion of the workers are covered by EPL. Therefore, when studying the effects of EPL in developing countries, it is imperative to consider the EPL coverage rather than the aggregated effects (see Bertola et al., 2000 and Boeri, 2011). To conclude, the relative abundance and the very low cost of labor in developing countries provide benefits that are more than enough to offset the increased costs associated with EPL, which, at least theoretically, allows radical innovations to be highly profitable.

CONCLUSION

From China to India through Africa and to Brazil, there is a large collection of literature on the impact of EPL on employment, innovation and productivity; but the results are not conclusive. It is arguable that a lack of conclusion may indicate an underlying complexity which is yet to be understood. Moreover, the inconclusive aspect of the debate, being drawn from wide differences observed in the results obtained by researchers using sometimes the same data, does not serve the need of public policies that each paper always appeals to. In fact, the notion of EPL is by essence an inter-disciplinary topic which should not be studied only through an economic lens. It is therefore not surprising that the most common mistake observable in this literature review is of legal nature, as the concept that the law on the book is different from the law in practice is often ignored, which eventually leads to erroneous conclusions. One can also observe a lack of awareness of the role that the informal labor market plays in the EPL equation. Even though the informal labor force is a growing alternative source of manpower, it is virtually ignored in the literature on EPL. In fact, some scholars even referred to the firms' recourse to the informal labor market as a form of "innovative compliance".

To summarize, after exploring the literature on EPL in Brazil, India, China and Africa, the only thing that is known with certainty is that "it is not known for certain" whether EPL has any impact on employment, innovation or productivity for any of these countries.

REFERENCES

Adhvaryu, A., Chari, A. V., & Sharma, S. (2013). Firing Costs and Flexibility: Evidence from Firms' Employment Responses to Shocks in India. *The Review of Economics and Statistics*, *95*(3), 727–740. doi:10.1162/REST_a_00305 PMID:24357882

Aghion, P., Burgess, R., Redding, S., & Zilibotti, F. (2006). *The unequal effects of liberalization: Evidence from dismantling the license raj in india*. St. Louis, MO: Federal Reserve Bank of St Louis. doi:10.3386/w12031

Aghion, P., Burgess, R., Redding, S. J., & Zilibotti, F. (2008). The Unequal Effects of Liberalization: Evidence from Dismantling the License Raj in India. *The American Economic Review*, *98*(4), 1397–1412. doi:10.1257/aer.98.4.1397

Aghion, P., & Howitt, P. (1998). *Endogenous Growth Theory*. Cambridge, MA: MIT Press.

Ahsan, A., & Pagés, C. (2009). Are all labor regulations equal? Evidence from Indian manufacturing. *Journal of Comparative Economics*, *37*(1), 62–75. doi:10.1016/j.jce.2008.09.001

Akerlof, G. A. (1982). Labor Contracts as a Partial Gift Exchange. *The Quarterly Journal of Economics*, *97*(4), 543–569. doi:10.2307/1885099

Aleksynska, M., & Eberlein, F. (2016). Coverage of employment protection legislation. *IZA Journal of Labor Policy*, *5*(1), 17. doi:10.1186/s40173-016-0073-x

Almeida, R., & Carneiro, P. (2006). *Enforcement of regulation, informal labor, firm size and firm performance*. St. Louis, MO: Federal Reserve Bank of St Louis.

Almeida, R., & Carneiro, P. (2009). Enforcement of labor regulation and firm size. *Journal of Comparative Economics*, *37*(1), 28–46. doi:10.1016/j.jce.2008.09.004

Almeida, R. K., & Carneiro, P. (2007). *Inequality and employment in a dual economy: Enforcement of labor regulation in brazil*. St. Louis, MO: Federal Reserve Bank of St Louis. doi:10.1596/28270

Almeida, R. K., & Susanlı, Z. B. (2012). Firing Regulations and Firm Size in the Developing World: Evidence from Differential Enforcement. *Review of Development Economics*, *16*(4), 540–558. doi:10.1111/rode.12003

Amin, M. (2009). Labor regulation and employment in India's retail stores. *Journal of Comparative Economics*, *37*(1), 47–61. doi:10.1016/j.jce.2008.07.001

Anant, T. C. A., Hasan, R., Mohapatra, P., Nagaraj, R., & Sasikumar, S. K. (2006). Labor Markets in India: Issues and Perspectives. In J. Felipe & R. Hasan (Eds.), *Labor Markets in Asia: Issues and Perspectives* (pp. 205–300). Basingstoke, UK: Palgrave Macmillan. doi:10.1057/9780230627383_5

Autor, D., Kerr, W., & Kugler, A. (2007). *Do employment protections reduce productivity? evidence from U.S. states*. St. Louis, MO: Federal Reserve Bank of St Louis. doi:10.3386/w12860

Baker, D., Glyn, A., Howell, D., & Schmitt, J. (2004). *Unemployment and labor market institutions: The failure of the empirical case for deregulation*. St. Louis, MO: Federal Reserve Bank of St Louis.

Baker, D., Glyn, A., Howell, D., & Schmitt, J. (2005). Labor market institutions and unemployment: assessment of the cross-country evidence. In Fighting Unemployment: The Limits of Free Market Orthodoxy. New-York: Oxford University Press.

Banker, R. D., Byzalov, D., & Chen, L. (2013). Employment protection legislation, adjustment costs and cross-country differences in cost behavior. *Journal of Accounting and Economics*, *55*(1), 111–127. doi:10.1016/j.jacceco.2012.08.003

Barros, R. P., Corseuil, C. H., & Bahia, M. (1999). *Labor Market Regulation and the Duration of Employment in Brazil*. Discussion Paper 676. Rio de Janeiro, Brazil: IPEA.

Barros, R. P., Corseuil, C. H., & Foguel, M. (2001). *The Impact of Regulations on Brazilian Labor Market Performance*. Inter-American Development Bank.

Barros, R. P., Corseuil, C. H., & Gonzaga, G. (1999). *Labor Market Regulation and the Demand for Labor in Brazil*. Discussion Paper 656. Rio de Janeiro, Brazil: IPEA.

Berdugo, B., & Hadad, S. (2012). How Do Firing Costs Affect Innovation and Growth when Workers' Ability is Unknown? Employment Protection as a Burden on a Firm's Screening Process. *European Journal of Comparative Economics*, *9*(1), 3–30.

Bertola, G. (1991). *Flexibility, investment, and growth*. Cambridge, MA: National Bureau of Economic Research, Inc. doi:10.3386/w3864

Bertola, G. (1994). Flexibility, Investment, and Growth. *Journal of Monetary Economics*, *34*(2), 215–228. doi:10.1016/0304-3932(94)90050-7

Bertola, G., Boeri, T., & Cazes, S. (2000). Employment protection in industrialized countries: The case for new indicators. *International Labour Review*, *139*(1), 57–72. doi:10.1111/j.1564-913X.2000.tb00402.x

Besley, T., & Burgess, R. (2004). Can Labor Regulation Hinder Economic Performance? Evidence from India. *The Quarterly Journal of Economics*, *119*(1), 91–134. doi:10.1162/003355304772839533

Bhalotra, S. R. (1998). The Puzzle of Jobless Growth in Indian Manufacturing. *Oxford Bulletin of Economics and Statistics*, *60*(1), 5–32. doi:10.1111/1468-0084.00084

Bhattacharjea, A. (2006). *Labor market regulation and industrial performance in India: A critical review of the empirical evidence*. St. Louis, MO: Federal Reserve Bank of St Louis.

Bhattacharjea, A. (2009). The Effects of Employment Protection Legislation on Indian Manufacturing. *Economic and Political Weekly*, *44*(22), 55–62.

Boeri, T. (2011). Institutional reforms and dualism in European labor markets. Handbook of Labor Economics, 4.

Boeri, T., & Garibaldi, P. (2007). Two Tier Reforms of Employment Protection: A Honeymoon Effect? *Economic Journal (London)*, *117*(521), F357–F385. doi:10.1111/j.1468-0297.2007.02060.x

Boeri, T., & Jimeno, J. F. (2005). The effects of employment protection: Learning from variable enforcement. *European Economic Review*, *49*(8), 2057–2077. doi:10.1016/j.euroecorev.2004.09.013

Cairns, D. S. S. (2015). New Formalities for Casual Labor: Addressing Unintended Consequences of China's Labor Contract Law. *Washington International Law Journal*, *24*(1), 219–252.

Casale, G., & Perulli, A. (2014). *Towards the Single Employment Relationship: Comparative Reflections*. Oxford, UK: ILO.

Chan, A. (2003). A 'race to the bottom': Globalisation and China's labor standards. *China Perspectives, 46*, 41–49.

Chan, C. K.-C., & Nadvi, K. (2014). Changing labor regulations and labor standards in China: Retrospect and challenges. *International Labour Review*, *153*(4), 513–534. doi:10.1111/j.1564-913X.2014.00214.x

Cooper, R., Gong, G., & Yan, P. (2013). *Costly labor adjustment: General equilibrium effects of china's employment regulations*. Cambridge, MA: National Bureau of Economic Research, Inc. doi:10.3386/w19324

Cooper, R., Gong, G., & Yan, P. (2015). Dynamic labor demand in China: public and private objectives. *RAND Journal of Economics, 46*(3), 577-610. doi:10.1111/1756-2171.12098

Cuñat, A., & Melitz, M. J. (2007). *Volatility, labor market flexibility, and the pattern of comparative advantage*. St. Louis, MO: Federal Reserve Bank of St Louis. doi:10.3386/w13062

D'Souza, E. (2010). The employment effects of labor legislation in India: A critical essay. *Industrial Relations Journal, 41*(2), 122–135. doi:10.1111/j.1468-2338.2009.00558.x

Davis, S. J., & Henrekson, M. (1995). *Industrial policy, employer size, and economic performance in Sweden*. Cambridge, MA: National Bureau of Economic Research, Inc. doi:10.3386/w5237

Dollar, D., Iarossi, G., & Mengistae, T. (2002). *Investment Climate and Economic Performance: Some Firm Level Evidence from India*. Development Research Group, The World Bank, Working Paper No. 143.

Dougherty, S., Frisancho, V., & Krishna, K. (2013). *State-level labor reform and firm-level productivity in India*. New Delhi, India: Brookings-NCAER India Policy Forum.

Dougherty, S., Robles, V. F., & Krishna, K. (2011). Employment protection legislation and plant-level productivity in India. Paris: Organization for Economic Cooperation and Development (OECD). doi:10.1787/18151973

Dutta Roy, S. (2004). Employment dynamics in Indian industry: Adjustment lags and the impact of job security regulations. *Journal of Development Economics, 73*(1), 233–256. doi:10.1016/j.jdeveco.2003.01.003

Elbadawi, I., Mengistae, T., & Zeufack, A. (2006). Market access, supplier access, and Africa's manufactured exports: A firm level analysis. *The Journal of International Trade & Economic Development, 15*(4), 493–523. doi:10.1080/09638190601037567

Fallon, P., & Lucas, R. E. B. (1991). The Impact of Changes in Job Security Legislations in Industrial and Zimbabwe. *The World Bank Economic Review, 5*(3), 395–413. doi:10.1093/wber/5.3.395

Fallon, P., & Lucas, R. E. B. (1993). Job Security Regulations and the Dynamic Demand for Industrial Labor in India and Zimbabwe. *Journal of Development Economics, 40*(2), 241–275. doi:10.1016/0304-3878(93)90085-2

Fox, L., & Oviedo, A. M. (2013). Institutions and Job Growth in African Manufacturing: Does Employment Protection Regulation Matter? *Journal of African Economies*, *22*(4), 616–650. doi:10.1093/jae/ejt017

Freeman, R. B. (2005). Labor market institutions without blinders: The debate over flexibility and labor market performance. *International Economic Journal*, *19*(2), 129–145. doi:10.1080/1016873050008067 5

Friedman, L. M. (1977). *Law and Society: An Introduction*. Prentice Hall.

Garibaldi, P. (1998). Job flow dynamics and firing restrictions. *European Economic Review*, *42*(2), 245–275. doi:10.1016/S0014-2921(97)00062-7

Gong, G., & Hu, G. (2016). The role of returns to scale in measuring frictions in resource allocation: Revisiting misallocation and manufacturing TFP in China. *Economics Letters*, *138*, 26–29. doi:10.1016/j.econlet.2015.11.014

Griffith, R., Harrison, R., & Macartney, G. (2007). Product Market Reforms, Labor Market Institutions and Unemployment. *Economic Journal (London)*, *117*(519), C142–C166. doi:10.1111/j.1468-0297.2007.02039.x

Griffith, R., & Macartney, G. (2014). Employment Protection Legislation, Multinational Firms, and Innovation. *The Review of Economics and Statistics*, *96*(1), 135–150. doi:10.1162/REST_a_00348

Gupta, P., Hasan, R., & Kumar, U. (2009). *Big reforms but small payoffs: Explaining the Weak Record of Growth and Employment in Indian Manufacturing*. St. Louis, MO: Federal Reserve Bank of St Louis.

Gust, C., & Marquez, J. (2004). International comparisons of productivity growth: The role of information technology and regulatory practices. *Labour Economics*, *11*(1), 33–58. doi:10.1016/S0927-5371(03)00055-1

Gwatidzo, T., & Moyo, B. (2014). Impact of employment protection legislation on employment and exporting in select African countries. *Development Southern Africa*, *31*(2), 299–321. doi:10.1080/0376835X.2014.880877

Habyarimana J. (2008). *The Role of Labor Regulation in Explaining the Low Growth in Employment in South Africa.* Washington, DC: The World Bank.

Hartwell, C. A. (2010). Employment Protection Legislation and Labor Markets in Transition: Assessing the Effects of the Labor Code in Armenia. *European Journal of Comparative Economics*, *7*(2), 413–445.

Hoek, J. (2002). *Labor Market Institutions and Restructuring: Evidence from Regulated and Unregulated Labor Markets in Brazil.* William Davidson Institute, University of Michigan, Working Paper, 484.

Holmes, T. J. (1998). The effect of state policies on the location of manufacturing: Evidence from state borders. *Journal of Political Economy, 106*(4), 667–705. doi:10.1086/250026

Hopenhayn, H., & Rogerson, R. (1993). Job turnover and policy evaluation: A general equilibrium analysis. *Journal of Political Economy, 101*(5), 915–938. doi:10.1086/261909

Howell, D. R., Baker, D., Glyn, A., & Schmitt, J. (2006). Are protective labor market institutions at the root of unemployment? A critical review of the evidence. *Capitalism and Society, 2*(1), 1–71.

Hsieh, C.-T., & Klenow, P. J. (2009). Misallocation and Manufacturing TFP in China and India. *The Quarterly Journal of Economics, 124*(4), 1403–1448. doi:10.1162/qjec.2009.124.4.1403

Islam, I., & Nazara, S. (2000). *Minimum Wage and the Welfare of Indonesian Workers. Occasional Discussion Papers Series 3.* Jakarta: ILO.

Kucera, D. (2003). Effects of Labor Standards on Labor Costs and FDI Flows. In J. Bhagwati & H. Corbet (Eds.), *Labor Standards in an Integrating World Economy.* Washington, DC: Cordell Hull Institute.

Li, J. (2008). China's New Labor Contract Law and Protection of Workers. *Fordham International Law Journal, 32*(3), 1083–1131.

Lisi, D. (2008). *Analysis of employment protection legislation: A model with endogenous labor productivity.* St. Louis, MO: Federal Reserve Bank of St Louis.

Messina, J., & Vallanti, G. (2007). Job Flow Dynamics and Firing Restrictions: Evidence from Europe. *Economic Journal (London), 117*(521), 279–301. doi:10.1111/j.1468-0297.2007.02057.x

Mitra, D., & Ural, B. P. (2008). Indian manufacturing: A slow sector in a rapidly growing economy. *The Journal of International Trade & Economic Development, 17*(4), 525–559. doi:10.1080/09638190802250282

Mortensen, D. T., & Pissarides, C. A. (1999). Unemployment Responses to 'Skill-Based' Technology Shocks: The Role of Labor Market Policy. *Economic Journal (London), 109*(455), 242–265. doi:10.1111/1468-0297.00431

Naghavi, A. (2007). Asymmetric Labor Markets, Southern Wages and the Location of Firms. *Review of Development Economics*, *11*(3), 463–481. doi:10.1111/j.1467-9361.2007.00355.x

Nickell, S., Nunziata, L., & Ochel, W. (2005). Unemployment in the OECD Since the 1960s. What Do We Know? *Economic Journal (London)*, *115*(500), 1–27. doi:10.1111/j.1468-0297.2004.00958.x

Paes, B., Corseuil, C. H., & Gonzaga, G. (2015). *Labor market regulations and the demand for labor in brazil*. St. Louis, MO: Federal Reserve Bank of St Louis.

Poschke, M. (2009). Employment protection, firm selection, and growth. *Journal of Monetary Economics*, *56*(8), 1074–1085. doi:10.1016/j.jmoneco.2009.10.013

Rodrik, D. (1996). Labor Standards in International Trade: Do They Matter and What Do We Do About Them? In R. Lawrence, D. Rodrik, & J. Whalley (Eds.), *Emerging Agenda for Global Trade: High Stakes for Developing Countries*. Washington, DC: Overseas Development Council.

Rubery, J. (2011). Towards a gendering of the labor market regulation debate. *Cambridge Journal of Economics*, *35*(6), 1103–1126. doi:10.1093/cje/ber001

Sachs, J. D., & Warner, A. M. (1997). Sources of Slow Growth in African Economies1. *Journal of African Economies*, *6*(3), 335–376. doi:10.1093/oxfordjournals.jae.a020932

Saint-Paul, G. (1996). *Dual Labor Markets: A Macroeconomic Perspective*. Cambridge, MA: MIT Press.

Saint-Paul, G. (1997). Is labor rigidity harming Europe's competitiveness? The effect of job protection on the pattern of trade and welfare. *European Economic Review*, *41*(3–5), 499–506. doi:10.1016/S0014-2921(97)00017-2

Saint-Paul, G. (2002). Employment protection, international specialization, and innovation. *European Economic Review*, *46*(2), 375–395. doi:10.1016/S0014-2921(01)00093-9

Samaniego, R. M. (2006). Employment protection and high-tech aversion. *Review of Economic Dynamics*, *9*(2), 224–241. doi:10.1016/j.red.2005.10.002

Schivardi, F. (2000). Labor Market Rigidities, Unemployment and Growth. *Giornale degli Economisti e Annali di Economia*, 115–141.

Shapiro, C., & Stiglitz, J. E. (1984). Equilibrium Unemployment as a Worker Discipline Device. *The American Economic Review*, *74*(3), 433.

Sharma, A.N. (2006). Flexibility, Employment and Labor Market Reforms in India. *Economic and Political Weekly, 41*, 2078-86.

Shyam Sundar, K.R. (2005). Labor Flexibility Debate in India: A Comprehensive Review and Some Suggestions. *Economic and Political Weekly, 40*, 2274-85.

Smith, B., Brecher, J., & Costello, T. (2006). Multinationals to China: No New Labor Rights. *Multinational Monitor*, *27*(6), 34–37.

Smith, J. C. (2000). Nominal Wage Rigidity in the United Kingdom. *Economic Journal (London)*, *110*(462), C176–C195. doi:10.1111/1468-0297.00528

Sofi, I. A., & Sharma, P. (2015). Does Employment Protection Legislation Matter in Dualistic Labor Market? Panel Evidence from Indian Manufacturing Sector. *Labor Studies Journal*, *40*(2), 149–168. doi:10.1177/0160449X15587829

Song, Z., Storesletten, K., & Zilibotti, F. (2011). Growing Like China. *The American Economic Review*, *101*(1), 196–233. doi:10.1257/aer.101.1.196

van Schaik, T., & van de Klundert, T. (2013). Employment protection legislation and catching-up. *Applied Economics*, *45*(8), 973–981. doi:10.1080/00036846.2011.613784

World Bank. (2008c). *Enterprise Survey*. Washington, DC: The World Bank.

Yan, P. (2015). What did China's labor contract law do to its private manufacturing firms? *China Economic Journal*, *8*(2), 158–171. doi:10.1080/17538963.2015.1070492

KEY TERMS AND DEFINITIONS

Employment Protection Legislation (EPL): Refers to all types of employment protection measures that govern the hiring and firing of workers, their treatment on the job (including holidays, sick leave and maternity issues, and other related issues, such as workplace safety), whether grounded primarily in legislation, court rulings, collectively bargained conditions of employment, or customary practice.

Innovation: Refers to the process of transforming knowledge into new products (goods or services) with a view to improving a firm's performance.

Knowledge-Based Economy: Is defined as an economy in which information, technology, and knowledge play a fundamental role in the production and distribution process.

Labor Market Flexibility: Can be understood as the capacity and willingness of labor to respond efficiently and rapidly to changes in market conditions, such as a shock in the demand for labor and the wage rate.

Labor Market Rigidity: Refers to prevailing employment practices and environmental policy conditions which limit employers' options with respect to the volume of work, firing costs, minimum wage, notices, lack of opportunity for part-time and flexible-hours work, location, etc.

Productivity: Can be defined as the ratio of a volume measure of output per period to a volume measure of input (capital, energy, personnel, etc.) used in a production process during that period.

ENDNOTES

1 See Freeman (2005) for a good summary of the issue.

2 Legal culture is a set of ideas, attitudes, beliefs, expectations and opinions about law.

3 For instance, the National Labor Committee investigated the cost of labor for some multinational companies in developing countries and found that subcontractors of companies like Wal-Mart and K-Mart pay as low as 15 cents an hour in Nicaragua, Disney pay 57 cents in Haiti; whereas workers of Nike, Esprit and Disney are not only underpaid, but denied the right to unionize.

Chapter 3
Regulating Occupational Health and Safety in EU and China:
From a Comparative Law Perspective

Kai Liu
Jiangsu Normal University, China

ABSTRACT

Occupational health and safety (OHS) is an important aspect of the labour protection field. This chapter compares OHS legal regimes of China and EU. Comprehensive workplace health and safety legislations of the two systems are described, and the different aspects, including for example, legislative aim, the legislation structure, general obligation, OHS insurance, moral harassment, law enforcement, etc., are detailed. Based on the analysis, conclusions are made and policy recommendations from both legislation aspect and enforcement aspect are provided.

INTRODUCTION

The EU Workplace accident and disease prevention have been the focus of law-making activity in European Union (EU) since the creation of the common market in 1950 when the European Coal and Steel Community begins to unite European countries economically and politically in order to secure lasting peace. In more than half a century, the EU occupational health and safety (OHS) law grew from nothing into the present legal system (Liu & Liu, 2015), which centers on the Framework Directive 89/391(see hereafter). The modern Chinese occupational health and safety

DOI: 10.4018/978-1-5225-4134-9.ch003

law started from the foundation of the People's Republic of China in 1949 and has formed system centering on the Work Safety Law (WSL) and Occupational Disease Prevention Law (ODPL). This research is set to compare the two systems and see from what aspects the Chinese system may benefit from the EU system. To serve this purpose, the OHS rules and their application in the EU law and the Chinese law are compared in this chapter. The aim of the comparison is to investigate whether what convergences and divergences exist between the EU system and the Chinese system. Answering these questions might provide some clues to understand how the OHS are regulated respectively in China and EU, and as such is requisite for providing potential recommendations for improving the Chinese system. As commented by Örücü, the comparative lawyer must discover and describe uniformities and differences on the basis of the information s/he has collected and described. (Örücü, 2006). This comparative research is ordered in three topics: the convergences, divergences and the variables between OHS systems of the two jurisdictions. Among them, the variables concern the differences, as divergences do. However, variables concern the factors that are of either non-legal nature or legal nature but not OHS law nature. Based on the comparison, a conclusion would be drawn.

Before analyzing the legal systems, it is necessary to know some information about their economic and labour market contexts in order to better understand the differences between the two jurisdictions. Here three important economic labour market indicators are presented. Regarding EU, according to the data published by the EU's statistical agency --- the Eurostat, the total number of labour force was 218,375,000 people in 2016 (Eurostat, 2016), the unemployment rate was 9.6% (Eurostat, 2017), and the labour participation rate 72.9% (Organisation for Economic Co-operation and Development, 2015). Correspondingly, the data's of China are 806,460.14 (World Bank, 2016), 4.02% (People's Congress, 2017), and 71.0% (World Bank, 2016).

LEGAL SYSTEMS

The EU

EU's regulation of OHS was traced back to the foundation of the European Coal and Steel Community. (Hale,1984; Liu & Liu, 2015; Majone, 1993). According to Liu and Liu, the evolution of the EU/EC has defined the progress OHS protection. Over the decades spanning from the beginning of ECSC, through establishing EEC and through several rounds of enlargements, to the final establishment of the EU, it can be observed that the technique of legislative intervention evolved from safeguards, based on detailed and highly technical normative acts, to a different kind of regulation which is more based on general protection duties and principles (Liu & Liu, 2015).

Nowadays, OHS has already become one of the key focus areas of law-making activity since the creation of the common market (Liu & Liu, 2015). The EU OHS system is built the landmark Directive 89/391. In general, the Directive 89/391/EEC lays down employers' general obligations to ensure workers' health and safety in every aspect related to work, 'addressing all types of risk' (Sabel & Zeitlin, 2008; Liu & Liu, 2015). It is also a Framework Directive that established general principles, including risk assessment, avoidance, substitution and prevention. The Directive served as a basis for later individual directives dealing with specific issues such as those on workplaces, personal protective equipment, work equipment, manual handling of loads and display screen equipment (Nicholson, 2002; Liu & Liu, 2015). The individual Directives define how risks are to be assessed, and the setting and measuring limit of values at the workplace. Article16 paragraph 3 of the Framework Directive states that its general provisions shall apply in full to all the areas covered by each individual Directive (See Article16, paragraph 3 of the Framework Directive). Until the day of writing, in total 19 directives have been adopted, which are compiled in the European Agency for Safety and Health at Work (EASHW) 's website (European Agency for Safety and Health at Work, 2017). According to EASHW, these directives are categorized into six topics: (a) Workplaces, equipment, signs, personal protective equipment; (b) Exposure to chemical agents and chemical safety; (c) Exposure to physical hazards; (d) Exposure to biological agents; (e) Provisions on workload, ergonomical and psychosocial risks; and (d) Sector specific and worker related provisions (European Agency for Safety and Health at Work, 2017), as shown in the following table. The individual directives define how to assess these risks and, in some instances, set limit values for certain substances or agents. According to EU system, all the directives shall be transposed into domestic law of Member States (MS), in order to ensure that national law is fully in alignment with EU OHS legislation.

Generally, the EU OHS system formulation is seen as a social dimension of European integration (Majone, 1993) --- which has been actively pursued during the past fifty years. It is at least partly through the adopting of OHS legislations that the capacity of the European Union to effect patterns of social exclusion is potentially deployed (Walby, 1999). The FD where the system centers on establishes general principles for managing safety and health, such as responsibility of the employer, rights/duties of workers, using risk assessments to continuously improve company processes, and workplace health and safety representation. All subsequent Directives within the meaning of Article 16 (1) of the Framework Directive follow these common principles. The Directive 89/391 established a general duty for employers to assess and prevent or reduce risks to safety and health at work. Indeed, the general

Table 1. Daughter directives under the framework directive

Area	Directive
Workplaces, equipment, signs, personal protective equipment	Directive 2009/104/EC – use of work equipment
	Directive 99/92/EC - risks from explosive atmospheres
	Directive 92/58/EEC - safety and/or health signs
	Directive 89/656/EEC - use of personal protective equipment
	Directive 89/654/EEC - workplace requirements
Exposure to chemical agents and chemical safety	Directive 2009/161/EU - indicative occupational exposure limit values
	Directive 2009/148/EC - exposure to asbestos at work
	Directive 2006/15/EC - indicative occupational exposure limit values
	Directive 2004/37/EC - carcinogens or mutagens at work
	Directive 2000/39/EC - indicative occupational exposure limit values
	Directive 98/24/EC - risks related to chemical agents at work
	Directive 91/322/EEC - indicative limit values
Exposure to physical hazards	Directive 2013/59/Euratom - protection against ionising radiation
	Directive 2013/35/EU - electromagnetic fields
	Directive 2006/25/EC - artificial optical radiation
	Directive 2003/10/EC - noise
	Directive 2002/44/EC - vibration
	Directive 96/29/Euratom - ionizing radiation
	Directive 90/641/Euratom - outside workers in controlled areas (ionizing radiation)
Exposure to biological agents	Directive 2000/54/EC - biological agents at work
Provisions on workload, ergonomic and psychosocial risks	Directive 90/270/EEC - display screen equipment
	Directive 90/269/EEC - manual handling of loads
Sector specific and worker related provisions	Directive 2010/32/EU - prevention from sharp injuries in the hospital and healthcare sector
	Directive 94/33/EC - young workers
	Directive 93/103/EC - work on board fishing vessels
	Directive 92/104/EEC - mineral-extracting industries
	Directive 92/91/EEC - mineral-extracting industries – drilling
	Directive 92/85/EEC - pregnant workers
	Directive 92/57/EEC - temporary or mobile construction sites
	Directive 92/29/EEC - medical treatment on board vessels
	Directive 91/383/EEC - fixed-duration or temporary employment relationship

duty fails expressly to mention against moral harassment at work. Yet, according to Liu's research, the current position of the European Commission is that moral harassment is covered under this directive. This is because, under the terms of Article 6(1), employers are obliged to assess all the risks, including, inter alia, those related to chemical agents, work equipment and the design of workplaces. The list is not exhaustive and the national legislation enacted in application of this directive has been extensively used in relation to workplace violence (Liu, 2015). The EU system has paid considerable attention to occupational health and safety in small to medium-sized enterprises (SMEs), which are a key sector in EU's economy and are vital to achieving EU economic goals (Hämäläinen, 2008).

According to Champoux and Brun, the nature of the OHS problems in small firms and the factors explaining the higher relative risk level are a topic of primary interest, for two reasons: firstly, they are more fragile financially; and secondly, their owner-managers tend to be personally responsible for virtually all management functions in their firms without any management training (Champoux & Brun, 2003).

To combatting this problem, the EU advocates the OHS services, which are external services and can provide professional OHS preventative services to SMEs. The model of preventive OHS service advocated by the EU Framework Directive 89/391 is an integrated one in which the pro-vision of occupational medicine, safety, hygiene, ergonomics, and work psychology is part of a 'holistic' approach towards the prevention of injury and ill-health and the improvement of working conditions and the working environment (James & Walters, 2002). A further distinctive feature of this approach is that workers and their representatives are centrally involved in both the oversight of the operation of such services and in carrying out the risk assessments that are the procedural basis to current approaches to health and safety management (James & Walters, 2002). The transposition of the EU directives led many countries to produce and to implement new laws and regulations, in order to conform to EU system. According to Jacinto and Aspinwall, the EU member states acted at different speeds and with different levels of detail, mostly depending on their own ''state-of-the-art'' and stage of development (Jacinto & Aspinwall, 2004).

China

The legislative structure of OHS in China is based on the Constitution. Its Article 42 provides:

By using various means, the state creates conditions for employment, strengthens labor protection, improves working conditions and, on the basis of expanded production, increases remuneration for work and social benefits... The state provides necessary occupational training to citizens before they are employed.

Furthermore, the structure consists of laws, administrative regulations, local regulations, departmental rules, local rules and OHS standards. Among them, two major OSH laws are Work Safety Law (WSL), and Occupational Diseases Prevention Law (ODPL), which functions as the foundation of the whole OHS system and deal respectively with safety and health issues at workplace (Brown, 2009). Other relating laws include Mines Safety Law (MSL), Labour Law, Labour Contract Law, Fire Protection Law, Emergency Response Law and Criminal Law. The major regulations are Regulations on Coal Mine Safety Inspection, Special Regulations of the State Council on Preventing Coal Mine Accidents, Regulations on Safety Management in Construction Projects, Regulations on the Safe Administration of Hazardous Chemicals, Regulations on Fireworks and Firecracker Safety Management, Regulations on Work Safety Licenses, Regulations on Civil Explosive Products Safety Management, Regulations on Special Equipment Safety Inspection, Regulations on Safety Supervision and Management of Agricultural Machinery, Regulations on Ascertaining Administrative Responsibility in Extraordinarily Serious Safety Accidents, Regulations on Work Injury Insurance, and Regulations on Reporting, Investigation and Handling of Work Safety Accidents, as compiled by International Labor Organization in its LEGOSH database. (LEGOSH Database, 2014).

With respect to the two primary laws, namely the Work Safety Law and the Occupational Disease Prevention Law. According to Pringle and Frost's compilation, the Work Safety Law stipulates 14 basic systems and/or measures. The important ones are: (a). A production unit must meet all the relevant laws, regulations, and industry-specific laws (such as the Coal Safety Law), otherwise it may not undertake production activities; (b) An enterprise must appoint an individual who is responsible for all aspects of safety; (c) An enterprise must also implement a safety management organization or individual; (d) An enterprise must implement a system of education, training, and assessment of safety knowledge of OHS directors (that is, personnel with overall responsibility), OHS managers, and workers; (e) Enterprises must implement a system of three simultaneous [OHS] measures at all stages of all projects; that is, OHS measures should be evident at the planning stage, during construction (of plant and so on), and when production is under way; (f) Production units must register exceptionally dangerous hazards with the local safety inspectorate; (g) Enterprises must implement a safety management system specifically addressing workplaces where explosives, working at height, and other dangers are involved (Pringle & Frost, 2003).

According to Su's compilation, the Occupational Disease Prevention Law (ODPL), adopted in 2001, defines the occupational health rights of workers, the obligations and duties of employers to protect the health of their employees, the responsibilities of the governments at various levels, and trade unions' representation in workers' health protection. The law stipulates basic principles governing the prevention and control of occupational disease, protective measures, hazards monitoring and management in workplaces, diagnosis of occupational disease, health authority inspections, and the liabilities incurred by those violating the law and control of occupational disease, protective measures, hazards monitoring and management in workplaces, diagnosis of occupational disease, health authority inspections, and the liabilities incurred by those violating the law (Su, 2003).

COMPARATIVE OBSERVATION

In the previous sections, the legal systems in regulating OHS in EU and China were discussed. The legislative frameworks and how the laws are implemented in the two countries with regard to what respective roles played by public enforcement agencies, the workers' representing bodies, as well as the individual workers are identified. Following the comparative methodology proposed in the first Chapter, this section summaries the convergences and divergences by 'analogy, distinction and contrast' and identifies the variables that may give rise to the divergences presented above. By situating China in its current transitional phase, the context of contemporary China is also assessed by referring to the experiences of the EU to produce a better understanding of the uniqueness of Chinese problems.

Convergence

Mapping out convergence is important. The comparative study would benefit from the findings of convergence because it can help understand to what extent the Chinese system is similar to that of the EU. The OHS legal systems in the EU and China present some converging features, which are summarized below. This converging process is advanced both by domestic demands, such as increasing publicity of industrial accidents and emerging new occupational risks, and by the common OHS legal norms.

First, based on an examination of the legal policies in the China and EU in the field of regulating OHS, it is clear that the protecting workers from occupational hazards are gaining prevalence in the two jurisdictions' political and legal agendas, which can be observed in three aspects. First, both jurisdictions have adopted a statutory framework to combat occupational hazards and to secure a healthy and safe working environment. OHS in China are mainly legislated into two distinct systems, namely the safety work system and the occupational diseases control and prevention system.

Second, both systems are of relevance with prescriptive approach. Since its creation in 1950s, the EU witnessed a prescriptive approach, which focused on providing in some cases OHS technical standards directly and in many more cases mandating the Member States to provide technical standards (Liu, 2015). The prescriptive approach was dominant until the introduction of the Framework Directive 89/391, (Liu, 2015), which was influenced by the UK's Health and Safety at Work etc Act 1974. The latter adopted goal-oriented elements recommended by *the Robens Report*. One prominent character of the Chinese legislation is of large number of prescriptive provisions. The difference is that the EU traditionally took use of the prescriptive approach, while China still utilizes it.

Third, both jurisdictions have endorsed some commonly accepted principles and underpinning values that govern the protection and promotions of OHS. These principles and values include the realization of the imposition of the OHS obligation primarily on the employer, the establishment of specialized public agency to enforce OHS laws, and the realization of adopting a comprehensive legislative system to battle occupational hazards. Although the EU and China show different attitudes toward the way of formulating the provisions in their respective legislation systems, both of their approaches indicate an attempt to realize the requirements of securing a healthy and safe workplace.

Fourth, both jurisdictions are of political will at the central level. Even at its creation, the EU saw OHS as an essential area to regulate and an area of relevance with the community's integration. The development of EU OHS also implies that OHS has been one of the few social domains, which remain highly centralized. (Liu, 2015). In this context, it is arguable that EU is of great political will to regulate the OHS. Protecting workers against occupational hazards is highly of interests of a socialist country as China. This is already stipulated as in the supreme law, the Chinese Constitution. In different congress meetings and state council meetings, preventing occupational accidents and "securing the safety of labors' lives and property" have been addressed. In this context, China is never short of political will at least at the central level to protect and promote OHS, although there has been a lack of driving force --- including factors of different aspects (the legal aspect is a well-functioning legal system) --- which would turn political will into effective OHS management.

Fifth, OHS regulating in the EU and China faces some common challenges. The emerging potential OHS hazards introduced by new technologies, materials, and substances, have threatened OHS regulating. Although psychological and psychosocial problems are becoming dominant occupational risks, both of the two systems have not recognized these hazards in their legislations. However, it should be noted that some

EU Member States, for example, Sweden, the Netherlands, France, UK, Germany, and Austria, among other things, have already statutorily recognized these risks as workplace hazards, and moreover there are academic speculations that the EU law would in the not far further recognize these risk as workplace hazards. The EU's trend at this point would be further discussed in the following part.

Divergence

Despite the converging features between the EU and China, the legislation and the adopted approaches in the two jurisdictions present different answers to the research questions formulated in Chapter 1. hese differences include the role of worker participation, the regulating mental health at workplaces, the attitude towards the psychological and psychosocial problems at the enforcement level.

Economic Interests May Not Endanger the Health of an Employee

As a developing country as China, would the economic growth inevitably a priority in the social-economic context. However, this is also presented in the legal wording of OHS regulations, including the two primary legislations, the Safety Work Law and the Occupational Disease Prevention Law. In comparison, this is not observed in the OHS legislations at both the EU level and the Member States level. According to Barnard's analysis, the EU bases its OHS legislative activities also partly on the economic concerns: one of the main economic justification is to create "a level playing field", by depriving those countries with low OHS standards of a perceived competitive advantage over those countries with higher standards and thus greater costs (Barnard, 2013). Nevertheless, in no case would the OHS legislations be enacted for promoting economic growth, and would the economic growth be expressly provided as the legislative purpose. Also, through the examinations of the Member States' national laws, which should be at least theoretically in line with the EU legislations, no wording relating economic growth promoting is found. The rationale behind is simply because the OHS law is of nature social law. It cannot protect the workers' OHS rights, while promoting the economy, as the two issues are in industrial practice contradictory to each other, and could not be made at the same time. As stated in the *1974 Council Resolution on Social Action Programme*, which sees OHS law as a measure aimed at the humanization of the workers' living and working conditions with particular reference to improvement in health and safety conditions at work.

The System: Unified vs. Separated

The EU legislative system is built based on an integrated approach, reflected in its integrated framework Directive 89/391. This legislative system deals with both the OH and OS. Correspondingly, the transposed legislations in Member States are of unified nature and deals with both the OH and OS. This involves a basic framework of primary legislation establishing general principles and some specific requirements (Barnard, 2013). Examples include the Denmark's *Working Environment Act 1975*; Greece's *Health and Safety of Workers' Act 1985*; Ireland's *Safety, Health and Welfare at Work Act 1989*; the Netherlands' *Working Environment Act 1980*; and UK's *Health and Safety at Work Act 1974* (Barnard, 2013). It is also the case with their respective enforcement systems, which are also integrated and responsible for implementing the whole OHS laws and securing the compliance by inter alia the employers.

OHS issues are dealt with in a different way in China. The legislative framework is statutorily divvied into OH and OS systems, respectively headed by two basic laws: the Occupational Disease Prevention Law and the Safe Production Law. Under this legislative framework, the supervision system is correspondingly separated, and mainly include health administrative department and work safety administrative department. And, these two regulatory departments are both authorized by laws and respectively assume their duties and responsibilities.

Both Chinese scholars and scholars from outside have different opinions vis-à-vis whether the Chinese system is adaptive and elastic enough to meet current and future challenges. Zhou holds that the OH enforcement power distribution to the health department is not in line with the need of actual development of OH, and the objective administrative system in China. (Zhou, 2010). Instead, the primary OH enforcement responsibility should be distributed to safety administration. Only OH issues relating to the occupational disease treatment, and rehabilitation would be left to the health department as the health system, in his view, possesses sufficient expertise and resources for the above issues (Zhou, 2010). Li and Zhang argue that separation approach in OHS has caused contradictions and overlaps in two parallel legislative systems (Li & Zhang, 2012). Bingan Li thinks the separated legislative framework has caused unnecessarily rising size of the OHS standards as different administrative departments are empowered according to the legislative framework to promulgate standards within their respective jurisdictions (Li, 2013).

From the enforcement perspective, Zong et al hold the view that the segregation in the OHS system has caused has caused the unnecessary rise of the cost of enforcement, as well as the cost arising from compliance with laws on the part of the employers (Zong. et al., 2011). This viewpoint is also shared in: Zhang et al.'s research. (Zhang et al., 2010). From the OHS management perspective, Wu and Chi points out that the separation of OH and OS may cause ineffective convergence of occupational hazards source management, early prevention, process management and consequences response (Wu & Chi, 2015). In the legal domain, the above mentioned ineffective convergence in the enforcement of occupational health and safety laws may weaken the supervision capacities. Furthermore, they point out that the lack of harmonized legislation and unified supervision would result in the conflict of regulatory departments' function and poor coordination (Wu & Chi, 2015).

Based on the above opinions, it is arguable that the lack of harmonized legislation and unified supervision has caused to some extent the conflict of regulatory departments' function and poor coordination, and also from the compliance perspective, the ineffective convergence of occupational hazards source management, early prevention, process management and consequences response.

General Obligation Approach

Although the regulating OHS by the EU/EC started as early as its creation, the approach that was adopted was based on binding normative instruments with the aim of standardizing national laws, and this technique was widely used until the 1990s (de la Vega, 2013). Since the 1989 Directive 89/391, the general obligation approach has been put in place, together with greater use of soft law instruments. In the EU system, general obligation, the general obligation provisions have all been introduced to ensure that the principal parties involved (primarily the employer, and to a less extent, the employee, and other parties) in all work processes are subjected to a range of overlapping and interlocking duties requiring them to ensure the workplace is safe and without risks to health. Under the general obligation approach, both employers and employees have specific statutory obligations in relation to workplace health and safety that must be followed. This is combined with the greater role of private individuals (workers and/or their representing bodies) in the drafting of the workplace instruments (de la Vega, 2013). Moreover, this ideal of general obligation may not be easily achieved without the EU's desire for risk assessment. As a matter of fact, the EU puts risk assessment as one of the primary means underpinning the general obligation approach. In this sense, it is seen as the key method in self-regulation, and is presented as one of the crucial means in order to avoid occupational accidents.

The general obligation approach can hardly be found in the Chinese system. The present legal provisions are mainly detailed, restrictive and prescriptive, specifying the minimum standards that the employers should comply. The minimum standards are mostly prescriptive technical requirement of the production activities, such as scaffolding safety, prevention of falls, etc. Most standards for health and safety are compulsory. This sharp difference with the EU system is because the Chinese regulations and standards are based on the perspective approach rather than general obligation approach. The prescriptive approach is also called "deemed to comply" or "command and control". The Chinese legislation under this approach is, as opposed to ends, primarily concerned with type and quality of materials, method of manufacturing, and workmanship. The system attempts to standardize the work process using prescriptive rules and procedures usually backed by the monitoring of compliance and by sanctions for non-compliance. In parallel, due to absence of general obligation, the Chinese system fails (also does not need) to adopt risk assessment mechanism.

The Role of Occupational Insurance

Although the EU legislative system does not include providing occupational insurance as mandatory requirement, all the Member States have mandated so in their national legislations, although the differences in doing so are found. The legislations of in some EU countries have included workplace insurance as integral part of "social security health insurance schemes", and those of the other countries have prescribed a separate insurance scheme specific for OHS. In the first case, if a work-related illness, or an occupational accident injury occurs, the rules on sickness apply. Many of the legislations of the Member States include the occupational insurance in the mandatory health insurance, for example, the Netherlands, Sweden and UK; the others in the social security scheme. Despite the differences, one character at least is common. That is

In the three countries, which are chosen for study in this research, if the workers think there is a gap between the amount they are compensated by the occupational insurance scheme and that they expect, they can go to court to seek extra compensation to fill the gap. It should be kept in mind that the frequency of going to court varies among the three countries. In the Netherlands, and Sweden, as discussed before, it is very rare that workers start the procedures by themselves. Instead, the trade unions will do this on their behalf.

In comparison, the occupational accident insurance scheme commenced implementation as late as in 2004. China fails to run a mandatory universal health insurance system, as the legislative framework has itself limits in relation to the coverage of employees and the nature of injury. According to the current Chinese system regulating the insurance, the most fundamental requirement for the employee is to prove they have or had a labour relationship with the employer at the time of the accident or onset of illness. In this context, the employer is reluctant to sign written labour contract, which would become the most obvious proof for the existence of the labour relationship in order to not avoid providing the insurance for the workers, for the reason that the insurance is financed by employer-paid.

According to a 2010 published literature, in the Delta River industry area, only 65 percent of the workers had labour contracts and only 73 percent had work injury insurance (Brown, 2010). For those who are not covered by occupational insurance, have to seek compensation by "unusual means", such as attracting public social media's attention, which is reflected in the case of Tseng Hei-tao (Liu, 2013).

The Role of Moral Harassment

At the union level, the Community has until now not adopted special legislation vis-à-vis moral harassment (Liu, 2015). As discussed before, the Framework Directive fails to include moral harassment as workplace hazards. However, it does require employers to 'adapt the work to the individual, especially as regards the design of work places, the choice of work equipment and the choice of working and production methods, with a view, in particular, to alleviating monotonous work and work at a predetermined work-rate, developing a coherent overall prevention policy which covers technology, organization of work, working conditions, social relationships and the influence of factors related to the working environment'. In this sense, there is a reference to, and provision for, risks related to the psychosocial work environment. Also, the European legislators have taken use of policy approaches - to define moral harassment as a violation of dignity, as well as to combine sexual and gender harassment with "mobbing," and bullying of all workers (Liu, 2015). Furthermore, according to the compilation by Martino et al., the European Parliament's 'Resolution on Harassment at the Workplace 2001/2339 (INI)' includes the following:

calls on the Member States, with a view to counteracting bullying and sexual harassment at work, to review and, if appropriate, to supplement their existing legislation and to review and standardize the definition of bullying;

urges the Commission to consider a clarification or extension of the scope of the framework directive on health and safety at work or, alternatively, the drafting of a new framework directive as a legal instrument to combat bullying and as a means of ensuring respect for the worker's human dignity, privacy and integrity; emphasizes in this connection the importance of systematic work on health and safety and of preventive action;

In this context, although without specifying what form it should take, the EU commission recognizes that psychological harassment and violence at work require legislative action (International Labour Organization, 2004).

At the member state level, countries such as UK, Sweden, the Netherlands, Belgium, Germany, Austria, Spain, Luxemburg, and France have developed specific legal regimes to expressly protect in their laws the workers from harassment at work. In Member States like Greece, there is still no specific legislation to combat the phenomenon. However, the victims can be fully protected by the institutional anti-discrimination law (Vlagopoulou, 2017). According to EU's report, as of 2004, as many as twenty three then Member States (Austria, Belgium, Cyprus, the Czech Republic, Denmark, Estonia, Finland, France, Germany, Hungary, Ireland, Italy, Lithuania, Luxembourg Malta, the Netherlands, Poland, Portugal, the Slovak Republic, Slovenia, Spain, Sweden and the UK) stated that they had employment legislation that dealt with Sexual Harassment/Harassment based on sex (McGolgan, 2004).

In contrast, moral harassment is until the day of writing never considered an occupational hazard in China (Liu, 2015). China has adopted a legal system against this concern based on not specific OHS moral harassment provisions, but instead provisions of other non-OHS laws, including mainly the right to reputation provisions in General Principles of Civil Law (Article 101) and in the Penal Code (Article 246). Moreover, in this system, the scope of moral harassment is much narrow, compared to that in the EU Member States' system, as it is largely limited to including no much more than sexual harassment.

The Quality of Law Enforcement

Rule of law constitutes one of the EU's essential elements and good governance. The EU has a good reputation in terms of the rule of law, the law is generally enforced to a satisfactory level in the EU Member States, particularly in the "old members". It should be noted that there is a noted imbalance existing within EU regarding this issue, because the *status quo* in the "new members" --- the Member States ascended since 2004 --- is basically not equitably at a high level as in the old members. Nonetheless, generally, in combination with that the EU strengthens the protection of the rule of law and fundamental rights in the EU, the non-compliance with the law is not commonly observed in the Community.

In comparison, although the situation is continuously improving, there is a well-known gap between the 'law in books' and the 'law inaction' in China (Li, 2014). That is so called in Chinese "laws are not well executed or strictly executed although they are well enacted"(有法不依,执法不严). To develop the economy, local governments tend to avoid strengthen the inspection and control to compel the employer's compliance with laws, in order to make way for promoting economic growth. This problem is closely related to and aggravated by the problem mentioned in the section 3.2.1 in this chapter. That is, economic growth is statutorily recognized that as a priority.

The Role of Workers' Representing Bodies

In Europe, civil society has been traditionally playing a vital role in promoting the whole society's advancement. This role has begun to play even before it was recognized by legislations. It is also the case with the worker's representing bodies which play a vital role in the OHS enforcement system. Public awareness of occupational protection has been raised by constant social movements, including the early working class movements of the late 19th century and, to add a further dimension to this, the modern social movement beginning in the 1970s when the number of work-related accidents and illnesses remained high, after twenty years from the launch of the fundamental freedoms of movement (de la Vega, 2013).Nowadays, it is argued that a prominent feature of the EU model is its emphasis on encouraging civil society to participate in the development, implementation, and enforcement of OHS policy, as demonstrated in the employer-employee cooperation approach in its system. In other words, the EU system relies not exclusively on a centralized state inspectorate to enforce OHS laws, by supplementing the inspectorates with mandated workplace OHS committees. There committees, though bearing different titles in different Member States, generally operate with delegated public powers, including for example the monitor, and in some measure, are empowered to enforce, compliance with the regulatory regime.

In contrast, the awakening of public awareness of the OHS protection in China occurred later, especially after the occurrence of serious occupational accidents or outbreaks of occupational diseases. Nevertheless, public awareness of OHS protection remains at still a considerably low level. In a largely Party-state country as China (Yu, 2007), civil society (i.e., individuals and organizations that are outside the governmental apparatus) is seen as being "relatively underdeveloped" (Percival, 2013; Nicholas, 2012; Yu, 2007). Trade union system is basically of half-official status, and not granted independent position. The relationship between the Chinese trade union system, and the communist party and the state is seen in the research by Hishida et al. (Hishida et al., 2010)

At the workplace level, trade union is not empowered to be actively involved in OHS, neither is any other form of worker's representing body, if any. Therefore, the role of workers' representing bodies in participating in OHS is not observed in China in the same way that it is in the EU.

Variables

OHS is never merely a separate material sphere; instead, they are interconnected with their surroundings and enmeshed in social-economic and legal contexts. Having observed the divergences between the EU and China regarding OHS legislation and practice, this section identifies several variables in the contexts that may explain the divergences found above.

OHS Policy-Making in Social-Economic Contexts

Although both jurisdictions have conducted intensive OHS policy-making, their starting points differ significantly. In a post-developed society as the EU, OHS protection is deemed as an intrinsic component of civic life and a crucial means of achieving public welfare of not only the workers but also the whole society members. OHS protection is firmly grounded as a fundamental purpose of the industries, whereas the economic growth is considered a by-product, at least secondary to the public welfare.

In comparison, in China, the social-economic contexts in which OHS is situated are, however, not similarly opportunistic and poetic. Instead, the GDP-based assessment model of local officials' performance pushes these officials to expressly or implicitly allow the employer enterprises in their jurisdictions to bypass OHS requirements to reduce production costs and in some cases even help the employers avoiding potential compensation liabilities to injured or ill workers. For example, see case Tseng Hei-tao (Liu, 2013).

Compared to the OHS protection in EU, this issue in this East Asian country is seen as being more pressured. Well-documented factors include the increasingly expanding size of industries, the large working population, a comparatively poor economic basis and the comparative poverty. The following statistics may be illustrative: The size of China's GDP is exceeding10 trillion USD as of 2014. China processes 21% of the world's population, and around 400 million workers. The China government has until the day of writing never published statistics over the total number of the workers. So, it is made reference here to the statitiscs by China Labour Bulletin, a Non-Government Organization with high credibility. (China Labour Bulletin, 2017).

The annual GDP growth rate, though decelerating since 2012, has been on average nearly 10% in the past three decades (International Monetary Fund, 2017; World Bank, 2017). China has achieved a rapid economic development, especially in industrial field. China has become the world's largest manufacturer, with its manufacturing output surpassed the U.S. and Japan (Wu & Chi, 2015). Despite their benefits, the expanding industries have been increasingly put the workplace at risk and hazards to human health arise. In this context, China is facing unprecedented pressure with regard to OHS protection.

Operation of Administrative Power and Public Trust in General

Although reforms have been initiated in recent years aimed at the transformation to a limited government, China has a long history of an omnipotent government (Fan. et al., 2014; Morgan. et al., 2010). Lacking a separation of powers, the government historically served the administrative as well as the judicial functions (Morgan. et al., 2010).

In China, however, multiple factors impede the exercise of administrative power in an accountable way, including the absence of laws specifying procedural rules governing the administrative power exercise, a lack of channels through which citizens may seek to enforce the rights given to them by law, and a lack of public participation and transparency. The impediments are elaborated in a more detailed way in the research by Ostry et al. (Ostry. et al., 2003). In this context, the government can freely, though to a varying extent from region to region, switch between roles as the exerciser and the supervisor of power, which creates room for rent seeking.

Judicial Independence and the Predicament of the Courts

Indeed, the state of judicial independence in China remains elusive (Michelson & Li, 2012; Peerenboom, 2010; Kinkel & Hurst, 2011). Yet, Michelson and Li argue that most scholars agree that the Chinese legal system remains fundamentally fused to the state bureaucracy and subject to some important measure of political interference and control (Michelson & Li, 2012). This is also the case for OHS-related cases in China. In contrast, this deferential attitude does not derive from judicial respect for agencies' professional knowledge under the rationale of rule of law, as it is in the EU. In the Chinese system, this attitude derives from the courts' comparatively inferior role in terms of administrative power (Peerenboom, 2010). As a result, the courts are supposed to work in tandem with governments for the purposes of policy advocacy and social control.

Inappropriate interference in judicial work by governments has led to a phenomenon in which local courts are not willing to handle cases against where governments explicitly or implicitly protect the enterprise because of economic development concerns and do not have the ability to adjudicate such cases neutrally and independently (Liu, 2013). The predicaments and impediments that courts confront in China are not found in the EU, where the rule of law and independency of courts are well respected (Sadurski. et al., 2006).

Assessment of Contexts: Understanding the Transition in China

Having analyzed the convergences, divergences and variables between the EU and China, the next question will address how to assess these contextual similarities and disparities to better understand the distinctive features of the current transition in China.

Since 1978, China has stunned the world with its one of the world's biggest economic booms. The Chinese economic miracle closely relates to the development model to which China adheres (Ma, 2015). However, the "China model" has, in the recent years, received more criticism on inter alia democratic representation, and human rights issues (Chang, 2014) and the cost is seen as huge and unsustainable (Huang, 2008). In the OHS field, this cost would be that economic growth also increases occupational risks without inter alia enough increasing legal protection (Zhao. et al., 2012).

Examining the EU's OHS policies, one can observe a clear shift in the late 1980s. Before that, the prescriptive approach to rule-making, with focus on specification standards, intensively shaped the landscape of the EU's legislations. However, the following shift in regulating OHS signaled an awareness of fundamental problems akin to the prescriptive approach, when it comes to prevention of workplace accidents.

In comparison, China began to introduce reforms in the late 1970s with the end of the Cultural Revolution, which had brought about immeasurable economic losses and social turbulence to the China. Since then, China has made economic growth its main priority (Dorn & Wang, 1990). This priority was also echoed by massive grass-rooted people; they were desperately in desire of improving their livelihoods and quality of life. In parallel, the economic growth priority is systematically established in the Chinese administrative system, where economic growth performance has significant impact on the promotion prospects in the local officials promotion tournament (Wang, 2007; Cao, 2006). In the other words, the whole Chinese society from both the government and the civil society are to some extent "kidnapped" by the imperative of economic growth for the preservation of political stability. In this sense, OHS regulating should be considered not only as a material entity but also as a basis for economic growth and furthermore as a basis for the sovereignty's legitimacy.

Nonetheless, with society becoming increasingly pluralized and workers beginning to desire a better quality of life and a better workplace, economic growth cannot completely sustain the legitimacy challenge in the new era. The derogation of the workplace health and safety and the occurrence of the industrial accidents, and the prevalence of the occupational diseases are occurring at an alarming rate. In order to alleviate the social conflicts and smooth China's transition, the authority has revitalized and employed traditional values and ideologies. The most recent one is 'harmonious society' brought forward in 2004 as the governing ideologies for contemporary China (Guo & Guo, 2008; Zhao & Lim, 2010; Ma, 2015). Yet, it can be asserted that harmony may only be a mirage as long as it is built on the current OHS regulating model. In this context, making a commitment to workplace health and safety and delivering on its promise before it is too late might be the foremost priority for furthering the unavoidable transition process in China.

CONCLUSION

Through the compression observation between the Chinese system and the EU system, this section will conclude what conditions would be reached in order to establish an effective OHS legal system. The results arising from this section would be the basis for proving legal and policy recommendations for improving the Chinese system.

General Obligation Approach Plays a Vital Role in Improving the Effectiveness of OHS Law

First, general obligation approach can bring down the size of the OHS laws as shown in the EU OHS system part. The causes of workplace incidents are typically complex and may involve a series of events, which are of varying probabilities. Under the prescriptive approach, to cover the situations as many as possible, a regulator has write rules or standards as many as possible, correspondingly. However, with the introduction of general obligation, the regulator does not need to provide rules to cover all the situations (which is also impossible to achieve). Instead, the regulator only need to mandate the general obligation applicable to parties (primarily the employer) in all workplaces.

Second, the operation of modern businesses involves the use of sophisticated management and technical systems. It is unlikely that a regulator, no matter how well versed he or she may be in the businesses, will possess sufficient knowledge to be able to write and enforce regulations that keep up with all of the latest technical developments. However, under the general obligation approach, the general obligation would be the primary line to check whether the employer and the other parties have complied the law, and as such simplify the process of formulating the law and enforcing the law, as repeatedly shown in the EU part, the Sweden part, the Netherlands part, and the UK part.

Third, there is no means of designing or operating to a calculated level of risk. Even if it could be shown that the use of a different type of ladder is of very low risk, for example the OHS rule has to be followed. In this context, the prescriptive approach is very labor intensive and costly both to the regulator and the regulated industry and can be cumbersome for mature industries, as shown in the Chinese system part. The general obligation approach allows for the overlaps of accountability. It mandates all the employers have a duty to identify hazards, assess risks, and eliminate or control risks to the OHS of the workers. Given the resource restraints, it can be useful for organizations to prioritize risks and plan their actions so that they can make their workplaces healthier and safer.

A Harmonized OHS Legal System

A harmonized system would regulate OHS more effectively and protect workers against workplace hazards more efficiently. First, the harmonized legislative system would lead to a harmonized enforcement system. As demonstrated in the EU system, the EU and its Member States (for example, the three countries chosen in this research) have adopted a harmonized law, dealing with both health and safety, and correspondingly, the Member States have established a harmonized enforcement system to implement the laws. In contrary, separated legislative system would lead to separated enforcement system, as is presented in the Chinese system part. That the statutory protection of OH and OS, which are presented in two important existing laws: Production Safety Law and the Occupational Disease Prevention Law, two enforcement systems are responsible for implementing the two laws respectively.

Second, a harmonized system helps to avoid public agencies' function conflicts and unnecessary confusions to the employers. As a matter of fact, the OH and OS are closely related, which cannot be artificially separated, and both of them are serving the workers' safety and health. The Chinese approach to separate the two parts results in the conflict of regulatory departments' function and poor coordination. This further lead to that the enterprises sometimes would confuse that which department assumes regulatory function. Like in the China's case, regarding the supervisory power distribution between the work safety department and the health department has caused confusions to the employers. In parallel, the regulatory vacuum would be induced because of this status. However, a harmonized system would effectively avoid this problem because of the existence of only one legislative system and one supervision system.

Third, at the enterprise level, a harmonized system can protect workers better. According to Wu and Chi, the separation of occupational health and occupational safety in China has in fact caused to the employers the ineffective convergence of occupational hazards source management, early prevention, process management and consequences response (Wu & Chi, 2015). The ineffective convergence at the enterprise level in turn leads to degrading the actual protection level the employer could provide for the workers (Wu & Chi, 2015). In contrast, a harmonized system would effectively avoid the above situation by ensuring the uniformity and consistency of hazards source management, early prevention, process management and consequences response, and ultimately helps the employer provide a satisfactory level of protection.

Workers Actively Contribution to Health and Safety Workplaces Can Lead to a Lower Occupational Risk Level and Accident Rates

The previous discussion has shown that a resolution to the effectively promoting workplace OHS is not as simple as ensuring the law compliance while according the public inspectorate more powers or vice versa. In contrast to the traditional focus on command-and-control as presented in the Chinese system, and in the before-1980s EU system, the regulation of OHS activities necessitates: a more delicate balance between the state and the workplace, and the employer and the employee; and a deeper quest for the cooperation at the workplace level.

Previous studies have shown that the prevalence of the command-and-control would eliminates the link between thinking and doing: at the country level, the government thinks- the workplace parties do, and at the enterprise level, the management thinks - workers do, and lead to that employees and unions are kept at arm's length from decision making because their interests are assumed to be limited to achieving higher pay and benefits. This is not in line with the fact that the employer does not have the solutions to all health and safety problems, while workers and their representatives have the detailed knowledge and experience of how the job is done and how it affects them (European Agency for Safety and Health at Work, 2012). Workplaces in which workers actively contribute to health and safety often have a lower occupational risk level and accident rates (European Agency for Safety and Health at Work, 2012). According to the previous studies, this is also witnessed in the European system. Some countries as Sweden and the Netherlands have begun to promote workers' participation in OHS as early as the end of WWII. At the EU level, since the shift, the countries witness a growth in worker's participation, although in the country as the Netherlands it might be also partly caused by the labour inspectorate being understaffing (Jaspers & Pennings, 2013). The need to promote worker involvement in OHS is widely accepted not only at the EU level, but also at international level (see International Labour Organization Convention concerning Occupational Safety and Health and the Working Environment, No 155 of 1981).

The participatory mechanisms usually provide for the workers and/or the workers presenting bodies (in most cases, in the form of OHS delegates and OHS committees) the right to be consulted when any changes to the workplace affect, and the right to (together with the employer) produce agreements, and other forms of supporting documentation produced that regulate the workplaces. This documentation may even create mandatory rights and obligations as long as it is empowered by the statutory laws. For example, as shown in the Netherlands case, the agreements can deal with workplace moral harassment issues.

In this sense, promoting workers' participation can be a powerful tool to improve the existing OHS system to be adaptive enough to workplace needs, effective to combat against OHS hazards, and stable enough to accommodate diversified workplace interests and claims.

The Key to Sufficiently Compensate the Occupationally Injured or Ill Workers Rests in Occupational Insurance

Priz brothers note that the occupational insurance is by nature a crafted "historic compromise" and "the compromise established that the liability of an employer towards workers who were injured or made ill on the job was essentially no-fault" (Priz & Priz, 2010). They further point out the workers receive, through the insurance mechanism, the compensation for their medical costs and lost wages (Priz & Priz, 2010). Prior to the introduction of this solution, injured and/or ill workers had to take legal action based on tort system against their employers for compensation, which created a system where workers found it difficult, costly and time-consuming to get compensated for the costs of occupational injury and illness (Priz & Priz, 2010).

In this sense, the divergences between the EU and China in terms of occupational insurance indicate gap between the two jurisdictions in compensating the workers, in cases that they are injured and/or become ill. The Chinese system fails to establish a comprehensive insurance system. As commented by Larson and Larson, the right to compensation benefits depends on one simple factor: the existence a work-connected injury and/or illness. (Larson & Larson, 2008). However, a mere elevation of the emphasis on the occupational insurance in name, such as dictation of the legal wording that a universal occupational insurance be established, does not necessarily increase the capacities of the insurance scheme. Instead, corresponding measures must be taken to improve the general context in which a particular institution is situated.

First, desirable effective scheme needs to be built on the premise that the employers are financially motivated to provide the employees the insurance. The current scheme that put the premiums paying liability completely on the employer would definitely reduce the employer's motivation as the employers might become financially overburdened. It is also not fair if this responsibility is shifted to the employee. Given the general situation that China has a rich government and a poor working class. (The Economist, 2015; Zhou, 2010; Wang & Zheng, 2013). In this context, a practical solution might be the government provides subsidies for the insurance premiums. As a consequence, the law should impose a statutory a subsidy-providing responsibility on the employer. Second, the various involving parties should be accorded the powers in case insurance is not provided. This means that the labour inspectorate, employers, employees and/or their representing bodies need to be equipped with their respective institutional functions. Particularly, the trade union should be accord sufficient powers to compel the employer provide sufficient insurance.

REFERENCES

Barnard, C. (2013). *EU employment law*. Oxford, UK: Oxford Press.

Brown, R. C. (2009). *Understanding labor and employment law in China*. Cambridge, UK: Cambridge University Press. doi:10.1017/CBO9780511642258

Cao, J. (2006). *Macroeconomics*. Beijing: Tsenghua Press.

Champoux, D., & Brun, J. (2003). Occupational health and safety management in small size enterprises: An overview of the situation and avenues for intervention and research. *Safety Science*, *41*(4), 301–318. doi:10.1016/S0925-7535(02)00043-7

Chang, X. (2014). *Society Building: A China Model of Social Development*. Cambridge, UK: Cambridge Scholars Publishing.

Chinese Government. (n.d.). *China annual report 2017*. Retrieved June 17, 2017, from https://www.google.nl/url?sa=t&rct=j&q=&esrc=s&source=web&cd=1&cad=rja&uact=8&sqi=2&ved=0ahUKEwicxtm967HKAhXIwA4KHWn7BAUQFggdMAA&url=http%3A%2F%2Fwww.clb.org.hk%2Fschi%2F&usg=AFQjCNFB67hJAZowulv8TTLkdyAYqu5nLQ&bvm=bv.112064104,d.ZWU

De la Vega, B. V. (2013). Occupational health and safety: An EU law perspective. In E. Ales (Ed.), Health and safety at work: European and comparative perspective (pp. 1-32). Alphen aan den Rijn: Kluwer Law International.

Dorn, A. J., & Wang, X. (1990). *Economic reform in China: problems and prospects*. Chicago: University of Chicago Press.

European Agency for Safety and Health at Work. (2012). *Worker representation and consultation on health and safety: an analysis of the findings of the European survey of enterprises on new and emerging risks*. Retrieved June 17, 2017, from https://osha.europa.eu/en/tools-and-publications/publications/reports/esener_workers-involvement

European Agency for Safety and Health at Work. (2017). *European directives on safety and health at work*. Retrieved June 17, from https://osha.europa.eu/en/safety-and-health-legislation/european-directives

Eurostat. (2016). *Employment and unemployment data*. Retrieved June 17, 2017, from http://ec.europa.eu/eurostat/web/lfs/data/database

Eurostat. (2017). *Unemployment statistics*. Retrieved June 17, 2017, from http://ec.europa.eu/eurostat/statistics-explained/index.php/Unemployment_statistics

Fan, S., Kanbur, R., Wei, S., & Zhang, X. (2014). *The oxford companion to the economics of China*. Oxford, UK: OUP Oxford. doi:10.1093/acprof:oso/9780199678204.001.0001

Guo, B., & Guo, S. (2008). *China in search of a harmonious society*. Lanham, MD: Lexington Books.

Hale, A. R. (1984). Is safety training worthwhile? *Journal of Occupational Accidents*, *6*(1-3), 17–33. doi:10.1016/0376-6349(84)90026-9

Hämäläinen, R. M. (2008). *The Europeanisation of occupational health services: A study of the impact of EU policies*. Retrieved June 17, 2017, from https://helda.helsinki.fi/bitstream/handle/10138/20390/theeurop.pdf?sequence=1iitattu

Hishida, M., Kojima, K., Ishii, T., & Qiao, J. (2010). *China's trade unions - how autonomous are they?: a survey of 1811 Enterprise Union chairpersons*. London: Routledge.

Huang, Y. (2008). *Capitalism with Chinese characteristics: Entrepreneurship and the state*. Cambridge, UK: Cambridge Press.

International Labour Organization. (2003/04). *Moral harassment: Work organization to blame?* Newcastle upon Tyne, UK: Labour Education.

International Monetary Fund (IMF). (2017). *People's Republic of China and the IMF*. Retrieved June 17, 2017, https://www.imf.org/external/country/chn/

Jacinto, C., & Aspinwall, E. (2004). A Survey on occupational accidents reporting and registration systems in the European Union. *Safety Science*, *42*(10), 933–960. doi:10.1016/j.ssci.2004.07.002

James, P., & Walters, D. (2002). Worker representation in health and safety: Options for regulatory reform. *Industrial Relations Journal*, *33*(2), 141–156. doi:10.1111/1468-2338.00225

Jaspers, T., & Pennings, F. (2013). Occupational health and safety in The Netherlands: A shift of responsibilities. In E. Ales (Ed.), Health and safety at work: European and comparative perspective (pp. 1-32). Alphen aan den Rijn: Kluwer Law International.

Johnstone, R., Quinlan, M., & Walters, D. (2005). Statutory occupational health and safety workplace arrangements for the modern labour market. *The Journal of Industrial Relations*, *47*(01), 93–116. doi:10.1111/j.1472-9296.2005.00160.x

Kinkel, J., & Hurst, W. (2011). Review essay—access to justice in post-Mao China: Assessing the politics of criminal and administrative law. *Journal of East Asian Studies (Seoul)*, *11*(3), 467–499. doi:10.1017/S1598240800007414

Larson, L. K., & Larson, A. (2008). *Workers' compensation law: cases, materials, and text.* Leiden: LexisNexis.

LEGOSH Database. (2014). *China – 2013.* Retrieved June 17, 2017, http://www.ilo.org/dyn/legosh/en/f?p=14100:1100:0:NO:1100:P1100_ISO_CODE3,P1100_YEAR:CHN,2013:NO

Li, B. (2013). Research on the occupational health guardian system. *Academic Journal Graduate School Chinese Academy of Social Sciences*, *34*(06), 25–28.

Li, L. (2014). It is necessary to break through the status quo that "power is superior to law" in order to build rule of law in China. *The Qiushi Journal*, *14*(5), 33–37.Li, J., & Zhang, L. (2012). Research on health and safety law: From the human rights perspective. *Law and Society*, *22*(03), 87–90.

Liu, K. (2013). Conundrums in the legal protection of migrant workers' health rights and relative resolutions: Implications from the case of Tseng Hei-tao. *Medicine, Health Care, and Philosophy*, *16*(3), 543–553. doi:10.1007/s11019-012-9445-1 PMID:23073738

Liu, K. (2015). Comparative study of regulating the moral harassment: Lessons for China. *Occupational Medicine & Health Affairs*, *3*(4), 66–72.

Liu, K., & Liu, W. (2015). The development of EU law in the field of occupational health and safety: A new way of thinking. *Management and Labour Studies*, *40*(3&4), 207–238. doi:10.1177/0258042X15624990

Ma, Y. (2015). *Resolving conflicts between conservation and recreation in protected areas a comparative legal analysis of the United States and China* (PhD Dissertation). Erasmus University Rotterdam.

Majone, G. (1993). The European community between social policy and social regulation. *Journal of Common Market Studies*, *31*(2), 153–170. doi:10.1111/j.1468-5965.1993.tb00455.x

McGolgan, A. (2004). *Report on sexual harassment in the workplace in EU Member States*. Retrieved June 17, 2017, from http://www.justice.ie/en/JELR/SexualHrrsmtRpt.pdf/Files/SexualHrrsmtRpt.pdf

Michelson, E., & Li, K. (2012). *Judicial performance without independence: the delivery of justice and political legitimacy in rural China*. Prepared for Workshop on Works-in-Progress on Chinese Law, Center for Chinese Legal Studies, Columbia Law School.

Morgan, H. M., Černič, J. L., & Milligan, L. (2010). *Perspectives on power: an inter-disciplinary approach*. Cambridge, UK: Cambridge Scholars Publishing.

Nicholas, J. (2012). *21st century China: Does civil society play a role in promoting reform in China?* Center for Democracy, Development and the Rule of Law Thesis.

Nicholson, P. J. (2002). Occupational health in the European Union. *Occupational Medicine*, *52*(2), 80–84. doi:10.1093/occmed/52.2.80 PMID:11967350

Organisation for Economic Co-operation and Development. (2015). *Labour force participation rate*. Retrieved June 17, 2017, from https://data.oecd.org/emp/labour-force-participation-rate.htm

Örücü, A. E. (2006). Methodology of Comparative Law. In J. M. Smits (Ed.), *Elgar encyclopedia of comparative law* (pp. 446–447). Cheltenham, UK: Edward Elgar Publishing. doi:10.4337/9781847200204.00047

Ostry, S., Alexandroff, A. S., & Gomez, R. (2003). China and the long march to global trade: the accession of China to the World Trade Organization. Psychology Press, 2003, 171-174.

Peerenboom, R. (2010). *Judicial independence in China: Lessons for global rule of law promotion*. Cambridge, UK: Cambridge University Press.

People's Congress. (2017). *The Government Working Report 2017*. Retrieved June 17, 2017, from http://www.gov.cn/zhuanti/2017lhzfgzbg/

Percival, R. V. (2013). The role of civil society in environmental governance in the United States and China. *Duke Environmental Law & Policy Forum*, *24*, 141.

Pringle, T. E., & Frost, S. D. (2003). The absence of rigor and the failure of implementation: Occupational health and safety in China. *International Journal of Occupational and Environmental Health*, *9*(4), 309–316. doi:10.1179/oeh.2003.9.4.309 PMID:14664482

Priz, E., & Priz, S. M. (2010). *Worker's compensation: a field guide for employers*. Charleston, SC: Book Surge Publishing.

Sabel, C. F., & Zeitlin, J. (2008). Learning from difference: The new architecture of experimentalist governance in the EU. *European Law Journal*, *14*(3), 271–327. doi:10.1111/j.1468-0386.2008.00415.x

Sadurski, W., Czarnota, A., & Krygier, M. (2006). *Spreading democracy and the rule of law?: the impact of EU enlargement for the rule of law, democracy and constitutionalism in post-communist legal orders*. Dordrecht: Springer Science & Business Media. doi:10.1007/1-4020-3842-9

Su, Z. (2003). Occupational health and safety legislation and implementation in China. *International Journal of Occupational and Environmental Health*, *9*(4), 302–308. doi:10.1179/oeh.2003.9.4.302 PMID:14664481

The Economist. (2015). *Yuan for all*. Retrieved June 17, 2017, from http://www.economist.com/news/leaders/21641203-chinas-loans-foundering-governments-may-seem-challenge-imf-biggest-risks-are

Vlagopoulou, M. (2017). *Psychological harassment in the workplace ("mobbing") in Greece and its legal implications*. Retrieved June 17, 2017, from http://www.globalhrlaw.com/resources/psychological-harassment-in-the-workplace-mobbing-in-greece-and-its-legal-implications

Walby, S. (1999). The new regulatory state: The social powers of the European Union. *The British Journal of Sociology*, *50*(1), 118–140. doi:10.1080/000713199358842 PMID:15266677

Wang, G., & Zheng, Y. (2013). *China: development and governance*. Singapore: World Scientific.

Wang, Z. (2007). *Improving the economic growth model*. Beijing: Social Sciences Academic Press.

World Bank. (2016). *Labor force participation rate*. Retrieved June 17, 2017, from http://data.worldbank.org/indicator/SL.TLF.CACT.ZS

World Bank. (2017). *GDP growth*. Retrieved June 17, 2017, http://data.worldbank.org/indicator/NY.GDP.MKTP.KD.ZG

Wu, F., & Chi, Y. (2015). Regulatory system reform of occupational health and safety in China. *Industrial Health*, *53*(3), 300–306. doi:10.2486/indhealth.2014-0119 PMID:25843565

Yu, H. (2013). Jiajn Li's argument that "laws are not well executed or strictly executed although they are well enacted" undermines the law's credibility. *China Renda Journal*, *24*(05), 48–52.

Yu, Y. (2007). The role of future of civil society in transitional China. *Polish Perspectives*, *12*(1), 15–18.

Zhang, Z., Zhang, M., & Xie, S. (2010). The research on the possibilities of integrating the occupational safety and health law. *China Information Technology*, *10*(8), 263–264.

Zhao, J., Tu, E. J., McMurray, C., & Sleigh, A. (2012). Rising mortality from injury in urban China: Demographic burden, underlying causes and policy implications. *Bulletin of the World Health Organization*, *90*(06), 461–467. doi:10.2471/BLT.11.093849 PMID:22690036

Zhao, L., & Lim, T. S. (2010). *China's new social policy: initiatives for a harmonious society*. Singapore: World Scientific.

Zhou, J. (2010). *China's peaceful rise in a global context: a domestic aspect of China's road map to democratization*. Lanham, MD: Lexington Books.

Zhou, Y. (2010). *Occupational safety and health law*. Beijing: Higher Education Press.

Zong, L., Zhang, Z., Zhang, M., & Xie, S. (2011). The research on the integration of occupational safety and health law in china. *Journal of Xi'an Shiyou University*, *23*(1), 32–34.

KEY TERMS AND DEFINITIONS

Convergence: A similarity between different legal systems.

Divergence: A difference between different legal systems.

Ergonomical Risks: The aspects of a job or task that impose a biomechanical stress on the worker.

General Obligation: An occupational health and safety law approach that focus more on imposing obligations of general nature rather than providing prescriptive rules.

Moral Harassment at Workplace: Vexatious behavior that manifests itself in the form of conduct, verbal comments, actions, or gestures at the work environment.

Occupational Health and Safety: A multidisciplinary field concerned with the safety, health, and welfare of people at work.

Psychosocial Risks: The aspects of a job or task that impose psychosocial harm to working population.

Chapter 4
Economic Variations and Their Impact on Labor Legislation Throughout History in Argentina

Andrea Isabel Franconi
Universidad de Buenos Aires, Argentina

ABSTRACT

Throughout history, Argentina has undergone a series of profound economic variations, which, as such, have produced a strong impact on labor legislation and social security. The access key in Argentina to labour law protection is the existence of a relationship of dependence. This turns to be an inclusive and exclusive condition because it divides strictly the labour market and the labour force inherent in two different areas, namely, the subordinate workers (who are included in the labour protection system) and the rest of the employees, including among the latest, the ones involved in non-typical forms of employment contracts. For such purposes, it is important to analyze different periods of time, selecting the more significant ones to see the evolution of Argentinean labour legislation. It is also relevant to describe the consequences caused by economic and political variations on collective bargaining in order to understand the composition of the actual labour force in Argentina.

DOI: 10.4018/978-1-5225-4134-9.ch004

INTRODUCTION

Throughout history, the Argentine Republic has undergone a series of profound economic variations which, as such, have produced a strong impact on labour legislation and social security.

As the mechanisms for labour flexibilization become stronger, the work force diversifies in such way that more sectors become excluded from the granted protection provided by the hard core of the public labour policy.

During the 90s, there appeared new types of contracts which allowed the employer to receive the professional services from a worker but securing a reduction of cost during these period and / or securing a mechanism for ending the labour relationship without undergoing high indemnification costs.

During the last years, it can be observed, a new paradigm to create more freedoms to hire; and its counterpart, the decrease in protective labour legislation as a rigid core.

It is herein intended to show the economic and political analysis of the facts (highlighting that it exceeds these document the full development of themselves, there are going to be taken as examples those who have a strong relevance in the subject herein discussed) that gave place to the regulatory management attached to the labour law and the social security from the Argentine Republic and its modifications.

For such purposes it is worth mentioning different periods, from which it has to be highlighted: 1) what occurred in 1976, with the military governments, the liberal treatment on the economy from the country and the suppression of trade unions and its main outcome, the signing and validity of collective labour agreement; 2) the 90s and the arrival of new neoliberal criteria to the country with the introduction of new para-labour hiring conditions, such as the modifications connected to the social security system, tending to a privatization of companies and state services and 3) the modification of the criteria of interpretation of the National Supreme Court of Justice in relation to employment and its rights.

Also, it is worth mentioning that in accordance with the economic and political period, there has been in the Argentine Republic a development of the social actors involved who achieved to have a permanent collective negotiation.

Unions have acquired a high level of importance in Argentine working relationship system due to the signing of collective labour agreements. Its treatment, creation, development and content, as the necessity for approval from the state authority, have special relationship with the content of individual relationships and also with the individual labour agreement. This is why, the great impact caused by economic and political variations on this heteronomous law from the country cannot escape this chapter.

The main purpose of this chapter is to analyze these aspects, from the individual labour law up to the collective labour relationships, in order to be able to understand the way in which economic variations have had an impact in the creation of Labour Legislation in Argentina.

Main Focus

In Argentina, the access key to labour law protection is the existence of a relationship of dependence. This turns to be an inclusive and exclusive condition, because it divides strictly the labour market and the labour force inherent, in two different areas, namely, the subordinate workers (who, are included in the system of labour protection) and the rest of the employees, including among the latest, different forms of employment contracts or rendering services that do not have at first sight all the proper characteristics of dependency, and that forms of employment contract, for that reason are excluded from the legislative protection.

Labour Contract Law 20744 establishes the Labour Contract as the rendering of services, or the performance of certain work in favor of another, in a relation of dependence, for a certain period of time in exchange of a compensation. Being the principal item the "dependency".

In times of economic crisis, it has been a common practice to make legislation changes that allowed employers an easy way out from the work relationship; whether it be by reducing indemnification costs, developing contracts which permit to establish a preconceived period of time, or, not granting the employees all the rights foreseen in the labour law.

This is how, the principle from section 14 bis from National Constitution, which begins with the phrase: *"Work in its diverse forms shall be protected by the laws..."* seems to be reduced to a simple statement which limits to the employment relationships sector included in the labour relationship and in accordance to certain hiring modality.

The differentiation herein made of the labour market has been used along the different periods as a scape mechanism during economic crises to have an unprotected work force.

Until these days, this theme has usually been developed from the historical perspective, but not including the analysis of the situation from the intern labour law point of view and it's consequences on the creation of the labour force as well as the Employment Legislation in Argentina.

The Evolution of Labour Law in Argentina

The story of Labour Law in Argentina starts with those immigrants who came to these lands chasing better life conditions. Most of them were living in the middle of the war (Second World War) especially in Europe.

In view of this situation, the arrival of immigrants to the country brought the ideological content of those who have experience the development and the consequences of the capitalist mode of production and the social conflict that it generated

The arrival of new workers with trade union training or with socialist or communist orientation accelerated the training time for the working class and their awareness raising.

Several factors interacted to produce this phenomena. Among them: the economic structure change, caused by the incipient process of industrialization; the vertiginous increase and the modification on population, caused by the mass arrivals of immigrants; the deterioration of labour conditions and life from the working class, worsened by the great crisis from 1890; also, the awareness raising, of the condition of being a social class; the appearance and dissemination of rebellious ideologies, which arrived with the immigration from Europe, capable of awakening workers legitimate aspirations of social justice; the organization of the first workers´ union, with a reformist or revolutionary program and international connections.

In Europe and in the United States of America the social issue was there since the middle of the XIX century. That was when the working class started the struggle to achieve emancipation. This struggle was acquiring international dimensions.

In Argentina, the change of paradigm manifested itself since the constitution of the first working associations: graphic workers in 1867, bakers in 1886, train drivers and smokers in 1887. At the same time, labour conflicts began. These ended up in strikes. Among the first strikes there can be mentioned: the one from graphic workers in 1874 and in1878, from train employees in 1888 and from carpenters, cabinetmakers and similar in 1889. These have multiplied during the past decade.

During the following years, they decreased but reappeared during the new century: in 1902 twenty six partial and one general conflict occurred. In November from the same year, powered by anarchism, the biggest general strike until then occurred in Latin America. In 1907, only in Buenos Aires, they added up to 231, and in 1910 up to 29857.

The Fist Argentine Regional Working Congress adopted the same agenda as the International Working Congress from Paris from 1889. Together with the *Club Vorwärts*, founded in 1882 by German Socialists, it requested to the National Congress to limit the working hours up to eight, to forbid those under fourteen years old to work and a reduction of six hours to those who were between fourteen and eighteen years old, to have an uninterrupted weekly rest of thirty-six hours at least, the abolition as a general rule of working during night shifts, the prohibition to employ women to work in unhealthy industries or in pieces of works, the constant inspection of factories and work places, and the sanitary of workers houses, compulsory insurance against accidents at work, the creation of an arbitrary court, etc.

This new situation caused a strong impact on the traditional groups of power that belonged to the "*80s Generation*" [Generación del 80] who tried to redirect it through the legal via.

Different figures and groups of people that wished to solve the social issued through pacific means came up with the proposal of modifying the law. This ended up converging in the great project of the National Labour Law from 1904.

On September 6th, 1905, the Executive Power passed Law 4661. It was considered the first law with a modern orientation. It was the starting point for a new approach in what has to do with Labour Law. Law 9688 from accidents at work.

In 1988 Domingo O. Moyano had already discussed the issue by stating in his doctoral thesis that:

...governments are obliged to oppose to effective ways for the sad consequences of work depreciation. To alleviate suffering from the working class for me it is more important that the restriction of a job and the land ownership generalization are two big ways of improving the social position of the disowned classes.

The constitutional reform from 1949 granted the power to the Congress, for the first time, to approve a Social Code (Section 68, Subsection 11). The conventional constituent Arturo Sampay stated that this right not only included the traditional system of the labour agreements but also, the collective part of labour issues and the social prevention system (Tissembaum, 1958).

Once the reform was annulled, the following, from 1957, kept the power of the Congress to approve the code, which was renamed as Work and Social Security. Likewise, it added a section that would be of extreme importance for the regulation in Argentina, Section 14 bis. This section has three paragraphs that includes part of the social rights that were once included in the Constitution from 1949, individual workers' rights, collective labour rights and social security rights.

Now, the code had a principle of implementation in 1974 with the passing of law 20.744, Labour Contract Law, but it was limited to Individual Labour Law, having an inclusive and exclusive character, because only relates to work performed as an employee under a relationship of dependence.

Originated in a draft from the General Confederation of Labour it was passed on September 20th from the same year.

Taking everything into account,

-apart from the coding, which actually constitutes one chapter of it- grants the common basis of regulations, unless in those cases of exclusion expressly provided. Its rules, in the same conditions provided by the law, shall be applicable for all the labour agreements perform [...] notwithstanding the fact that the most favorable applicable law for the worker shall be the one enforced, as an accepted principle by the law, this shall imply being subject to those relations projected as laws from the Nation. The professional regulations or basis statutes shall receive the fundamental principles of the law [...] but shall deal with the modalities that each labour relationship has disciplined by them.

This new regulatory text was supposed to be the cornerstone of the labour law system in the Argentina, however, as it is going to be showed hereinafter, it has suffered profound modifications along the history due the changes, not only because of the political context of the country but also more specifically because of the economic aspect of it.

1970 Economic Crisis: Effects in Labour Legislation

Since the mid-70s, the rights granted in the labour agreement began to be questioned as they were said to be excessive, especially by the business sector. The debate about the deregulation and adaptation of Labour Law began and extended up to the 80s.

The world economic crisis from the 70s gave origin to a "new", "crisis time", "emergency" Labour Law; in many cases it was doomed to its own extinction. In the presence of a strong manifesting lack of movement in legal-formal expansiveness of the concept of subordination, in disagreement with the socio-economic data, and in the rigidity of its rules, not adequate for the managerial levels and for small enterprises, the labour institutions, once created during a period of growth and consolidation of economic relationships, turned to be incompatible with recession periods and a structural generalized unemployment as the one from that moment.

This was how, regulatory laws from the contract were modified by the facto government in 1976. It suppressed the prevalence of uses and customs that were more favorable for the employee over the laws and any other collective agreement; softened the system of legal presumptions, which interfered in the application of the bona fide principle; eliminated the automatic and proportional readjustment system from basic salaries in accordance with increases in the living salary; modified the provisions that protected women, which effectively limited the chances of women to get a job; reduced from one year to six months the maternity period, and the advance notice; kept the compatibility between the Contract Law and Special Laws, but limiting its application to the compatibility with the nature and modality of each activity and its specific legal regime; derogated for state companies and for those of public services the rules that exceeded the applicable rights of the Contract Law, changing what used to be the "floor" of employees to be their "ceiling". (Vialard, 1991)

In Argentina, the issued was stated in terms of deregulation, adaptation, of making more flexible a regulation originated in the public labour policy. The argument was that every restriction manifested the power of direction and business organization, safeguarding the justice of decisions and the respect for the worker dignity, it is contrary to the promotion of the investment and the necessity of an industrial counterclaim.

There has been given on its favor the eligibility to replace old relationships as regards production adjusting them to the new requirements of the productive forces; a possibility for the company to adjust employment, working and production conditions with the agility required adapted to the changing conditions from the economic system and the technological innovations; allowing the provision of goods and services of higher quality at a cheaper price; adjusting labour relationships to new socioeconomic circumstances or to those that did not caught the attention in the past due to their lack of importance, increasing productivity requirements and those of the not stationary demand, as an answer to the unemployment crisis; which reduce or avoid the risk of losing workforce; increasing employers´ freedom to improve productive resources.

Faced with these favorable arguments, the request of flexibility is answered highlighting the need to respect the principles of protection from Labour Law, from which depends that the negative effects from the crisis or those related to the new rules imposed by the globalization of the economy do not fall over the weakest: the workers.

On this subject, Podetti considered that it is not a crisis of the Labour Law in general, but a crisis of its classic formulation, which took place between 1943 and 1976. In his opinion, is the identity of the first one that must be preserved *in accordance with the validity of social justice, common good and the protecting principle. It is through fidelity for the values within the above mentioned that, whichever are the inevitably changes required to be adopted in face of new socioeconomic, political, technological and cultural circumstances, that Labour Law shall be able to maintain its identity and way of being; and it shall be the servant in the aspiration of a progressive and fair society. (Humberto, 1990).*

The 90s: Economic Formulation Mechanisms and Their Effect

In a crisis, as for instance those which are frequently seen in the Argentine Republic, relationships start to get tense. On the one hand, employees may want to ask for a raise on their salaries (if it is an inflationary situation) or if they are worried about their working situation, they may ask for more protections. On the other side, employers may say that due to the crisis it is impossible to raise salaries, or guarantying that there are not going to be any dismissals. They need to have certain profitability in their business.

During the 90s, mechanisms of labour flexibility were developed through diverse legislation changes, what is more, said mechanisms were included in every collective agreement signed at that moment.

Since then, a huge transcendental change occurred. Finds its way into the debate, a very subtle idea: if the labour contract (flexible at that moment) granted protections for the employee (which after a while will be translated into costs and limits for the employer), the easiest way to ignore this situation was by avoiding any working engagement.

This was how a process of "dismantling" the labour contract began. Its immediate conclusion was, if the hiring was performed outside the labour contract, it was not protected by any regulation, and Labour Law could not be applied.

The relation between a labour contract and a service lease contract has being doing a swinging. The history of Labour Law is mainly the story of the transformation of the old lease or service agreement from Napoleonic codes applied on the modern labour contract, regulated and protected by labour legislation. In this growing process, the hiring of certain services turned to be a remain form used only for exceptional services, and generally provided by those with sufficient power of negotiation (university graduates, advisors, etc)

As highlighted by Montoya Melgar, we are now in presence of a "plurality of productive worlds" which are constantly asking for different answers: the expansion self-employed work – states Melgar – renew in our days the requests about their protection, which matches in a way with the reorganization of the proposal of the concept of dependence; whether by going back to the widest idea of "economic dependence" a characteristic from new levels of social legislation, by enlarging the concept of dependence thorough subordination notions, created by those Italian jurists, or by applying the concept of cuasi employment created by the Germans; notions from abroad which were elabourated with the clear objective of enlarging the scope of application of Labour Law apart from its classic content.

In Argentina, during the 90s, a profound process of reformation of labour legislation began. In said decade, the productive reconversion, together with the economic opening and the deregulation, produced in Argentina, on one side, the reduction of the number of salaried worker permanently and, on the other side, the increase of open unemployment, of the worries of the employees who are working and of the fragile number of salaried job posts. (Beccaria y Lopez, 1997: 10-11).

The Law 24.013 (National Labour Law) was one of the first laws that implemented the flexible labour policies. It allowed the collective agreements to calculate working hour´s base on averages. Following this criteria- a clear mechanisms of labour flexibility- the daily limit is 8 working hours and the weekly limit is 48 hours. Instead of controlling it each day or week, it could be calculated in a longest period of time, for instance, in 3 or 6 months' time, or even in a year time. The employer could compensate period of excess with other inferior periods, avoiding having to pay extra money with any charges that may include.

This rule showed an unusual degree of flexibility as it did not determine any maximum term (in a year´s time) which was going to be the basis for the calculation of the average, leaving the collective agreement free to choose the period of time which is going to be analyzed.

Any regime with these characteristics allowed companies to make an intensive use of their workforce during the period of time the markets of products require. However, even though this mechanism could be highly advantageous in terms of productivity for the employers, it could also mean overwhelming workdays for their employees.

In 1995, the Law 24.465 on labour flexibility was passed. It was modified in 1998 by Law 25.013. This law extended the trial period from one to three months, expandable up to six by the collective agreement. During this period, the contract could be terminated without expressing any reason or compensation. It regulated the part-time labour contract, and that of training with a duration from three to twenty-four months.

It adopted special promotion modality for those above forty years old, disabled, women and ex combatants from Malvinas, for a minimum of six months and a maximum of two years' time, being the employer exempt to pay only half of their contributions to the social security system.

The lack of honesty about the hiring conditions caused irregular situations. As for instance, the use of temporary work agencies with a different purpose from what they were authorized by the labour legislation, or the framing of typical labour relationships in special legal forms: the rendering of a service, fix term jobs and temporary jobs. The probed existence of such abnormalities, imposed by the economic situation, was another cause of complaint to modernize the law, especially the new hiring modalities. (Zanini, 1990).

The Law 25.250 was passed in year 2000. This law turned work even more unstable. It established a trial period of from 3 to 6 months, the latest is for small companies, allowing it to be extended from 6 to 12 months thought the collective agreement.

As regards collective agreements (as it is going to be explain herein), it blocked the negotiation per activity, demanding requirements which were impossible to obtain, imposing in the facts a decentralization by company; it revoked implicitly one guiding principle of the most favorable law applicable, by stating that in case of agreement concurrence of different fields, the one applicable shall be the one from the smallest field, even though it is not the most favorable. This provision caused strong complaints from chambers of small enterprises. It enabled to "unhook" the collective agreement as a request from the employer and the trade union, which means no application of the agreement for such activities which are unhooked from it. It revoked the rule of ultraactivity from the collective agreements for those in force as for those who are to be entered into; and it replaced regulation decree of strikes with a legal provision that was such ambiguous, that it allowed the Labour Ministry to decide education to be considered essential to restring the right to strike, departing thus from international criteria.

The process of legislative transformation would finish, in what respect diseases and working accidents, with the passing of Working Risk Law (WRL) [*Ley de Riesgos de Trabajo*] on September 3rd 1995, which would restring the rights to access social security benefits provided therein, among others, and during the following years many clauses of this law were declared to be unconstitutional by the Nationals Courts of Justice.

Argentinean Supreme Court of Justice Decision (2015): Public Economic Order Over Public Labour Order?

New strategies of production, the transformation of labor culture from the new economy, case law criteria more flexible which weaken the sacred principle from past (like for instance, the unrenounceability of labor rights), the introduction of standards of social security reserved for Independent work to the world of economically dependent work, the idea that the unemployed have to look for -and settle with- any kind of job when in front of economic crises, contribute to strengthen a labor relationship system with more and more restrictive spaces for the workers protected by Labor legislation.

The foregoing can be seen in the latest case law decisions which have settled a new change in the matter. For that reason, it is extremely important to bring into the present those emblematic records regarding protection o lack of protection of working rights in Argentina.

Cairone Case

The decision from the Argentinean Supreme Court of Justice on the matter of "Cairone c. Hospital Italiano" (Cairone, 2015) in which the first and second grade Labour Court decisions were nullified, turned to be important to understand the change of paradigm on the situation of Labour Law in Argentina.

In light of the terms used by the substitute prosecuting attorney (Irma Adriana García Netto) to whom two other Ministers made reference to (Elena I. Highton de Nolasco and Juan Carlos Maqueda); and of the voting, on his own grounds, from the President of the Court (Ricardo Luis Lorenzetti) said situation was allowed due to the following:

For arbitrary it is rendered null and void, the decision allowed on the claim from the heirs of the anesthesiologist doctor against the plaintiff as it requested that there was a binding labour contract between themselves, raising the sentence amount, by considering that the personal provision of services from the latest turned operative the presumption mentioned in section 23 from Labour Contract Law (LCL) as the a quo did not gave a correct treatment to the claim in accordance with the outcomes of the case and the applicable law. This requirement must have been imposed with more rigidity on the sub lite taking into account the economic outcome of the sentence.

Votes from Judges Highton de Nolasco and Maqueda, out of the ruling from the Attorney General to whom they make reference to.

The facts: Shortly, Courtroom I from the National Labour Court of Appeal confirmed the judgment given by the court of origin (number 76), allowing the case for the heirs of the anesthesiologist, Julio Cesar Estala. He had a labour relationship with Hospital Italiano as anesthesiologist doctor for thirty two years. During this years, the provision of services was habitual and stable. As a staff physician he was one of the many elements from that business machinery. That is why, his condition of dependent employee was recognized by the court of origin.

However, the outcome of the Supreme Court on this subject was to dismiss the case on such criteria. Leaving years of industriousness and effectiveness recognition with not effect.

This is a clear representation of the private sector empire (which precedes the public) were autonomy governs individual wills and the contractual rule which derives as its logic outcome: pacta sunt servanda ("agreements must be kept"). What takes us to section 1197 from the Civil Code: "*The parties are submitted to the covenants in any contract as they are to the law itself.*"

On the contrary, as it has been pointed out,

...it is all about that what is acquired or obtained by an employee in a protected field, or better, through or by means of a mechanism prepare for his protection (public laws or collective autonomy) cannot be then validly dispose in a different unprotected field or while exercising a mechanism (the one of individual autonomy) which cannot but only strengthen the inequality of its position or of its hypo-sufficiency. (Ramirez, 2007)

This is one of the main reasons that encourage labour public order.

Be it understood that, it is not about violating the contractual freedoms that employers have, but to have the space used by those freedoms inside the frame of individual relationships of work preceded by a socially responsible behavior. This behavior shall be able to give privileges to the man as it is and in its creative and transforming function, as a sustained value in a democratic society. It is because of this that the State, as guarantor of such values, shall set the necessary boundaries to seal the interstices through which the contractual freedom may want to slip away to run far from the framework that safeguards the essential conditions for a decent job. (Goldin et al, 2013)

In the end, what is intended to be explained is something that after a century shall be already understood, Labour Law tries to guarantee freedom and real equality (not just formally speaking).

On the other side, it is a must to analyze the argument about the "economic consequences", used by tree ministers from the Supreme Court (one of them based on his own legal basis, and the other two, making theirs the decision from the Attorney General) to blame the Courtroom I of not having taken into account this to arrive to the final decision.

The vote from Dr. Lorenzetti said that the court of origin should have taken into consideration, apart from the legal and social consequences, the economic consequences "*... to exceed the case, and that the judges cannot ignore, because it affects the entire hiring system*". And, on the other side, the decision from the

Attorney General, states that: *"Said requirement must have prevailed more strictly in the sub lite, in connection with the transcendence of the economic outcome of the ruling ($4,572,156.64)."*

It has to do with a theory known as consequentialism, which comes from the Economic Analysis of Law (EAL). In accordance with this theory, the issue on legal indetermination could be solved with the principle of economic efficiency:

Judges shall understand that for those cases to be tried that have an indetermination in the applicable laws, they shall turn to, not the analogous laws or the general principles of law, but to act in a consequentialist way. This means to fill those regulatory gaps with protect reasons by economic efficiency. (Barbarosch, 2011)

That said, those who reject these theories, ensure that they are inadequate from a regulatory point of view, and what is more, also from an interpretative point of view. It has to be considered that the purposes of private law are much more varied and constrictive that efficient. The economic model of law does not get the deontic o regulatory aspect of the legal system.

In that sense, it is paradoxical that law, and then, labour law, shall be limited to be the guarantor from the market; or, clearly and simply, a substitute in such cases when the negotiation cannot be fulfill due to different obstacles. And it turns to be paradoxical because,

The relationships of social power are translated into the subordination of those who work for the capitalistic owner, who organizes it and directs it. And the laws are used to regulate diversely said special social power, but never to the point of confuse them with the social power that preceded them. (Goldin et al, 2013)

In other words, it is about moralizing the economy. It is about getting the economy rid of its mercantile unique and recurrent idea on work as a transactional commercial object. This is a fact that still today survives in an unequal power relationship between workers and employers, and which the Economic Analysis of Law will never have in consideration.

Labour legislation (for Supiot) needs to have a stage with guarantees from the State of people as a dogmatic value or cornerstone from the institutional building. The State,

As cornerstone of our institutional building, is the immortal representation of the attributes of the human being expurgated from its negativity. Unique, because it is

not equal for every man; sovereign, because it is not subdued to nobody but itself; and public spirit that never dies, because its physical body is the people which regenerated incessantly. As transcendent person and holder of exorbitant prerogatives from Common Law, the State is the ultimate guardian of the legal identity of living or fiction creatures which submit to it. Without this cornerstone, out anthropologic staging shall fall down. (Supiot, 2007)

The role of the State as the guardian of the society and the legal good, while using, through its judges, the Economic Analysis of Law while interpreting and applying Labour Law, makes a clean sweep of this legal branch and submits the labour legislation to the reign of economy.

To solve the conflict between capital and employment, it put all of them together and convened those in charge of the capital decision, ignoring the origin of Labour Law, its foundation, its purpose and its functions. The Court has renounced, as a power from the State, to constitute itself as the guarantor of the society and legal good. And it has overlooked work as "a humanizing technique tool". And all this in pursuit of "*… a simulated market, to adopt a solution that may have been adopted by the market if there were not any obstacles for its functioning*" (Barbarosch, 2011).

Therefore it has become notorious that the latest labour law decisions from the Supreme Court of Justice of Argentina have changed and their point of view follows the economic analysis of law through consequentialism. When what we should expect from our judges is the complete opposite, in order to prevent giving up the labor force to the "laws" of economy that globalization suggests in the markets.

State Intervention in the History of Collective Negotiation in Argentina

It is worth mentioning, apart from the individual aspect of Labour Law evolution, those events that occurred in the collective aspect of labour relationships in Argentina. Where the labour movement, its management and its contribution has been decisive while planning the current scenario of workers´ situation.

Originally, the collective labour agreements, were admitted as civil law contracts (for example, 1906 Agreement on Graphic Industry, then there appeared to this group of pioneers train workers and lately maritime workers).

From 1943, the negotiation was boosted and even more with the passing of Decree 23.852/45, which as it regulated the professional workers associations established the Union Right of collective negotiation even defining as "disloyal practice" the corporate refusal to negotiate.

It is worth highlighting that, said rule only allowed to exercise said right (by this time, section 14 bis from the National Constitution still did not existed) to the most representative institution with union status. In 1956 the Decree/ Law 9.270/56 enlarged said right to all those registered associations. Laws 14.155 and 20.165 restricted again these power conferring it only to those associations with union status (same criteria which has been followed by Laws 22.105 and 23.551).

In respect of the collective negotiation effects, it was not until 1953, with the passing of Law 14.250 -today in force with the modifications from Laws 23.545 and 25.877- after some modifications which today revoked, that it was established a legal statute on its matter.

With the coming of economic and social crises, the State used this instrument to influence collective relationships, apart from the usage of the union status assignation.

September 1955 revolution, which interrupted the democratic elected government, interfered with the unions and the labour conditions were determined by administrative authorities exclusively.

Decree-Law 2.739/56 extended the agreements in force and established an increase in the salaries taking into account what it will be decided in future agreements. Decree 6121/56 stated that new agreements shall have a validity period of 18 months. However, with Decree 824/57 it was decided an extension of all previous agreements.

Once the democratic government took up again control it was stated, with Decree 290/58 and 312/58, the restitution of the union status and the freedom of collective negotiation. Maybe from 1958 up to 1967 it was developed, for the first time, the fullest union freedom and of collective negotiation in Argentina, without any legal interferences or powers of the government over social actors.

Since 1967, with the so-called Argentine Revolution, another dictatorship that interrupted democratic life and union life; rules which violated collective autonomy were passed and passed on to the hands of the state the management and regulation of labour relationships. This began with Decree-Law 17.224 (B.O. 5/4/67) which, with the only intention of neutralizing the effect of inflation, took under its control the fixing of raising salaries, making equal all conventional salaries. This process continued with Decree-Laws 18.016, 18.887 and 18.888, allowing the negotiation but limited and conditioned.

In this context, with the new regime agreements were closed in 1971 and then, with the convocation of Law 19.872, those from 1973. That means, that only in 1/2/71, by rule of Decree-Law 18.887/70, the necessity to go back to the regime of Law 14.250. However, the State kept on directing wage policy (see Decrees-Laws 19.220/71, 19.403/71 and 19.589/72).

Finally, when the democratic government started to rule again in 1973, Law 20.517 (passed in 6/7/73) brought back Law 14.250. However, it had limitations related to the National Commitment Act which, on its side, established the guidelines for salaries and prices up to 1975.

By Decree 901/73 the terms of duration of the collective conventions were extended as long as the act was in force. The government kept controlling the prices and salaries policy (see Decrees 1.012/74, 1.448/74 and 3.567/75) triggering the negotiation of new collective agreements, under the Law 14.250 since 1/06/75.

However, decree 3.032/75, suspended the effects of conventional clauses which established adjustments in salaries until it was established and approved the National Wage Institute Project, from the Productivity and participation (tripartite body), but Decree 2.720/75 which foreseen this, was revoked with Decree 13/75. So this body never could start its operations.

With the arrival of the new military dictatorship, altering the development of union lives, Law 21.476 was passed – subject which will be analyzed later on – which according to Krotoschin has been the more acute intervention from the State.

As Etala stated, salaries policy in Argentina, during this period, was marked by a strict regulation from the state (1976). At the same time, Decree 9/76 from the Military Board eliminated any union activities that were not administrative. Law 21.476 extended the periods of the agreements but modifying and even partially revoking them.

To all these measurements Law 21.367 was added, section 5 of this law, stated that any salary modification could be done through the National Executive Power (NEP). Establishing fines for those business men who grant forbidden raisings. Section 7 of this rule suspended its validity, and also that of every rule or conventional or legal disposition that established organisms or commissions with a participation or integration of social parties with powers to establish or readjust salaries.

As Jorge Rodriguez Mancini concurred (1990)

despite the prohibition on the negotiation of collective agreements inside the system of Law 21.307 negotiations that allow the modification of salaries portraying thousand ways to elude the prohibition herein mention appeared, first timidly and later on more strongly, with the participation of union association representation, even of those which were intervened by the government...

This shows the unstoppable strength of the collective negotiation. On 26/8/82, with Decree 438/82, the advisory "technical commissions" integrated with representatives from the State, from workers and from employees was authorized to study the systems and regimes existing in employment and salaries matters and to advice on the adjustment of them, leaving the Labour Ministry with the power to validate the agreements the representatives of all the areas may present. (Etala, 1976)

This new and present democratic process evolved gradually to the re-instauration of the freedom for collective negotiation, but with the limitations already imposed in an inflationary economic context.

This was how when a democratic government took office on 10/12/83 the Decree 367/83 was passed fixing salaries from 01/01/84. This fixation of salaries continued (see, among others, Decrees 859/84, 1.161/84, 3.458/84, 103/86, etc).

Law 23.126 gave back the validity of agreements, however, section 2 of this law authorized the State to suspend the application of certain provisions which were not able to be fulfilled by the companies.

Decree 2.224/85 (B.O. 25/11/85) established a compulsory system of voluntary acceptance for the revision of the collective agreements reintroduced by Law 23.126; however, being able to agree dispositions which did not inferred negatively on the costs.

During the presidency of Dr. Alfonsin, until the implosion of the system in December 2001, the same politic on the respect for collective freedoms was secured. Even though in reality there were some limitations.

In such sense, it can be mentioned Law 23.928 of Convertibility, which prohibited any monetary upgrading and revoked any conventional provision which said the opposite to what was established in the law; and, subsequently, decree 1334/1991 which limited the homologation of collective agreements not to include provisions in what has to do with increasing salaries or formulas based on productivity indexes.

Decree 470/93 from 18/03/93 modified Decree 199/88 opening the possibility of articulated negotiation in different levels. This rule modified the restrictive approach of Decree 1334/91, as it anticipated that

for the purposes of homologation, the Ministry...shall take into account if the agreement... includes any provision which violates any public order law, Laws 14.250 and 23.928, and if productivity criteria, investments, incorporation of technology, trainings were taking into account...,

a pessimistic and permissive formula.

Likewise, the famous decree 1553/1996 can be mentioned, which empowered the application authority to take away the homologation of collective agreements, which leaded to an unconstitutionality issued raised by some members of CGT. This issued had a favorable answer from the Argentinean National Labour Court. And the scope of the homologation act was limited for the State; eliminating completely the official amendment at any given time just by the fact that there were some modifications in the conditions which leaded to the determination of the decision. Also, it was explained that this should have been performed thought a law passed by the Congress modifying Law 14250.[1]

Likewise, at a time, the CGT, filed a complaint against the government before Freedom of Association Committee due to a violation in ILO International Convention Number 98. In what has to do with the passing of decrees 1553, 1554 and 1555 from year 1996 (Case 1887). The Experts Committee stated the following:

...the hope that in the Collective Agreement Project reformation herein mentioned the government shall revoke the provisions that conditioned the necessary homologations by the administrative authorities from the CGT, exceeding the level of the company, linking productivity, investment, new technology incorporation and training criteria.

Another interesting restriction to the autonomy of negotiation is that from section 25 from Law 24.013 (National Employment Law) which established, clearly stating the state interference, the obligations for the commissions that negotiate collective agreements to argue on the following subjects: a) the incorporation of new technology and its effects on labour relationships and employment; b) the implementation of training systems to make easier the versatility of employees; c) rank systems and functional mobility; d) the incorporation of an appropriated relationship on productivity improvements; e) the increase of productivity and the raising of real salaries; g) the incorporation of mechanisms of relevant information and consultations; h) the guidelines for mandatory recurrence negotiation shall be regulated in case of a business crisis, following a special procedure.

In March 2000, Law 25.250 was passed, with significant modifications on collective matters, specially, in promoting decentralization; stating in each case, the prevalence of smaller scope agreements against those with a biggest scope; and the fall of the ultra-activity system provided by Law 14.250 in the beginning, among other initiatives which showed many frustrated initiatives from the 90s.

Law 25.877, mentioned before, reintroduced the system of the most favorable law and the ultra-activity of labour law collective agreements.

Thus, it can be seen that in Argentina there are many cases in which the State tried to limit the collective negotiation, imposing conditions for negotiation or the issues to be negotiated. In general, the limitations of the negotiations or to let the parties negotiate on several issues have been seen in laws or decrees conditioned by an economic situation (for instance, limitations on the issue about salaries), or in long periods of economic crisis or government policies that were introduced as the only way out for serious situations the country was undergoing.

CONCLUSION

The story of Labour Law makes reference to the story of the formation and development of the legal system, establishing certain limits and conditions to the "expropriation" of the fruits of man´s work and to the powers of direction that this contract grants to the beneficiary of said fruits (the employer). This is how there appears a regulated network of guardianships and of benefits which protect the "subordinated" party in the contractual relationship.

Labour Law seems to be a set of rules – originally of state source and then the result of the collective bargaining- which recognizes the lack of freedom of those who are hired, a lack that is at the same time a consequence of an economic necessity- as the resignation of freedom that implies the submission to the hierarchical powers of the employer. And, from that acknowledgments, displays a number of rules and designs a set of legal, technical media to set limits on the exercise of the supremacy position of the employer as in the submission of freedoms from the employee.

The differentiation of the labour market previously made and mentioned, has been used throughout the diverse periods as an escape mechanism during the economic crisis to generate a work force with no protection.

As the mechanisms to make work more flexible were more accentuated, the work force diversified in such way that more areas were excluded from the protection provided by the hard core from the public labour policy.

What is more, the advance achieved on the heteronomous law, and in the negotiation, has been seen in certain periods and in accordance to the political and economic situation, surrounded by a certain behavior from the State which intended not to recognize the content of the undertaken commitments by signing different labour collective agreements.

Indeed, collective negotiation in Argentina underwent strong attacks from the State among the different periods of our history and according to the economic and political system. Also, it was the center of legislative restrictions which could be seen especially in the loss of the democracy of the ruling government.

The dynamic, the story and the specific characteristics of our labour relationship system have always meant a strong intervention from the state and a strongly marked regulation, which cannot disappear from one day to another. A change like this on this matter cannot be performed isolated, but it would require many other modifications of the labour law.

From the individual labour law as to that of the collective labour relationships, there can be seen the strong impact that economic variations have in the creation of labour legislation in the Argentine Republic.

The intervention from the State –throughout its different forms- has to be built as the guarantor of the minimums provided by the law as regards working conditions.

As a consequence, finding the exact point of intervention of the State and the parties that make the negotiations, among those not always clearly discernibly parameters, constitutes a delicate task which means commitment, willpower, intelligence and open deliberation among the involved social partners.

REFERENCES

Barbarosch, E. (2011). *La seguridad jurídica en la decisión judicial. ¿Utopía o realidad?* Buenos Aires, Argentina: La Ley.

Etala, J. J. (1976). *La política salarial desde mayo de 1976 en adelante.* Buenos Aires Argentina: D.T.

Goldin, A. O., Alimenti, J. F., & Caparrós, F. J. (2013). *Curso de Derecho del Trabajo y de la Seguridad Social.* Buenos Aires, Argentina: La Ley.

López, J. (1998). *Derecho Colectivo del Trabajo.* Buenos Aires, Argentina: La Ley.

Mirta Griselda and others v Sociedad Italiana de Beneficencia en Buenos Aires – Hospital Italiano s/dismissal. CSJ 1468/2011 (47-C), Recurso de Hecho de 19/02/2015.

Moyano, D. (1868). *El trabajo.* Buenos Aires, Argentina: D.T.

Podetti, H. A. (1990). *Cambio social y adaptabilidad del Derecho del Trabajo.* Buenos Aires, Argentina: D.T.

Podetti, H. A., (1990). Cambio Social y Adaptabilidad del Derecho del Trabajo [Social Change and Adaptability from Labour Law]. *DdelT, L, 1990-B*, 2519-2526.

Ramírez Bosco, L., & Rodríguez Mancini, J. (2007). *Ley de Contrato de trabajo.* Buenos Aires, Argentina: La Ley.

Rodríguez Mancini, J. (1990). *La negociación colectiva.* Buenos Aires, Argentina: Astrea.

Supiot, A. (2007). *Homo Juridicus, un ensayo sobre la función antropológica del derecho.* Buenos Aires, Argentina: Siglo XXI Editores Argentina S.A.

Tissembaum, M. R. (1958). *La reforma constitucional de 1957. Las disposiciones de Derecho del Trabajo y de la Seguridad Social.* Buenos Aires, Argentina: D.T.

Vázquez Vialard, A. (1991). *Cincuenta años en la evolución del Derecho del Trabajo Argentino*. Buenos Aires, Argentina: Academia Nacional de Derecho y Ciencias Sociales.

Zanini, P. J. (1990). Reflexiones acerca de la necesidad de la modernización integral del Derecho Laboral. Buenos Aires, Argentina: D.T.

KEY TERMS AND DEFINITIONS

Ex Combatants From Malvinas: Soldiers who participated during the War in Malvinas Islands in the year 1983.

Generation of '80: Was the governing elite in Argentina from 1880 to 1916. Members of the oligarchy of the provinces and the country's capital, they first joined the League of Governors (*Liga de Gobernadores*), and then the National Autonomist Party. They filled the highest public political, economical, military, and religious positions.

Labour Contract Dismantling: Also called "labour deregulation," consists of using simulated juridical forms, substituting labour forms, in order to deny labor rights to the employees.

Labour Flexibilization: Labour flexibilization refers to the changing work practices and legislation by which firms no longer use internal labour markets or implicitly promise employees lifetime job security, but rather seek flexible employment relations that permit them to increase or diminish their workforce and reassign and redeploy employees with ease.

Privatization: The process of transferring ownership of a business, enterprise, agency, public service, or public property from the public sector (a government) to the private sector. It also means the government outsourcing of services or functions to private firms.

Quasi-Employment: Type of labour relation in which the employee has features that belongs to a self-employed worker, but, also others, that refers to a subordinated worker. In Spain it is called "T.R.A.D.E.," meaning self-employed economically dependent worker.

Temporary Work Agency: Organization that matches employers to employees in an employment situation where the working arrangement is limited to a certain period of time based on the needs of the employing organization. In Argentina it has to fulfill specific requirements and conditions to be legal.

Trial Period: Period in the labour contract during which the employee can be dismissed without receiving an economic compensation.

Unhook From the Collective Agreement: Measure that allows the businessman "fulfilling a series of specific requirements" to modify the work conditions that were established in a labour collective agreement.

ENDNOTE

1 C.Nac.Trab. sala 3, CGT v. Estado Nacional. DT 1997-A-.

Chapter 5
Labor Protection in Mexico:
Recent Reforms and Future Challenges

Jose Ernesto Rangel Delgado
University of Colima, Mexico

Antonina Ivanova Boncheva
Universidad Autonoma de Baja California Sur, Mexico

ABSTRACT

If one looks for a representative emerging economy to examine the different effects of labor reforms, Mexico provides an important case study. In order to boost economic recovery, the government promoted infrastructure spending, transfers to development banks, support to small and medium-sized enterprises, and to the export sector. As usual labor-management relations are uneven in Mexico and union issues can be complex, to reduce the negative consequences related to the sharp increase of unemployment, the government tried to focus more on the generation of employment introducing several measures such as training and temporary jobs to facilitate the withdrawal of savings from the mandatory individual pension accounts, coverage of the medical insurance and maternity benefits for dismissed workers, among others. But, challenges such as the informal economy, minimum wage convenience, flexible labor contracts, entrepreneur vulnerability, and higher education labor market have to be faced.

DOI: 10.4018/978-1-5225-4134-9.ch005

INTRODUCTION

Latin American countries performed well both in economic and social terms during the first decade of the twenty-first century (Cornia, 2014). To different extents, they experienced positive economic growth as well as a sharp decline of poverty and inequality (Lopez-Calva and Lustig, 2010). Nonetheless, the arrival of the international crisis and the resulting changes in external conditions severely affected the region (Fernandez-Arias & Montiel, 2010). However, governments have been able to implement countercyclical fiscal policy to cope with the negative consequences of the crisis (Martorano, 2014a).

Not all the Latin American countries achieved the same results. Mexico is an emblematic case and its experience highlights the crucial role played by initial conditions. Indeed, the worsening of fiscal conditions pushed the Mexican government to embark on a process of fiscal consolidation since 2010. As a result, the Mexican economy (growth and employment) recovered slowly and poverty sharply increased.

Mexico was hit by the financial crisis in late 2008 after almost a decade of sustained economic growth. Although the Mexican exports were more diversified by products (in comparison to other Latin American countries), they were more concentrated by destination since exports to the United States accounted for more than 70 per cent of total exports. Thus, the drop of GDP recorded by the United States in 2008 (-0.3 per cent) and 2009 (-3 per cent) negatively hit the Mexican economy.

Beyond this, the international turbulence provoked a reduction in the financial flows from rich economies to the rest of the world. Private portfolio flows (as percentage of GDP) decreased by 1.9 points in Mexico between 2007 and 2008; they went up around 4 points in the following year and sharply declined by more than 6 points from 2009 to 2011.

On the other hand, foreign direct investments (FDI) were much less volatile. Between 2008 and 2009, on average FDI dropped by 1.2 percentage points from 3.3 to 2.1 per cent of GDP and slightly recovered in the following years. Mexico experienced a reduction of FDI by about 0.7 points over the period 2008 and 2009 and an increase by 0.3 points between 2009 and 2010 (CEPF, 2010). Mexico was also affected by the reduction of remittances that dropped from 2.6 in 2007 to 2 per cent of GDP in 2012.

These events generated important consequences. In particular, the unemployment rate rose by almost 2 points up to 5.5 per cent in Mexico (INEGI, 2016). The Mexican economy recorded a negative growth rate in the third quarter of 2008. The crisis reached its peak in Mexico in the first quarter of 2009 and the drop in GDP recorded was larger, though performance remained positive, at low values, from the second half of 2009.

This chapter explores the recent developments in the Mexican labor market and the labor protection normativity during the post-crisis period. The first part explores the impacts of the crisis on Mexican economy and the policy responses of the country to economic and financial effects. The second part assesses the changes in Mexican labor market and labor legislation, such as labor protection, medical insurance, old age unemployment, and labor-management relations. In the third part, we pay attention to the future challenges in Mexican labor markets: Informal economy, minimum wage, flexible labor contracts, vulnerable businesses and decent jobs for higher education graduates. Finally, we present some final reflections.

Impacts of the Crisis and Policy Responses in Mexico Before the Crisis

Notwithstanding the favorable external conditions, there are no doubts that a crucial contribution to the good economic and social performances of the 2000s was the adoption of a new economic model (Cornia, 2014). Indeed, the majority of Latin American countries implemented a set of fiscal and monetary policies that boosted economic development and promoted a sharp reduction of poverty and inequality (Cornia and Martorano, 2011).

The monetary policy was basically countercyclical. Indeed, "during periods of the bonanza, monetary authorities attempted to control the expansion in money supply, fall in interest rates and credit expansion triggered by export expansion and large financial inflows through an accumulation of reserves and sterilization" (Cornia, 2012, p. 26).

Mexico explicitly introduced an inflation targeting regime. The Mexican model targets an inflation rate of 3 per cent with a ±1 percentage point tolerance range. Moreover, the country adopted a floating exchange rate regime that allows authorities to correct it "under exceptional circumstances". As a result – during the last decade – inflation declined and remained at low levels in Mexico, while the exchange rate regime promoted stability and trade competitiveness (Martorano, 2014b).

With respect to fiscal policy, Latin American countries recorded positive results thanks to the ability to contain expenditure together with a growing capacity to mobilize revenue (Martorano, 2014a). As other countries in the region, Mexico was able to benefit from favorable terms of trade especially through state-owned companies operating in the export sector such as the Mexican *Pemex* (Cornia et al, 2011). Nonetheless, the capacity to generate revenue from taxes was very low. Mexico was the only Latin American country that recorded a drop-in tax/GDP ratio by about 2 points to 8.8 per cent over the same period (Cornia & Martorano, 2011).

Many factors facilitated the growing ability of Latin American countries to mobilize revenue via taxation as the good economic conditions, the process of economic formalization, the introduction of new technologies and, last but not least, the increase of tax morale and reduction of tax evasion. This performance was also assured by fiscal reforms that generated the so called "silent revolution" (Lora, 2007). For example, a fiscal rule was introduced by the Mexican government in 2006 which set a zero-target cash balance. Without doubt, this first generation of fiscal rules contributed to increasing the fiscal discipline in Mexico. However, they showed considerable limits during the recent crisis since they reduced the space for implementing countercyclical policy measures. Thus, Mexico partially reformed the rules in order to increase the fiscal space.

Fiscal sustainability was also assured by a sharp reduction of indebtedness and a rapid accumulation of international reserves. On average, the regional debt/GDP ratio decreased from 60 to 30 per cent between 2002 and 2007 (Martorano, 2014a). The Mexican debt/GDP ratio dropped by 8 points from 46 to 38 per cent over the same period (Table 1).

Impacts of the Financial Crisis 2008

After almost a decade of sustained economic growth, Mexico was hit by the financial crisis in late 2008. Although the Mexican exports were more diversified by products (in comparison to other Latin American countries), they were more concentrated by destination since exports to the United States accounted for more than 70 per cent of total exports. Thus, the drop of GDP recorded by the United States in 2008 (-0.3 per cent) and 2009 (-3 per cent) negatively hit the Mexican economy.

Beyond this, the international turbulence provoked a reduction in the financial flows from rich economies to the rest of the world. Private portfolio flows (as percentage of GDP) decreased by 1.9 points in Mexico between 2007 and 2008; they went up around 4 points in the following year and sharply declined by more than 6 points from 2009 to 2011.

Table 1. Fiscal indicators in Mexico, 2007

Primary Balance (% of GDP)	Target Primary Balance (a)	Structural Primary Balance (b)	Required Structural Adjustment (a-b)	Public Debt (% of GDP)	Currency Reserves (% of GDP)	EMBI Spreads
-0.51	0.83	-2.26	3.09	37.83	8.76	150

Source: Martorano (2014b)

On the other hand, foreign direct investments (FDI) were much less volatile. Between 2008 and 2009, on average FDI dropped by 1.2 percentage points from 3.3 to 2.1 per cent of GDP and slightly recovered in the following years. Mexico experienced a reduction of FDI by about 0.7 points over the period 2008 and 2009 and an increase by 0.3 points between 2009 and 2010 (CEPF, 2010). Mexico was also affected by the reduction of remittances that dropped from 2.6 in 2007 to 2 per cent of GDP in 2012.

Policy Responses to the Crisis in Mexico

In Mexico, monetary policy has been accommodating. After the reduction of inflation pressures, the Central Bank cut interest rates by 375 basis points to 4.5 per cent during the first half of 2009. Financial conditions improved after 2008 thank also to external support. In particular, "in October 2008 the establishment by the U.S. Federal Reserve of temporary liquidity swap facilities with the Banco de México of up to US$30 billion (extended in February and again in June 2009); and the approval in April 2009 by the IMF of a flexible credit line arrangement, with no conditionality, of approximately US$47 billion" (IMF, 2010; Ros, 2011, p. 174).

Yet, due to limited fiscal space, the Mexican stimulus package was smaller than in other Latin American countries (about 1.5 per cent of GDP in 2009). The Mexican authorities implemented several measures in different sectors. In order to boost economic recovery, the government promoted infrastructure spending, transfers to development banks, support to small and medium-sized enterprises, and to the export sector (OECD, 2009).

Crisis and Employment in Mexico

From November 2008 to January 2009, more than 541 thousand people lost their jobs in the urban areas of the country, representing an average of 5,885 dismissals per day, according to reports from the Institute Mexican Social Security (IMSS).

Labor Protection Normativity

The Official Gazette of the Federation published on April 1, 1970 aspects related to labor protection, which coincide with a worldwide trend towards the transformation of the state-centered economic model towards greater market participation and a neoliberal economic model. These, placed labor in a new working condition. This tendency was reinforced after the 2008 crisis giving rise to the Law of 2015, which in articles 47 and 51, shows legislation on both justified and unjustified dismissals.

Figure 1. Total jobs created per year (annual average)
Source: Prepared by the authors.

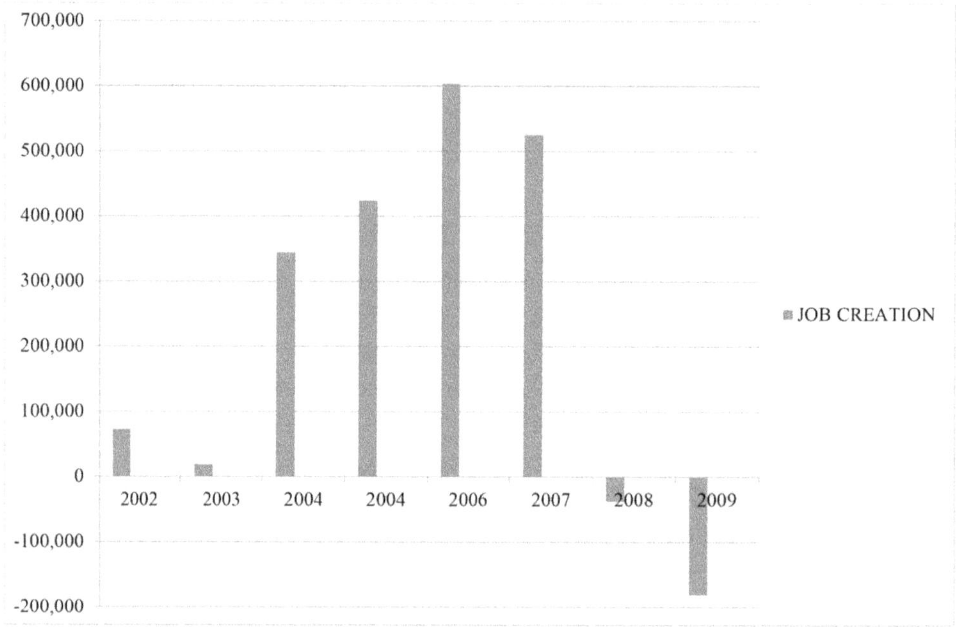

The Federal Labor Law (DOF, 2015a) has been conforming in the format that it currently presents over the years. As of 2008, aspects related to labor flexibility and other issues related to layoffs have been consolidated. A new form of job hiring is established in Mexico. This is biased by the temporary jobs positioning in front of the permanent jobs, and definition of the retirement as obligation of the Mexican Institute for Social Security (IMSS).

Two types of dismissal are recognized in the current law, those without responsibility for the employer and those without responsibility for the worker. Article 47 of the Law states fifteen causes of recess of the employment relationship without responsibility of the employer, while article 51 states ten causes of dismissal without responsibility of the worker. Likewise, the Law considers that the employer who dismisses the worker must give written notice, clearly referring to the conduct or reason that motivates the recess, and the date or dates in which they were committed. The notice must be delivered personally to the worker at the time of the dismissal or, to communicate it to the competent Conciliation and Arbitration Board, within five working days.

Medical Insurance and Maternity Benefits

The Social Security Act of Mexico (DOF, 2015b) is clear in terms of attention to the status of women workers' maternity. In its Chapter I, article 11, Sec. II Expresses that the maternity and sickness care system is mandatory. Therefore, workers have health insurance during their contribution to Social Security.

It can be observed, first, that the social insurance service, whether due to illness or maternity does not present substantial changes with financial crises. However, these may be influencing the disposition of financial resources for the granting of the service.

Maternity care in recent years is considering more flexibility for the exercise of the corresponding benefit. Thus, currently working mothers can choose to attend to the evolution of their pregnancy with an external doctor or to attend to the IMSS hospitals. Even from 1 December 2012 all male workers who become parents, whether for the birth of a child or the adoption of a minor, will enjoy a paternity leave of five working days with pay (IDC, 2013).

Since May 9, 2008, care for pregnancy was strengthened with the program "Healthy Pregnancy", aimed at ensuring the incorporation of all pregnant women into the social protection system. The maternal and perinatal health policies are enhanced in the prevention and promotion of maternal health. (National Development Plan and Maternal and Child Health Program). These measures have reduced maternal and infant mortality.

According to INEGI (2015) indicators "Between 1990 and 2013, the mortality rate in children under five in Mexico decreased from 41.0 to 15.7 deaths per thousand live births, and the infant mortality from 32.5 in 1990 to 13.0 deaths per thousand live births in 2013.

Following INEGI (2015), "... in the international context, many factors have influenced the relative success in reducing child mortality. On the one hand, the advances that appear to have played an important role in health are access to mass vaccination, strengthening breastfeeding and regular medical checks, and in the case of education, the expansion of preschool. These areas have also influenced progress in infrastructure, sanitation, access to drinking water and coverage of health services."

Because of the novelty of this benefit, there are doubts about its treatment in social security, so it is then indicated what the employer must do when granting these licenses to their employees. They should be given the same treatment as "leave with pay". As during the time when they will not attend to provide their services, the workers will receive their full salary, the employer must consider them as days actually worked and therefore pay the employer's contributions and corresponding credit repayments.

Old Age Unemployment Insurance

Retirement is one of the hot topics in complicated budget conditions, especially in an aging population, with descending birth rates.

The population pyramid of Mexico, for example, shows that 48.6% of the total population corresponds to men and that 51.4% correspond to women. But the most interesting is that of this population about 30% corresponds to the economically active population usually considered between 12 and 60 years of age. Between 10 and 20 years of age, for example, there is a population bulge, known as a "demographic bonus", which begins to decrease; the age corresponding to youth is until 29, where the population is notoriously beginning to decrease. According to the data of 2015 the total population is descending.

Currently, two Social Security laws apply: The Law of 1973 and the Law of 1997. Any worker hired prior to 1997 will be favored by the 1973 law, while any worker who has been hired will find himself under social security. Severance pensions in old age are granted to the insured who, having reached the age of sixty and sixty-five years, respectively, has the minimum contribution period provided for by the Social Security Law, has caused a discharge from the Mandatory Regimen of Social Security, is deprived of paid work, and is in force in their rights. The minimum period

Figure 2. Population pyramid
Source: INEGI-Population pyramid (2015). Retrieved from http://www.beta.inegi.org.mx/temas/estructura/

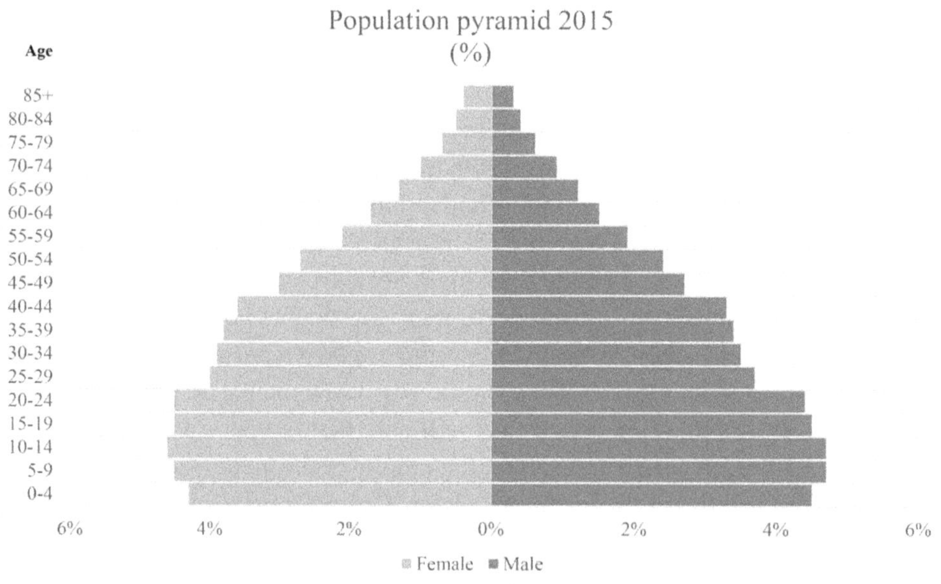

of contribution provided for by the above-mentioned ordinances is: 500 weeks of contribution (1973) and 1250 weeks of contribution (1997) ((DOF, 2015c).

Labor-Management Relations

The first labor union in Mexico was constituted in 1872. In the early 1930s, corporatism was in a frank process of consolidation with the emergence of the National Revolutionary Party founded by Plutarco Elias Calles. From there the workers' organizations are consolidated until the presidential term of General Lazaro Cárdenas, period in which the Mexican Constitution is applied with the greater reaches of social order.

In the 1970s, a new trend of development centered on market positions, particularly linked to economic neoliberalism, and pushed the unions towards a setback that placed them under different conditions that placed the defense of workers. Thus, by the year 2005 Mexico had 35 workers' organizations, generally classified as unions, confederations, associations, union groups or unions of workers.

In a new era of trade unionism, however, according to the Supreme Court of Justice of the Nation (UNAM, 2009, p. 13), "The union and the collective contract represent two of the most important labor law figures, in the defense of workers' security, their rights and the obtaining of better labor conditions. "

Hence, we can see that unionism is linked to the three periods mentioned above, showing different roles. A first period of construction and development, a second one of consolidation and achievements, and another of reversion and reshuffle to the new global market trends, in which the union's role has to adapt, showing a smaller influence the current economic processes.

Actually, labor-management relations are uneven in Mexico and union issues can be complex. Mexican labor law provides for collective bargaining; however, in practice, there is widespread use of so-called "protection contracts," which are collective bargaining agreements (CBAs) signed by the employers with unrepresentative unions, that in practice advocate more for the employer's interests than the workers.' These unions often enter workplaces even before enterprises open and without the knowledge of workers, and block the ability of independent unions to effectively and legitimately bargain collectively on behalf of workers. Many actors also note that the Mexican government wields unofficial veto power in the supposedly neutral and balanced tripartite arrangement of labor-business relations.

The large majority of labor unions in Mexico fall under the umbrella of the Confederation of Mexican Workers (Confederación de Trabajadores Mexicanos) or CTM, which is comprised of approximately 11,000 labor unions, almost all of which could be considered "protection unions." The CTM is the primary member organization in the labor arm of one of Mexico's major political parties, the Institutional Revolutionary Party (*Partido Revolucionario Institucional*) or PRI.

Workers have made numerous complaints of poor working conditions in maquiladoras and in the agricultural production industry. Low wages, poor labor conditions, long work hours, unjustified dismissals, lack of social security benefits and safety in the workplace, and lack of freedom of association were among the most common complaints. As a result, there have been several protests and boycott calls by farmworkers in northern Mexico, which have posed significant investment risks. In March 2015, farm workers in San Quintin, Baja California, walked out and staged protests to demand higher wages, access to social security, pay for overtime, parental leave, freedom of association, the right to collective bargaining, etc. Most recently in March 4, 2016, more than 3,500 workers went on strike in Lazaro Cardenas, in the state of Michoacán against steel maker ArcelorMittal in response to 300 alleged unfair dismissals and violations of their collective agreement (SDOIA, 2016). The strike affected the production of more than 8,500 metric tons of steel per day, and the Mexican labor authorities ruled that the strike was illegal.

In terms of labor dispute resolution mechanisms, the Conciliation and Arbitration Boards (CABs) in Mexico adjudicate all individual and collective labor conflicts. Although they have a tripartite structure with government representatives and equal numbers of worker and employer representatives, the CABs have been widely criticized as being biased in favor of management. The federal labor law sets out processes for dispute resolution over which the CABs preside, including a mandatory conciliation phase. If conciliation fails, the parties submit evidence and the CAB rules on the issue after a hearing. CAB resolutions are final, but a party may request an injunction, or '*amparo*' to the Constitutional court. "*Amparos*" are offered on limited constitutional grounds.

Governmental Initiatives to Generate Employment

To reduce the negative consequences related to the sharp increase of unemployment, the government tried to focus more on the generation of employment introducing several measures such as training and temporary jobs (Khanna et al, 2014). In particular, the Program for Job Conservation (*Programa de Preservación del Empleo)* was established, the Temporary Program of Employment (*Programa Temporal de Empleo)* was extended by about 40 per cent with respect to the original plan, and the National Service of Employment (*Servicio Nacional de Empleo)* was strengthened (Valencia Lomeli et al, 2013).

One example is provided by Gamez et al. (2014) analyzing the responses to the crises in the tourist sector in Los Cabos, one of the most famous Mexican resorts. In spite of experiencing a huge contraction (a loss of 250,000 or 25% of visitors in 2009), the reduction of employment in hotels of Los Cabos was not an immediate strategy to cope with the crisis. Almost 40% of hotels did not fire any of their employees and only 1 out of 5 fired 10% of their staff. That is, almost 60% of hotels kept their staff, although this was at the expense of the workers' income as a trade-off to keep their jobs. On the other hand, more than one third reduced their staff between 20–40% (Gamez et al, 2014). One of the policies to increase the performance of the personnel was to enhance the skills and knowledge building and create opportunities to apply these skills and knowledge. These were complemented by delegating more responsibility to lower-level management and allowing personnel to have more control over their own work. Of course, introducing some financial or non-financial incentives was considered to be important.

Mexico does not have a proper unemployment benefits system, but during the crisis the government issued regulations to facilitate the withdrawal of savings from the mandatory individual pension accounts (Robalino et al, 2014, pp. 111-112). Moreover, coverage of the medical insurance and maternity benefits for dismissed workers was extended from two to six months (Valencia Lomeli et al, 2013). Lastly, via the Insurance for Old Age Unemployment (*Seguro de Cesantía en Edad Avanzada)* the government guaranteed a pension to elderly people (aged 60 years and more) who became unemployed and had contributed at least for 24 years (Freije et al, 2014).

Through the 2009 National Agreement to Support the Household Economy and Employment, the Mexican government implemented several measures to help households facing economic difficulties. First of all, a reduction of the energy costs (gasoline, electricity fees, etc.) was implemented. However, one of the most important measures to protect poor households and children was related to the changes implemented in the Opportunities Program (*Oportunidades)*. First, the benefit was increased. Second, the government promoted an expansion in coverage of the *Oportunidades's* program with support from the World Bank. Similarly, the coverage rate for other programs such as the Program on Food Support (*Programa de Apoyo Alimentario)* and the *Habitat* was extended. Overall, the cost of social protection measures was about 0.40 per cent of GDP (Valencia Lomeli et al, 2013).

In view of this situation, the Ministry of Labor and Social Welfare seeks to promote articulation among labor market actors to improve employment opportunities; Prepare reports and formulate programs to promote the occupation in the country, as well as to ensure their implementation; And to guide job seekers towards the vacancies offered by employers based on their training and skills, mainly serving the disadvantaged population, such as: young people between the ages of 16 and 29, people with disabilities, seniors, women, pre-liberated people, people living in extreme poverty and food, and forming part of the National System for the Crusade against Hunger (SNCcH), beneficiaries of *Prospera*, Social Inclusion Program and population that is addressed in the National Strategy for the Prevention of Adolescent

Pregnancy. These activities include information on the supply and demand of employment to be linked according to the requirements of both parties.

Given the dismantling of value chains that has involved the new stage of economic construction in Mexico, other types of programs have been activated, such as the Temporary Employment Program, linked to the National Employment Service (Robalino et al, 2014, pp. 111-112), which has, among other objectives: Promote and design mechanisms for monitoring the placement of workers, as well as designing, conducting and evaluating specific programs to generate employment opportunities for young people and vulnerable groups.

However, since 2010 worsening of the fiscal balance pushed the government to promote a fiscal adjustment process cutting some current expenditure (excluding social programs), levying new taxes or raising existing ones. In particular, a new 3% levy was imposed on telecommunications (ECLAC, 2013).

In addition, the maximum individual and corporate income tax rate was raised temporarily from 28% to 30%; VAT was increased from 15% to 16%; and the tax on gaming and lotteries jumped from 20% to 30%. Levies on tobacco, beer and other alcoholic beverages were also raised temporarily (ECLAC, 2010).

Future Challenges

The Informal Economy

The Mexican Social Security Institute (IMSS) reports the creation of 732, 000 formal jobs in 2016, the highest number of the last decade (IMSS, 2017). However, the Mexican Statistics Bureau (INEGI) estimates that 59 percent of the workforce is engaged in the informal economy (INEGI, 2016). In the formal economy, there is a general surplus of labor but a shortage of technically skilled workers and engineers.

Table 2. Mexico: Countercyclical Fiscal Measures

Workfare (1)	Social Protection (2)	Fiscal Stimuli (3)
The temporary employment program at the federal level was expanded by 40% over what had been planned	Launch of the *Programa de Apoyo Alimentario* (PAL)	Public investments in infrastructures
Launch of Employment Preservation Program for protecting employment in vulnerable businesses	Expansion of *Oportunidades* Program.	Support to private sector

Source: Adapted from Powell (2012).

Figure 3. Percentage of unprotected labor by economic sphere
Source: Prepared by the authors.

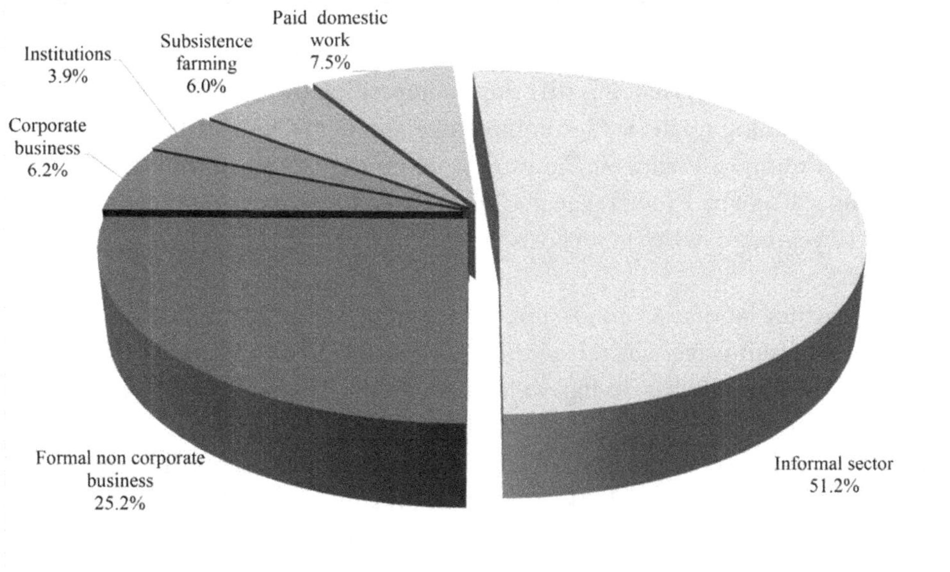

The informal economy, without labor protection, without benefits of any kind, which has only been favored by a comprehensive vision of medical care through Seguro Popular and other public healthcare institutions, has recently been considered a population in "Critical conditions of occupation", according to INEGI. This category reveals the rate of labor informality, which amounts to 57% of the total employed population for the first quarter of 2017.

Since the second quarter of 2008, INEGI reported the composition of unprotected labor according to the economic area, which can be seen in the following table, which shows the degree of inattention (informal) in the informal sector. This sector is not only affected by the lack of social protection, but also represents significant leaks in taxes for the government.

Table 3. Percentage of unprotected labor in total occupation

Absolute amount of unprotected labor	23 543 656
Absolute amount of occupation	43 866 696
Percentage of unprotected labor in total occupation	53.67

Source: INEGI (2008).

Minimum Wage

Mexico is in the process of changing its labor laws and practices to bring them in line with international norms. Mexican manufacturing operations in the textile and garment sectors are experiencing stiff wage competition from Central America and India, but are gaining relative wage competitiveness with China in high technology sectors. According to Financial Times (2017), hourly wages in Mexico in dollar terms are now 40 per cent lower than in China. That represents a stunning turnaround from just 12 years ago, when labor costs in Mexico were roughly 183 per cent higher than China's.

The tripartite National Commission sets the minimum wage each year. In 2016, Mexico's minimum wage was raised to MXN $73.04 (USD $4.10) per day, which continues to be less than a living wage in this OECD country (SDOIA, 2016). However, in 2017, a substantial increase above the range of inflation estimated by Bank of Mexico between 2 and 4% was implemented for the first time in many years. The increase is 9.58% from $ 73.04 to $ 80.04, or 6.58% above 3% of the country´s average inflation target, that could contribute to foster the domestic market and the purchasing power of the majority of Mexican workers (Sandoval Malori and Straulino-Rodríguez, 2016).

Nevertheless, during the last 36 years, the purchasing power of the minimum wage accumulated a loss of 72.8 percent. That is only three quarters of the value that the incomes of the occupied population had at the end of 70s (Santiago Reyes, 2011).

But Mexico is also, according to statistics from the Organization for Economic Cooperation and Development (OECD, 2016), the country with the lowest minimum wage in the bloc. The wages were characterized as "extremely low" and "much less than average" wages by CEPAL (2015) which in 2015 the organization estimated at 90 cents per hour; seven times less than in the United States ($ 7.2) or three times less than in Chile ($ 3).

Mexico works on the basis of a minimum wage that little or nothing reaches the support of the family economy and also in many cases Mexican citizens face the reality of working in low quality jobs and in conditions of occupational risk. Coupled all to conditions of corruption and social insecurity. For decades, the minimum wage has been far removed from the "adequate remuneration to meet the normal material, social and cultural requirements of a head of household, and to provide for the compulsory education of their children" as mandated by Article 123 Ap.VI of the Constitution (Moreno-Brid *et al.,* 2016).

Figure 4 shows the between the minimum wage and the consumer price index (CPI), for the low inflation period 2008-2015. This is the reality of almost all economic sectors (according to INEGI): Primary sector (agriculture, forestry, fishing and hunting); Secondary (extractive industry of electricity, manufacturing

Figure 4. Purchasing power of minimum wage versus consumer price index (CPI)
*Source: Adapted from Aguirre Botello (2017). Retrieved from http://www.mexicomaxico.org/voto/salmininf.htm_*

and construction); And tertiary, commerce, restaurants and accommodation services, transport, communications, mail and storage, professional services, financial and corporate services, social services, various services, government and international organizations, among others.

The total number of employees earning minimum wage, for example, in the primary sector amounts to 25.52% of the total employed population in the country in the first quarter of 2017; In the secondary sector a 61.37% percentage is detected; In the tertiary 12.60%, and others not specified 0.51% (INEGI, 2017).

Although the minimum wage has some positive role in matching incomes among groups of unskilled workers, for example, young and mature, men and women (OECD, 2016), there is no protection of purchasing power. The protection of workers by minimum wage is almost inexistent regarding the possibility of acquiring the goods and services of the basic basket. One of the results has been the constant contraction of the domestic market, due to the fall in purchasing power (Santiago Reyes, 2011). Another is the increase in wage inequality between skilled and unskilled workers, offset only by a progressive transfer strategy (as Opportunities Program and Social Security) that reduces inequality.

Flexible Labor Contracts

Since 1970s the contracts for a specific work or defined time began to proliferate as a result of the labor flexibility imposed by the neoliberal model, substantially reducing the contracts for an indefinite period. This generates impacts on benefits granted to workers, especially those related to the 1973 and 1994 IMSS law retirement, reinforced after the crisis in 2008.

The Mexican Congress enacted a sweeping labor reform bill into law on November 29, 2012. The law encompasses major changes to make Mexico's labor market flexible and incorporates modern statutes such as non-discrimination. Included in the 300 articles are provisions to ease the hiring-and-firing of workers, establish an apprenticeship system, establish an hourly wage system (heretofore, there was only a daily wage), and regulate outsourcing. The labor reform also prohibits job discrimination based on race, national origin, gender, age, disability, social status, health condition, religion, citizenship status, sexual preference, marital status, opinions, or any other category of discrimination that contradicts human dignity. It makes it illegal for employers to require pregnancy tests of their female workers and job candidates. The reform also restructures Mexico's labor courts and incorporates the International Labor Organization's (ILO) concept of decent work. [1]

Mexico's Secretariat of Labor, the *Secretaría del Trabajo y Previsión Social* (STPS) is responsible for enforcing labor laws and conducting inspections of workplaces. In 2014, the STPS carried out regular inspections of workplaces, using a questionnaire and other tools to identify victims of labor exploitation (INEGI, 2016). These inspections identified several industries as having a high incidence of child labor (agriculture, coal mines, and construction). In April 2014, Mexico's Congress passed a constitutional reform (enacted in June) to prohibit children under the age of 15 from working.

The Federal Labor Law was then updated in June 2015 and allows those between the ages of 15 and 17 to work no more than six daytime hours in nonhazardous conditions, and only with parental permission. The labor law includes a broad list of hazardous and unhealthy occupations that minors are prohibited from performing. According to the International Labor Organization, government enforcement was reasonably effective in enforcing these laws in large and medium-sized companies, especially in factories run by U.S. companies and in other industries under federal jurisdiction. Enforcement was inadequate in many small companies and in the agriculture and construction sectors, and it was nearly absent in the informal sector, in which most children worked.

SMEs and Other Vulnerable Businesses

Mexico, without being the exception, reports a total of about 90% of its companies as Small and Medium Enterprises (SMEs). It is precisely this type of company that is most at risk in usually unstable market economic situations. That is the main reason to structure "The Employment Preservation Program for protecting employment in vulnerable businesses".

As entrepreneurship is the brand that characterizes the current economy, the entrepreneur must be ready to face financial and operational problems, and according to Villafranco (2014), there are seven items that can make the difference between success and closure of a company: Strategic oriented to the capacity of the company to protect itself or adapt to the changes that may come; The ability to comply with laws and regulations that were omitted causing unexpected consequences; Financial factors, in the sense that the dimension of the debts acquired may not have been considered with fair average, causing lack of liquidity and leverage; Those of operational order that imply the lack of internal control structures in the organization; Environmental factors that imply the non-fulfillment of the requirements established by the law on environment, like the emission of pollutants; The lack of prevention and threats for an outdated use of ICTs; Factors related to poor management in the selection and location of employees (human resources).

In this respect, and in order to preserve employment in the face of the volatility of companies of such dimensions, Mexico has the Employment Preservation Program, whose purpose is to protect employment by strengthening practices that reduce costs companies face reductions in working hours instead of layoffs.

Another area of companies with a high vulnerability index is the one with an adverse economic environment, which faces easy changes in consumer preferences and is strongly oriented towards foreign trade, such as the automotive industry and electronics, among others. The workers in these sectors have such a specific level of specific knowledge and skills that it is preferable to keep them than dismiss them, given the cost of training that would imply, new workers, to the economic recovery (OIT, 2009)

Higher Education and Employment

In the various studies carried out, one can observe a labor demand that is based mainly on educational levels of high school and therefore faces a devaluation of the quality of skilled work, trained in institutions of higher education.

The 26.28% of the total of the underemployed population, counts on average level of high school and higher education at national level (INEGI, 2016). This means that a little more than a quarter of the population presumes acceptable qualification levels in a knowledge-based economy, in other words, that this economy, contrary to the high levels of coverage at these levels, does not reach to use graduates of upper and upper secondary education loosely. This, in other words, means the substantial devaluation of wages in the face of constant inflation, as well as the devaluation of the professions, which is often necessary to work more hours than their current occupation allows them. As is the case of university graduates who occupy positions formerly occupied by higher education levels (Rangel & Ivanova, 2012).

CONCLUSION

The complexity of the development of market economies is centered not only on their industrialization, but also on other factors such as environmental care, climate change, technological development, population aging, international trade and global value chains, impact on the labor protection and labor normativity in many countries.

Mexico has recently been considered as an emerging economy beyond it´s industrialization. It is member of the OECD, has signed treaties such as the Kyoto Protocol, and actively participates in the G20 and the Asia Pacific Economic Cooperation (APEC), among other international organization.

However, the labor income in the country is not guaranteed and often very low. Due to the unequal distribution of income, 47%, of the total population is close or below the poverty line. Additionally, with the recent policies of USA and the imminent renegotiation of NAFTA, Mexico faces the necessity to generate jobs before the eventual return of compatriots abroad. To affront the same challenge, the minimum wage must be raised in order to develop the domestic market and decrease the dependence on foreign demand.

In Mexico, financially speaking, the retirement begins to generate a serious problem, not enough wealth is generated to face the payment of an aged labor. Oil prices, which have a negative impact on the generation of foreign currency incomes, the eventual application of taxes on remittances from the United States, may reduce this significant source of foreign exchange for the Mexican economy.

In general, international labor rights are recognized in Mexican law and the country has extensive occupational safety and health regulations and technical standards. However, important legal ambiguities exist with regard to collective bargaining and many rights are not respected in practice. According to labor rights activists, employers in all sectors sometimes used the illegal 'hours bank' approach–requiring long hours when the workload is heavy and cutting hours when it is light–to avoid compensating workers for overtime. In addition, many companies evaded taxes and social security payments by employing workers informally. The law prohibits most forms of discrimination; however, discrimination in employment or occupation continues to occur against women, indigenous groups, persons with disabilities, LGBT persons, and migrant workers.

The existing law enforcement is one of the main challenges that Mexico faces. Other important ones are to dignify the minimum wage, to guarantee the incomes and the rights of the temporary workers and to protect the employment in vulnerable businesses, such as SMES (including informal economy), and create decent jobs for higher education graduates.

Nowadays Mexico is in process of changing its labor laws and practices to bring them in line with international norms. Reforms of employment protection should be considered as part of a comprehensive package that includes an adequate safety net for the unemployed and effective re-employment services.

It is true that the abrupt changes that the country has had to face have placed it on a new development path. External developments and foreign markets are shaping the public policy, but the internal market should not be left out. Both give spaces for an occupation of the labor and for improving the conditions of labor protection. And finally, public policies and labor law enforcement must be based on the principles of social and economic inclusive and sustainable development, human rights and equity, according to the UN (2015) sustainable development goals.

REFERENCES

Aguirre Botello, M. (2017). *Evolución del salario mínimo en México de 1935 a 2017*. Retrieved from http://www.mexicomaxico.org/voto/salmininf.htm

CEPAL. (2015). *Panorama Social de América Latina 2015*. Retrieved from http://www.cepal.org/es/publicaciones/panorama-social-america-latina-2015-documento-informativo

CEPF (Centro de Estudios de las Finanzas Públicas). (2010). *Inversión Extranjera y Empleo*. Retrieved from http://www.cefp.gob.mx/publicaciones/nota/2010/mayo/notacefp0152010.pdf

Cornia, G. A., Gomez-Sabaini, J. C., & Martorano, B. (2011). *A new fiscal pact, tax policy changes and income inequality: Latin America during the last decade*. Working Paper Series UNU-WIDER Research Paper (2011/70).

Cornia, G. A. (2012). *Inequality Trends and their Determinants: Latin America over 1990-2011*. Working Paper Series UNU-WIDER Research Paper (2012/09).

Cornia, G. A. (2014). *Falling Inequality in Latin America: Policy changes and Lessons*. Oxford University Press. doi:10.1093/acprof:oso/9780198701804.001.0001

Cornia, G. A., & Martorano, B. (2011). Democracy, the New Left and Income Distribution: Latin America over the Last Decade. In V. E. Fitzgerald, J. Heyer, & R. Thorpe (Eds.), *Overcoming the Persistence of Inequality and Poverty*. London: Palgrave Macmillan. doi:10.1057/9780230306721_8

Diario Oficial de la Federación, D. O. F. (2015a). Ley Federal del Trabajo. Última reforma publicada el 12 de junio de 2015.

Diario Oficial de la Federación, D. O. F. (2015b). Ley del Seguro Social. Última reforma publicada el 12 de noviembre de 2015.

Diario Oficial de la Federación, D. O. F. (2015c). Reglas de operación para el programa de apoyo al empleo. Novena sección.

ECLAC. (2010). *Economic Survey of Latin America and the Caribbean, 2009–2010*. ECLAC, Santiago de Chile.

ECLAC. (2013). *Fiscal Panorama of Latin America and the Caribbean Tax Reform and Renewal of the Fiscal Covenant*. ECLAC.

Fernández-Arias, E., & Montiel, P. (2010). *The Great Recession, 'Rainy Day' Funds, and Countercyclical Fiscal Policy in Latin America*. Department of Economics Working Papers (2010-17). Williams College.

Financial Times. (2017). *Want cheap labour? Head to Mexico, not China*. Retrieved from https://www.ft.com/content/bddc8121-a7a0-3788-a74c-cd2b49cd3230?mhq5j=e1

Freije, S., López-Acevedo, G., & Rodríguez-Oreggia, E. (2014). Effects of the 2008–09 Economic Crisis on Labor Markets in Mexico. In A. Banerji, D. Newhouse, P. Paci, & D. Robalino (Eds.), *Working through the Crisis: Jobs and Policies in Developing Countries during the Great Recession*. Washington, DC: World Bank.

Gámez, A., Ivanova, A., & Compiranon, K. (2014). Tourism and Economic Crisis Management within APEC. Cases: Phuket (Thailand) and Los Cabos (Mexico). *International Journal of Sustainable Development and Planning*, *9*(2), 143–157. doi:10.2495/SDP-V9-N2-143-157

IDC on line. (2013). *Permiso de paternidad efectos ante el IMSS*. Retrieved from http://www.idconline.com.mx/seguridad/2013/02/06/permiso-de-paternidad-efectos-ante-el-imss

IMF. (2010). *Mexico: Arrangement under the Flexible Credit Line and Cancellation of the Current Arrangement. Country Report 10/81*. Washington, DC: International Monetary Fund.

IMSS. (2017). *Puestos de trabajo afiliados al Instituto Mexicano del Seguro Social (IMSS) al mes de diciembre de 2016 No.011/2017*. Retrieved from http://www.imss.gob.mx/prensa/archivo/201701/011

INEGI. (2008). *Encuesta Nacional de Ocupación y Empleo, segundo trimestre de 2008*. Retrieved from http://www3.inegi.org.mx/sistemas/infoenoe/Default_15mas.aspx?s=est&c=26227&p=

INEGI. (2015a). *Estadísticas a propósito del día del niño (30 de abril)*. Retrieved from http://www.inegi.org.mx/saladeprensa/aproposito/2015/ni%C3%B1o0.pdf

INEGI. (2016). *Encuesta Nacional de Educación y Empleo (ENOE)*. Retrieved from http://www.beta.inegi.org.mx/temas/empleo/

INEGI. (2017). *Población ocupada según sector de actividad económica, nacional trimestral*. Retrieved from http://www.inegi.org.mx/sistemas/BIE/CuadrosEstadisticos/GeneraCuadro.aspx?s=est&nc=597&c=25586

Khanna, G., Newhouse, D., & Paci, P. (2014). Fewer Jobs or Smaller Paychecks? Aggregate Crisis Impacts in Selected Middle-Income Countries. In A. Banerji, D. Newhouse, P. Paci, & D. Robalino (Eds.), *Working through the Crisis: Jobs and Policies in Developing Countries during the Great Recession*. Washington, DC: World Bank.

López-Calva, L. F., & Lustig, N. (2010). *Declining inequality in Latin America: A decade of progress?* Brookings Institution Press.

Lora, E. (2007). *The State of State Reform in Latin America*. Stanford University Press.

Martorano, B. (2014a). *From Volatility to Stabilization: Cyclicality of Fiscal Policy in Latin America over the Last Decades*. Working Papers-Economics (WP07/2014), Universita' degli Studi di Firenze, Dipartimento di Scienze per l'Economia e l'Impresa.

Martorano, B. (2014b). *Pre-crisis Conditions and Government Policy Responses: Chile and Mexico during the Great Recession*. Innocenti Working Paper (2014-15), UNICEF Office of Research, Florence.

Moreno-Brid, J. C., Garry, S., & Krozer, A. (2016). Minimum Wages and Inequality in Mexico: A Latin American Perspective. *Revista de Economía Mundial*. Retrieved from http://www.redalyc.org/articulo.oa?id=86647324006

OCDE. (2015). *Employment Outlook 2015*. Paris: Organización para la Cooperación y el Desarrollo Económicos. Retrieved from http://ifuturo.org/documentacion/Employment%20outlook%202015.pdf

OECD. (2009). *OECD Review of Budgeting in Mexico 2009, Supplement 1*. Paris: OECD.

OECD. (2016). *Making the most of the minimum: statutory minimum wages, employment and poverty, Chapter 2, Employment Outlook 2016*. Retrieved from https://www.oecd.org/employment/emp/2080222.pdf

OIT. (2009). *Trabajo decente un mundo mejor comienza aquí. Notas sobre la crisis*. Retrieved from http://www.ilo.org/wcmsp5/groups/public/---americas/---ro-lima/documents/article/wcms_limd2_9_es.pdf

Powell, A. (2012). *The World of Forking Paths: Latin America and the Caribbean facing global economic risks*. Washington, DC: Inter-American Development Bank.

Rangel Delgado, J. E., & Ivanova Boncheva, A. (2012). *The Crisis in two Pacific Rim Economies: Higher Eduation and Employment in Mexico and Thailand*. Southampton, UK: Witpress.

Robalino, D. A., Newhouse, D., & Rother, F. (2014). Labor and Social Protection Policies during the Crisis and the Recovery. In A. Banerji, D. Newhouse, P. Paci, & D. Robalino (Eds.), *Working through the Crisis: Jobs and Policies in Developing Countries during the Great Recession*. Washington, DC: World Bank.

Ros, J. (2011). The Economic Crisis of 2008–09 and Development Strategy: the Mexican Case. In M. Haddad & B. Shepherd (Eds.), *Managing Openness: Trade and outward-oriented growth after the crisis*. Washington, DC: World Bank. doi:10.1596/9780821386316_CH14

Sandoval Malori, S., & Straulino-Rodríguez, P. (2016). 2017 Increase to Daily Minimum Wage for Mexico. *Ogletree Deakins*. Retrieved from https://ogletree.com/shared-content/content/blog/2016/december/2017-increase-to-daily-minimum-wage-for-mexico?utm_source=Mondaq&utm_medium=syndication&utm_campaign=View-Original

Santiago Reyes, M. (2011). Los salarios en México. *Análisis Político*. Retrieved from http://library.fes.de/pdf-files/bueros/mexiko/08742.pd

SDOIA. (2016). *Investment Climate Statement Mexico-Labor. US Embassies Abroad*. Retrieved from https://www.export.gov/article?id=Mexico-Labor

UN. (2015). *Sustainable Development Goals*. Retrieved from https://sustainabledevelopment.un.org/?menu=1300

UNAM. (2009). *Los Sindicatos en México*. UNAM.

Valencia Lomelí, E., Foust Rodríguez, D., & Tetreault Weber, D. (2013). *Sistemas de protección social en América Latina y el Caribe*. ECLAC, Santiago de Chile.

Villafranco, G. (2014, August). 7 riesgos mortales para la operación de una Pyme. *Forbes*.

KEY TERMS AND DEFINITIONS

Basic Basket of Goods and Services: Basket of goods refers to a relatively fixed set of consumer products and services valued on an anual basis and used to track inflation in Mexico. The basket of goods is used primarily to calculate the consumer price index.

Consumer Price Index (CPI): Is a measure that examines the weighted average of prices of a basket of consumer godos and services and services, such as transportation, food, and medical care. It is calculated by takingprice changes for each item in the predetermined basic basket and averaging them. Changes in the CPI are used to assess price changes associated with the cost of living. The CPI is one of the most frequently used statistics for identifying periods of inflation and deflation.

Flexible Labor Contracts: Labor market flexibility is a firm's ability to make changes to their workforce in terms of the number of employees they hire and the number of hours worked by the employees. Labor market flexibility also includes areas such as wages and unions. A flexible labor market is one where firms are under fewer regulations regarding the labor force and can therefore set wages (i.e., no minimum wage), fire employees at will, and change their work hours. A labor market with low flexibility is bound by rules and regulations such as minimum wage restrictions and requirements from trade unions.

Informal Economy: The informal economy or shadow market is generally defined as economic activities, enterprises, and workers that are not regulated or protected by the state. Illegal activities are typically excluded from the definition of the informal economy, as are goods and services produced within the home.

Labor-Management Relations: Collective bargaining is the process of negotiating the terms of employment between an employer and a group of workers. The terms of employment are likely to include items such as conditions of employment, working conditions and other workplace rules, base pay, overtime pay, work hours, shift length, work holidays, sick leave, vacation time, retirement benefits, and healthcare benefits.

Minimum Wage: A minimum wage is a legally mandated price floor on hourly wages, below which non-exempt workers may not be offered or accept a job.

Small and Medium Enterprises: A microenterprise will usually operate with fewer than 10 people and is started with a small amount of capital. Most microenterprises specialize in providing goods or services for their local areas. Small and midsize enterprises are businesses that maintain revenues, assets, or a number of employees below a certain threshold. Every country has its own definition of what is considered a small and medium-sized enterprise. In Mexico, the definition is the following: (1) Industry: small from 11 to 50, and médium from 51 to 250 persons; (2) Trade: small from 11 to 30, and médium from 31 to 100 persons; and (3) Services: small from 11 to 50, and médium from 51 to 100 persons.

ENDNOTE

1 The full text of the reform law can be found at http://www.stps.gob.mx/bp/micrositios/reforma_laboral/ref_lab.html

Chapter 6
Brazil's Employment Regulation and Outsourcing:
A Precarious Option

Roberta Ferme Sivolella
Universidade do Estado do Rio de Janeiro (UERJ), Brazil

ABSTRACT

This chapter analyzes the evolution of employment regulation in Brazil in order to understand the current moment that it is experiencing. In the current political, economic, and social crisis scenario, the protection system, which is historically valid and justified by the intense social inequalities, is questioned as the country is trying to deal with the urgencies of a big economic downturn without trust of local and international investors in internal market. An intensely advanced legal and judicial system in terms of constitutional principles and guarantees faces a number of structural problems that affect its effectiveness, while at the same time, in the middle of the scenario, the effectiveness and immediacy of the legal and judicial solutions becomes urgent. This chapter finally aims to analyze, in a historical and systematic way, and through statistical data related to employability, GDP and litigation linked to the subject of labor relations, how this Latin "giant" stands and seeks the solution between proposals for legislative reform.

DOI: 10.4018/978-1-5225-4134-9.ch006

INTRODUCTION

Brazil is really "in the spotlight", standing out in national and international headlines, either due to its current troubled political scenario, or because of a false propaganda of being the dreamland for tourists.

Behind the jargon "beach, samba and soccer" (and now, corruption) there are millions of Brazilians eager for what the political and economic future hold. Historically, the dominance of a society based on the market, mixed with a culture of deep application of non-compliance mechanisms, have generated an intense crisis that pushed the political and economic boundaries, and destabilized the already fragile framework of labor guarantees actually observed.

Under the paradox of a comprehensive - and rated as highly protectionist - labor legislation, Brazil has been experiencing the reality of a high rate of failure to comply with laws and of conflicts that achieves the Judiciary, aggravated by the use of precarious forms of work and attempts to "tailor" solutions in jurisprudence to situations outside the law. In this context, an enormous reform in labor laws becomes to increase this discussion.

What are the origins and the limits of casualization of labor law in Brazil? Ultimately, what are the (wrong) choices that led to uncertainty and calamity, which affect not only the labor market, but also the institutions of law in Brazil?

This work does not aim to reach a single answer. However it assuredly encourages the reflection about such an important topic affecting the reality of the current Brazilian labor market.

A CYCLICAL HISTORY OF LOSS OF JOB SECURITY

The State Fragmentation Reaches the Worker's Life

In Brazil, the history of labor law expresses in its evolution the very concept of the relationship it aims to provide. As a result of the large discrepancy between the subjects that make up the working relationship, the economic hierarchy and the social inequality permeating the history of the Brazilian society are also reflected on the way their social and political subjects behave, as well as on their legislation.

There is no doubt there is a reciprocal relationship of "cause and effect" among relationships covered by the branch of law studying the expenditure and the use of the workforce and its nuances, and each historical moment involved. Not accidentally, the regulation of labor relations, in analysis of its higher flexibility or rigidity, shows a pendular and cyclical movement, sometimes tending towards a greater regulation and supervision by the State, sometimes tending towards a greater flexibility and freedom of settling its provisions between the parties to the contract.[1]

In Brazil, this cyclical effect was also present. As a result of a serious social crisis of the early twentieth century, deepened by the economic crisis that followed the First World War, many social movements erupted, reflecting the collective trade union movement that was being formed. These events caught the attention of the public power in the sense that the old liberal model and the individualist policies would not win the approval and the vote of the population, then in a democratic Republican-regime. [2]

Brazil joined thus the so-called interventional phase, in which the state, under the promise of a highly protective system and maintainer of social rights, had the control over any initiative on collective level. The famous "Vargas Age" had its beginning, where strict and dictatorial use of the police power, with the granting of a Constitution based on the fascist Italian system, and the dissolution of the National Congress (1937), happened together with the creation of numerous unprecedented labor guarantees.

The Consolidation of the Labor Law, created in 1943, represented the culmination of such guarantor-interventionist movement, combining chapters aimed at protecting workers subjected to particular conditions of work and at protecting women, with high intervention in the formation of trade unions and even in their decisions. The Consolidation of the Labor Law, known in Brazil as CLT, is a great tool and basis of labor law used to the present day, consecrating the *contract of indefinite duration*[3] and *stability* [4] (now superseded by the FGTS system – the severance pay indemnity fund system) as a rule and regency model for labor relations. It also consecrated important limitation to private will, which cannot override the provisions of the labor protection laws, to collective bargaining, nor to the related court decisions.[5]

The following decades experienced the military dictatorship period (1964-1985), represented by the apex and at the same time, the decline of the interventionist model through its most extreme and armed expression. As expected, within the cyclical and pendulous logic already mentioned, the violence of the system as well as its extreme character led to the urgency of a democratic autonomy, as an exponent of political freedom. In the 70s, the keynote of the neoliberal society that preached the self-determination of the economic market already dominated the world, being felt in labor relations, including Brazil.

The 1988 Constitution, principled and detailed to the extreme, reflected the aspirations of a society that rewarded by an ideological support, and at the same time, by the freedom of choice. From Oct/05/1988, protection against arbitrary dismissal was included in the list of classically respected social rights in Article 7 of the Brazilian Greater Charter of 1988 in its item I. The workers' rights as a whole, in turn, were classified as social rights explicitly in art. 6 of the same title, and therefore immutable clauses that cannot be changed by constitutional amendments to the detriment of workers (art. 60, § 4, n. IV CRFB / 88).The social value of work and the dignity of the human person, in turn, were listed in Article 1 as principles inherent to the Democratic State of Law.

However, the high load of values and of principles given to the promulgated constitution (reflection of the fear of a new camouflaged state intervention), led to gaps in relation to recurrent social situations, so that, although large in their devices (one of the most extensive in the world- started with 245 articles and 1627 devices), the Brazilian Constitution already has almost 100 Constitutional Amendments. The logic of the need for legislation to regulate infra factual situations of the labor market, therefore, remained, not always attentive to the dictates of the Greater Charter or even to the outdated Consolidation of the Labor Law (CLT).

Since the 70's, by the way, the neoliberal society have dictated global reality, preaching the self-determination of the economic market, from the perspective in which the State control over the economy generates obstacle and inefficiency to the development of capital.6 In Brazil, new ways of working more flexibly arose in response to such market economy, out of the ordinary working relationship protected by law. Still in the late 60's, the Decree-Law 200/67 allowed the intermediation contract of manpower in Public Administration, subsequently leaving the Law 5645/70 specify which public services could be outsourced, namely: "the activities related to transport, conservation, custody, lifts operation, cleaning and other similar". The Federal Law 6.019/1974 legalized temporary work, legitimizing the temporary employment agency to "make available to other companies, temporary workers, qualified, paid and assisted by them" to "meet the temporary need for replacement of its regular personnel and permanent or extraordinary extra services."

In practice, however, a number of "extralegal" situations continued to occur. Roberto Fragale Filho, Labor Judge of the Regional Labor Court of the 1st Region, tells in his article entitled "Brazilian's Fissured Workplace- David Weil's Vignettes in the New World"[7] the situation that occurred in 1978 in Tatuí, São Paulo, where workers without any kind of disability were hired fraudulently to work at Ford of Brazil, a subsidiary of the Ford Motor Company, through the philanthropic association AVAPE (alleged entity intended for people with physical disabilities). Upon performance of the Labor Prosecution Office (hereinafter MPT), Ford was required to hire all 280 workers as employees and ordered both Ford and AVAPE to pay R$ 400.000.000,00 (= US$ 126,855,240.00) to be applied on public policy for disabled people in the city of Tatuí.[8]

The context of the economic crisis of the 80s, caused by the oil crisis of 1973 and 1979 and by the abundant supply of foreign credit, created an external debt and an unprecedented recession, causing low growth of the Gross Domestic Product (hereinafter GDP in the medium insignificant level of 1.7% per year), abrupt currency devaluation to 30% in 1979 and inflation reaching the 100% mark in 1980.[9] The intense unemployment generated increased even more forms of contracting with displacement of responsibility for labor charges, generating demand for the Judiciary and the Legislature.

In 1983, in turn, Federal Law 7.102/1983 legalized the work intermediated by surveillance companies, signaling the tendency to allow subcontracting in peripheral activities. Such tendency was mirrored by the case through the issue of Precedent 256 of the Higher Labor Court of Appeals – TST, which provided that "except in cases of temporary work and surveillance service, provided for in Laws No. 6,019, of 01/03/1974, and 7,102 of 20/06/1983, it is illegal hiring workers through a third company, forming the employment directly with the borrower services." Thus, consolidating the understanding of the possibilities of labor intermediation restricted to those situations provided by law. Still, the understanding was in contrast and exceptional to the general rule of the Labor Code in Article 2, which provides that the employer is "the company, individual or collective, which, assuming the risks of economic activity, hires, pays salaries and directs personal service provision."

A number of situations inconsistent with the legal dictates, however, began to be brought to the yoke of the Judiciary, signaling a strong trend of a "flexibility" of the market practice, although in inofficious model and not embraced by the legal dictates[10]. Many of them even came from irregular contracting relationships with public entities.

Some sparse laws were used to unsuccessfully try to meet the legislative lack as the means of labor intermediation that was consolidated to be called "outsourcing".

Law 8,863/94 extended the outsourcing hypothesis for the entire area of property security, public or private, including for individuals. Law 8,949/94, in turn, introduced the sole paragraph of art. 442 of the Labor Code encouraging outsourcing through cooperatives, stating that "whatever the field of activity of the cooperative society, there is no employment relationship between it and its members, or between them and the services that makers." Such an overly broad concept, of course, stimulated the simulated signings.

Telephony services and utility companies, in turn, had outsourcing allowed as defined in the Law 9,472 97 and 8,987/95, respectively.

In 1994, the Superior Labor Court issued the Precedent 331, to consolidate jurisprudential guidelines on outsourcing, reaffirming its possibilities related to temporary work and surveillance services and expanded it to maintenance and cleaning services, establishing also the concept of intermediate and final activities. Despite being literal expressions, it is concluded that, respectively, of activities embedded in the core of the company and those ancillary activities, there is to date no legal definition to the concepts.

The first draft of Precedent 331 of the Higher Labor Court of Appeals - TST[11] also established that the "third party" worker does not have any link with the Public Administration direct, indirect or through foundation (behold, conducting public tender is required - Article 37, II, Federal Constitution of 1988). Finally, it is considered as a liability unfulfilled obligations by the employer, that is, if the principal debtor is overdue, it would be possible to run the secondary responsible in the outsourcing.

In September 2000, the wording of the Precedent under discussion was amended to include the possibility of subsidiary accountability of the Public Administration, restricted to cases in which it had participated in the court proceedings and it was stated in the order. The actual wording, however, apparently was opposed to paragraph 1 of article. 71 of Law 8666 of 1993, the "law of bidding" ("Default of the contractor, with reference to labor, tax and commercial charges does not transfer to the Public Administration responsibility for payment ..."), which led a deadlock to be decided by the Supreme Court on 24/11/2010. At that time, it was declared the constitutionality of art. 71, § 1 of the Law of bidding, which led to the TST, once again, to change the wording of Precedent 331, indicating that the responsibility of the Public Administration due to outsourcing is not objective, but depends on the proof of guilt, and including the item that extends the application of the said joint liability to all condemnation object titles, without exception.

Nonetheless, in the expansion of the wording of the latest version of Precedent 331 - still maintained - quite a stir is still ongoing. Either due to the lack of determination of the concepts "intermediate" and "final" activities, which generate endless possibilities of labor intermediation, or by choice of law, which elected a subsidiarity criterion, rather than solidarity, to blame the intermediary. Indeed, the second option would inhibit outsourcing, or at least take the borrowing firm to choose the supplier with more zeal, simplifying and speeding up executions, and therefore the satisfaction of labor credit[12].

The Brazilian labor planning keeps, however, waiting for legal rules from the institute, for which is being processed currently, by Bill 4.302/98 and Bill 4334/04.

The intense and constant influence of the economy in labor relations is indubitable, integrated into its core by the eternal dichotomy between capital and labor. The development of the society and the human being - before isolated in scattered groups in a subsistence economy - is intertwined with the development of the economic science itself, through relations of exchange between larger groups that needed, for their own development, to carry out exchange of goods and knowledge. The notion of trade and the "market" as a form of capital expression and relationships involving that ultimately arise with the notion of work as an activity that, compared to its historical treatment, supports the idea of the product of human labor as value.

There is a growing tendency today to focus on the economic aspect of the issues, considered more urgent by the established political order. According to Lukacs, the most relevant effects of the application of capitalist principles are the fragmentation and "commodification" of social relations, understood in a separate and isolated way from the context, as a form of hegemony; and the postmodern position is the same.[13] The defense of the man himself, character and subject of guaranteed primordial rights, emerges as a challenge against the ideological avalanche caused by a neoliberalism that has not recognized or managed to keep much of the social achievements arduously achieved by the struggles of social movements.

In today's society called "market society", labor cost reduction mechanisms are presented as instruments/main strategies in a context of crisis. Inevitable is to conclude, therefore, that the quantitative and the dispensing procedure, e.g., or the "ease" of terminating the employment contract, in each system, ultimately functions as a way of measuring the contrast between the progressive value of labor law and the State of the free market economy.[14] By one side, the need of giving priority to guarantees and continuity of employment, as a way to stabilize and to mitigate the effects of the financial interest on the dignity of the worker. On the other hand, the tendency towards more flexible labor relations as a way to keep your source embodied in the offer of employment maintained by the so-called "health of the company."

The construction of a volatile contract model with the responsibility transferred to third parties, with less charges, certainly came to conform to such reasoning, fitting perfectly in a country of recent democracy, full of social inequality and eager for any form of employment (or underemployment) offered. The fear of social misery in a society where the vital needs of citizens are not accessible to everyone on an equal basis, combined with a culture of noncompliance, where people are confident in the slowness and inefficiency of Justice, certainly aggravates this situation.

The relaxation of labor laws, with the uncertainty created by the absence of clear regulations about the chances of exception to the traditional employment contract, becomes the means by which the highest rank taken by the capital strength departs more and more its social positioning sub-levels, in a big wheel driven by the increased dependence in a vicious cycle of submission and acceptance, by the class that holds the workforce and their own condition of dignified existence subjected the sole discretion of an entity embodied by financial interest. The so-called "subjective hope" is generated, which fits to the "subjective probabilities".[15] It is the "awareness of a social insignificance",[16] which leads to social passivity and resignation as the key that opens the gates of the control room of economic strength, which guides at its own pleasure the social relations contrary to the fundamental guarantees.

By recognizing the "worthlessness" of their work, the worker loses the moral link that stimulates them to produce and to claim their production. The dignity that comes from work and their indispensability give way to "product" of short duration and the worker must also "thank" and submit to the scanty opportunity that was offered to use their workforce to an undervalued price.

The "inferiorization" of the labor force value and the loss of consciousness that this is *essential* to the maintenance of the means of production, and not only dependent on this, generates an intense shock in the social balance, and disproportionately increases the already pre-existing discrepancy between hypo-sufficiency of whom undertakes its workforce and hyper-sufficiency of whom - only with the supply of the first - can keep increasing the power of wealth creation and the structuring of social mobility.

Certainly, the need to preserve the health of the company is vital to ensure, on the other hand, the maintenance of jobs and to provide the continuity of benefits to the employee. The interdependent relationship is irremovable and certainly leads to the adoption of certain more flexible forms of employment. In many developed countries, by the way, this flexible model is the rule, without having to pay attention to the balance of the system or to a successful State model. The apparent balance, however, falls to the ground when the disadvantaged sections of society are examined, subjected to conditions that violate the dignity and the social value of the work at the expense of maintaining a stable economy.

The judiciary's role also ends up being part of this "economic" model of Labor Law. A clear example is the recent research carried out based on accounting expert reports in labor claims related to Banks. It was concluded that, considering the likely cost of the overtime pay, the average duration of the process, the interest rates and the inflation adjustment applicable to Brazilian labor claims in contracts for labor relations in period of more than five (5) years, it is more economical for banks to wait for the judicial decisions, especially with regard to funding for overtime, because the cost is lower in court than during the contract period[17].

Banking institutions even appear as one of the most frequent litigants in terms of labor outsourcing. So much so that there are a number of understandings resulted from the case law concerning the matter [18] in an attempt to halt the easing of labor rights through economic practices that take advantage of the legal vacuum, and the volatility of the jurisprudential understandings.

The above picture is further aggravated when considering the State fragmentation and the intense political crisis in Brazil today. If the cyclical movement, as showed, affects labor law and the guarantee of social rights, its violation is constantly sought through the state and its intervention. So, to whom we turn when the State structure itself is collapsing?

More precisely in the current year of 2016, the Brazilian government has been going through an intense crisis of governability, aggravated with the course of the investigation carried out by federal prosecutors, the "Lava Jato Operation." The investigation, started with a network of "money changers" who worked in several Brazilian states, has found the existence of a vast corruption scheme at Petrobras, a famous Brazilian state oil company, involving politicians from various parties and the largest contractors in the country. The Federal Public Ministry estimated a deviation of R $ 2.1 billion of Petrobras safes, having been found to assemble R$ 6.1 billion for losses caused by corruption in the balance sheet of the company in 2014[19].

The considerable impacts have not been restricted to the government limits and to the conduct of an impeachment process, still ongoing.[20] The first result found was the bankruptcy of several companies of manpower intermediation hired by Petrobras, living of their contracts with the State, many suspended due to budget cuts and the start of the investigation. The result was disastrous: thousands of workers laid off without any warranty or labor installment paid. Petrobras – the subsidiary responsible - follows the rules of Indirect Public Administration, given that its conviction has no understanding based on the Court, behold, according to the current wording of Precedent 331 of the C. TST, such condemnation depends on proof of guilt.[21]

In Macaé, in the state of Rio de Janeiro, a city that had its economy sustained by the oil industry and was home to thousands of employment contracts in outsourced companies hired by Petrobras, the consequences were devastating. The annual distribution of processes by Labor Court came to exceed the number of 7,000 per year and per "Vara"[22], mostly due to unjustified dismissal without any payment, delay of wages and prospect of satisfaction for uncontroversial values near zero.

Moreover, precisely at a time when the great increase in litigation rate due to the growth in unemployment (1.2 million workers were withdrawn from the formal market in 2015 because of the crisis), a large and efficient performance of the Judiciary is requires (in 2015, the Labor Court received nearly two million new cases in first instance, which exceeded the previous year by 7%), the government decided to hold a budget cut of 90% in investment expenditure and 29.4% in the cost of labor courts (Law 13,255 / 2016).[23] The most curious thing is that - the justification for such constant cut of the law - it was pointed out that the Labor Court generated many costs by virtue of being "protective" in relation to the employee. [24]

Meanwhile, Bill 4330/04 and Bill 4302/98 are underway which, in an attempt to end the legal uproar involving the limits and the concept of outsourcing, ended up by greatly expanding the hypotheses of the institute's application. From the start, it ends with the limitation of outsourcing of the main activity, legitimating in various devices situations that previously were already rejected by the judiciary, for reputable violation of labor rights. The last one was passed in the Chamber of Deputies, and now awaits final approval from the Senate in order to be submitted for presidential sanction and, thus, become effective.

Under Bill 4330/04, "The contract for the provision of services may relate to the development of inherent activities, accessory or complementary to the economic activity of the contractor." (Article 4, paragraph 2) and "contracts for the provision of services to third parties where the contractor is public administration, responsibility for labor charges is regulated by art. 71 of Law No. 8666 of June 21, 1993 " (Article 12). The one that was approval in the early stages of the legislative procedure (Bill 4.302/98) has also many dispositions that reduce worker's rights, by permitting a larger period for the temporary contractions, including the possibility to enlarger it by collective negotiation (Article 10). It also has an imprecise wording that can give ground to a terrible interpretation, by permitting the outsourcing of company´s core activity, increasing the risk of fraud (Article 4o-A).

When everything seemed to be the worst possible scenario, a new Bill called "Labor Reform" took shape in an incredible velocity. In less than six months, a minute with six pages (at that time called "Mini Reform") turned into a 55 pages Bill (number 6786/2016), changing and reducing many workers guarantees, including that considered Constitutional values. The total reduces of Unions' assistance in dismissal (including unrestricted collective dismissals), an almost unrestricted possibility to negotiate Constitutional rights without judge's intervention, and even the possibility to substitute salaries by utilities (as slavery used to happen in rural world) are just some of the scaring examples of this alarming Bill, reflecting an enormous step backward from guarantees arduously achieved throughout decades.

Undoubtedly, it represents a poor political choice generating a precarious labor law, and deprived of its fundamental guarantees.

CONCLUSION

Law should reflect the social reality of its time. On the other hand, one of the greatest means of measuring the effectiveness of the legal system of a society, as well as its control, originates from the social acceptance of its values. According to Konrad Hesse, the Constitution depends on the historical reality of its time, and the constitutional science must be aware of the forces that determine the State action. It should be observed that the Constitution, for numerous reasons, cannot be opposed to the cultural, economic and political reality. There is no denying, however, of the possibility that the legislative plan has in the conformation of the same reality.

The Constitution becomes an active force in carrying out the State tasks. To occur achievement and constitutional realization it is necessary to germinate and to flourish a *constitutional will (wille zur verfassung),* which depart from the general awareness and from those responsible for the constitutional order: the judges, the hermeneutics, and the scholars.[25]

Thus, it is understood as the effectiveness of a rule as one that generates a generic act of social acceptance, that is, citizens not endowed with powers delegated by the State to act in activities of public scope - the "ordinary" citizens – who must demonstrate, through their daily acts and customary practices, that there is practice of observance and obedience in the legal relations involving the values provided for constitutionally.

There is no doubt that the law cannot provide all concrete situations. There is no doubt, either, that for the maintenance of jobs in the face of economic collapse contexts, sometimes it is necessary to take some measures to protect the health of a company. Along with such certainty, however, it is the fact that the working conditions of contract workers have much higher precariousness rates than those of formal jobs, either with respect to lower wages or with respect to greater insecurity in the working environment.[26]

That said, what we cannot allow is that - under the supposed justification of the need to regulate factual situation - situations that have materialized fraud or "noncompliance" become legalized. When a legal rule does not reflect the social fact and the aspirations of the society for which it is,[27] the moment is to use the frameworks of the labor law and the principles that it aims to garnish. Or, indeed, a truly "precarious" option will occur, which neither the famous "Brazilian way" will be able to solve.

REFERENCES

Autran, A. (n.d.). *Folha Explica.* Retrieved March 06, 2016 from http://arte.folha.uol.com.br/poder/operacao-lava-jato/

Bordieu, P., & Passeron, J. C. (1992). *A reprodução: elementos para uma teoria do sistema de ensino.* Rio de Janeiro, RJ: Francisco Alves.

Dostoievski, F. (2011). *Gente Pobre.* São Paulo, SP: Associação Cultural Letra Selvagem.

Fragale Filho, R. (2015). Brazilian's fissured workplace: David Weil's vignettes in the new world. *Comparative Labor Law & Policy Journal*, *37*(1), 37–53.

Hesse, K. (1991). *A força normativa da Constituição*. Porto Alegre, RS: Sergio Antonio Fabris.

Hobsbawn, E. J. (2008). *A Era das Revoluções*: *A Revolução Francesa*. São Paulo, SP: Paz e Terra. Jurídico, C. *Cortes na Justiça do Trabalho preocupam TST e advogados*. Retrieved April 20, 2016. From http://www.conjur.com.br/2016-fev-28/cortes-orcamento-justica-trabalho-preocupam-tst-advogados

Lukács, G. (1982). *Estética 1. La peculiaridad de lo estético*. Barcelona: Grijalbo.

Marangoni, G. (2012). *Anos 1980, década perdida ou ganha?* Retrieved March 12, 2016 from http://www.ipea.gov.br/desafios/index.php?option=com_content&id=2759:catid=28&Itemid=23

Marcolino, A., Horie, L., Serrao, R. S., Peres, C. L., Roberto, D. O., & Oliveira, S. (n.d.). *Terceirização e Desenvolvimento- uma conta que não fecha*. Retrieved June 2, 2016 from http://www.cut.org.br/system/uploads/ck/files/Dossie-Terceirizacao-e-Desenvolvimento.pdf

Pinheiro, P. S. (1991). *Estratégias da Ilusão: A revolução mundial e o Brasil (1922-1935)*. São Paulo, SP: Companhia das Letras.

Romagnoli, U. (2008). Sobre el despido o la violencia del poder privado. In *Revista de Derecho Social Latino América* (Vol. 4-5, p. 9). Buenos Aires: Editorial Bomarzo.

Rousseau, J. J. (1998). *Julie ou La Nouvelle Heloise*. Paris: Preface Dialoguée.

Siqueira, G. S. (n.d.). *Anamatra ingress no STF contra cortes no orçamento da Justiça do Trabalho*. Retrieved April 1, 2016 from http://www.trt7.jus.br/index.php?option=com_content&view=article&id=2805:anamatra-ingressa-no-stf-contra-cortes-no-orcamento-da-justica-do-trabalho&catid=152&Itemid=302

Viana, M. T., Delgado, G. N., & Amorim, H. S. (2011). Terceirização- aspectos gerais. A última decisão do STF e a Súmula 331 do TST. Novos enfoques. Revista TST, 77(1), 54-84.

KEY TERMS AND DEFINITIONS

Anamatra: National association of labor magistrates.
CLT: Labor code.
IPEA: Institute of applied economic research.
TST: Higher labor court of appeals.
Vara do Trabalho: Is the name of each unity or trial court that any local labor court is divided.

ENDNOTES

1 It can be considered that, to achieve the "peak" of the flexibilization-intervention of the State, inevitably there are intense repercussions in other social niches (politics and economy in particular), which ultimately boost the cycle to its beginning in diametrically opposite direction. The Industrial Revolution is an example of such a premise, for which the low cost of labor and its maximum exploitation came to fit in with the need for financial investment focused on technological development. This operation, however, was so exacerbated it culminated in intense social crisis, injecting stimulus to the rise of revolutionary movements and creating a prominent focus system to the regulation of workers' rights. (Hobsbawn, E. J.- *A Era das Revoluções*: A Revolução Francesa").

2 A clear example of the influence of social actors and a quick response from the State within the "cycle" cited was the Law 1641 of 26 May 1907, that allowed the expulsion of foreigners who, for whatever reason, would compromise the national security or the public order. This law represented the concerns of the owners of means of production with the influence foreigners have in relation to national workers, bringing the resulting ideas of the Marxists and the international proletarian movement.(Pinheiro, P. S., *Estratégias da Ilusão.*: A revolução mundial e o Brasil (1922-1935).

3 Cf. Article 443 of the Labor Code - CLT:
"Art. 443 - The contract of employment may be agreed tacitly or explicitly, verbally or in writing and for a fixed or indefinite period.
Paragraph 1° - It is considered as a certain timeframe the employment contract whose duration depends on prefixed term or the execution of specified services or or performing certain event likely to approximate forecast. (Sole paragraph of Decree-Law No. 229 of 02.28.1967)

Paragraph 2º - The contract for a specified period will only be valid in the case of: (Included by Decree-Law No. 229 of 02.28.1967)
a) service whose nature or transience justify the predetermination of term; (Included by Decree-Law No. 229 of 02.28.1967)
b) business activities of a temporary nature; (Included by Decree-Law No. 229 of 02.28.1967)
c) experience contract. (Included by Decree-Law No. 229 of 02.28.1967) "

4 As article 492 of the Labor Code - CLT: "Art. 492 - Employee counting more than ten (10) years of service in the same company cannot be fired except for serious reason or circumstances of force majeure, duly proved."

5 As article 444 of CLT – The working contractual relations may be subject to free stipulation from the stakeholders in all that does not contravenes the protection provisions to work, the collective agreements applicable to them and the decisions of the competent authorities.

6 Invoking Rousseau's idea: "Man is too noble a being to serve simply as the instrument for others (...), men were not made for places, but places for men;" (Rousseau, J. J. *Rousseau- Julie ou La Nouvelle Heloise, . La première partie*).

7 As Roberto Fragale Filho exposed in "Brazilian's fissured workplace: David Weil's vignettes in the new world".

8 As quoted by FRAGALE FILHO, Roberto. Op. cit.

9 As data provided by IPEA- Institute of Applied Economic Research.

10 ROBERTO FRAGALE mentions that between 1988 and 1994, the annual amount of new cases doubled going from 1,044,469 to 2,048,944. Fragale Filho, R. Op. Cit.

11 As *Precedent 331 of the Higher Labor Court of Appeals – TST:*
"CONTRACT FOR SERVICES. LEGALITY (New wording of item IV and inserted items V and VI to the editor) - Resolution 174/2011, DEJT published on 27, 30 and 31.05.2011
I - The hiring of workers through a third company is illegal, forming the link directly with the borrower services, except in the case of temporary employment (Law No.6,019, of 01/03/1974).
II - Irregular hiring of workers by intermediary company does not generate employment relationship with the public authorities directly, indirectly or through foundation (article 37, II of the Constitution / 1988.).
III – There is no employment relationship with the borrower contracting security services (Law No. 7,102, of 20/06/1983) and cleaning and conservation services, as well as specialized services related to intermediate activities of the borrower, provided that personhood and direct subordination is absent.

IV - The breach of labor obligations by the employer implies the joint liability of the borrower of services as those obligations, provided that it has participated in the procedural relationship and also listed in the judicial enforcement.
V - The members of the Public Administration respond directly and indirectly in the alternative, on the same terms of item IV, if it is shown to culpable conduct in compliance with the obligations of Law No. 8666 of 21.06.1993, especially in the enforcement of contractual and legal obligations of the service provider as an employer. The aforesaid liability does not arise from mere breach of labor obligations by the company regularly contracted.
VI - The subsidiary liability of the borrower services covers all monies arising from the conviction for the period of employment provision.
Historic:
Precedent maintained - Res 121/2003, DJ 19, 20 and 21.11.2003.
Precedent amended (Item IV) - Res 96/2000, DJ 18, 19 and 20.09.2000.

331 (…)
IV - The breach of labor obligations by the employer implies the joint liability of the borrower services, as those obligations, including as the direct administration bodies, local authorities, public foundations, public enterprises and joint stock companies, since they have participated in the procedural relationship and have also been included in the judicial enforcement (art. 71 of Law No. 8666 of 21.06.1993).
The original version (revision of Precedent No. 256 - Res 23/1993, DJ 21, 28/12/1993 and 04/01/1994), was:

331 (...)
II - irregular hiring through intermediary company does not generate employment relationship with the public authorities Direct, Indirect or through Foundation (article 37, II, of the Constitution.).
(...)
IV - The breach of labor obligations by the employer, involves the joint liability of the borrower services, as those obligations, provided that they have participated in the procedural relationship and have also been included in the judicial enforcement.

12 In this way, Marco Túlio Viana, Gabriela Neves Delgado e Helder Santos Amorim. (TERCEIRIZAÇÃO – ASPECTOS GERAIS. A ÚLTIMA DECISÃO DO STF E A SÚMULA 331 DO TST. NOVOS ENFOQUES).

13 As indicated in LUKÁCS' artice, "*Estética 1.* La peculiaridad de lo estético".

14 Extracted from the article "Sobre el despido o la violencia del poder privado", Umberto Romagnoli.

15 This expression was used by Pierre Bordieu and Jean Claude Passeron in "A *reprodução*: elementos para uma teoria do sistema de ensino".

16 Valuing the only thing left – the possibility to do their work within the limits of legality and honesty – is a matter of mental stability. (DOSTOIEVSKI, Fiódor. "*Gente Pobre*. São Paulo: Associação Cultural Letra Selvagem, 2011, p. 205-206).

17 This very interesting study was scrutinized by TAMYRIS SCHNEIDER RIBEIRO and MARLOS AUGUSTO MELEK, judicial expert and Labor Judge, respectively, in Article "A DESMISTIFICAÇÃO DA SUPRESSÃO DAS HORAS EXTRAS E SEU IMPACTO NA FOLHA DE PAGAMENTO NO SETOR BANCÁRIO".

18 For example, the Precedent No. 239 TST: *"BANKING. EMPLOYEE FROM DATA PROCESSING COMPANY (incorporated the Case Law paragraphs 64 and 126 of SBDI-1) - Res 129/2005, DJ 20, 22 and 25.04.2005 It is a bank employee the worker from the data processing company who provides the service to a bank member of the same group, except when the data processing company provides services to bank and non-bank companies of the same group or to third parties," and the* Precedent No. 93 TST: "BANKING (maintained) Res. 121/2003, DJ 19, 20 and 21.11.2003 *It is part of the remuneration of the bank worker the financial advantage that he earned in the placement or sale of papers or securities of companies belonging to the same economic group, if this activity is carried out on time and in the workplace and with the consent, tacit or express, from the employer's bank."*

19 Data from the newspaper Folha de São Paulo's website.

20 On 05/11/16, the National Congress decided to conduct the impeachment proceedings, resulting in the removal of the elected President Dilma Roussef, and now, her substitute, President Michel Temer is still under trial, because of irregularities found during the last Presidential elections.

21 Examples of various judgments of the court where the subsidiary responsibility of Petrobras was cleared: TST - RR: 2334-60.2010.5.02.0362, ST - ARR: 863-48.2010.5.03.0049; RR 863-48.2010.5.03.0049, RR 871-34.2011.5.02.0011, RR 335-26.2014.5.11.0251,

22 "Vara do Trabalho" is the name of each unity or trial court that any local Labor Court is divided. For example: Labor Court in Macaé has 3 "varas do trabalho", each one responsible for the judgement of a group of claims.

23 As data showed in Conjur site.

24 The bizarre justification given in the Budget Law Project was seen as institutional retaliation, and rejected by public notice issued by the National Association of Labor Magistrates - ANAMATRA.

25 The concept was extracted from Konrad Heesse, in "A força normativa da Constituição".

26 For example, the study conducted by CUT (United Workers' Central) and DIEESE (the Inter-Union Department of Statistics and Socio-economic Studies) conducted in 2014, found that, in 2011, of the 79 deaths in the Brazilian electricity sector, 61 were employees of outsourced companies and between 2005 and 2012, 14 employees of Petrobras workers died in accidents in the exercise of their professions, while in the same period, 85 died outsourced. Extractec by "Terceirização e Desenvolvimento - Uma conta que não fecha".

27 So have said Émile Durkheim, in *As regras do método sociológico.*

Chapter 7
Employment Protection in South Africa:
An Analysis of Recent Labour and Social Security Legislative and Policy Developments

Avinash Govindjee
Nelson Mandela University, South Africa

ABSTRACT

This chapter tests the existing (labour and social security-related) legislation against the South African constitutional framework, as well as international and regional standards. The issues to be addressed specifically include the following: 1) Is the existing legislation pertaining to employment protection, unemployment, and work constitutionally compliant? 2) Is it correct to expect legislation (and state policy) to regulate matters such as job-retention and work creation (for example, by activating the workforce and through the creation of public works programmes), and if so, does the present statutory and policy framework address this expectation adequately? 3) To what extent is the legislation compliant with international standards and best practices, and are there fresh approaches to address the present malaise, perhaps emanating from regional standards and experiences? 4) Finally, are there any best practices or lessons learned through the South African experience that should influence developments in other emerging economies?

DOI: 10.4018/978-1-5225-4134-9.ch007

INTRODUCTION

South Africa's unemployment rate is presently 27,7%, with over 6,2 million persons classified as unemployed.[1] More than 2,2 million persons are "discouraged work-seekers", being available to work or start a business but unable to take active steps to find work as a result of unavailability of jobs, lack of skill or loss of hope of finding any kind of work.[2] In 2013, of the 1,5 million persons running non-VAT (value-added taxation) registered businesses, as many as 1,4 million were in the informal sector. Predominantly run by black Africans, persons aged 35-44 years and those with the lowest levels of education, the businesses are survivalist in nature and most often are formed as a result of unemployment and the inability of the individual to obtain an alternative source of income.[3]

Almost nine million people in South Africa are presently without work, despite being willing and able to work. The youth (aged 15-34) are particularly vulnerable in the labour market, with over 37% presently being classified as "unemployed". This is despite the Constitution of the Republic of South Africa, 1996, (the Constitution) promising the rights to human dignity and equality, to fair labour practices, to freedom of trade, occupation and profession and the right to social security including, for everyone unable to support themselves or their dependants, appropriate social assistance.

It is more than twenty years since this celebrated constitutional text came into operation. During that time, various pieces of legislation have been specifically enacted and / or amended for the purpose of regulating work, protecting those in employment and contributing to the alleviation of the harmful effects of unemployment. Legislation such as the Labour Relations Act, 1995, the Social Assistance Act, 2004, the Unemployment Insurance Fund Act, 2001, the Compensation for Occupational Injuries and Diseases Act, 1993 and the Employment Services Act, 2014 have all been designed, at least in part, with this in mind. Nevertheless, it is clear that South Africa continues to battle structural inequality, unemployment and persistent poverty.

This contribution interrogates this situation by providing a detailed critique of the applicable legislative and policy framework, including the most recent labour and social security statutory developments (such as the regulation of fixed-term employment contracts and the proposed introduction of return-to-work arrangements). The purpose of the analysis is to juxtapose the South African legislative approach with the existing realities of poverty, inequality and unemployment. The (labour and social security-related) legislation is tested against the constitutional framework, as well as international and regional standards.

The issues to be addressed specifically include the following:

1. Is the existing legislation pertaining to employment protection, unemployment and work constitutionally compliant?
2. Is it correct to expect legislation (and state policy) to regulate matters such as job-retention and work creation (for example, by activating the work force and through the creation of public works programmes) and, if so, does the present statutory and policy framework address this expectation adequately?
3. To what extent is the legislation compliant with international standards and best practices, and are there fresh approaches to address the present malaise, perhaps emanating from regional standards and experiences?
4. Finally, are there any best practices or lessons learned through the South African experience that should influence developments in other emerging economies?

THE CONSTITUTIONAL FRAMEWORK

The Constitution promises in its preamble the "improvement of the quality of life of all citizens" and aims, *inter alia*, to "free the potential of each person". Founded on the constitutional values of human dignity, the achievement of equality and the advancement of human rights and achievements,[4] the Constitution suggests that everyone has the right to have their dignity respected and protected[5] and the right to equal protection and benefit of the law.[6] Although the "right to work" is conspicuous by its absence, the Constitution provides that every citizen has the right to choose their trade, occupation and profession freely[7] and that everyone has the right to fair labour practices[8] and to have access to social security including, for persons unable to support themselves and their dependants, appropriate social assistance.[9]

In respect of socio-economic rights, the state is required to take "reasonable legislative and other measures, within its available resources, to achieve the progressive realisation of each of these rights",[10] a provision which has been interpreted on occasion by the Constitutional Court of South Africa. Various pieces of legislation have traditionally been associated with giving effect to the constitutional rights to fair labour practices and to have access to social security. For example, the Labour Relations Act, 1995, the Basic Conditions of Employment Act, 1997, and the Employment Equity Act, 1998 have typically been used to regulate employment relationships. The Social Assistance Act, 2004, the Unemployment Insurance Act, 2001, the Compensation for Occupational Injuries and Diseases Act, 1993 and the Occupational Health and Safety Act, 1993 are some of the core social security-based statutes that have applied in South Africa during the past two decades.

THE IMPACT OF SOUTH AFRICAN LABOUR AND SOCIAL SECURITY LEGISLATION ON EMPLOYMENT PROTECTION

The Labour Relations Act, 1995 (LRA)[11] gives effect to the constitutional right to fair labour practices by promoting and facilitating collective bargaining at the workplace and at sectoral level, by regulating the right to strike and the recourse to lock-out and by establishing a coherent dispute resolution framework to attend to labour disputes, including unfair dismissals and unfair labour practices. The stated purpose of the LRA is to "advance economic development, social justice, labour peace and the democratisation of the workplace by fulfilling the primary objects of this Act."[12] Importantly, the LRA promises every employee the right not to be unfairly dismissed and the right not to be subjected to unfair labour practices. Both the notion of "dismissal" and "unfair labour practice" are defined.[13] Importantly, reinstatement is considered to be the primary remedy for an unfair dismissal. In terms of section 193(2), the Labour Court or arbitrator *must* require the employer to re-instate or re-employ an employee following an unfair dismissal unless:

1. The employee does not wish to be re-instated or re-employed;
2. The circumstances surrounding the dismissal are such that a continued employment relationship would be intolerable;
3. It is not reasonably practicable for the employer to re-instate or re-employ the employee; or
4. The dismissal is unfair only because the employer did not follow a fair procedure.

In terms of recent amendments to the LRA, low-earning employees employed via triangular employment relationships or on fixed-term contracts of in excess of three months are considered to be permanent employees unless certain exceptions are applicable, providing a further form of employment protection through domestic legislation. In essence, these amendments have the consequence of elevating a limited duration (fixed-term) employment contract to the creation of a permanent employment relationship on terms and conditions of employment that are not inferior to other workers performing the same or similar work (again, unless specific exceptions are applicable).[14]

The Employment Equity Act, 1998, (the EEA)[15] focuses on achieving equity in the workplace by:[16]

1. "Promoting equal opportunity and fair treatment in employment through the elimination of unfair discrimination; and

2. Implementing affirmative action measures to redress the disadvantages in employment experienced by designated groups, in order to ensure their equitable representation in all occupational levels in the workforce".

Significantly, while affirmative action measures[17] implemented by an employer must include measures to identify and eliminate employment barriers, measures to further diversity in the workplace, reasonable accommodation for people from designated groups, including preferential treatment and numerical goals, the EEA stops short of implementing quotas or creating absolute barriers for people who are not from designated groups, and dismissals based purely on race, gender or the like would be considered to be automatically unfair, providing a further layer of employment protection to employees.

The Unemployment Insurance Act, 2001 (UIA)[18] established an unemployment insurance fund to which employers and employees contribute and from which employees who become unemployed (or their beneficiaries, as the case may be) are entitled to benefits.[19] This includes unemployment benefits, illness benefits, maternity benefits, adoption benefits and dependant's benefits.[20] In this way, the harmful economic and social effects of unemployment are (at least partially) addressed. Importantly, the Fund may be used for the "financing of the retention of contributors in employment and the re-entry of contributors into the labour market and any other scheme aimed at vulnerable workers".[21] To access unemployment benefits, the unemployed contributor must, at least in theory, be registered as a work-seeker with a labour centre and must be capable of and available for work.[22]

The Compensation for Occupational Injuries and Diseases Act, 1993 (COIDA)[23] entitles employees who meet with accidents or contract occupational diseases compensation, and provides payments to dependants in the case of deaths resulting from such injuries or diseases.[24] This Act is on the cusp of undergoing amendments, with a new chapter expected to be included in order to prioritise the notion of early return-to-work following the occurrence of an occupational injury or disease, accompanied by appropriate vocational rehabilitation and the introduction of a proper disability management system (and possibly including Return-to-Work Coordinators to liaise with medical professionals and injured / ill employees in order to ensure appropriate re-integration into the working environment).[25]

The picture that emerges from this cursory survey of selected employment-related legislation is that South African law seeks to provide various layers of protection to persons in employment. For example, unfair dismissals and unfair labour practices often result in orders of reinstatement. Employees employed via triangular employment relationships or those engaged in fixed-term contracts for longer than three months may be "deemed" to be permanent employees unless certain exceptions are applicable. Even the transformation imperative in South African employment law has been tempered in a fashion that protects existing employment relationships (and which prevents dismissals being justified on the basis of the need to ensure the demographic transformation of a workplace). In addition, unemployment benefits are paid to contributors who have lost their employment, subject to certain conditions.[26] Furthermore, proposed changes to COIDA place a greater emphasis on returning injured / ill workers to the workplace as soon as possible, rather than being satisfied with compensation payments alone.

What is apparent from this appraisal is that South African law offers a level of protection to people formally engaged in traditional employment relationships. There is also assistance for categories of vulnerable workers, including employees working in triangular employment relationships and those engaged via fixed-term contracts. Unemployment insurance and return-to-work initiatives, similarly, operate in a way that is mainly of benefit to former "traditional" employees. Initiatives to encourage and facilitate the employment of people presently unemployed are clearly more difficult to legislate. (Indeed, it is arguable that over-legislating in this area may result in stifling employment creation, and that urgent economic growth is a prerequisite for any meaningful gain in the number of persons employed.) Nevertheless, the South African parliament attempted to do just that be enacting the Employment Services Act in 2014 (the ESA).[27]

The purpose of this Act is to:

1. "Promote employment;
2. Improve access to the labour market for work seekers;
3. Provide opportunities for new entrants to the labour market to gain work experience;
4. Improve the employment prospects of work seekers, in particularly vulnerable work seekers;
5. Improve the employment and re-employment prospects of employees facing retrenchment;
6. Facilitate access to education and training for work seekers, in particular vulnerable work seekers;
7. Promote employment., growth and workplace productivity; and
8. Facilitate the employment of foreign nationals in the South African economy, where their contribution is needed -
    a. That gives effect to the right to fair labour practices contemplated in section 23 of the Constitution;

b. That does not impact adversely on existing labour standards or the rights and expectations of South African workers; and

c. That promotes the training of South African citizens and permanent residents." (S 2(1))

According to section 2(2) of the Act, the purpose is to be achieved by –

1. "Providing comprehensive and integrated free public employment services;
2. Coordinating the activities of public sector agencies whose activities impact on the provision of employment services;
3. Encouraging partnerships, including in the provision of employment services, to promote employment;
4. Establishing schemes and other measures to promote employment; and
5. Providing a regulatory framework for the operation of private employment agencies."

In theory, the employment protection dimensions of this new piece of legislation are significant. In respect of "job retention", for example, it is expected of the Minister of Labour to establish schemes to minimise the retrenchment of employees.[28] The Department of Labour is also expected to develop and operate an employment information system for "monitoring, evaluating, researching and analysing trends"[29] and must finance the provision of public employment services from its budget.[30] In addition, the Department is expected to provide the following public employment services free of charge to members of the public in a manner that is open and accessible:[31]

1. "Matching work seekers with available work opportunities;
2. Registering work seekers;
3. Registering job vacancies and other work opportunities;
4. Facilitating the placing of work seekers with employers or in other work opportunities;
5. Advising work seekers on access to education and training;
6. Advising workers on access to social security benefits;
7. Providing specialised services to assist vulnerable work seekers;
8. Facilitating the exchange of information among labour market participants, including employers, workers and work seekers, private employment agencies, Sector Education and Training Authorities and training providers…"

The ESA also provides for the creation of an "Employment Services Board" to advise the Minister on matters such as available work opportunities.[32] The Act simultaneously formalises the creation of a juristic person, Productivity South Africa, to promote employment growth and productivity and to promote a culture of productivity in the workplace.[33]

These developments constitute an unprecedented attempt by the legislature to attempt to "legislate" for employment creation and to supplement the traditional forms of dismissal protections contained in labour statutes. To some extent, the development addresses concerns that employment creation policy initiatives (such as the Department of Labour's Expanded Public Works Programme) occurred in a legislative vacuum, making it difficult for state inaction / inefficiency to be challenged through the courts. In terms of the ESA, the Labour Court has exclusive jurisdiction in respect of all matters arising from the Act, excluding the prosecution of criminal offences. In addition, the Labour Court is granted the authority to review any administrative action in terms of the Act on any grounds permissible in law.[34] It remains anomalous, however, that these statutory developments have occurred without a direct constitutional mandate for progressive employment creation on the part of the state, utilising available resources and via legislative and other measures (as is the case with a number of other socio-economic rights in the South African Constitution, including, for example, the rights to social security, housing, health care, food and water).

ANALYSIS

Is the existing legislation pertaining to employment protection, unemployment and work constitutionally compliant?

There is nothing to suggest that the above-mentioned legislation contravenes the Constitution. In fact, it is clear that the legislative framework broadly supports the constitutional promise of ensure that everyone enjoys the right to fair labour practices. What is perhaps more in issue is the missed opportunity of pegging this legislation on an enumerated constitutional right to work, as has occurred in various other jurisdictions.[35] Including such a right, coupled with an internal limitation ensuring that the state must take reasonable legislative and other measures, within its available resources, to achieve the progressive realisation of the right, would arguably have created a better platform for translating this national priority into financial and policy support for interventions directed towards addressing the unemployment crisis in the country. In addition, this approach would have had the added benefit of supporting a constitutionally consistent approach to the treatment of socio-economic rights, given that so many other state obligations which have significant financial implications have been provided for in the Constitution in this fashion (i.e. by being coupled with a similarly worded internal limitation).

Had such a right been included in this carefully circumscribed manner, the door would have been open to a more direct, continuous evaluation of state conduct to ensure the reasonable budgetary prioritisation of interventions directed towards reducing unemployment. Unreasonable state action would have been subject to court review and the courts could have played their part in ensuring that state attempts to address the challenges associated with employment protection and creation remain progressive in nature. Any retrogressive steps (such as the termination of a successful job creation project or policy) could have been struck down and the state would remain under pressure to channel available resources to address the issue.

It is also submitted that such an approach would have contributed towards giving effect to the preamble's promise of improving the quality of life, and supported various constitutional values, including human dignity and the advancement of human rights.

Finally in this regard, it must be noted that the relatively recent enactment of the ESA marks an important transition point, from dealing with employment creation initiatives from a policy (as opposed to a legislative) basis through various state programmes to creating legislative obligations on the state, with the Labour Court mandated to review any administrative action in terms of this Act on any grounds permissible in law.

Is it correct to expect legislation (and state policy) to regulate matters such as job-retention and work creation (for example, by activating the work force and through the creation of public works programmes) and, if so, does the present statutory and policy framework address this expectation adequately?

The argument with respect to this point is two-fold. Firstly, the constitutional scheme that South Africa possesses is one based on respect for the rule of law and a system of checks and balances subjecting state conduct to court intervention in appropriate circumstances (based on the expectation that the judiciary is best placed to interpret the Bill of Rights and evaluate state conduct in order to determine its reasonableness). That being the case, it is indeed necessary for the legislature to approach difficult matters such as employment creation on a principled basis, by formulating legislation and supplementing this, where necessary, through regulations and policy directives. As alluded to above, it would have been preferable if such developments occurred against the backdrop of a clear constitutional mandate, coupled with appropriate internal limitations. Nevertheless, such an approach is at least consistent with the constitutional scheme of the country.

Secondly, and assuming that it is accepted that addressing the employment challenges facing the country rank highly in terms of national priorities, the lack of a viable alternative approach to legislating for employment protection leaves few options for the state to consider. Prior to the ESA, for example, the state adopted a fairly non-interventionist approach (at least from a legal perspective) towards the economy's ability to create employment opportunities and reduce unemployment. That approach, no doubt coupled with many other factors including macro-economic instability and rising numbers of work-seekers, has seen the official unemployment rate remain fairly stagnant over a prolonged period of time. The ability of courts to evaluate the reasonableness of state measures (either in terms of their conceptualisation or implementation) was stunted, and court challenges in this arena were few and far between. Private employment initiatives, labour broking and private employment agencies operated with relative freedom, but the economy seemingly remained immune to attempts to stimulate the numbers of those enjoying productive work. The more recent statutory interventions suggest a fresh approach. The state appears more willing to assume (primary) responsibility for assisting those unable to support themselves and their dependants not just through social assistance (in the form of state grants) but through direct initiatives attempting to stimulate productivity, create employment opportunities and assist employment providers and job-seekers to find one another. Whether these lofty ideals are realisable in practice remain to be seen, and there is concern that the state bureaucracy will make many of the promises of the ESA, in particular, simply unrealisable.

But to simply reject the string of recent legislative developments, outlined above, in this manner, is also, perhaps, somewhat myopic. In other instances, such as the use of the UIA, and its excessive surplus of funds, to finance the retention of contributors in employment and the re-entry of contributors into the labour market, the legislative developments appear to be more easily translatable into concrete steps that have the effect of contributing to employment protection. A recent example of this is the successful partnership between the UIF and the CCMA to create a scheme directed towards reducing the number of retrenchments by subjecting at-risk workers to additional training and by reducing the wage bill of companies on the brink of retrenchment during short periods of need.[36] Similarly, the promised COIDA initiative of introducing return-to-work arrangements for persons suffering an occupational injury or disease appears eminently capable of yielding positive results. The beauty of these recent approaches, particularly when introduced by way of a clear legislative mandate, is the (often unwritten) judicial review safety-net that accompanies their introduction.

To what extent is the legislation compliant with international standards and best practices, and are there fresh approaches to address the present malaise, perhaps emanating from regional standards and experiences?

The recent developments sketched above, particularly in relation to the UIA, COIDA and ESA, should certainly be perceived, in part, as a demonstrated attempt to align domestic legislation with South Africa's international obligations. For example, some attempt has been made to align the UIA to international and regional standards. Most notable in this regard is the setting of the rate of maternity benefits at 66% of a (female) contributor's earnings that will make the UIA compliant with the provisions of the International Labour Organisation Maternity Protection Convention, article 16(1) of the 2014 Southern African Development Community (SADC) Protocol on Employment and Labour and the 2007 Code on Social Security in the SADC.[37] The provisions in the ESA relating to private employment agencies also reflect an attempt to align South Africa's international obligations in terms of the ILO Unemployment Convention[38] to endeavours to co-ordinate at a national scale the operations of public and private employment agencies where they exist.[39] The proposed developments in relation to return-to-work arrangements give expression to various international standards, as encapsulated by the United Nations, the International Labour Organization and the International Social Security Association. South Africa's ratification of the United Nations Convention on the Rights of Persons with Disability (UNCRPD) and its Optional Protocol in 2007 has certainly contributed to developments in this regard, given that the UNCRPD contains several provisions which are of direct relevance and application to the establishment and functioning of a RTW policy in developing countries.[40] Various ILO instruments also provide significant insight into the nature of vocational rehabilitation measures and standards required, although South Africa has not ratified ILO instruments that make a significant contribution towards advancing an RTW agenda.[41]

More broadly, the South Africa Decent Work Country Programme represents the culmination of a consultative process between the ILO, the South African government, business and labour in order to internalise and operationalize key international principles which facilitate decent work enhancement in the country.[42] The priorities and strategic focus of the South Africa Decent Work Country Programme intersect with the ILO strategic objectives and key outcome areas.[43]

The most glaring anomaly, as argued elsewhere, is the Constitution's omission of a specified right to work despite the International Covenant on Economic, Social and Cultural Rights[44] giving explicit recognition to a right to work, which includes the right of everyone to gain his / her living by work freely chosen or accepted. The Committee for Economic Social and Cultural Rights has emphasised both the social and economic dimensions of a right to work and it has been argued that directly constitutionalising such a right would be the ultimate expression of the notion of transformative constitutionalism and would facilitate the various legislative and policy developments aimed at achieving poverty alleviation through minimising unemployment insecurity.[45] In addition, despite the attempt to align the UIA with international and regional standards, there are several examples of non-compliance with various ILO Conventions.[46]

As far as regional standards are concerned, the SADC Protocol on Employment and Labour confirms that State Parties should adopt "proactive policies and measures towards inclusive economic and social development so as to absorb the majority of the labour force into productive employment and income-generating activities".[47] In addition to affording preferential employment opportunities for the youth, women and persons with disability, State Parties are expected to adopt measures to stimulate and support job creation initiatives and to ensure adequate protection against loss of employment, including protection against arbitrary and/or unfair dismissal.[48] Given the particularly low level of youth employment, it is certainly true that "proactive policies and measures" are required to address the impasse. While the SADC Protocol on Employment and Labour does not provide further direction on measures that may be suitable in this regard, the Protocol at least serves to underline the importance of fresh, focused, employment creation initiatives for this particularly vulnerable group.

CONCLUSION: ARE THERE ANY BEST PRACTICES OR LESSONS LEARNED THROUGH THE SOUTH AFRICAN EXPERIENCE THAT SHOULD INFLUENCE DEVELOPMENTS IN OTHER EMERGING ECONOMIES?

The final issue for consideration relates to whether or not there are any core lessons emanating from South Africa which ought to influence developments in other jurisdictions. The South African experience reflects a dynamic approach towards employment protection. Despite the absence of a clear constitutional basis for legislation in this arena, the recent developments outlined above demonstrate the extent to which a coherent legislative approach, aligned with international standards, has emerged. Whether and to what extent this approach is going to contribute to reducing unemployment and its adverse effects is difficult to determine. At least three broad areas may be identified at this stage as emerging "best practices":

Firstly, the South African approach to socio-economic rights in general, in terms of which the state is expected to take reasonable legislative and other measures within its available resources to achieve the progressive realisation of rights remains of interest to developments in other emerging economies. It provides a measurable benchmark against which state action can be assessed and, importantly, opens the door for the judiciary to serve the function of assessing the reasonableness of the measures attempted.

Secondly, multi-actor state responsibility and inter-governmental partnerships (as well as public-private partnerships) and collaborations (as occurred in the Training Layoff Scheme involving the Ministry of Labour, the Commission for Conciliation Mediation and Arbitration and private sector employers undergoing a retrenchment exercise) is likely to become increasingly relevant for purposes of co-crafting of solutions to the multi-faceted challenges of employment creation and protection.

Finally, in this regard, the enactment of the ESA in South Africa is a potentially significant development, given its co-emphasis on regulating private employment agencies, public employment creation and productivity. The manner in which this legislation is utilised, the mobilisation of resources to support its objectives and the role of the courts in assessing the progress made, will be observed with keen interest, particularly given that other initiatives have seemingly failed to impact significantly on people on the periphery of formal employment.

REFERENCES

Compensation for Occupational Injuries and Diseases Act, 1993 (Act 130 of 1993)

Employment Equity Act, 1998 (Act 55 of 1998)

Employment Services Act, 2014 (Act 4 of 2014)

Govindjee, A., & Dupper, O. (2011). Constitutional perspectives on unemployment security and a right to work in South Africa. *Stellenbosch Law Review*, *22*(3), 775–803.

Labour Relations Act, 1995 (Act 66 of 1995)

Mpedi, L. G. (2014). *Understanding Unemployment Insurance Law*. Cape Town, South Africa: Juta.

Olivier, M., & Govindjee, A. (2015). A critique of the Unemployment Insurance Amendment Bill, 2015. *Potchefstroom Electronic Law Journal*, *8*(7), 2739–2776.

Olivier, M., & Govindjee, A. (2017). Improving return to work and disability management in the developing world: Pointers emanating from international instruments, standards and guidelines. *Bulletin of Comparative Labour Relations*, *97*, 193–218.

Statistics South Africa. (2014). *Survey of Employers and the Self-employed 2013*. Retrieved June 8, 2017 from www.statssa.gov.za/publications/P0276/P02762013.pdf

Statistics South Africa. (2017). *Quarterly Labour Force Survey: Quarter 1*. Retrieved June 8, 2017 from www.statssa.gov.za/publications/{0211/P02111stQuarter2017.pdf

The Constitution of the Republic of South Africa, 1996

Unemployment Insurance Act, 2001 (Act 63 of 2001)

KEY TERMS AND DEFINITIONS

Dismissal: Termination of employment, with or without notice, in accordance with the provisions of section 186 of the Labour Relations Act, 1995.

Fixed-Term Contract: Employment contract containing a stipulated termination date.

Right to Work: A justiciable entitlement to obtain remunerated work from the state.

Socio-Economic Rights: Rights traditionally classified as "second-generation," including economic, social, and cultural rights such as the right to have access to housing, the right to have access to healthcare, the right to education and labour rights.

Triangular Employment Relationships: Employment involving a temporary employment service provider or "labour broker"; an employee and a client.

Unfair Labour Practices: Unfair conduct on the part of an employer in matters such as promotions, demotions, suspensions, provision of training, or benefits.

ENDNOTES

1 Statistics South Africa *Quarterly Labour Force Survey: Quarter 1: 2017* (2017) accessed at www.statssa.gov.za/publications/{0211/P02111stQuarter2017.pdf (accessed on 8 June 2017). Unemployed persons are those (aged 16-64 years) who: a) were not employed in the reference week; and b) actively looked for work or tried to start a business in the four weeks preceding the survey interview; and c) were available for work; or d) had not actively looked for

work in the past four weeks but had a job or business to start at a definite date in the future and were available.

2 Statistics South Africa (2017) 19.

3 Statistics South Africa *Survey of Employers and the Self-employed 2013* accessed at www.statssa.gov.za/publications/P0276/P02762013.pdf (2014) v (accessed on 8 June 2017).

4 S 1 of the Constitution.

5 S 10 of the Constitution.

6 S 9(1) of the Constitution.

7 S 22 of the Constitution. The practice of a trade, occupation or profession may be regulated by law.

8 S 23(1) of the Constitution.

9 S 27(1)(c) of the Constitution.

10 S 27(2) of the Constitution.

11 Act 66 of 1995.

12 S 1 of the LRA. The "primary purposes" include giving effect to obligations incurred by the country as a member state of the International Labour Organisation: s 1(b).

13 In section 186 of the LRA.

14 See, in general, ss 198A and 198B of the LRA. Differences in the quality or quantity of the work, the seniority of the employees or their qualifications would be examples justifying differential treatment.

15 Act 55 of 1998.

16 Section 2 of the EEA.

17 Defined in section 15 of the EEA.

18 Act 63 of 2001.

19 S 2 of the UIA.

20 S 12 of the UIA.

21 S 5(d) of the UIA.

22 S 16 of the UIA.

23 Act 130 of 1993.

24 See long-title to the COIDA.

25 See in general in this regard Olivier and Govindjee "Improving return to work and disability management in the developing world: Pointers emanating from international instruments, standards and guidelines" in R Blanpain (ed) *Bulletin of Comparative Labour Relations* (Kluwer, 2017) (accepted for publication and in press).

26 The period of unemployment must last longer than a specified period; the reason for the unemployment must be due to, among other things, termination of the contributor's contract of employment by the employer, the dismissal

of the contributor, the expiry of the contributor's fixed-term contract and the like; an application for benefits must be lodged at an employment office within a six-month period; the applicant must be registered as a work-seeker with a labour centre and the applicant must be capable of and available for work: see in general, LG Mpedi "Understanding Unemployment Insurance Law" *Juta's Pocket Companions* (2014) 53.

27 Act 4 of 2014.

28 S 7(1). This may include schemes to provide for turn-around strategies, lay-offs, re-training or alternative employment opportunities: s 7(2).

29 S 11.

30 S 12(1). In addition, money may be allocated for this purpose from the UIF, from COIDA, from money generated from the registration of private employment agencies and via the receipt of grants and donations.

31 S 5(1). The Department may also provide vocational and career counseling; assessment of work seekers to determine suitability and any other related life skills to secure employment or other forms of work.

32 Ss 21-23.

33 See, in particular, ss 31-33.

34 S 48.

35 See, in general, A Govindjee and O Dupper "Constitutional perspectives on unemployment security and a right to work in South Africa" *SLR* (vol. 22 no.3) (2011) 775-803.

36 See A Govindjee and O Dupper (2011) 787.

37 Convention 183 of 2000.

38 ILO Unemployment Convention 2 (1919) ("ILO Unemployment Convention"). Ratification took place on 20-02-1924.

39 A Govindjee and O Dupper (2011) 786.

40 See M Olivier and A Govindjee "Improving return-to-work and disability management in the developing world: Pointers emanating from international instruments, standards and guidelines" in R Blanpain (ed) *Bulletin of Comparative Labour Relations* (2017) (in press).

41 *Ibid*. In fact, South Africa has been criticized for failing to incorporate international instruments such as the UNCRPD adequately into its legal framework, leaving workers' compensation laws leaning in a lopsided fashion towards compensation as opposed to rehabilitation.

42 RSA *Decent Work Country Programme* 4 as referred to in Govindjee and Dupper (2011) 790.

43 *Ibid*.

44 Signed by South Africa in 1994 and ratified in 2015.

45 Govindjee and Dupper (2011) 802.

46 See in general M Olivier and A Govindjee "A critique of the Unemployment Insurance Amendment Bill, 2015" *PER* (2015) vol. 8 no. 7 2739-2776.

47 Article 15(a).

48 Article 15.

Chapter 8
Employment Protection Legislation and Unemployment in Botswana

Happy Siphambe
University of Botswana, Botswana

Mavis Kolobe
University of Botswana, Botswana

Itumeleng Primrose Oageng
University of Botswana, Botswana

ABSTRACT

Botswana has experienced phenomenon economic growth and structural transformation since independence. Despite the achievement in terms of economic growth, the country has had challenges with unemployment averaging 20% and being quite high for youth. The labour laws have changed over time to conform to international standards. The current changes have, however, not been positive in terms of labour relations with the transition from consultative system to collective bargaining almost forestalled. The labour movement has been quite weak. The labour laws have had mixed impact on employment and the labour market and employment creation. The chapter makes key recommendations on how Botswana's labour environment can be transformed based on international experience. Key recommendations are towards employment creation and improving the social dialogue space, especially for labour as the weaker party. This should go a long way in increasing labour productivity and dealing with the persistent problem of poor work ethic.

DOI: 10.4018/978-1-5225-4134-9.ch008

INTRODUCTION

At independence in 1966, Botswana had a very small labour force made mainly of low skilled and lowly educated Batswana who were mainly migrant labourers to the South African mines. The country had very little in terms of industrialisation due to limited manufacturing and services industries. A few years after independence, the country went through structural transformation due mainly to the profitable exploitation of diamond mines discovered just after independence. The revenue from the diamond allowed the country to invest heavily in infrastructure and human capital resulting in a highly transformed labour market.

The result of the changes in the economic sphere has been transitions and structural changes in the composition of the workforce. This is characterised by dualism between the modern formal sector and the informal sector. There was also transformation from an agricultural based economy to one driven by mining and services sectors. There has also emerged a persistent and high level of unemployment averaging about 20 percent with youth unemployment of more than 40 percent. Part of the problem of youth unemployment is due to limited job opportunities and skills mismatch.

While there were structural changes in both the economy and the labour market, the country also experienced major changes in terms of industrial relations due to evolving labour laws and regulations. In particular the labour relations were transformed from consultative structures to semi tripartite structures meant for negotiation. The current situation is one of chaos with very hostile labour relations and an evolving set of laws meant to not only make labour market much more flexible but also meant to weaken the bargaining power of the workers. This chapter therefore provides an analysis of the various labour market changes that have evolved in Botswana's labour market and provide policy proposals on the way forward in terms of the current labour relations quagmire from both an international perspective and that applicable to Botswana's own unique situation.

MAIN FOCUS OF THE CHAPTER

Economic and Structural Changes of Botswana's Economy-Challenges of Economic Diversification

The economy of Botswana has largely been driven by mineral revenues and to some extent by private sector investment. The mineral revenue accounted for 51.3 percent of total government revenue in 1985 increasing to 59.3 percent in the year 2000. In the 42 years of independence, between 1966 and 2007/08, the real growth of GDP averaged 8.7 percent per year. The non-mining GDP growth was 10 percent in 2011 and the mining GDP growth rate was -2.2 percent (Republic of Botswana, 2013). Unlike other developing mineral rich economies, the economy seems to have avoided the "Dutch Disease"- a phenomena that renders the non-mining sector uncompetitive. A plausible explanation may be that the Pula has been devaluated a few times to make it competitive relative to other currencies. The revenue from diamond sales was also wisely invested in terms of human development and the surplus invested in the Pula fund.

Between the years 1966 and 2016, there has been a notable change in the composition of Botswana`s gross Domestic Product (GDP). Table 1 also shows that at the time of independence (1966), the mining sector was non-existent. With the discovery of minerals especially diamonds in the late 1960's, the mining and quarrying sector strikingly increased from nothing in 1966 to 44.7 percent in 1990. Since the 2008 global financial crisis, the contribution of the mining sector to total GDP has been decreasing, attributed mostly to the decline in demand and price for diamonds. Even with the decline in demand for diamonds, the mining sector still remains among the major contributors to GDP (accounting for 14.7 percent of total GDP in 2012 and 11.9 percent in 2016). This shows how the mining sector is an important component of GDP; hence government expenditure (as government relies heavily on revenues from the sector). Most importantly, during this period, there has been growth in various non-mining sectors in particular Trade, Hotels & Restaurants. Currently, the non-mining sectors (excluding government) contribute

Table 1. Share of GDP by economic activity–selected years 1966 to 2016 (percentages)

Economic Sector	1966	1990	1997	2008	2012	2016
Agriculture	42.7	4.7	3.4	2.0	1.9	1.6
Mining and quarrying	-	44.7	38.9	26.7	14.7	11.9
Manufacturing	5.7	4.9	5.0	5.6	6.4	6.0
Water and electricity	0.6	2.4	1.8	1.2	0.5	0.8
Construction	7.8	7.1	5.7	5.2	7.6	7.5
Trade, hotels and restaurants	9.0	7.0	10.1	14.1	17.5	20.6
Transport	4.3	2.7	3.2	4.2	5.4	6.0
Financial and business services	20.1	7.1	10.0	12.2	14.6	14.8
General government	9.8	12.3	14.0	12.2	13.2	13.0
Social and personal services	-	3.6	3.8	5.4	6.9	7.0
Total Value Added	100.0	96.5	95.9	88.8	88.7	89.2
Adjustment items	-	3.5	4.0	11.2	11.2	10.8
GDP	100	100	100	100	100	100

Source: Bank of Botswana annual reports, 2001 and 2017

about 63 percent of total value added, compared to 39.5 percent in the year 1990. This shows that government efforts to diversify the economy away from the mining sector have been fruitful. Despite this impressive performance in the non-mining sectors, the share of agricultural sector and water and electricity has been decreasing over the years. From Table 1, the agricultural sector moved from being the major contributor of GDP at 42.7 percent in 1966 to the second least contributor at 1.6 percent in 2016. The decline is attributed to recurring droughts and animal disease (especially foot and mouth disease) in the country. The agricultural sector is labour intensive and a significant employer in developing countries; therefore a decline in the share of GDP in the agricultural sector has implications for employment and poverty in the economy. Water and electricity continues to contribute very little to total GDP in the economy, despite receiving a big share of the total government development budget in most years.

Botswana's Labour Market: Its Evolution, Current Status and Unemployment Challenges

This section of the chapter provides information on the labour market over time to its current form. We provide analysis of the labour supply and demand and the unemployment. The current structure of the labour market to some extent determines the nature of employment regulations and how these regulations impact on employment creation over time. The analysis is dictated by the limitation of more current data which is due to the fact that the labour force survey is currently being produced every 10 years. Starting 2017 there are plans to produce labour market data every quarter which should make the analysis easier in future.

Labour Force Participation

The economically active population constitutes the labour force which is comprised of the employed and the unemployed persons and in Botswana it is defined as those individuals aged 12 years and above[1]. Employed persons refers to those who did some work in the reference period either for payment in cash or in kind (paid employees) or who were in self-employment for profit or family gain as well as persons temporarily absent from these activities but definitely going to return to work (e.g. on leave or sick). The unemployed are made up of those who are currently not working but are either actively seeking for jobs or discouraged job seekers. The not economically active population is made up of students, retired persons, sick and housework (Central Statistics Office, 2008a). A measure of the extent of utilization of labour force is the Labour Force Participation Rate (LFPR), which is defined as:

$$\frac{LF}{P} x100$$

where

LF = labour force, and
P = relevant population (Batswana aged 12 years and above).

The labour force participation rate in Botswana has generally been rising over time for both males and females. In 1995/96 the population aged 12 years and above was 950,793 with an economically active population of 528,108, making a labour force participation rate of 56 percent. For 2005/06 the population aged 12 years and above was 1,153,228 and the labour force was 787,962, making a labour force participation rate of 68 percent, which was a twelve percentage point increase in participation between the period. In terms of gender, the participation rate rose from 61 percent to 72 percent between 1995/96 and 2005/06 for males, which was an 11 percentage point increase between the periods. Statistics Botswana revised the working age group from 12-64years to 15-64 years in the 2009/10 BCWIS to accommodate both the international practice (ILO) and national needs on employment information. Hence for the year 2009/10, the labour participation rate (59.1 percent) was recorded to be lower than the participation rate in 2005/06). For females, the participation rate rose from 51 percent to 65 percent between 1995/96 and 2005/06, being a 14 percentage point increase. The participation rates for women increased much faster than that of men as society began to develop and the education of women also increased. Figure 1 shows labour force participation rates by age group for 1995/96,2005/06 and 2009/10. The general pattern is for that of an inverted "U", where the participation rates rise with age, reaches a peak at around 35-39 before beginning to decline again. The general pattern is also one of higher labour force participation rates for 2005/06 for each age group than in 1995/96. This as indicated is also mainly driven by more women participating in the labour market than in the previous period (Central Statistics Office, 2008a). Figure 2 shows the labour force participation rate by gender for 2009/10. Males generally have a higher participation rate for all ages but the gap increases with age. This generally indicates that among older Batswana, women tended to participate less in the labour market than the much younger cohort.

Figure 1. Labour force participation rate: 1995/96;2005/06 and 2009/10
Source: Labour Force Survey, 1995/96; Labour Force Survey, 2005/06 and Botswana Core Welfare Indicators Survey, 2009/10

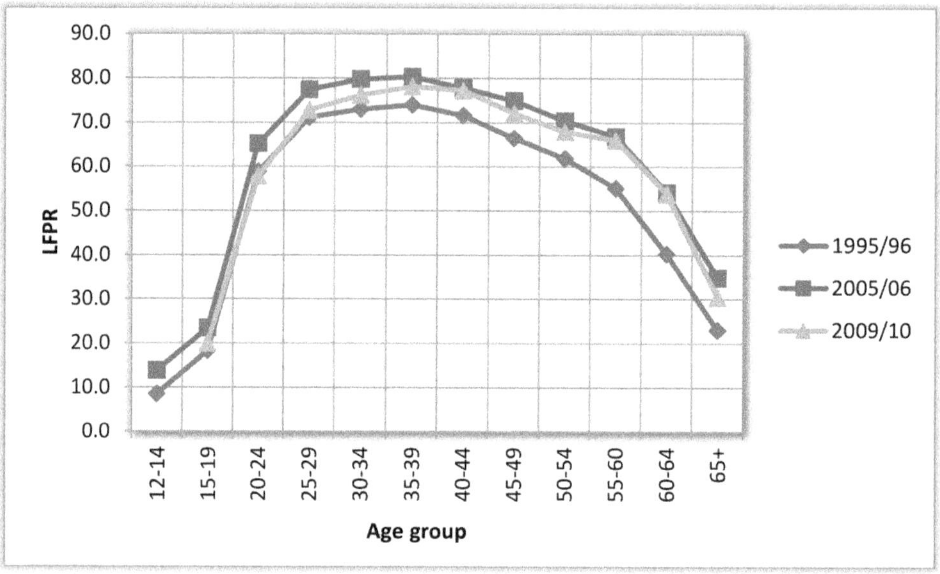

Figure 2. Labour force participation rate by gender and age 2009/10
Source: Botswana Core Welfare Indicators Survey, 2009/10

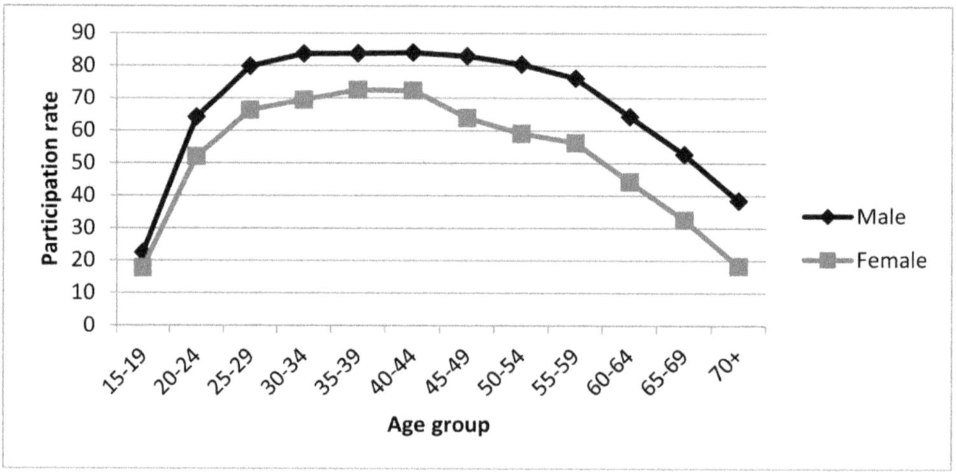

Employment in the Formal Sector

Botswana economy is characterised by a weak link between the sector driving the growth of the economy, mining and employment. Table 2 shows the sectoral distribution of formal sector employment between 1980 and 2015 on the basis of enterprise surveys. The share of agriculture in total formal sector employment declined from 5.2 per cent in 1980 to 1.6 per cent in 2015. Currently, the mining sector has the relatively smaller share of output than in the past (about 12 per cent of GDP), and its contribution to employment has also fallen from 8.6 per cent in 1980 to about 3.2 per cent in 2015. The small share of mining in employment reflects its capital-intensive nature, and, therefore, the limited opportunities for employment creation in this sector. The shares of manufacturing, commerce, finance and business services as well as education by non-government providers in total employment increased substantially between 1980 and 2015.

A similar breakdown of employment distribution by industry is provided from the two Labour Force Survey data sets and the Core Welfare Indicator Survey data set by industry, sector, education, occupation, training, gender, and region. In the 2009/10 BCWIS those currently employed were 579,429, of which 54 percent were males and 46 percent were females. Figure 3 shows the distribution of currently employed by industry. Main employers in 2009/10 are agriculture (26 percent), public administration (11 percent), public administration (16 percent), wholesale and retail (10 percent) construction (7 percent), real estates (7 percent) and manufacturing (6 percent)[2]. In 1995/95 public administration had the largest share of industrial employment at 17 percent, followed by agriculture with 16 percent. The mining sector, which has been the driving force in terms of output and export earnings also declined from a share of 4.4 percent in 1995/96 to 2.6 percent in 2005/06 and 2.5 percent in 2009/10.

In terms of employment by gender based on the 2009/10 BCWIS, females dominate in Hotels and restaurant (73 percent), Finance (60 percent), private household (72 percent), education (63 percent), health (64 percent), wholesale and retail (62 percent) and local government (62 percent). Women are least represented in mining and quarrying (17 percent), construction (15 percent) and electricity and water (20 percent). In general, females are increasingly dominating in most industries, even though there is still some major signs of occupational segregation. In terms of location, 45 percent of those employed were employed in the rural areas in 1995/96 and in 2005/06. The urban areas absorbed the rest of the workers at 55

Table 2. Number of paid employees in the formal sector by economic activity, 1980-2015 (selected years)

Economic Activity	Number of Persons Employed [Percentage Share]							
	1980	**1985**	**1990**	**1995**	**2000**	**2005**	**2008**	**2015**
Agriculture	4,300	4,000	6,400	4,500	5,800	5,554	5,563	6,637
	[5.2]	[3.4]	[3.1]	[1.9]	[2.2]	[1.9]	[1.8]	[1.6]
Mining and Quarrying	7,200	7,300	8,100	8,100	7,900	9,270	11,538	12,773
	[8.6]	[6.3]	[3.9]	[3.5]	[3.0]	[3.1]	[3.7]	[3.2]
Manufacturing	5,600	9,900	24,300	24,200	29,800	32,397	36,135	37,316
	[6.7]	[8.5]	[11.6]	[10.4]	[11.2]	[10.8]	[11.6]	[9.2]
Electricity and Water	1,500	1,900	2,100	2,500	2,900	2,430	2,819	4,752
	[1.8]	[1.6]	[1.0]	[1.1]	[1.1]	[0.8]	[0.9]	1.2
Construction	13,400	11,500	31,000	22,400	27,300	24,364	22,097	22,877
	[16.1]	[9.8]	[14.8]	[9.6]	[10.3]	[8.2]	[7.1]	[5.7]
Commerce	10,400	18,300	38,300	45,500	47,600	55,979	60,269	48,906
	[12.5]	[15.7]	[18.3]	[19.5]	[17.9]	[18.7]	[19.3]	[16.5]
Transport and Communication	3,400	5,700	8,500	8,700	9,900	12,608	12,195	13,457
	[4.1]	[4.9]	[4.1]	[3.7]	[3.7]	[4.2]	[3.9]	[3.3]
Finance and Business Services	4,300	6,800	14,700	17,700	18,300	21,763	25,302	28,598
	[5.2]	[5.8]	[7.0]	[7.6]	[6.9]	[7.3]	[8.2]	10.3
Community and Personal Services	2,400	3,900	8,200	9,800	4,300	5,137	5,707	8,588
	[2.9]	[3.3]	[3.9]	[4.2]	[1.6]	[1.7]	[1.8]	[2.5]
Education	1,300	1,900	2,100	3,800	6,200	7,850	9,638	10,181
	[1.6]	[1.6]	[1.0]	[1.6]	[2.3]	[2.6]	[3.1]	[3.0]
Government (Local and Central)	29,500	45,600	65,100	86,200	105,200	121,364	11,9778	88,487
	[35.4]	[39.0]	[31.1]	[36.9]	[39.7]	[40.6]	[38.5]	[32.2]
Total	83,400	116,800	209,000	233,400	265,300	298,715	311,164	341,115

Source: Various Central Statistics Office *Statistical Bulletins*

percent in both years. For 2005/06, the cities/towns employed 26 percent of the labour force, while urban villages employed 30 percent of the total labour force. Within the rural areas, a majority of the workers (56 percent) were employed in the agricultural industry. The other significant sectors of employment in the rural areas are wholesale and trade (9 percent), public administration and education at 7 percent each, and manufacturing and private households at 5 percent each. Clearly agriculture is still the significant industry of employment. The sector is however one of the lowest in terms of average earnings, only paying higher than private households. The 2005/06 estimated the earnings for agriculture workers at an average of P366 per month. It is also well documented that agriculture has low productivity partly due to the unfavourable climatic conditions facing the country and poor work ethics. Reducing poverty through this sector is therefore a major challenge given the very low earnings and general low productivity of the sector.

Figures 4 show the distribution of currently employed by sector of employment. In 1995/96, the major employer was government with 33 percent. The second largest employer was the private sector with 32 percent. Parastatals employed the least employees with a share of 4 percent[3]. By 2005/06 the private sector had grown in terms of employment and was now the dominant sector with 42 percent of the total labour force. Government employment had on the other hand declined in terms of share from 33 percent in 1995/96 to 21 percent in 2005/06 making it the third largest employer in 2005/06. Subsistence farming is the second largest sector of employment with 24 percent share to total employment. What is a major challenge is how to sustain employment in Botswana given the pressure from international organizations such as IMF for Government to downsize its size. Absorption of the employees from the downsizing exercise if it happens will need to be absorbed into other key productive sectors of the economy and therefore the need for labour market policies and programmes that provide for retraining, provision of information on available jobs, etc.

Figure 3. Distribution of employees by industry: 1995/96,2005/06 and 2009/10
Source: Labour Force Survey, 1995/96; Labour Force Survey, 2005/06 and Botswana Core Welfare Indicators Survey, 2009/10

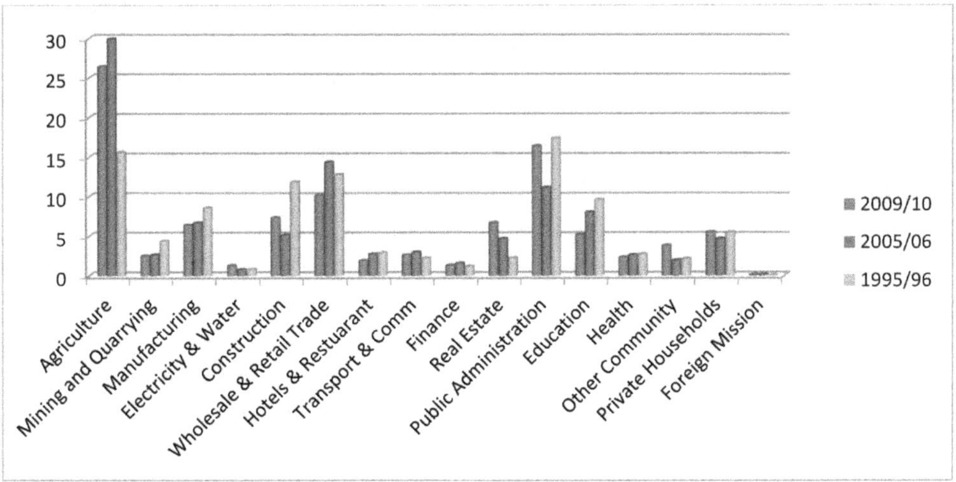

Figure 4. Distribution of currently employed by sector. 1995/96 and 2005/06
Source: Labour Force Survey, 1995/96 and Labour Force Survey,2005/06

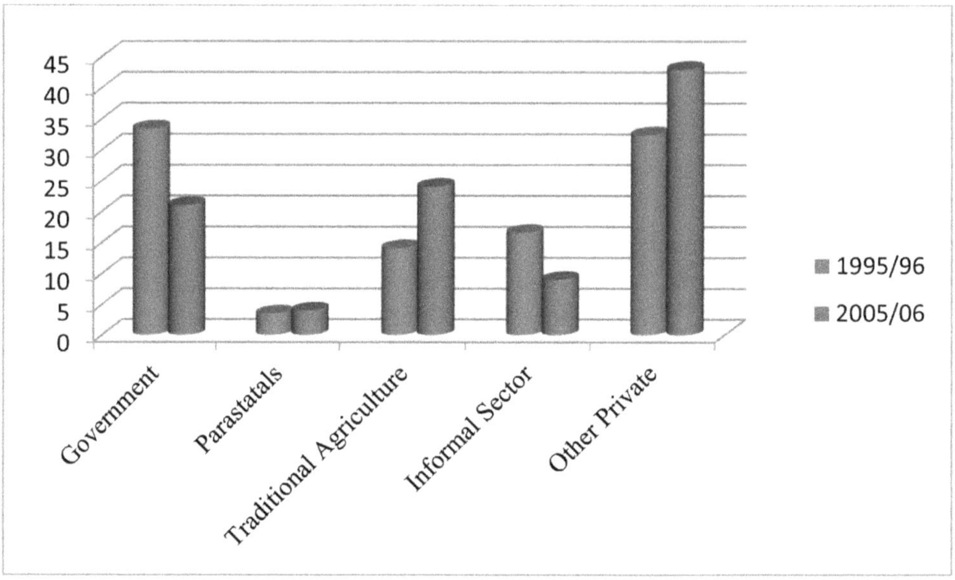

In terms of gender, females dominate only in government at 52 percent. The private sector has an almost equal share of male and female workers. Parastatals have the least female employees with 36 percent of women employed in the sector. In terms of distribution of employment by sector and location (figure 5), most of the government employees are in the urban villages (43 percent). Those in the rural and urban villages are 32 percent and 27 percent respectively. A larger share of parastatal employees is in the urban areas at 72 percent. Private households and subsistence agriculture have bigger shares of employees in the rural areas at 68 percent and 82 percent respectively. A larger share of private sector employment is in the urban areas and urban villages at approximately 36 percent each (Central Statistics Office, 2008a).

Figures 6 show the distribution of employees by employment status for 1995/96, 2005/06 and 2009/10. In 1995/95, 80 percent of the workers were paid employees. The second largest was own farm/lands with employees at 9 percent. In 2009/10 the workers in paid employment made up 68 percent share. The second largest share is in own farm/lands but now with a larger share of 9 percent share to employment. Self-employment, both with employees and without had also grown marginally from 3 percent and 7 percent to 4 percent and 9 percent respectively by 2005/06. However, between 2005/06 and 2009/10 it decreased to the 1995/96 share of total employment.

Figure 5. Share of employment by sector and location
Source: Labour Force Survey, 2005/06

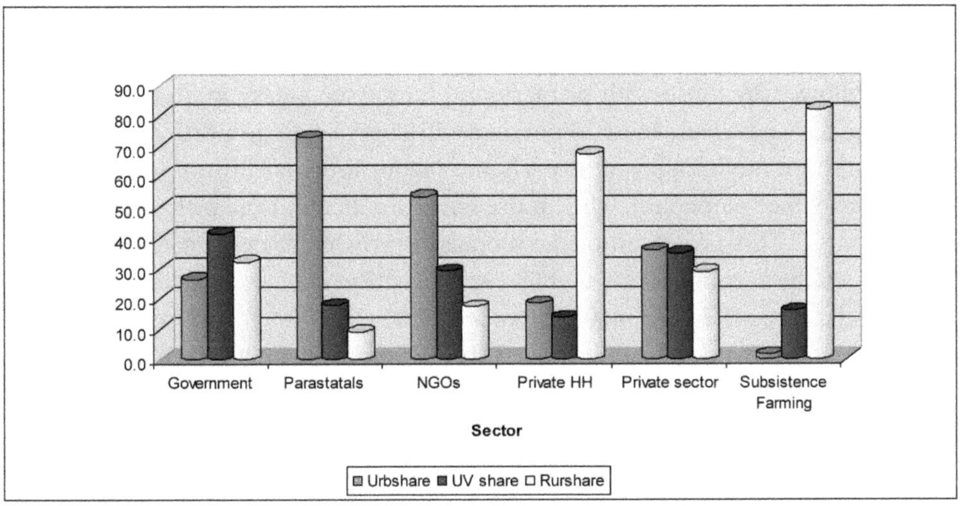

Figure 6. Employment by status: 1995/96; 2005/06 and 2009/10
Source: Labour Force Survey, 1995/96; Labour Force Survey, 2005/06 and Botswana Core Welfare Indicators Survey, 2009/10

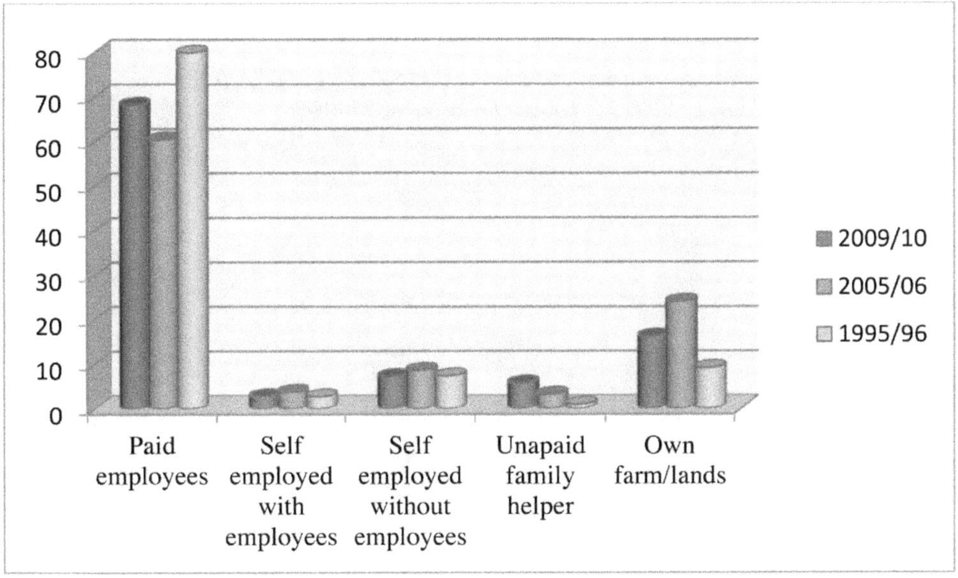

Figure 7 shows the distribution of currently employed by education level for 1995/96 and 2005/06. For 1995/95 the biggest proportions of employees were those with primary education at 38 percent, followed by those with junior certificate at 24 percent. For 2005/06 the largest group was those with junior certificate at 27 percent followed by those with primary and senior secondary at 26 percent each. Those who have never attended school made up a very small proportion of 4 percent of the total currently employed. Clearly the labour force is shifting towards those with at least junior secondary, while those with no education and primary education are decreasing. This is a result of the increased investment in education over time that has seen the enrolment rate increasing. Transition rates from primary to junior secondary have been 97 percent while that for students moving from junior secondary to senior secondary education increased from 49 percent in 2004 to 66 percent in 2008 and it was targeted to reach 70 percent by end of National development plan 9 (Republic of Botswana, 2009).

Figure 8 shows the distribution of workers by occupation and gender. Females dominate in clerical work at 74 percent, service workers at 55 percent and technical and associate professionals[4] at 53 percent. Females are less represented in plant machine operators and craft and related workers at 9 percent and 24 percent respectively. This indicates that there is still a significant occupational segregation along gender lines. In terms of distribution of employees by occupation, the dominant occupation is

Figure 7. Employment by education level: 1995/96 and 2005/06
Source: Labour Force Survey, 1995/96; Labour Force Survey, 2005/06

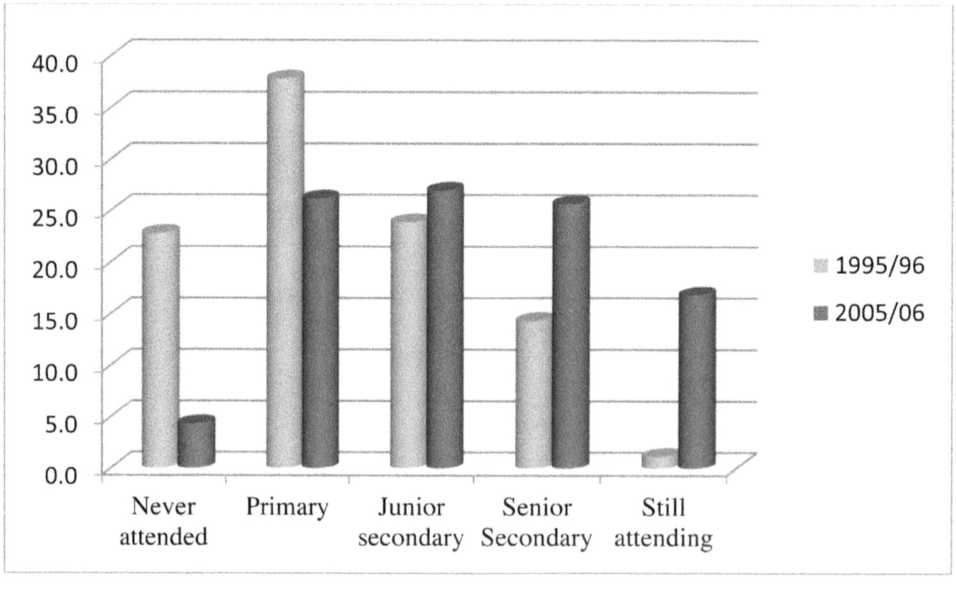

Figure 8. Currently employed by occupation and gender: 2009/10 (percentage within occupation by sex)
Source: Botswana Core Welfare Indicators Survey, 2009/10 data

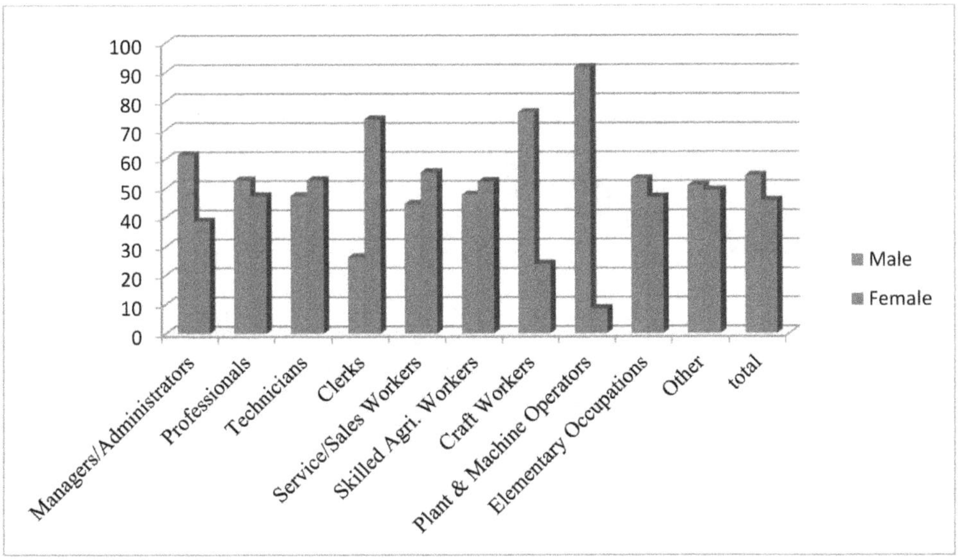

elementary occupations with 31 percent, followed by service/sales at 15 percent and skilled agricultural workers at 14 percent. In terms of currently employed workers by training, a majority of them (71 percent) indicated that they had no training. Amongst the 29 percent that had training, most of them at 51 percent had training at certificate level, followed by diploma at 25 percent. Degree was the lowest with 24 percent. The distribution in terms of training is shown in figure 9.

Employment in the Informal Sector

A major feature of the developing country's labour market is the existence of the informal sector, which presents these labour markets as being dualistic in nature. Experience of the developing countries has shown that the informal sector is an important aspect of their economies, especially in terms of employment creation. Apart from its dynamic links with the formal sector, there is recognition that it is almost impossible for the formal sector to create all the required jobs for the expanding young labour force. Finding what the nature and dynamics of the informal sector in any labour market analysis is therefore very important for policy making. Among the major factors responsible for its growth is the inability of the formal sector to create enough jobs for the increasing labour force, and the increase in labour supply from the rural areas migrating to the urban areas in search of jobs. The informal

Figure 9. Distribution of workers by type of training: 2009/10
Source: Botswana Core Welfare Indicators Survey, 2009/10 data

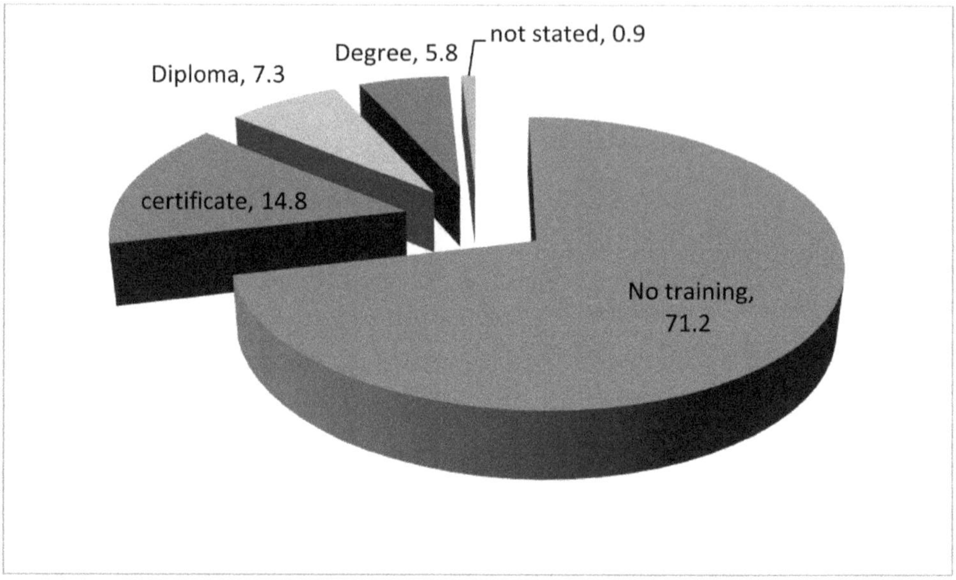

sector in Botswana has grown over time and is dominated by women who are mostly in trade and retail related activities. Most of the employees in informal activities have no training and therefore no skills and are mostly residing in the urban areas of Botswana.

In terms of Botswana's Labour Force Surveys and Informal Sector Surveys, the informal sector was defined as companies that satisfied the following criteria both in 1995/96 and 2005/06:

- Not registered as a company or with any professional association
- Employing less than 10 employees
- Informal accounts or none
- Expenditure not easily distinguished from household expenditure
- Employees casually hired
- Often temporary or mobile or in owner's home/plot.

Also included under informal sector were domestic servants and other private household workers.

The total estimated numbers of informal sector workers in 2005/06 was estimated at 77,392. This is about 10 percent of the total labour force. In 1995/95, employment in the informal sector was 57,240, which was still about 10 percent of the total labour force.

In nominal terms the informal sector grew between the two periods, which probably reflects the inadequate employment growth in the formal sector. About 60 percent of those in the informal sector as their main activity are women. Forty percent of the informal sector workers are employed in wholesale and retail. The second largest is real estate with 21 percent followed by manufacturing with 11 percent of total employment (Figure 10). Fifty five percent of the informal sector employees are in the urban areas, while those in the rural areas make up 45 percent of the total informal sector labour force. Fifty percent of the informal sector workers are self-employed without employees, while 23 percent have paid employees.

In terms of education, a majority of the informal sector employees have primary and junior certificate at about 30 percent of the total informal sector labour force each. Eighty-three percent of those having informal activities as their main activity have not had any form of training. Most of the informal sector business is found in the cities/towns and urban villages at 36 percent share of each. This correlates with the relatively high unemployment rates in these areas and therefore the sector is likely to be occupied by those who are unable to find formal sector jobs. The rural area is however also now having a significant number of informal activities at 28 percent of the total. The majority of those residing in the urban areas are females at 54 percent. There is clearly a segmentation of the labour market in Botswana, with the formal labour market dominated by men on one hand and the informal sector being dominated by women on the other. The other feature of that segmentation is in the form of education and training. As Figure 11 shows, the majority of the employees in the informal sector have junior and primary education at 53 percent of the total number of employees. The second largest group is those with Cambridge certificate at 26 percent. Moreover, most of the employees in the informal sector at 89 percent had no training. It is therefore quite likely that those who choose to enter the informal sector do not have the skills and education to enter the formal sector, confirming the duality of Botswana's labour market.

The informal sector needs to be supported in terms of dealing with some of the major constraints such as lack of access to finance through provision of targeted finance. There is also need to provide infrastructure for the informal sector to allow the sector to grow and absorb more of the labour force. This is important given the inability of the formal sector to absorb all the labour force in Botswana. This will require deliberate active labour market policies working on the demand side of the labour market.

Figure 10. Business in informal sector by industry
Source: Informal Sector Survey, 2007

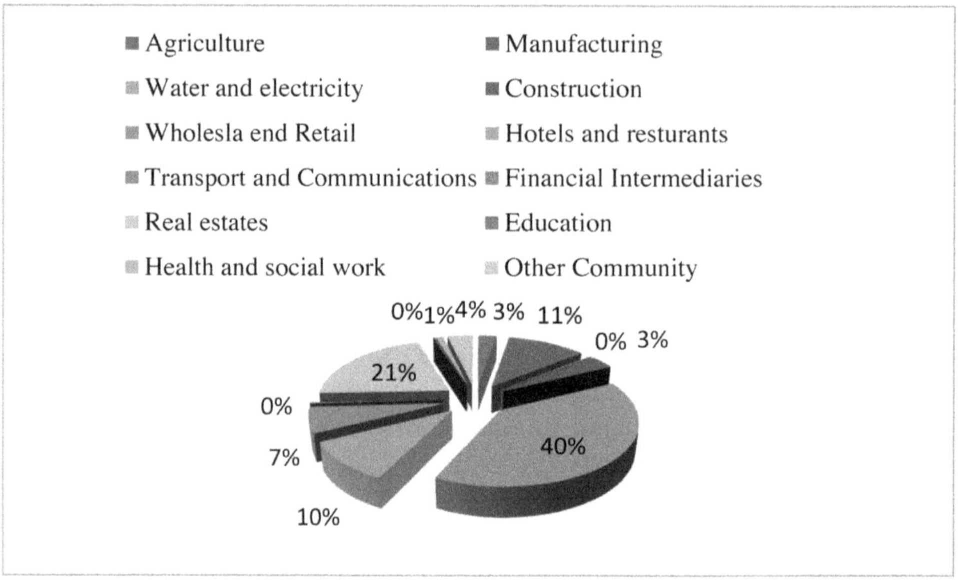

Figure 11. Informal Sector employees by highest education level
Source: Informal Sector Survey, 2007

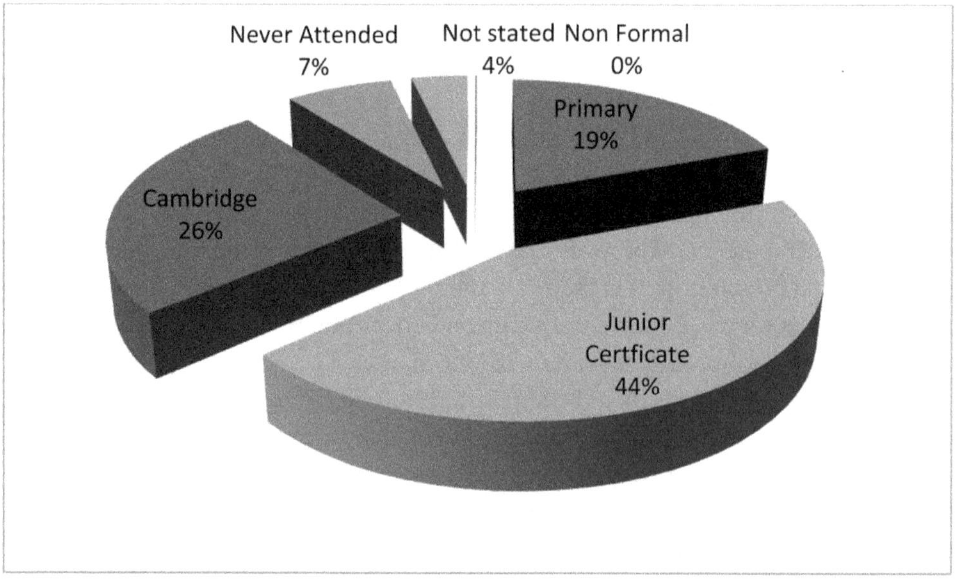

Employment, Unemployment and Labour Force: Persistently High Unemployment

Table 3 summarises the changes in labour force over time. The labour force has been growing over time reaching close to one million in 2013. Unemployment has generally increased from a small figure of 10.2 percent in 1981 to an average of 20 percent in the mid 199os to the current period. The unemployment is stabilising at about 20 percent in the current period and showing no signs of decreasing despite many government efforts. The unemployment is relatively high for women and for the youth in general. There is also significant underemployment of labour estimated at 10 percent of the labour force. Unemployment in general weakens the bargaining power of labour and therefore reduces the effectiveness of any positive labour laws such as minimum wages.

Botswana's Labour Market Regulations and Laws, Evolution and Current Status

In the last few decades, there have been debates over the issue of international labour relations. As governments sign up to international trade agreements, some of their

Table 3. Summary of labour force and unemployment over time

Year	Labour Force	Employed	Unemployed	Unemployment Rate
1981	315475	283249	32226	10.2
1991	441203	379938	61265	13.9
1993/94	499527	391804	107723	21.6
1995/96	439933	345405	94528	21.5
1998	556918	441215	115703	20.8
2000	574161	483432	90729	15.8
2001	562897	453385	109512	19.5
"2002/03"	606826	462366	144460	23.8
2004	756145	570329	185816	24.6
"2005/06"	653192	539150	114042	17.5
2008	679471	514422	183047	26.2
"2009/10"	710600	584251	126349	17.8
2011	801520	642065	159455	19.9
2013	900338	720296	180042	20

Source: Statistics Botswana, 2016

constituencies include, among others, labour agreements that would oblige them to adhere to certain laws protecting workers' rights. Some believe that these laws might be applied unfairly, in ways that might harm the workers they are intended to help. However, there are strong reasons to support the demand for labour laws and standards as a means for workers to organise and express their rights in a good platform because they lead to improved quality of work (Luce, 2005).

How has the changing labour market and labour market and regulations affected Botswana's industrial relations? Botswana is one of the countries that are committed to improved quality of work through addressing the socio-economic dimensions that are critical to the world of work. Being a member of some international bodies such as International labour organisation (ILO) has significantly contributed to the attainment of its objectives. Botswana's commitment to improved quality of work is shown by its adoption of Labour laws and regulations which is an important means of implementing ILO standards and putting the concept of decent work into practice (International Labour Organisation, 2011).

The conditions of employment in Botswana are regulated through national labour laws which include the Employment Act, Trade Unions and Employers Organizations Act, Trade Dispute Act, Public Service Act and Workers Compensations Act among others (Botswana Federation of Trade Unions, 2012). Since becoming a member of ILO in 1978, the country has made significant progress towards implementation of these national labour laws. For example, the Employment Act and the Trade Dispute Act among others have been in operation since 1982 and 2003 respectively.

However, even though Botswana has done a good job in enacting these labour laws, it has had to amend some of them because the government had too much control on the country's labour relations. For instance, the government was the one that decided the parameters within which unions could recruit and collective bargaining was under its supervision which did not sit well with organised labour in the country. Trade unions therefore, mounted pressure on the government to amend these laws to create a friendly environment for all the stakeholders (Mwatcha, 2015).

The most significant amendments include the amendments to the Trade Union and Employers' Organisation Act, the Employment Act and the Trade Dispute Act, which made commendable attempts to liberalise the labour relations in Botswana (Mwatcha, 2015). The amendment of these acts brought some of the Botswana labour laws in line with some international conventions (Botswana Federation of Trade Unions, 2009).

These Acts together with other forms of legislation such as ILO conventions ensure that there is cooperation between the government, employers' and workers' organisations. Furthermore they guarantee the weaker party amongst these three social partners for the protection and basic rights in order to be in a fair position when negotiating salary and working conditions. The working together of these social partners brings about a wholesome approach to tackling the challenges of work and in creatively using the available opportunities to achieve the ultimate benefits (Blackburn, 2006).

Evolution and Current Status of Botswana Labour Laws

The first legislation in the Bechuanaland Protectorate (what Botswana was called then before independence) was the Trade Union and Trade Dispute Proclamation of 1942, which legalized trade unions. The legislation provided for what could be regarded as paternalistic protection of workers, but made inadequate provision for the settlement of industrial disputes. Twenty one years later, the employment Act, No.15 of 1963 was enacted, but still failed to provide for the settlement of disputes. In 1969, the Trade Unions and the Trade Dispute Proclamation and Employment Act No. 15 of 1963, were replaced by the Trade Unions Act No. 24 of 1969, the Trade Dispute Act No. 28 of 1969 and the Regulations of Wages and Conditions of Employment Act of 1969 (Friedrich Ebert Stiftung, 2008).

Botswana's accelerated developments in the 1980's required major changes to these Acts and labour laws in general, including its labour law framework for the private sector. The provisions of some of the Acts were inadequate in terms of meeting the labour needs of the new economic order. The Employment Act, of 1982, for example contained gender discriminatory provisions in the section on gender (Kalula, *et al*, 2008).

The labour laws in Botswana are now being assessed in terms of their suitability and implications as Botswana's economy shifts from being public sector led economy to being private sector led economy in terms of both output and employment generation. This is because labour relations in the public sector in Botswana have been fundamentally different from those in the private sector. Botswana subscribes to a system of labour and employment which is referred to as a "strict public and private law divide" where private service and public sector employment are regulated by two separate legal orders. Public service in Botswana is governed by Public Service Act, Public Service Regulations and General Orders, whereas private sector employment is governed by the Employment Act (Mogapaesi, 2014).

This chapter discusses four major pieces of legislation governing labour relations and the rights and activities of trade unions in Botswana and these are the Employment Act, the Public Service Act, Trade Dispute Act and Trade Unions and Employers' Organizations Act. The chapter also discusses ILO Conventions ratified by the Botswana Government and the minimum wage legislation.

Employment Act (CAP 47:01)

It sets out the basic minimum terms/conditions of employment for private sector, parastatal corporations and public employees. It is the chief legislation that regulates employment relationships in the private sector. It regulates almost all important elements that accrue to an employment relationship such as remuneration, various types of leave and dismissals (Mogapaesi, 2014).

The beneficiaries of the Employment Act must fall within the definition of an employee, which with the 2004 amendments have been broadened as "an employee is any person who has, either before or after its commencement, entered into a contract of employment for the hire of his labour provided that expression does not include members of the Botswana Defence Force, Botswana Police Service, Local Police Force and the Prison Service." This means public officers and those employed by a local authority are now free to form and belong to unions, which was not the case in the past.

The limitation of this definition is that the Botswana Defence Force, Botswana Police Service, Local Police Force and the Prison Service are excluded from the definition of employees. In effect, they do not enjoy the rights and freedoms other employees do, for instance, the right to unionize. However, they do have associations who engage in consultations with the employing authorities and try to represent the armed forces employees interests (Friedrich Ebert Stiftung, 2008).

Amendments that are associated with the Employment act go as far as the early 1990s. Five key areas in the 1982 Employment Act were amended in the 1990s and these are: i) the right to work and job security; ii) aspects of work obligations; iii) gender-discriminatory provisions; iv) remedies and jurisdiction of the labour department and v) changes at work with reference to severance benefits (Kalula, *et al*, 2008). Furthermore, Botswana's amended Employment Act of 2003 provided for a Labour Advisory Board (Section 143). It included advising the Minister on any proposed principal or subsidiary legislation, reviewing dispute prevention and resolution procedures and advising on the constitution of the Panel of Mediators and Arbitrators (Section 148).Thus, the establishment of the Panel of Mediators and Arbitrators is done in consultation with the Labour Advisory Board.

One amendment that was welcome with open arms was on section 23 of the Employment Act that concerns restrictions of the grounds upon which an employer may terminate the employment contract by adding sexual orientation and health status (including HIV/AIDS status) as prohibited grounds of discrimination. It also introduced a new section 23(e), which provides more general protection against discrimination. That is the employee's race, tribe, place of origin, social origin, marital status, gender, sexual orientation, colour, creed, health status or disability; or any other reason which does not affect the employee's ability to perform that employee's duties under the contract of employment (International Labour Organisation, 2014).

There are many other amendments that have been made to the Employment Act but it should be noted that it is still lacking in some aspects. One of the key areas in the Employment Act that still needs to be fully addressed are sexual harassment in the workplace and child labour. There are no provisions in the Employment Act that outlaw sexual harassment in the private sector, neither does it make provision for a procedure to deal with incidents that include such conduct. Sexual harassment refers to the forcing of an employee to have sex with a boss or supervisor because of fear of losing a job or otherwise being penalized at work. It can also refer simply to comments or jokes made about or to employees that have sexual connotations and with which he or she is not comfortable. This is unacceptable behaviour and some trusts, enterprises and organisations have already included rules against this in their contracts or Conditions of Service (International Labour Organisation, 2013).

Botswana has a code of conduct for the private sector but it is not well marketed and well distributed. Most people are not even aware it exists. The Code of Good Practice on Sexual Harassment in the Workplace was formulated under section 51 (1) of the Trade Dispute Act and it empowers the Minister of Employment, Labour Productivity and Skills development, in consultation with the Labour Advisory Board, to publish among other things, Codes of Good Practice that serve as guidance for employers, employees and their organisations. The Code is not contained within the Trade Disputes Act, but exists as a separate document kept by the Office of the Commissioner of Labour, which has the responsibility of ensuring its accessibility to employers.

It specifies that all companies should subscribe to codes of conduct regarding sexual harassment. This encourages employees to report unwanted, unsolicited and/ or repeated verbal or sexual advances, sexually derogatory statements or sexually discriminatory remarks made by a director, manager or employee of a business in respect of another employee whether inside or outside premises of the business, which are offensive or objectionable to the recipient or which cause the recipient discomfort or humiliation. The codes provide for timely investigation of such reports and severe penalties for repeated offenders (Botswana Confederation of Commerce Industry and Manpower, 2006).

This code of conduct as already stated is not well known and is certainly not enough to address the grievances of workers in the private sector and therefore Botswana has to include in its regulations, specifically in the Employment Act since it caters for the private sector, the labour laws that prohibits sexual harassment in the workplace in order to promote decent work which Botswana does not only subscribe to, but has, as at February 2011 together with its social partners concluded in the Decent

Work Country Programme (BDWCP). The government has been requested by the Committee of Experts on the Application of Conventions and Recommendations (CEACR) to take the necessary steps to include provisions on sexual harassment as part of the Employment Act but its incorporation and implementation in national law has been occurring at a staggering slow pace (Mogapaesi, 2014).

With regard to child labour, the available statistics indicate that child labour is still persistent in the country despite the fact that Botswana has ratified all key international conventions concerning child labour, including the ILO Convention No.182 on the Elimination of the Worst Forms of Child Labour (International Labour Organisation 2011). According to the Employment [Amendment] Act (sections 107-110), no child less than 15 years of age shall be employed in any capacity whatsoever. However, a child aged 14 years and not attending school may be employed on light work not harmful to his/her health or development. Those under 18 may not be employed in work underground, at night, in work that is harmful to health and development, or that is dangerous or immoral. The Ministry of Employment, Labour Productivity and Skills Development is responsible for enforcing these child labour laws.

The Labour Force Survey (2005/06) shows that child labour affects some 20% of all Botswana children (82,400), in particular in the geographically spread out rural areas (International Labour Organisation, 2011). In 2013, Botswana made a minimal advancement in efforts to eliminate the worst forms of child labour. The Government continued its Stay-in-School Program which focuses on training educators and social workers to explain the importance of education to student and parents and in the process help them to overcome issues preventing children from attending school. The Government also funds and participates in a working group with NGOs to develop a list of hazardous occupations that should be prohibited for children, and to develop other laws related to child labour. Children in Botswana however, continue to engage in child labour in cattle herding in rural areas and domestic service in urban areas. Key gaps remain in the country's legal framework against child labour, and enforcement of existing laws is insufficient (Bureau of International Labour Affairs, 2013).

For Botswana to comply with international labour standards, the Ministry of Employment, Labour Productivity and Skills Development should enforce the child labour law by making sure that those who are below the age of 15 do not participate in any paid economic activities or be employed in any capacity. Child labour can however continue to be recorded in the labour force survey for purposes of measurement of its magnitude and structure and related matters.

The Public Service Act

The Public Service Act has been amended several times and the most recent amendment was in 2008 and was launched on the 1st of May 2008 by the Directorate of Public Service management (Motshegwa & Tshukudu, 2012). This new Public Service Act is known as the Public Service Act No.30 of 2008. It was done for the explicit purpose of aligning the country's labour laws with the International Labour Organisation (ILO) standards. The Act now complies with the ILO Conventions on Freedom of Association and Protection of the Right to Organize Convention; the Right to Organize and Collective Bargaining Convention; and the Labour Relations Convention, which is a good step with regard to improving the terms and conditions of service for government employees. The Act consolidated the public service in Botswana from being fragmentally regulated by various pieces of statutes into one unified service. Previously, there were four pieces of legislation governing employment in the Public Service and these were the Public Service Act CAP 26:01, Unified Local Government Service Act, Teaching Service Act and Tribal Land Act Part II (a) to II (f) of the tribal Land Act (Mwatcha 2015).

The objective of the new Act was to provide for a single legislation governing employment of all employees of Government. The use of separate laws resulted in inconsistencies in the conditions of service and uncoordinated relationships between Government as an employer and some civil servants. However, even the new unified Act had its own problem. Many loopholes were identified in the new Act and within a short period during its implementation some amendments were made. One major problem of the Act is the fact that, in its implementation, some unions were excluded as their registration was questioned and derecognised and this caused a rift between government and unions (Motshegwa & Tshukudu, 2012). Other problems of the Act are related to the teaching staff in terms of their time. Teachers, for instance, argued that they should not work beyond 4:30 pm except if that is treated as overtime. And yet the job of a teacher is one that requires working hours that are flexible.

These problems arose mainly because it is difficult for the new Act to contain everything as we may wish, i.e., collective labour law and administrative labour law and therefore, it is in the best interest of the country that when implementing labour laws in Botswana the government should reflect on South African labour relations. In South Africa, two complementary pieces of legislation are used in line with meeting ILO standards. The Labour Relation Act 66 of 1996 (LRA) and the Basic Conditions of Employment Act 75 of 1997 (BCEA) are the key statutes that were introduced in South Africa to create a more cooperative labour relations system (Taylor 2008).

The new Public Service Act resulted in the formation of the Public Service Bargaining Council (PSBC), an independent body that is responsible for all negotiations between government and civil servants. The Public Service Bargaining Council has been going through difficult times due to lack of clarity on what is acceptable conduct and it also had been critiqued for not being inclusive, as it did not include other government unions that are affiliated to BFTU and not to BOFEPUSU. The government and unions should account for the selective implementation of Public Service Bargaining Council (PSBC) so that it can be in line with international standards since at the moment it is not functioning as it is supposed to be. Furthermore both workers and government have to work out guidelines to facilitate the smooth functioning of the bargaining council. Two fundamental rights that need to be respected are the requirement for good faith bargaining and the right to strike. Since the 2011 public sector strike there has been several attempts to curtail these rights from the government side which has led to the total collapse of the PSBC.

Trade Disputes Act (Cap 48:02)

The Trade Disputes Act outlines the trade disputes settlement mechanism at both individual and collective level. It is based on a tripartite labour law which involves the government, workers and employers, and it provides legal guidelines for the protection of both workers' and employers' rights and also provides a basis for negotiations and social dialogue (Muqtada, 2013).

The Act also establishes the Office of the Labour Commissioner, which heads and oversees the settlement of trade disputes by appointed mediators and arbitrators. Disputes are referred to the Commissioner for mediation or arbitration before being tried in a court of law. The Act also establishes the Industrial Court, which serves a specialist function of settling trade disputes and securing and maintaining good industrial relations in Botswana (Mogapaesi, 2014).

The Industrial Court was established by the Trade Disputes (Amendment) Act (1992) as an independent institution for resolving disputes that could not be settled by the government machinery. It replaced the office of the Permanent Arbitrator, previously established under Section 17 of the 1982 Trade Disputes Act. Judges of the Industrial Court are appointed in the same way as those of the High Court. The Commissioner of Labour may refer a dispute mediated under the Act to the Industrial Court for determination.

The Industrial Court is a specialized court that has exclusive jurisdiction to hear all trade disputes properly brought before it. The decisions of the Industrial Court are binding on the parties to the dispute and have the same effect as the decisions of the High Court of Botswana. Unlike the labour department, the Industrial Court does not have the power to entertain disputes of interest, such as wage disputes.

The current law uses the term industrial action to refer to lock outs, strikes or actions short of strikes. It does not, however, entrench the right to strike. That is, strike action, as a right accruing to employees is not embodied in any written law. It follows, therefore, that the position of the law remains unclear on what constitutes a lawful strike and/or the circumstances under which strike action will be lawful, particularly in non-essential services. As regards, the so-called essential services, the legislature has made a vague attempt at outlining the procedure that should be followed before employees in essential services engage in a strike (Friedrich Ebert Stiftung, 2008).

The lack of the same provisions with regard to non-essential services notwithstanding, the Industrial Court has held that the fact that the law is silent on the right to strike does not mean that such right is not recognized in Botswana. Furthermore a strike in non-essential services will be deemed to be lawful until it is declared otherwise in terms of the Trade Disputes Act. In both situations (essential and nonessential services), however, the strike should be in furtherance of a trade dispute as defined within the Act.

In 2011 public officers in Botswana embarked on an industrial action for the first time in the history of the country, lasting almost two months. On 17 June 2011, (seven days after the last day of the strike) the Minister of the then Labour and Home Affairs passed Statutory Instrument 49 amending the Trade Dispute Act and designating certain additional services as essential. The newly designated services were the veterinary services, teaching services, transport services, telecommunications services, diamond sorting, cutting and selling services and all support services in connection to these services.

This amendment was strongly opposed by the unions and opposition parties who saw it as government's encroachment into the rights of workers. Their efforts did not pay off as the recent amendment of the Trade Disputes Act has made teaching services, veterinary services, diamond sorting, cutting and selling services essential service. This mean that workers in essential services are exempt from taking part in the last resort measure of industrial action as their professions are deemed too important to go out of provision (Bagwasi, 2016). As for the ILO, it is indecisive in determining whether Botswana labour laws granting public servants the right to strike are in compliance with ILO standards that Botswana committed herself to (Cohen & Matee, 2014).

On issues of social dialogue in the country it has been established that even though Botswana has been a member of the ILO since 1978, it was only in 1997 that Botswana ratified the five Core Conventions on social dialogue and tripartism. It can be argued therefore, considering that only 15 years have passed, that Botswana still does not have a tradition of social dialogue and tripartism (Mogalakwe & Siphambe, 2013). Most trade unions and labour analysts contend that Botswana's current tripartite structures such as NEMIC and High Level Consultative Council (HLCC) are relatively weak because representation is skewed in favour of business and less favourable to labour.

On his address to parliament regarding NDP 11, the Minister of Employment, Labour Productivity and Skills Development, stated that Government will continue engaging social partners for harmonious and peaceful industrial relations to promote socio-economic growth and development in the country. To achieve this they intend to establish an independent dispute resolution structure, a National Tripartite Social Dialogue Structure and develop a National Employment Policy (Bagwasi, 2016). This will address the issue of current weak tripartite structures in the country. Perhaps, when implementing the aforementioned structures in Botswana, the government should reflect on the South African model used for tripartite consultative arrangements. South Africa uses a model known as the National Economic Development and Labour Council (NEDLAC) for its tripartite consultative arrangements. This model, even though, it has its weaknesses, has proven to be very successful. NEDLAC bring together government, organised business, and labour and community groupings at national level for a social dialogue to discuss and reach a consensus on issues of social and economic policy.

Trade Unions and Employers' Organizations Act

The Trade Unions and Employers' Organizations Act lays down the roles of the Registrar of Trade Unions and Employer organizations, the registration of Trade unions, federations of trade unions and employer organizations and all the procedures that are followed when registering these unions and organizations. It also spells out the rights and liabilities of trade unions, federations of trade unions and employer organizations. Furthermore, it covers membership, officers, employees and trustees and other issues like constitution and notification of other matters, finance, recognition of registered trade unions as negotiating bodies and others (Motshegwa & Tshukudu, 2012).

The Trade Unions and Employers' Organizations Act (Cap 48:01) came into force on 1st September, 1984 and was amended on 23rd April, 2004. One of the key 2004 amendments was to allow public servants to unionize for the first time, with the exception of the Botswana Defence Force, the Botswana Police Service, the Local Police and the Prisons Services. Before the amendment, public officers and persons employed by local authorities did not qualify to be members of and/or to join trade unions except where they belonged to the so-called industrial class (Friedrich Ebert Stiftung, 2003).

By allowing public servants to unionize for the first time, Botswana proved to be better than countries such as Lesotho whereby although the provision of the 1992 Code on Freedom of Association applies to workers and employers in all sectors, the Public Service Act of 2005 of Lesotho prohibits public service employees from becoming members of any union registered under the 1992 Code, classifying their work as essential service. Botswana has followed the likes of South Africa among other countries. But more need to be done to make sure these goes beyond just paper and become reality especially to the workers as a party that has not enjoyed collective bargaining and the right to strike for most of the post-colonial period.

Ratified ILO Conventions by Government of Botswana

Botswana as a member of the ILO has made a momentous progress toward the implementation of the international labour standards. There are 15 ILO conventions (including all the 8 core or fundamental conventions) which have been ratified by Botswana with the last ratification made in 2000 (Botswana Federation of Trade Unions, 2012). The ratified conventions are as follows:

- Fundamental Conventions: 8 out of 8
- Governance Conventions (Priority): 1 of 4
- Technical Conventions: 6 of 177

Botswana still has 174 unratified conventions and these include among others; Labour Inspection convention, Radiation Protection Convention,Occupational Safety and Health (OSH) Convention, and the Promotional Framework for Occupational Safety and Health Convention, Migration for Employment Convention and Equality of treatment (Social security) Convention (International Labour Organisation, 2013). But it's important to note that others are a work in progress such as the one for Occupational Health and Safety as it is scattered in a lot of Ministries and also practiced in the private sector.

With regard to the ratified conventions, there are gaps that have been identified particularly by ILO's Committee of Experts on the Application of Conventions and Recommendations (CEACR) in respect to the implementation and compliance of some of the ratified conventions. Botswana has over the years failed to adequately respond to the concerns and requests made by this Committee. This failure may be attributed to the capacity constraints within the Department of Labour and Social Security as well as the inability to monitor compliance by the social partners (Botswana Federation of Trade Unions, 2012).

Minimum Wage Legislation in Botswana

The issue of minimum wage is an issue at the heart of the labour movement in Botswana. The concerns are about the minimum wage itself and the effectiveness of the policing methods being deployed by government. It is important to have a minimum wage to minimize worker exploitation by employers. The minimum wage applies to specified industries in terms of the Employment Act, namely, building, construction, quarrying, garage or motor trade, road transport, hotel, catering or entertainment trade, manufacturing, service or repair, wholesale or retail distributive trade and watchmen industries (Friedrich Ebert Stiftung, 2008). The current minimum wage for most industries as of 2016 is P5.46 per hour.

In 2005, the new revised National Policy on Incomes, Employment, Prices and Profits which was approved in Parliament in April, 2007 introduced a statutory minimum wage for domestic workers and the agricultural sector which was not there in the initial Incomes Policy. It took effect on 1st April 2008 and the minimum wages agreed upon were as follows: P408 per month at P1.70 per hour for the agricultural sector and P508 a month at P2.10 per hour for the domestic worker. It is now around P620 per month for agricultural workers and P3.03 per hour for domestic service.

Minimum wages are currently set in relation to the cost of living, the poverty level, levels of productivity and unemployment levels. The major issues regarding minimum wages is the monitoring of compliance of the minimum wage regulations by employers given that the Department of Labour and Social Security does not have adequate staffing to do regular inspections. Self-enforcement can be provided through educating both the workers and employers to make sure that each party is aware of their right and privileges.

Relationship Between Employment Regulations and Employment Outcomes in Botswana

The employment regulations in Botswana have an impact on employment outcomes in Botswana. Firstly, the minimum wage in Botswana which is set between P620 and P1200 across occupations has had an impact on the supply of labour especially in the agricultural sector and domestic services. The minimum wage for the agricultural sector is P620 per month whereas for domestic services it is approximately P680.00. This is seen as too little as some of the government welfare programmes, in particular the labour based programme-*Ipelegeng* provides a remuneration of P540 for ordinary members and P620 for supervisors and better working conditions (currently individuals in *Ipelegeng* work from 0730-1245 and provided with breakfast). With the cost of living in urban areas estimated to be over P2000 per month (Friedrich Ebert Stiftung, 2008) many individuals opt for *Ipelegeng* which allows them to engage in informal sector in the afternoons to supplement their incomes. As such there is a shortage of supply in the labour market in occupations with a minimum wage considered to be too little. With stringent procedures in acquiring work permits for foreigners in occupations for unskilled labour (which is abundant in Botswana), most employers have resorted to acquiring services from illegal immigrants (mostly from Zimbabwe), who are willing to work at the set minimum wages. This has however led to exploitation of such workers, as they are not protected by any labour laws in Botswana. On the demand side, Siphambe (2003) has shown that the minimum wages in Botswana are set at a level low enough not to deter employment creation and retention of existing workers.

Secondly, the employment act leaves room for employer preferences towards men in terms of wages. Since, the hiring and promotion in the private sector allows for men and women to negotiate their wages, this leaves room for a discriminatory pay system. In fact, Kolobe, Bakwena, & Siphambe (2015) found that men earn significantly more than females in the privete sector. Most of the gender pay gap (86%) was attributed to discrimination, not differences in characteristics (experience, education etc). However, this is not the case in public sector, were the wage structure is fairly standardised, leaving little or no room for new workers to negotiate on pay.

Thirdly, most national labour laws, such as the Employment Act, endeavour not to discriminate against creed, race, sex or origin in Botswana. However, there have been cases of such discrimination against migrant workers especially those from the neighbouring Zimbabwe. The collapse of the political and economic governance in Zimbabwe has had some devastating impacts on labour migration to Botswana. This has become a common feature and poses challenges and it is believed that these migrant workers may add to the already high unemployment in Botswana. The negative public perception of labour migration does not only underline the feeling that migrants are taking jobs away from the local labour force but has ultimately a negative impact on overall working conditions. Given the absence of enforceable labour standards on wages, occupational safety and health, migrant domestic workers in Botswana are more likely to accept wages and work conditions which can be considered as exploitative (Solidar, 2010).

The relatively high unemployment rate in Botswana has had the effect of weakening the worker's bargaining power which has resulted in industrial strikes being few. The positive side has been an attractive environment for investment. Ironically foreign direct investment is not increasing at the required pace despite this positive industrial relations due to other factors such as the small market, high costs of doing business and poor work ethics of the workforce.

The employment regulations in Botswana are more on making it relatively difficult to fire workers. This reduces the flexibility of the labour market in terms of responding to the external shocks such as rising unemployment and poor work ethics. The protection on workers is also highly reinforced by a liberal social protection system that takes care of workers in cases where they lose their jobs. There is however lack of some of the usual active labour market protection laws such as unemployment benefit and reasonable insurance leaving most of the workers vulnerable. While the country has done very well in terms of economic growth, the growth has not been transferred into human wealth as a number of Batswana some of whom are unemployed and underemployed are missed out in the development process. These weaknesses are evident from the high income inequality with a current Gini coefficient of 0.61, being amongst the highest in the world. There is therefore need to transform the economy to increase employment opportunities and diversify the economic dependence on the capital intensive mining activities.

CONCLUSION

Botswana is committed to improved quality of work and this has been shown by its adoption of labour laws and regulations among other things. The country is mandated to promote rights at work; productive and decent employment opportunities; enhance social protection and strengthen social dialogue which is line with the Botswana Decent Work Programme that the country has subscribed to since 2011. Therefore, despite the inadequacies identified in our discussion above on labour laws, the government plays an important role in labour relations in the country. There have been a lot of amendments to labour laws and regulations to align them with international standards; however there are still some areas that need to be strengthened in order to sufficiently protect the rights of both workers and employers. Some suggestions to improve the legal framework for industrial relations were discussed in the chapter and therefore, in line with these suggestions, the following recommendations are made:

- Botswana has an unequal industrial relations space which is partly due to low union density, high unemployment rate and low job growth. The situation tends to make the workers the weaker part in any engagement with the employer and the state.
- Women are increasing their participation in the labour market despite them facing relatively higher unemployment rate and being segmented to certain jobs and occupations. There is need for some transformation to allow for more women empowerment. Except in the private sector, the relatively low average wages of women are more to do with differences in human capital investments than with discrimination. A major way of equalizing women labour market outcomes will require the economy to be diversified and more jobs created in the other sectors that have a potential to employ more women. Some of the

sectors that have the potential are tourism, textile, agro processing and other manufacturing not based on heavy metal and steel.

- The issue of child labour has to be addressed. There is need for the Government and social partners to eliminate the worst forms of child labour in Botswana.
- Sexual harassment in the workplace has not been adequately addressed in the law as it covers the public sector only. The problem with the legal framework in Botswana is that the Employment Act is silent on the issue of sexual harassment. There should be a law that regulates sexual harassment in the Employment Act as it caters for both public sector and private sector employees.
- It is imperative that Botswana strengthen social dialogue and tripartism between employers and trade unions. Botswana's industrial relations were for most period after independence unequal as there was absence of collective bargaining and low union density as the public service was by law not allowed to form and belong to unions. There is need to develop social dialogue towards collective bargaining and away from the traditional consultative system so as to enforce tripartism and social dialogue. This requires reorganising the current social dialogue structures to accommodate all stakeholders equitably. Botswana could benchmark on the National Economic Development and Labour Council (NEDLAC) used in South Africa for its tripartite consultative arrangements.
- Government and trade unions have to work out guidelines to facilitate the smooth functioning of the bargaining council. They should also ensure that all concerned parties in the bargaining council are fairly represented and not left out.
- There is need to cultivate a culture of collective bargaining especially in the public sector. This requires respect for two fundamental rights being bargaining in good faith from both parties and not curtailing the right to strike on the part of the workers. The current designation of certain cadre such as teachers to be classified as essential services is an attempt on part of the employer to limit the power of unions strength through the strike. To build trust among the parties and also allow for respect between parties there is need to remove these impediments.
- The country should come up with all the necessary measures to enforce minimum wage legislation in the country to address the issue of non-compliance by employers.
- The minimum wage should be set such that it does not discourage people from looking for employment and matches the living expenses.

REFERENCES

Bagwasi, T. (2016). *Gov't Changes Approach on Unions*. Retrieved, July 24, 2017, from http://www.weekendpost.co.bw/wp-news-details.php?nid=3184

Bank of Botswana. (2001). *Bank of Botswana Annual Report 2000*. Gaborone: Bank of Botswana.

Bank of Botswana. (2017). *Bank of Botswana Annual Report 2016*. Gaborone: Bank of Botswana.

Blackburn, D. (2006). The role, impact and future of labour law. *Labour Education, 2-3*, 143-144.

Botswana Confederation of Commerce Industry and Manpower. (2006). *A Code of Conduct for the Private Sector.* Retrieved July 24, 2017, from http://bb.org.bw/downloads/code_of_conduct-Final.pdf

Botswana Federation of Trade Unions. (2009). *State of Information Technology in the Botswana Federation of Trade Unions: Challenges, Opportunities and Needs.* Author.

Botswana Federation of Trade Unions. (2012). *A Country Report on Botswana Decent Work Country Programme*. Retrieved July 23, 2017, from http://actrav-courses.itcilo.org/en/a105067/country-reports/bftu-botswana/at_download/file

Bureau of International Labour Affairs. (2013). *2013 Findings on the Worst Forms of Child Labour*. Retrieved July 24, 2017, from https://www.dol.gov/ilab/reports/child-labor/findings/2013TDA/2013TDA.pdf

Central Statistics Office. (2008a). *2005/06 Labour Force Survey Dissemination Seminar Summary Report*. Author.

Central Statistics Office. (2008b). *2005/06 Labour Force Survey Report*. Author.

Cohen, T., & Matee, L. (2014). Public Servants' Right to Strike in Lesotho, Botswana and South Africa-A Comparative Study. *Potchefstroom Electronic Law Journal*, (17): 4.

Friedrich Ebert Stiftung. (2003). *Trade Unions in Botswana: Country Report*. Author.

Friedrich Ebert Stiftung. (2008). *Trade Unions in Botswana: Country Report*. Author.

International Labour Organisation. (2011). *Social Protection Floors for Social Justice and a Fair Globalisation*. Report ILC. 101/IV/1. ILO.

International Labour Organisation. (2013). *Social Protection Floors and Gender Equality: A brief overview*. ESS Working Paper no 37. ILO.

International Labour Organisation. (2014). *Database of national labour, social security and related human rights legislation*. Retrieved July, 24, 2017 from http://www.ilo.org/dyn/natlex/natlex4.detail?p_lang=en&p_isn=842

Kalula, E., Ordor, A. O., & Fenwick, C. (2008). *Labour Law reforms that Support Decent Work: The Case of southern Africa. Issue paper No 28. International Labour organization (ILO).*

Kolobe, M., Bakwena, M., & Siphambe, H. (2015). Analysis of Gender Wage Differentials: The Case of Botswana's Labour Market. *Asian-African Journal of Economics and Econometrics*, *15*(2), 127–146.

Luce, L. (2005). *The Case For International Labour Standards: A "Northern" Perspective.* IDS Working Paper 250. Institute of Development Studies.

Mogalakwe, M., & Siphambe, H.K. (2013). *Review of Social Dialogue Status and Relevant Policies in Botswana and Assessment of Effectiveness of Trade Union Engagement in Policy Dialogue: Final Draft*. International Labour Organization (ILO).

Mogapaesi, T. (n.d.). *Sexual Harassment in the Workplace: Lessons for Botswana from a South African Perspective* (Unpublished Master's Dissertation). North-West University, Potchefstroom Campus.

Motshegwa, B., & Tshukudu, T. T. (2012). Deep Rooted Conflicts and Industrial Relations Interface in Botswana. *Journal of Public Administration and Governance*, *2*(3), 118–133. doi:10.5296/jpag.v2i3.2349

Muqtada, M. (2013). *Botswana: A national Employment policy: Revised draft.* Academic Press.

Mwatcha, M. P. (n.d.). *Botswana Labour Relations System: Lessons from 2011 Public Sector Strike* (Unpublished Master's Thesis). University of Witwatersrand, Johannesburg, South Africa.

Republic of Botswana. (2013). *Mid-Term Review of NDP 10*. Gaborone: Government Printers.

Siphambe, H. K. (2003). Understanding Unemployment in Botswana. *The South African Journal of Economics*, *71*(3), 480–495. doi:10.1111/j.1813-6982.2003.tb00082.x

Solidar. (2010). *Domestic Workers' Rights- Botswana*. Retrieved July, 24, 2017 from http://www.solidar.all2all.org/IMG/pdf/b5_2010_domestic_workers_report_botswana.pdf

Statistics Botswana. (2013). *Botswana Core Welfare Indicators Survey 2009/10*. Gaborone: Statistics Botswana.

Statistics Botswana. (2016). *Selected Statistical Indicators 1966-2016*. Gaborone: Statistics Botswana.

Taylor, I. (2003). As Good as it gets? Botswana's Democratic Development. *Journal of Contemporary African Studies*, *21*(2), 215–231. doi:10.1080/02589000305446

KEY TERMS AND DEFINITIONS

BCWIS: Botswana core welfare indicators survey.

BFTU: Botswana federation of trade unions.

BOFEPUSU: Botswana federation of public sector unions.

CEACR: Committee of experts on the application of conventions and recommendations.

CSO: Central statistics office, now Statistics Botswana.

DWCP: Decent work country programme.

GDP: Gross domestic product.

HLCC: High level consultative council.

NDP: National development plan.

NEDLAC: National economic development and labour council.

NEMIC: National employment, manpower, and incomes policy council.

PSBC: Public service bargaining council.

ENDNOTES

1 Internationally the Labour force is defined as people aged 15-64 who were either working or looking for work.

2 Note that these would not necessarily tally with those presented in Table 2 given that the LFS data includes the informal sector and subsistence agriculture employees.

3 Parastatals include a wide range of enterprises owned at least 50% by the Government, either profit making or non-profit making.

4 These comprise of teachers, nurse, and others that are traditionally dominated by females.

Chapter 9
The Social Protection Agenda and the Burden of Responsibility and Sustainability:
A Review of the African Dilemma

Moses Adesola Adebisi
University of Ilorin, Nigeria

ABSTRACT

Social protection represents part of the global agenda of the International Labour Organization in its concerted attempt to improve and promote global labour standards, labour rights as human rights, and reduce poverty. The situation of African countries is precarious given the poor state of their economies, poor national incomes, and the widespread state of poverty. In addition, most African countries south of the Sahara have poor databases on vital statistics, security insecurity, mono-cultural economies, and the failure to effectively entrench governance and democratic institutions and reforms, amongst others. How could the problem of corruption, graft, theft of public funds, and the cumbersome bureaucratic bottlenecks that are so prevalent in Africa be minimized if not eliminated? The chapter, therefore, anchors its analysis on two African countries: Nigeria and Ghana. But how can social protection be funded in a sustainable way? These are the objectives that are being pursued in this chapter.

DOI: 10.4018/978-1-5225-4134-9.ch009

INTRODUCTION

Defining Social Protection

Social protection has generated intense debates and gained currency within governmental and non-governmental organizations and systems at local, regional and international levels and discourses. Increase in poverty, unemployment, discrimination, deprivation and social exclusion especially in developing countries provided the necessary impetus and motivation for the global attention that is being given to social protection. More importantly, political crises and ideological conflicts e.g. religious extremism have led to a number of failed states and increased vulnerability of the populace to the afore-mentioned problems. In many of these developing countries,the majority of the citizenry falls within the informal sector, hence are uncovered by social protection which "remained a privilege of public servants" (Rohregger, 2010). She states further: "Due to the dominance of the informal sector, which employs many of the people in developing countries, only a few private sector employees have so far been included in the state systems of social protection"(ibid.). This shows that the majority of the populace in these countries is highly vulnerable to the myriads of socioeconomic and political problems which bedevil their societies. Therefore, the urgency and necessity of social protection/ social security cannot be easily ignored given the vital roles it can play.

According to Rohregger (2010) social protection has social, economic and poverty-reducing functions and goals. Quoting BMZ (2009:8), Barbara Rohregger highlights the basic political function of social protection thus:

The political function of social protection systems is to ensure social equilibrium. Social protection systems strengthen social cohesion, enhance the legitimacy of the political system and can prevent social conflict to be successful in this, social protection systems must be designed and implemented so that they particularly benefit poor and disadvantaged groups. (Rohregger, ibid.)

Meanwhile, the failure of social protection systems and policies to capture the vast majority of the population in these developing countries has been attributed to a number of factors, ranging from "financial resources, policy design and implementation details and political economy factors" (Bastagli, 2013). The developing countries need to do more in its promotion and implementation of social protection systems and policies if they are to reduce poverty, promote equality, increase prosperity and above all bring happiness to the majority of the populace. A number of constraints are in the way of achieving these objectives especially when looking at it from global comparative perspectives in terms of developed versus developing countries' developmental parameters. Hence, the paper addresses the social protection issues here by employing international standards and practices, although with some caution given the basic social, cultural and political realities and differences across the regions, as the barometric media for gauging or assessing local and regional social protection practices and policies in the selected countries of Africa.

CONCEPTUAL FRAMEWORK

Although social protection narratives have been vocally presented in major development discourses, it remains relatively a new application in some geo-political zones of the world. Such applications or policies that target social welfare provisioning for the poor in terms of poverty reduction, empowerment, healthcare and the promotion of prosperity amongst the poor in the society are relatively new. Therefore, conceptualizing social protection shows some variations in the adjectival and semantical deployment of concepts in the delineation of the scope or coverage of social protection. Devereux and Sabates-Wheeler (2004) suggests that current definitions of social protection range from the narrow, which sees social protection in the garb of what they call old-style social welfare provided to the poor people such as widows, orphans and the disabled persons; to the broader approach that includes such things as education, health subsidies, job creation and microcredit programme for those that they consider to be poor but not necessarily of the lowest social strata; and to the more political or transformative definitions that extent the scope of their definitions to cover such areas as equity, empowerment, economic, social and cultural rights. From these definitional confusions or inadequacies, these authors rely on what they call agency definitions of social protection provided by various sources. These definitions may suffice for our purpose in the analysis being presented here. Norton, Conway and Foster (2000) in their *Working Paper*143 for Overseas Development Institute (ODI) defines social protection as ''public action taken in response to levels of vulnerability, risk and deprivation which are deemed socially unacceptable within a given polity or society''. Similarly, Devereux and Sabates-Wheeler (2004) quote the World Bank's (2004), definition of social protection ''...a collection of measures to improve or protect human capital, ranging from labor market interventions, publicly-mandated unemployment or old-age insurance to target income support. Social protection interventions assist individuals, households, and communities to better manage the income risks that leave people vulnerable''. Furthermore, these authors quote the International Labour Organization's (ILO by van Ginneken, ed., 1999) definition of social protection as ''the provision of benefits to households and individuals through public or collective arrangements to protect against low or declining living standards''. Finally, Devereux and Sabates-Wheeler presents Asian Development Bank's (ADB) Ortiz (2001) definition that says social protection is ''the set of policies and programs designed to reduce poverty and vulnerability by promoting efficient labour markets, diminishing people's exposure to risks, and enhancing their capacity to protect themselves against hazards and interruption/loss of income''. These definitions provided by these authors no doubt provide adequate analytical tools for the purpose of this chapter that seek to explore the state of social protection in the Sub-Saharan region and responsibility can be shared and sustainability can be achieved both in the short and the long run. Given the peculiar economic and political circumstances of these countries, to what extent can they orchestrate an enduring and sustainable social protection programme that can actually target and deal with poverty reduction? This calls for an international platform that provides the institutional and legal frameworks upon which methodical, sustainable and targeted social protection best practices programs can be based.

THE UNITED NATIONS: PROVIDING INSTITUTIONAL FRAMEWORK AND SUPPORT

The practice of social protection has been in place in many countries of the world for a very long time. Therefore, there is little conceptual ambiguity and debate in understanding what social protection is all about. From the perspective of the *United Nations*, social protection constitutes a human right issue. Cichon, et al (2011) observed that the *Universal Declaration of Human Rights* by the UN in 1949 established the legal and moral basis of social protection. These authors point at Article 22 of the *Declaration* and quote:

Everyone as a member of society, has the right to social security and is entitled to the realization, through national effort and international cooperation and in accordance with the organization and resources of each State, of the economic, social and cultural rights indispensable for his dignity and the free development of his personality.

Furthermore, these authors (ibid.) refer to Article 25 of the same Universal Declaration of Human Rights of 1949 quoting:

(1). Everyone has the right to a standard of living adequate for the health and well-being of himself and of his family, including food, clothing, housing and medical care and necessary social services, and the right to security in the event of unemployment, sickness, disability, widowhood, old age or other lack of livelihood in circumstances beyond his control. (2). Motherhood and childhood are entitled to

special care and assistance. All children, whether born in or out of wedlock, shall enjoy the same social protection.

The UN, in articles 22 and 25 of its 1949 Universal Declaration of Human Rights, unambiguously and unequivocally established the naturality and universality of social protection as human right that requires communal, governmental and international action and protection. Therefore, these articles bind member nations who are also signatories to this Universal Declaration of Human Rights to a moral obligation ensuring that their citizens are covered by social protection as a way of poverty alleviation.

The Food and Agricultural Organization (FAO), an organ of the United Nations, in its *Policy Brief* identified four types of social protection (cf: Greenblott, 2008): 1. ''Protective social assistance for the poor such as disability benefits and old age pensions. 2. Preventive measures to avert poverty such as food for work schemes, school feeding programs, as well as measures to safeguard health, including ART and prevention of mother-to-child transmission (PMTCT) programs 3. Promotional income enhancement through activities including life skills, vocational and agricultural training for youth, as well as increasing access to credit through microcredit opportunities. 4. Transformative addressing of social inequality and exclusion through awareness campaigns, stigma reduction campaigns, psychosocial support and therapy, and policies and laws to protect OVC, e.g. protection of inheritance rights'' (Greenbolt, 2008). These forms of social protection could provide the much needed safety nets for the poor and vulnerable children and other individuals in the society. Most of the sub-Saharan countries, many of whom have monocultural economies especially based on oil and other basic minerals exports are unable to puts such safety nets in place for the poor and vulnerable persons in their countries because of governance challenges due to inter-ethnic and inter-cultural conflicts, corruption, expensive political systems, nepotism, tribalism, and poor maintenance culture, amongst others. For instance, some of the countries like Nigeria that are dependent on the export of petroleum resources have been bedeviled by drastic drop in oil revenues as result of the free fall in the global oil prices in the recent years.

SOCIAL PROTECTION IN NIGERIA: POLICIES, PROGRAMS AND CHALLENGES

One of the very first steps at the social protection in the area of the educational rights of children in Nigeria was taken by the *Action Group* political party government of the Western Region of Nigeria, led by the late Chief Obafemi Awolowo in 1955. The introduction of universal free basic primary education and its implementation for about eleven years until it was abruptly abrogated by the 1966 military coup, gave the region the prime position as far as educational attainment and development in Nigeria is concerned. Millions of children in the Western Region had an unprecedented opportunity for education paid for by the government. Today, the region now referred to as *South-West* (comprising of six states: Lagos, Ogun, Oyo, Ogun, Ondo and Ekiti) is the educationally most advanced region in Nigeria. However, the overthrow of the civilian government by the military brought about its own challenges due to prolongation of military rule that lacked democratic decision-making processes. Between January 1966 and May 1999, there were seven military coups and counter-coups. During the period, little or no attention was paid to social protection matters as the rate of poverty, destitution, unemployment, crime, corruption and insecurity escalated. Meanwhile, the military rule in Nigeria which ostensibly purports to be corrective of civilian misrule especially corrupt practices such as electoral malpractices, ethnicity, nepotism, and tribalism, amongst others, ended up being worse than the civilian government.

Meanwhile, studies have shown that subsequent Nigerian government, civil or military, over the years merely paid lip service to the very important issues relating to social protection with dire consequences for socio-economic development, prosperity and social and national security. For instance, Nigeria made a lot of money from oil revenue between 1960 and today but, there is little to show for it in terms of development and welfare provisioning for the citizens especially the vulnerable: young and old. Revenue statistics suggest that Nigeria made over US$600 billion from oil sales since 1960 but much of it has been lost to theft or misappropriation by military rulers, politicians and bureaucratic officials of government. According to Obi Ezekwesili, Nigeria's former Finance Minister and also a former top notch at the IMF-World Bank Group, in a paper presented at the 52nd Annual General Conference of the Nigerian Bar Association, NBA, corruption is a major problem that bedevils the Nigerian oil industry. The paper states that:

1. Between 1960 and 2012, an estimated sum of US$400 billion of oil revenues that Nigeria earned was lost to theft or mismanagement by government leaders: military rulers, politicians and bureaucratic officials of government. This report is based on or corroborated by Television journalist's (Monjola Sotubo, 2015) report which quotes *IRN Security*, a global crude oil security watchdog as saying: "From the $600 billion in oil revenue that has flowed into the government's account since the country's independence in 1960, an estimated $400 billion has been diverted, misspent or stolen".
2. That 20% of annual capital expenditure ends up in private pockets;
3. That in addition to this, 1% of the population gets over 80% of the oil revenues;

4. Furthermore, Ezekwesili substantiated her claim with *Transparency International*'s report that "Global Financial Integrity estimates that between 1970 and 2008, Africa lost more than $850 billion *to illicit financial outflows*" (italics mine).
5. She concluded that to fight corruption in governance, the judiciary and civil society must "let character be their destiny".

In their study of social protection in Nigeria conducted on the auspices or sponsorship of *Overseas Development Institute* (ODI), Holmes, Akinrimisi, Morgan and Buck (2011), are agreed that in spite of the huge amount of revenues that had accrued from oil sales since 1960 there is little to show for it on the ground in terms of development or poverty reduction and so on. They state in this report that:

the strong economic growth that the country has experienced has not served to substantially reduce poverty, inequality or instability. The poverty has doubled in the past 20 years and, although rates have decreased in recent years, the Gini coefficient is high (43.8 as of 2005) and 54% of the population lives in poverty... approximately 75 million people.

The study further highlights the key points of their findings on the state of social protection in Nigeria as follows:

1. That social protection as a response to poverty is emerging in Nigeria and that it receives support mainly from government and development partners;
2. That programme remains extremely small-scale in the context of high numbers of poor people;
3. That building institutional knowledge and capacity will be important to generate political and financial support to scale up existing program.
   (Source: Holmes et al, *Project Briefing* No 59, 2011).

In 2004, the People's Democratic Party-led Federal Government introduced a number of reforms in the labour and health sectors to cushion the effect of economic hardships and reduce poverty within the population now estimated at about 180 million people. The Labour Law Act 2004 and its amendments were rejected by workers because it was designed to weaken trade unions by making membership of trade unions and payment of 2% check-off dues voluntary. However, the regime of Olusegun Obasanjo (1999-2007) witnessed an era of improved welfare packages for civil servants as a result of wage increases. The period also witnessed the establishment of the National Health Insurance Scheme (NHIS) that requires workers to pay only 10% of medical treatments at both public and private hospitals. This covers the cost of treatment for couples who are employees and four of their children under the age of eighteen. However, as pointed out earlier by Holmes et al (2011), these measures are emergent in Nigeria. The coverage is still very insignificant giving Nigeria's high population of around 180 million people.

On the 29th of May 2006, the Federal Government of Nigeria (FGN) under the leadership of President Mohammadu Buhari inaugurated an audacious N500b social protection programme aimed principally at addressing the social and economic challenges faced by the underprivileged and vulnerable persons in Nigeria. This effort according to *The News (*May 29, 2016*)* was major address of Buhari's Democracy Day broadcast to the Nigerian nation. Excerpts from the broadcast as quoted by the news magazine reads as follows:

I am happy to formally launch, by far the most ambitious social protection program in our history. A programme that both seek to start the process of lifting many from poverty, while at the same time creating the opportunity for people to fend for themselves. In this regard, N500 billion has been approved in the 2016 budget for social intervention program in five key areas.

The news magazine lists these five key areas as:

1. **Job Creation:** This is intended to provide job opportunities for 500,000 teachers and 100,000 artisans throughout the country.
2. **School Feeding Program:** Under this scheme, about 5.5 million children are to benefit from nutritious meals through the school feeding program intended to achieve three basic objectives: improve learning outcomes, school enrolment as well completion rates.
3. **Conditional Cash Transfer Scheme:** This scheme is designed to provide financial support of up to a million naira to those described as vulnerable beneficiaries as a way of complementing government's enterprise programme which aims to benefit about 1,000,000 million market women, 400,000 artisans and also about 200,000 farmers across the country.
4. **The Education Grant Scheme:** Under this scheme, the federal government intends to provide financial grants to students studying science courses such as technology, engineering, and mathematics.
5. Lay a solid foundation for human capital development for the future generation.

However, more than one year after the launch of the social protection programme, little has been achieved especially in the areas of meeting the set objectives. For instance, out of the 500,000 teachers to be recruited, only about 300,000 have been engaged as at 2016, while the remaining 200,000 plus the 100,000 artisans slated for engagement remain outstanding. As at today (2017), more than 2,000,000 applicants had applied for the remaining vacancies to be filled. The snail speed of government business and the shortfall in oil revenues might be the cause of the delay in further engagement of applicants. This social protection programme, aimed at reducing poverty, create employment opportunities and reduce social and economic inequalities, is still in its infancy and on-going. Also, the Buhari Administration is in its third year and therefore it might too early to undertake a fair and objective assessment of its impact or effectiveness.

However, statistics have shown that Nigeria has one of the poorest expenditure on social protection as a percentage of its Gross Domestic Product, GDP. According to Hagen-Zander and Holmes (2012), Nigeria's expenditure in annual budgetary terms is less than 1% (approximately about 0.25%) of its GDP, which is less than those of Ethiopia, Malawi and Kenya, in a descending order from the top. Nigeria recently came of economic recession in a marginal proportion due to the collapse of oil prizes from which it derives about 95% of it national revenue. It runs a federal system of government that is more unitary in nature because it controls the lion share of the national revenues and other national institutions. Meanwhile, the problem with Nigeria in terms of putting in place an enduring, sustainable and efficient social protection system has nothing to do with human and material resources because it has one of the best developed human capital resources, a large pool of professionals and highly advanced economic and market structures on the African continent. Widespread bureaucratic corruption has left it with derelict infrastructure and near-bankrupt economy (Adebisi, 2015).

SOCIAL PROTECTION IN GHANA: HISTORICAL ORIGIN, PRACTICE, AND CHALLENGES

The history of social protection in Ghana dates back to 1965 with the enactment of the Social Security Act of 1965 (Abebrese, 2015). According to the author, social protection legislation and programme began in Ghana with the enactment of the Social Security Act of 1965. This was followed in chronological order by, Social Security Law of 1991, Ghana Growth and Poverty Reduction Strategy (GPRS I) of 2002-2005, National Health Insurance Scheme (NHIS) of 2003, Ghana School Feeding Programme (GSFP) of 2005, Ghana Growth and Poverty Reduction Strategy (GPRS II) of 2006-2009 and National Social Protection Strategy (NSPS) of 2007.

Like Nigeria, Ghana made huge income from cocoa and gold exports between the 60's and the 70's but the collapse of the Ghanaian economy led to the mass exodus of many Ghanaian workers, especially highly-skilled professionals who left the country in search of greener pastures in other countries. Ghana had had its own measure of military rule that literally plundered its economy before the coming of Flight Lieutenant John Jerry Rawlings in the early 1980s to sanitize the political system of the country. Rawlings' exemplary leadership and strict punishment for graft and corruption coupled with externally-induced economic reforms by the IMF-World Bank Group brought some sanity to the system. The question now however, is that what happens to the governance of the economy and the political system after the departure of Jerry Rawlings? This is the question of sustainability. Who finances the economic reforms continuously when external sources of funds end on the basis of negotiable agreements and conditionalities? This is the sustainability question that faces most developing countries as far as social protection matters are concerned. Ghana's Gross Domestic Product (GDP) stands at GHC44, 608.1 million, an increase over the 2015 record of GHC37, 351.3 million (*Ghana Statistical Services).* The economy relies on IMF regulation and loans with stringent conditionalities that makes it difficult for Ghana to meet its social protection obligations to its citizens as required. Both the Ghanaian and Nigerian governments at different times have introduced the school feeding programme that provide a meal per pupil per day at the primary school level, but the scale is limited and the extent to which the programme can be sustained remains a question of time or a matter of conjecture. This feeding programme is no doubt a key index of social protection floor which to some extent addresses an aspect of the needed support for the basic human rights of the poor. According to Honourable Nana Oye Lithur, Ghana's Minister for Gender, Children and Social Protection, before the social protection programme in Ghana were not well coordinated, poorly finance and limited in impact. He claims that they are better organized having refined the old system that saw a move towards a more integrated social protection system. Lithur (2013) lists the following as the *main components* of Ghana's National Social Protection Strategy (NSPS):

- Livelihood Empowerment Against Poverty (LEAP) cash transfer program (flagship) implemented under Ministry of Gender, Children and Social Protection.
- Labour Intensive Public Works implemented under the Ministry of Local Government and Rural Development.
- The Exempt Category under the National Health Insurance Scheme implemented under Ministry of Health.
- Pro-Poor interventions for poor peasant farmers including Block Farming under the Ministry of Food and Agriculture

INTERVENTION COMPONENTS OF THE NATIONAL SOCIAL PROTECTION STRATEGY (NSPS)

- Free school uniforms and exercise books implemented under ministry of Education
- School feeding programme under Ministry of Local Government
- Education Capitation Grant under Ministry of Education.
- Local Enterprise and Skills Development Programme (LESDEP)
- National Youth Employment Programme/Ghana Youth Employment and Enterprise Development Programme.

Furthermore, Lithur (2013) states that some of the achievements of the school feeding programme component of Ghana's social protection include increases in the number of school pupils fed per day and school enrollment, attendance and retention rate. For instance, he claims that more than 1.6 million hungry pupils were fed with nutritious meal per school day; also that school enrollment, attendance and retention have been recorded at about 80%, while about 38, 751 farmers are benefiting from the school feeding programme through the cultivation of 30, 973.8 hectares of farmland. There is no doubt some challenges for Ghana's social protection given the huge financial requirements. Ofori-Ado (assessed July 07, 2015) identifies the Government of Ghana as the major source of funding for it social protection programme with some support from its Development Partners such as foreign governments and other donor agencies. Statutory payments such as taxations form the main source of funding for the National Health Insurance Scheme (NHIS) and Schools Capitation Grants, while funding for the School Feeding Programme and The LEAP Programme comes mainly from the donor agency sources, such as World Bank Loan, UNICEF and DFID. For instance, the LEAP budget funding arrangements for 2013 was GHc 44,000,000.00 ($22,000,000.00), with the World Bank and DFID contributing about 50% in the sum of $5,000,000.00 and $6,000,000.00 respectively (source: Ofori-Ado, ibid.). Finally, Ofori-Ado identifies four basic challenges facing social protection in Ghana today as:

1. Fragmented and uncoordinated social protection interventions;
2. Limited GoG (Government of Ghana) budget allocations and frequent delays in release of funds;
3. Weak targeting and M&E methods used by most SP programmers;
4. Limited and unclear roles of CSOs in monitoring.

GENERAL OVERVIEW: CHALLENGES AND PROSPECTS OF SOCIAL PROTECTION IN AFRICA

The greatest challenges facing many African countries today revolve around the problem of poor management of the economy, political instability and the urgency of institutionalizing democratic norms and structures, corruption, a weak judiciary, dwindling revenue sources amongst others. The genesis of some of these problems can be linked to the colonial and neo-colonial experience of economic pillage and disarticulation of the domestic modes of production of the African societies. European conquest and domination of Africa, dating back to around 1444 when the Portuguese landed on the west coast of Africa and established the first European contact with Kingdom of Benin. The granting of independence at the end of the colonial rule by the European powers left the African societies, their economic and political structures and institutions helplessly dependent on the former. Therefore, the priorities of the colonial masters were political control and economic exploitation of the vast and highly needed natural resources of Africa. Nearly sixty years after independence, countries like Nigeria, Ghana and Kenya to mention but a few are still heavily dependent on their former colonial masters or the western nations generally for technology, economic aids and grants for social welfare budgeting and programme implementation. The Nigerian economy recently came out of recession due to large scale mismanagement and the collapse of the oil prices that saw revenues from oil plummeting to some of the lowest levels in about forty years. The consequences of these are for the poor to take the hit of poverty, diseases and collapsed infrastructure to the extent that in 2006, 28 out of 36 states that make up the Nigerian federal system were unable to pay their workers' salaries, with some of them owning up to eleven months in arrears.

SOCIAL PROTECTION IN AFRICA AND THE SUSTAINABILITY QUESTION

The future of social protection in Africa is cloudy given the myriads of problems that constrained it over the years. In most African countries, financial responsibilities have been born mainly by the poorly funded governments with some support from donor agencies, such The World Bank and DFID. Similarly, many of these governments pay lip service to address the problem of the poor such as poverty reduction, employment creation, education for the poor and disadvantaged children, micro credit for poor farmers, diseases and so on. In countries like Nigeria, budgetary allocation to social protection is less than 1% in 2006/2007 (Hagen-Zander and Holmes, 2012). Many African countries are reliant on commodities exports that are prone to unstable market forces. Both Nigeria and Ghana face similar economic situations. While Nigeria depends largely on petroleum exports, Ghana relies on cocoa, gold and in recent times some petrol dollar revenue. Nigeria currently faces the challenges of power generation and supply with an average daily generation of fewer than 4,000 megawatts, in a population of about 180 million people. The manufacturing sector has virtually collapsed because of high running costs in the absence of regular supply.

Therefore, sustaining social protection requires some drastic and concerted efforts that will energize the domestic economy and transforms it from an import-dependent economy to an export-oriented one. This will reverse the direction of foreign exchange flow. The Domestic economic boom could provide adequate financial resources for funding social provisioning/social protection programme that target such things as poverty reduction amongst others.

A number of steps have been taken in Nigeria to deal with the problem of corruption in public office. These are:

1. **The Economic and Financial Crime Commission, EFCC:** One of the steps that have been taken since the inception of the Buhari administration is the renewed fight against graft or corrupt practices. Nigeria's anti-corruption watchdog, The Economic and Financial Crime Commission (EFCC) has prosecuted many high profile political figures, military generals, government contractors and top civil servants.
2. **Extradition Treaties:** The administration has signed some extradition treaties with some countries considered to be safe havens for money launderers and criminals. The treaty Nigeria signed with the Government of the United Arab Emirates (UAE) is very important for its war against corruption.
3. **Bank Verification Number (BVN):** The introduction of Bank Verification Number (BVN) by the Central Bank of Nigeria, CBN. The BVN code number is compulsory for all bank account holders in Nigeria. This enables the apex bank to easily trace every financial transaction by all linked accounts and any illicit transfer of funds can be traced in real time.
4. **Treasury Single Account (TSA):** Against previous practices where government Ministries, Departments and Agencies (MDAs) operate several accounts through which public funds are easily siphoned or laundered, the new TSA policy now in force restricts all government taxes, monies and all other payments to be lodged in a single account in the public treasury. The TSA now makes it easy for the government to monitor the expenditure patterns of the MDA's, thereby curtailing corruption and other illicit financial transactions by government functionaries.

CONCLUSION

The central concern of this chapter has been the state of social protection in Africa with particular emphasis on two African countries: Nigeria and Ghana. Crucial to the discussion here is the dilemma faced by the African countries with respect to how the burden of financial responsibilities are shared or can be shared in the future and what these countries can do to sustain social protection program in the long run. The problem of the economic downturn, mismanagement of the economy and dependence on commodity export constitute some of the greatest challenges that affect social protection program in Africa. These African countries could do better in the future in their social protection practices and program if some of the steps taken by Nigeria as highlighted above can be employed in order to reduce graft and economic mismanagement against the backdrop of global best practices and improvement in governance and accountability.

REFERENCES

Abebrese, J. (2015). *Social Protection in Ghana: An overview of existing programmes and their prospects and challenges*. Fredrich Ebert Stiftung. Retrieved from http//:library.fes.de/pdf-files/bueros/Ghana/10497.pdf

Adebisi, M. A. (2015). The Political Economy of Oil Price Deregulation and the Subsidy Fraud Crisis: A Study of Systematic Bureaucratic Corruption in Nigeria. *Journal of Energy, Technology and Policy*, *5*(9), 2015.

Avato, J., Koettl, J., & Sabates-Wheeler, R. (2009). *Definitions, Good Practices, and Global Estimates on the Status of Social Protection for International Migrants*. Social Protection and Labor: The World Bank; SP Discussion Paper no. 0909. Retrieved from http//:library.fes.de/pdf-files/bueros/Ghana/10497.pdf

Bastagli, F. (2013). *Feasibility of Social Protection Schemes in Developing Countries*. European Parliament: Director-General for External Policies of the Union. EXPO/B/DEVE/FWC/2009-01/Lot5/34, February.

Boon, E. K. (2007). Knowledge Systems and Social Security in Africa: A Case Study of Ghana. *Tribes and Tribals*, *1*(Special), 63–76.

Cichon, M., Behrendt, C., & Wodsak, V. (2011). *The UN Social Protection Floor Initiative: Moving Forward with the Extension of Social Security*. Retrieved from library.fes.de/pdf/ipg-files/2011-2/05_a_cichon.pdf

Devereux, S., & Cipryk, R. (2009). *Social Protection in Sub-Saharan Africa: A Regional Review.* Centre for Social Protection Institute of Development Studies. Retrieved from https://www.ids.ac.mc/files/dmfile/SocialProtectioninSubSaharanAfrica.pdf

Devereux, S., & Sabates-Wheeler, R. (2004). *Transformative Social Protection.* IDS Working Paper 232. Institute of Development Studies, University of Sussex, UK. Retrieved from www2.unicef,org/socialpolicy/files/Transformative_Social_Protection.pdf

Ezekwesili, O. (2012). *Corruption, National Development, The Bar and The Judiciary*. Paper presented at the 52nd Annual General Conference of the Nigerian Bar Association.

Garcia, A. B., & Gruat, J. V. (2003). *Social Protection/Social Justice-A life Cycle of Continuum Investment*. Retrieved from http://www.ilo.org/public/english/protection/download/lifecycle/lifecycle.pdf

Greenblot, K. (2008). *Four Types of Social Protection. Protecting Africa's Future: Livelihood-based social protection for orphans and vulnerable children (OVC) in east and southern Africa.* Food and Agriculture Organization of the United Nation (FAO). Regional Emergency Office for Southern *Africa.*

Hagen-Zander, J., & Holmes, R. (2012). *Social Protection in Nigeria.* Overseas Development Institute (ODI).

Holmes, R., Akinrimisi, B., Morgan, J., & Buck, R. (2011). *Social Protection in Nigeria: an overview of programmes and their effectiveness*. Overseas Development Institute (ODI); Project Briefing No 59, September.

Lithur, N. O. (2013). *Social Protection in Ghana: History, Challenges and Opportunities. Honourable Nana Oye Lithur. Paper presented at the Minister for Gender*, Children, and Social Protection.

Norton, A., Conway, T., & Foster, M. (2000). *Social protection concepts and approaches: implications for policy and practice in international development.* Working Paper 143, London Centre for Aid Public Expenditure, Overseas Development Institute (ODI).

Ofori-Ado, L. (n.d.). *Social Protection Landscape in Ghana*. Retrieved from www.interreseaux.org/IMG/pdf/presentation_SOCIAL_PROTECTION_LANDSCAPE_IN_GHANA.pdf

Omilola, B., & Kaniki, S. (2014). *Social Protection in Africa: A Review of Potential Contribution and Impact on Poverty Reduction*. Study Report, UNDP. Retrieved from www.za.undp.org/content/dam/south_africa/docs/mdgs/SocialProtectioninAfrica-A Review of Potential Contribution.pdf

Rohregger, B. (2010). Social Protection and Governance. Discussion Papers on Social Protection. Deutsche Gesellschaft fur Technische Zusammenarbeit (GTZ) GmBH German Technical Cooperation.

Sotubo, J. (2015). *$400bn oil money stolen since independence-UK firm*. Retrieved from www.pulse.ng/news/business/in-nigeria-400bn-oil-money-stolen-since-independence-uk-firm-id3745342.html

The News. (2016). *Buhari formally launches N500b Social Protection Programme*. Retrieved from http://thenewsnigeria.com/2016/05/buhari-formally-lauanches-n500b-social-protection- programme/

van Ginneken, W. (Ed.). (1999). Social Security for the Excluded Majority. Case Studies of Developing Countries. Geneva: International Labour Office (ILO).

World Bank. (2004). Retrieved from http://wbln0018.worldbanl.org/HDNet/hddocs.nsf/c207c7f854bd0a098525660b007a272d/fb93d792069e704e8525681900d7bc?OpenDocument

KEY TERMS AND DEFINITIONS

Bank Verification Number (BVN): This is a bank code that is attached to every bank account in Nigeria. This helps to trace every financial transaction from one account to the other, locally or internationally. It is designed to help curb financial fraud in the public service and also curb illicit financial transactions by criminals.

Corruption: This is a process of circumventing due process thereby taking undue advantages of public resources such as position, money or outright stealing of public resources as a result of one's position, power, or influence.

Development Partners: These are foreign governments, institutions such as banks, non-governmental organizations, that provide financial or technical support for poor countries in the development processes.

Economic and Financial Crime Commission (EFCC): The EFCC is Nigerian government agency established to fight graft and other corrupt practices especially within the public service.

Empowerment: This is the process of enhancing the social and economic standing of an individual in the society. This can be done through social protection policies and program such as providing employment opportunities, financial and education supports, amongst others.

Extradition Treaties: These are international agreements entered into by foreign government as means of curbing crimes and preventing criminals from using those countries that are signatories to these treaties as safe havens for stolen monies or foe evading justice.

Health Insurance: This is policy scheme that reduces the financial burden or responsibility of the citizen of a country especially workers and the poor.

Poverty: This is a condition of relative deprivation, especially economic deprivation, when people suffer from want of basic necessity of life: food, shelter, clothing, and housing.

Treasury Single Account (TSA): This is corruption fighting method that requires all public ministries, departments, and agencies, MDAs, in Nigeria to bank their allocations with a single account created by the federal government. The TSA is domiciled in the Central Bank of Nigeria.

Chapter 10
Employment Protection Legislation in Haiti:
An Overview

Samir Amine
Université du Québec en Outaouais, Canada

Wilner Predelus
Université du Québec en Ouatouais, Canada

ABSTRACT

The merit of employment regulations in a market economy is often measured by their effectiveness in facilitating job creation without jeopardizing the notion of "decent work," as defined by the International Labor Organization (ILO). Consequently, the recent literature on employment legislation has extensively focused on the flexibility of the labor market, as a fair middle ground is always necessary to avoid undue distortions that can negatively impact the economy and worker's wellbeing. This chapter analyzes the provisions of the labor law in Haiti and how it affects job security and flexibility to observe a flexible structure that rather benefits employers. Notably, labor law in Haiti may have in fact rendered workers more vulnerable because these labor legislations were enacted on the assumption that employers and workers are on the same footing when it comes to industrial relations, while historic facts do not support such an assumption.

DOI: 10.4018/978-1-5225-4134-9.ch010

INTRODUCTION

According to the World Bank, Employment Protection Legislation (EPL) is designed to "*create conditions that are more conducive to job creation, protecting employment and improving working conditions*" (World Bank, 2007a). However, in emerging and developing economies, EPL requirements often remain merely statements of desirable goals as their enforcement is generally challenged by rampant corruption and a lack of manpower (see, for example, Dollar et al., 2002; Li, 2008 and D'Souza, 2010). In Haiti, there are additional challenges in transforming EPL into a useful socioeconomic tool as the labor legislations are, by any standard, far too complicated for its relatively inchoate economic system. Labor relations in Haiti are governed by the general provisions in the *Haitian Civil Code (Code civil Haïtien)*, as well as the special provisions enshrined in the *Haitian Labor Code* (HLC) *(Code du travail Haïtien) such as those relating to* labor standards and unionization. Framed to protect and regulate wage-earning industrial and agricultural workers, many of the provisions of the HLC are modeled on the 22 ILO conventions on labor standard ratified by Haiti. This Labor Code, which was inspired by international standard, has given rise to a very sophisticated administrative structure designed for its enforcement, and is enacted on the assumption that employers and workers are on the same footing in industrial relations. Although in theory the provisions of the Code cover every aspect of the notion of decent work, as promoted by the ILO, they are by no means the result of a long empirical evolution of the Haitian labor law. This paper analyzes the provisions of the Haitian labor law in relation to job security, that is, those governing the hiring and firing of workers and their treatment on the job, so as to understand the role of EPL in the Haitian labor market.

The rest of the paper is organized as follows: Section 2 provides a brief overview of the current economic and legal context of Haiti; Section 3 analyzes the provisions for the hiring and firing of workers; Section 4 looks at the treatment of workers on the job; and Section 5 concludes.

ECONOMIC AND LEGAL CONTEXT

For the past decades, the Haitian economy has been in a tailspin. As domestic political unrests raged and per capita income stagnated, unemployment rates have skyrocketed and the general social welfare has significantly deteriorated. For example, the unemployment increased sharply from7.2% in 1998 to reach a historic high of 16.8% in 2007, before gradually decreasing to 13.2% in 2016, a level that is almost twice that of 1999 (see Figure 1 below: Solid line). As for the GDP per Capita, it started plummeting from 2000 to reach a trough of USD 1,502 in 2010 before it

Figure 1. Unemployment rates in Haiti; GDP per capita, PPP 2011 Constant US Dollars 2000-2016

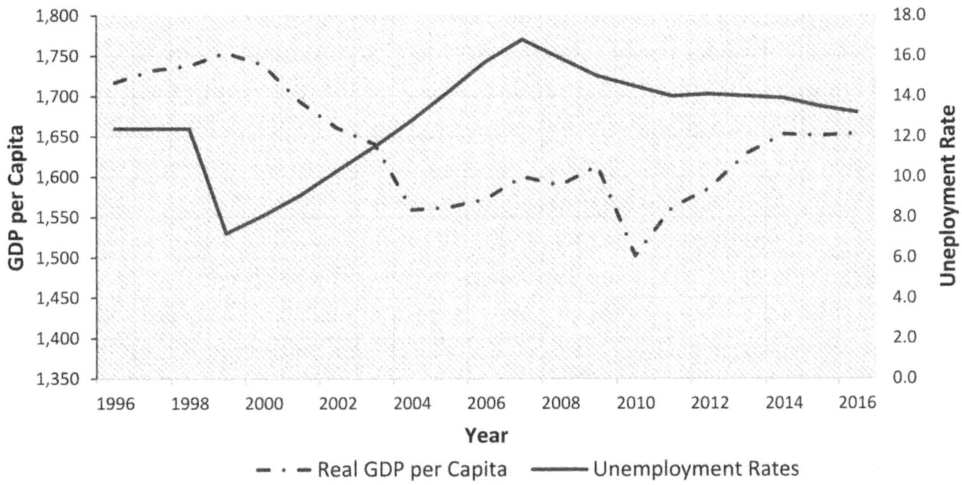

Source: International Labour Organisation, ILOSTAT Database / World Bank national accounts

rebounded. However, as of 2016, it remained well below its 1999 level (see Figure 1 below: Dash dot line). In fact, the steep fall observed in the tourism sector at the beginning of the 1980s, followed by a drop in the agricultural production, marked a new era in the economic perspective of Haiti as economic players started to turn to the apparel sector in search of new economic opportunities. *The Haiti Hemispheric Opportunity for Partnership Encouragement* (HOPE) *Act* enacted in 2006 by the Congress of the United States has expanded the preferences established under the *Caribbean Basin Economic Recovery* (CBER) *Act* for Haitian apparel, thus fuelling the hope of a renaissance of the labor market. As of 2013, the apparel sector has expanded considerably, creating no less than 65.8% of the total employment in the formal economy in 2013 (IMF, 2015).

At the same time, Better Work (2014) observes that the Haitian apparel sector attracts an overwhelming percentage of women, who were employed in up to 65% of the jobs created in 2013. The expansion of the apparel sector largely accounted for the increase in the participation of women in the labor force, as women have progressively increased their total participation rate (see Figure 2 below: Long dash line) over the recent years to narrow the gap with that of men (see Figure 2 below: Solid line)[1]. Yet, the apparel sector still has a long way to go to challenge poverty and unemployment as Haiti's value added in this sector, which hired only 41,000 workers in 2015, is only 3 percent (IMF, 2015). Although Hornbeck (2010) observes that the mix is slowly shifting toward the production of more complicated woven goods, the preferences that Haiti has enjoyed under HOPE and HELP (Haiti

Economic Lift Program) have not been exploited fully to justify the hope vested in the apparel sector, which contributes to as much as more than 90% of the total exports of the country (US International Trade Administration), and 10% to Haiti's Gross Domestic Product (GDP) (Better Work 2016). It remains to investigate how the legal environment makes contribution, if any, to this new economic reality.

Although HLC aimed at protecting and regulating industrial and agricultural wage earners, only a very small percentage of Haitian workers have directly benefited from its provisions because the working population in Haiti comprises mostly self-employed small retailers and farmers rather than wage-earning workers. Moreover, HLC has never been updated since its enactment in 1984 to take into consideration the new trends in the labor market, nor has it been amended to update some pecuniary provisions, which can negatively impact labor relations and undermine the enforcement of HLC. A prime example being the effects of the high inflation rates experienced by Haiti over the last few decades. Official statistics released by the International Labor Office revealed that, between 1984, the year in which HLC came into force, and 2016, the price level had increased by more than 5,000 percent[2], a staggering rate that is yet generally believed to be an underestimate[3]. Despite the high inflation rate, monetary fines imposed by HLC for non-compliance have never been reviewed. For instance, several sections of HLC, specifically Sections 133; 158; 222; 223; 229; 251; 253 etc. impose non-compliance fines varying from HTG 1,000 to HTG 5,000; which are equivalent today to approximately HTG 75,000 and HTG 200,000 after the adjustment for inflation. Therefore, applying the fines as stipulated in HLC at their nominal values today can be likened to hitting the offending individual or

Figure 2. Labor force participation rate in Haiti 1996-2016

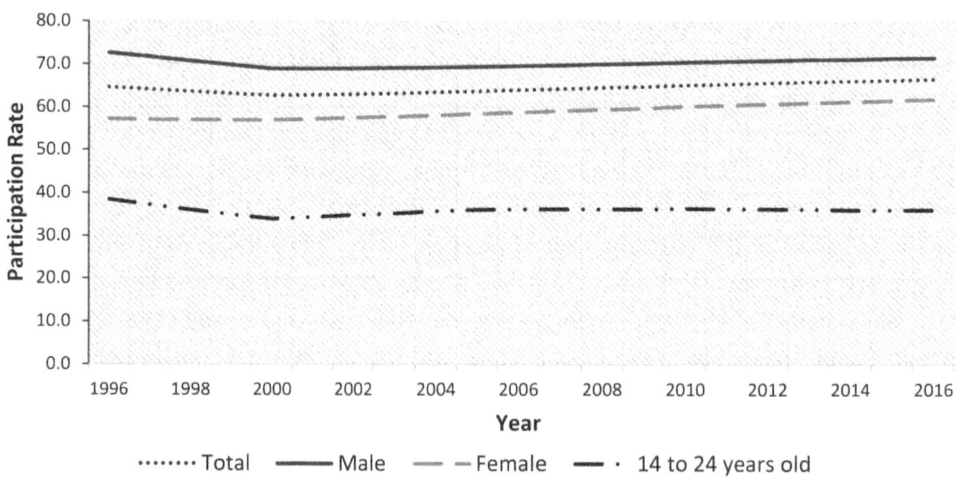

Source: International Labor Organization, ILOSTAT Database

entity with a wet noodle on the wrist, for the fines are far from being stiff enough to deter non-compliance of the HLC.

Besides being outdated, the HLC continued to face enforcement issues more than three decades after it has come into force, as much of the administrative structure for its enforcement is either deficient or squarely missing. For instance, Chapter IV of the HLC proposes for hiring labor inspectors with the authority to enforce the laws and regulations regarding labor conditions, health and safety standards, worker protection, etc. as stipulated under HLC. However, the existence of the administrative structure required for the enforcement of such labour laws is confined to the capital Port-au-Prince, thus severely limiting the geographical extent to which the laws can be effectively applied. For example, should a need for a labor dispute to be heard by the Special Tribunal of Labor (*Tribunal spécial du travail (SST))* arise in any part of the country, the parties involved would need to travel to Port-au-Prince for the case to be heard. The lack of legal infrastructure, coupled with a high illiteracy rate and a persistently elevated unemployment rate, poses a formidable challenge for the implementation of EPL in Haiti. As a former general and president of Haiti once commented: "constitution is written on paper and bayonet is made of iron", venting the precarious state of the rule of law. Haiti has yet a long way to go to turn the ideals embodied in the HLC into the reality as envisaged by the thoughtful framers who pieced the HLC together in the first place.

HIRING WORKERS UNDER HLC

In line with most other capitalist economies, HLC is designed to provide a clear path to mediate potential industrial conflicts between workers and employers. It provides a set of mechanisms that would not only protect the rights of workers, but would also offer employers and workers a legal framework to settle their dispute. In this regard, the HLC requires that any agreement between workers and employers be sealed by a verbal or written labor contract. Therefore, under Section 55 of the HLC, a verbal individual labor contract is as valid as a written one. To further protect the validity of verbal contracts and to prevent abuse, Section 23 of the HLC emphasizes that while the validity of a written contract can only be established by writing, any forms of proof are admissible in court to establish the validity of a verbal contract. Consequently, in case of a dispute involving a verbal labor contract, an investigation could well involve, for example, surveying other comparable workplaces where identical duties are performed so as to determine what the worker is entitled to. In any circumstances, under Section 53 of the HLB, the terms of a collective labor contract can be more generous for workers than what is prescribed by the HLC, but not the contrary.

Under the Section 55 of the HLC, employers are free to decide whether to hire employees on a permanent or temporary basis, as well as the length of the terms of the latter. However, no collective labor contract can be shorter than twelve months. This possibility for employers to enter into a determinate contract with workers without any legal obligation on their part, provides the employers with the flexibility of adjusting the size of their workforce according to seasonal variations in demand. Of note, even though dispatched work agencies are allowed under HLC, Haitian employers are yet to utilize this employment arrangement.

Once a labor contract is signed, the HLC gives the employers the authority of requiring the workers to perform any duties as long they remain legal and do not go against public order or good manners. As a result, the HLC aims to give the employers the maximum flexibility so that they can make use of their workforce as they see fit to meet operational objectives without overtly violating the workers' rights. In addition to the flexibility provided to employers under the HLC with respect to the nature of the duties, where an individual contract is concerned, employers enjoy the right to unilaterally decide the terms of the labor contract without any possibility for the worker to make a counter offer. This "take it or leave it" approach effectively renders an individual labor contract no more than an "adhesion contract". Consequently, it opens the door for some employers, especially those in small and medium-sized enterprises (SMEs) to hire according to their own subjective preferences rather than on the merits of the applicants, thus increasing the possibility of different forms of discrimination Due to the persistently high unemployment rate, many workers consider employment more a privilege than a right, and as a result, are very often willing to enter into a labor contract even if its terms are far below the HLC standards. Those cases are often undetected because, not only are the workers involved reluctant to report such practices to the authorities for fear of losing their job, but there is also a lack of effective supervision as prescribed in the HLC to prevent this kind of abuse. Such irregularities, however, are rarely found in collective labor contracts where employers do not have such power to unilaterally dictate the terms of labour contracts.

DISMISSING WORKERS UNDER HLC

One of employers' most feared elements of EPL is the inability to dismiss workers whenever they want or deem necessary. In theory, the higher the firing costs, the more stringent the EPL is and the more difficult it is for employers to adjust their workforce to meet operational objectives (see, for example, Saint-Paul, 1997 & 2002; Samaniego, 2006 and Cuñat and Melitz, 2007). The main reason behind the high firing cost in the emerging economies is the lack of social protections such as unemployment benefits, welfare, food rationing universal healthcare, etc. To fill the cracks in the social safety net, the government often resorts to using EPL, involving hefty fines with a view to discouraging firing.

Under the HLC, the termination of all labor contracts, whether individual or collective, verbal or written, permanent or temporary, must be subject to a prior notice from either the employers or the workers, depending on the party who decides to terminate the contract. The notice period varies according to the seniority of the worker, ranging from 15 days for a worker with three to twelve months of service to up to four months if the workers have been hired for ten years or more[4]. The party who abruptly terminates a labor contract without prior notice is liable to make a payment to the other party of the equivalent of the salary that would have been paid to the worker had a prior notice been given[5]. By making prior notice mandatory for both parties, both the employers and the workers would have adequate time to adjust to the new circumstances. However, under Section 44 of the HLC, prior notice is not mandatory if the worker has worked for the employer for less than three consecutive months, period during which neither the employer nor the worker have a binding obligation toward each other, or otherwise known as the probationary period.

Notwithstanding the prior notice requirement, both employers and workers can terminate a labor contract at any time for a valid and just cause, typically when at least one of the specific conditions stated in the HLC are met. For instance, if one party does not fulfill its obligations under the law or the contract, engages in an act of sabotage, lack of civility, etc., it would be unwise to require the aggrieved party to remain in a relationship that is either emotionally, physically or morally harmful. However, upon the termination of the labor contract, the aggrieved party would have the obligation to file a report with the Director General of the Office of Labor (*Directeur général du travail* (DGT) – the supervising body of the Ministry of Social Affairs and Labor (MAST) – explaining the rationale for the termination). Normally, the DGT would then be able to conduct an initial investigation, which, if found to be a genuine labor conflict, would then be forwarded for conciliation or arbitration All the cases that fail to be resolved following the completion of the conciliation or arbitration processes are, upon the request of any of the concerned parties, referred to the SST. Therefore, in summary, for employers the actual cost of firing under the HLC can be reduced to simply a matter of patience, for, once the prior notice is served to the workers, employers would have fulfilled all the duties required of them buy the law, and no further action is necessary. However, the need to serve a notice in the termination process can impose supplementary costs to employers, who might in turn need to further reduce their workforce due to unforeseeable events.

THE TREATMENT OF WORKERS UNDER HLC

In general, the notion of "treatment on the job" refers to the package of benefits to which the worker is entitled, whether it is payable fully or partly by the employer. These benefits may include vacation days, sick leave, parental leave, etc., which may be offered at two different levels under HLC. The first level is the minimum standard as defined by the Labor Standards Act (L*a Loi sur les normes du travail* (LNT)), while the second level is determined by employers and workers through a labor contract. However, in the spirit of ensuring fairness across the board, e.g. workers having comparable jobs in related industries would enjoy the same benefits, it is proposed that a third level, which is essentially a mix of standards as defined by LNT with inputs from both employers and workers, be adopted. Therefore, under this regime[6], a concerned union or even the MAST may request that the terms of an active collective labor contract as applied to a specific organization be made mandatory for all other employers in the same sector of business. It goes without saying that such a request is receivable only at the expiration of the labor contract it intends to replace. By serving the interests of both employers the workers, this new measure is an important innovation in the history of EPL in Haiti because it can, on one hand, save employers time by avoiding a long negotiation process, and on the other hand, encourage the growth of both wage and non-wage benefits for workers.

The wide range of wage and non-wage benefits available to workers under the HLC are, at their very minimum, a weekly paid off-work day following six consecutive days of continuous work over the course of seven days[7], no matter how many hours the worker provided over the week. In this case, employers who request the service of their workers during the weekly day off would have to pay the workers for extra time incurred, in addition to the regular wage for that day. The extra time wages are1.5 times of regular wage rate. This weekly paid day off, far from showcasing lavish labor conditions in Haiti where Haitian workers are on paid leave every week, reflects, on the contrary, the precarious financial situation of the workers. Instead of rewarding the workers' effort with a livable wage, the Legislator has resorted to co-opt with for a model that is deep-rooted in Haitian culture, where the workplace is an extension of the worker's family. As a result, the worker needs to rely on the employer to provide for their families even on the days they are not on the job. It follows that when somebody is sick or dies in the family, the worker expects financial support from the employers. In fact, employers do support workers in the Haitian culture. Tapping into the elements of traditional Haitian culture, the Legislator seeks to keep the wage levels very low so to prioritize a continuous and strong relationship between workers and their employers.

In addition to the weekly paid day off, permanent workers are entitled to an annual vacation leave of fifteen consecutive days (including thirteen workdays and two Sundays) after twelve months of service[8]. Temporary workers are also entitled to the same treatment as the permanent workers, but is given pro-rata according to the length of employment. Being aware of the potential risk of abuse in a society where a significant number of the population is illiterate and therefore does not know their rights, the Legislator goes further under the Section 123 of HLC to stipulates that the weekly day off, the holiday leave, sick leave and maternity leave not be deduced from the fifteen days of vacation. Under the HLC, workers are also entitled to receive every year a mandatory bonus which represents at least a twelfth of the worker's annual wage[9] every year between 24th and 31st of December. In case of dismissal, layoff or voluntary departure, the employer needs to release the bonus pay and the vacation pay to which the worker is entitled leading to the end of the labor contract on a pro-rata basis.

On top of a mandatory contribution to buy a no-fault insurance coverage for workers against illness and workplace accident, HLC also requires employers to contribute to the workers' old age pension plan at the level of 6% of their basic salary[10]. Both plans are administered by two public institutions, namely the National Office of Old Age Security (*Office national d'assurance-viellesse* (ONA)) and the Work Accidents Insurance, Sickness and Maternity (*Office d'assurance accidents du travail, maladie et maternité*" (OFATMA)) under the MAST. As a result of these coverages, workers reaching 55 years of age are entitled to a full pension after 20 years of service, and those who are injured at work (or become ill because of their job) are entitled to disability benefits and all the other protections as required by law. Actively insured workers are also granted the right to access the mortgage loan[11] service and the saving and loan services offered by ONA[12].

Concerning workplace accidents, the Legislator has adopted a very broad definition, which includes any accidents occurring on the regular route taken by the worker to and from work[13]. As the Haitian social safety net is not well developed, it seems that the Legislator intentionally provides this broad definition to protect the workers against other risks (such as an accident involving a car, which is covered exclusively by a public institution) for which they would otherwise not been covered for by the employers. This provision, however, further blurs the line between a worker's personal life and the workplace.

CONCLUSION

While the Haitian labor legislation provides Haitian workers with international standard protections covering their rights at work, it involves a very complex administrative structure for enforcement purposes. In addition, on request from the Director General of the Labor Bureau, free legal aid must be provided to workers in dispute. This legislation is inspired in part by the 22 ILO conventions on labor standards, which Haiti has ratified. The biggest issue, though, rests on the enforcement of the law, since in addition to the rampant corruption that paralyzes its institutions, the government has not provided for enough resources for fulfill this obligation. However, the gap between the elaborate requirements of HLC and the reality of the still embryonic state of the Haitian economy cannot be ignored. The fact that this legislation has never been amended despite having come into force some three decades ago is a potent indication of the struggle Haitian workers are having at achieving the more basic levels of employment protection. Furthermore, the assumption that employers and workers are on a level playing field in the labor market is problematic. Alarmingly, the explicit exclusion of the public service employees from the jurisdiction of the labor court could well be an indication that the government do not even trust its own dispute resolving institutions.

As the provisions of HLC are estimated to have covered only a very small percentage of the workers in Haiti, and that the it has never been correctly implemented or enforced since its enactment, it is difficult to have a full understanding of its economic and social impacts on the Haitian society. Nevertheless, HLC has an important impact on the labor relations of Haiti because it is considered a first step in making a meaningful contribution to the fundamental rights of the workers and encouraging employers to improve the welfare of their workers. While the integration of some specific Haitian cultural elements might be a departure from internationally accepted business practices, such a move can be justified as a thoughtful attempt to meet the general expectations of Haitian employers and businesses in order to facilitate their acceptance.

The assumption of the HLC framers according to which Haitian workers and employers are on the same footing when it comes to labor relations may be the key to help understand the challenge of being a worker in a country where unemployment rate has always been high.

REFERENCES

Better Work Haiti. (2014). *Garment Industry, 8th Biannual Synthesis Report Under the HOPE II. Legislation. Synthesis Report*. ILO/IFC.

Better Work Haiti. (2016). *Garment Industry, 13th Biannual Synthesis Report Under the HOPE II. Legislation. Synthesis Report*. ILO/IFC.

Cuñat, A., & Melitz, M. J. (2007). *Volatility, labor market flexibility, and the pattern of comparative advantage*. St. Louis, MO: Federal Reserve Bank of St Louis. doi:10.3386/w13062

D'Souza, E. (2010). The employment effects of labor legislation in India: A critical essay. *Industrial Relations Journal, 41*(2), 122–135. doi:10.1111/j.1468-2338.2009.00558.x

Décret du 24 février 1984 actualisant le Code du travail du 12 septembre 1961. Le Moniteur No 18-A du 5 mars 1984. Port-au-Prince.

Décret du 4 novembre 1974 créant le Service des prêts hypothécaires, Le Moniteur No 89 du 14 novembre 1974. Port-au-Prince.

Dollar, D., Iarossi, G., & Mengistae, T. (2002). *Investment Climate and Economic Performance: Some Firm Level Evidence from India*. Development Research Group, The World Bank, Working Paper No. 143.

Hornbeck, J. F. (2010). *The Haitian Economy and the HOPE Act. CRS Report for Congress*. Washington, DC: Congressional Research Service.

International Monetary Fund. (2015). *Haiti: Selected Issues*. IMF Country Report No 15/158. IMF.

Li, J. (2008). China's New Labor Contract Law and Protection of Workers. *Fordham International Law Journal, 32*(3), 1083–1131.

Loi du 25 août 1971 créant le Comptoir d'épargne et de prêts, Le Moniteur No 70 du 2 septembre 1971. Port-au-Prince.

Loi organique du Ministère des Affaires Sociale et du Travail (MAST) du 28 août 1967. Le Moniteur No 84-A du 28 septembre 1967. Port-au-Prince.

Saint-Paul, G. (1997). Is labor rigidity harming Europe's competitiveness? The effect of job protection on the pattern of trade and welfare. *European Economic Review*, *41*(3–5), 499–506. doi:10.1016/S0014-2921(97)00017-2

Saint-Paul, G. (2002). Employment protection, international specialization, and innovation. *European Economic Review*, *46*(2), 375–395. doi:10.1016/S0014-2921(01)00093-9

Samaniego, R. M. (2006). Employment protection and high-tech aversion. *Review of Economic Dynamics*, *9*(2), 224–241. doi:10.1016/j.red.2005.10.002

United States International Trade Administration. (n.d.). Retrieved from https://www.export.gov/article?id=Haiti-Apparel

World Bank. (2007). Armenia – Labor Market Dynamics: Volume 2. Human Development Sector Unit. Europe and Central Asia Region Report, 35361-AM. Washington, DC: World Bank.

KEY TERMS AND DEFINITIONS

Employment Protection Legislation (EPL): Refers to all types of employment protection measures that governs the hiring and firing of workers, their treatment on the job (including holidays, sick leave and maternity issues, and other related issues, such as workplace safety), whether grounded primarily in legislation, court rulings, collectively bargained conditions of employment, or customary practice.

Labor Code: Codification of the statutes, generally laws and decrees, respecting labor. Its main objective is to mediate industrial relations between workers and employers within a given society.

Labor Market Flexibility: Can be understood as the capacity and willingness of labor to respond efficiently and rapidly to changes in market conditions, such as a shock in the demand for labor and the wage rate.

Labor Market Rigidity: Refers to prevailing employment practices and environmental policy conditions which limit employers' options with respect to the volume of work, firing costs, minimum wage, notices, lack of opportunity for part-time and flexible-hours work, location, etc.

ENDNOTES

1 One must be very cautious when analyzing official statistics on women participation rate relatively to men's in a country like Haiti where the informal sector, in which women are overwhelmingly represented, plays an important role in the economy.

2 Obtained from the website of the International Labor Office on June 25, 2017 at 1:43 AM: http://data.worldbank.org/indicator/FP.CPI.TOTL?end=2016&locations=AE-HT&start=1977

3 Vital statistics for Haiti are meager, incomplete or contradictory.

4 See art. 45.

5 See art. 46.

6 See art. 60.

7 See art. 107.

8 See section 123.

9 See art. 154-157.

10 See Loi du 28 août 1967.

11 Décrêt du 4 novembre 1974.

12 Loi du 28 août 1971.

13 Loi du 28 août 1971.

Related References

To continue our tradition of advancing academic research, we have compiled a list of recommended IGI Global readings. These references will provide additional information and guidance to further enrich your knowledge and assist you with your own research and future publications.

Adeyemo, O. (2013). The nationwide health information network: A biometric approach to prevent medical identity theft. In *User-driven healthcare: Concepts, methodologies, tools, and applications* (pp. 1636–1649). Hershey, PA: IGI Global. doi:10.4018/978-1-4666-2770-3.ch081

Adler, M., & Henman, P. (2009). Justice beyond the courts: The implications of computerisation for procedural justice in social security. In A. Martínez & P. Abat (Eds.), *E-justice: Using information communication technologies in the court system* (pp. 65–86). Hershey, PA: IGI Global. doi:10.4018/978-1-59904-998-4.ch005

Aflalo, E., & Gabay, E. (2013). An information system for coping with student dropout. In L. Tomei (Ed.), *Learning tools and teaching approaches through ICT advancements* (pp. 176–187). Hershey, PA: IGI Global. doi:10.4018/978-1-4666-2017-9.ch016

Ahmed, M. A., Janssen, M., & van den Hoven, J. (2012). Value sensitive transfer (VST) of systems among countries: Towards a framework. *International Journal of Electronic Government Research*, *8*(1), 26–42. doi:10.4018/jegr.2012010102

Aikins, S. K. (2008). Issues and trends in internet-based citizen participation. In G. Garson & M. Khosrow-Pour (Eds.), *Handbook of research on public information technology* (pp. 31–40). Hershey, PA: IGI Global. doi:10.4018/978-1-59904-857-4.ch004

Aikins, S. K. (2009). A comparative study of municipal adoption of internet-based citizen participation. In C. Reddick (Ed.), *Handbook of research on strategies for local e-government adoption and implementation: Comparative studies* (pp. 206–230). Hershey, PA: IGI Global. doi:10.4018/978-1-60566-282-4.ch011

Aikins, S. K. (2012). Improving e-government project management: Best practices and critical success factors. In *Digital democracy: Concepts, methodologies, tools, and applications* (pp. 1314–1332). Hershey, PA: IGI Global. doi:10.4018/978-1-4666-1740-7.ch065

Akabawi, M. S. (2011). Ghabbour group ERP deployment: Learning from past technology failures. In E. Business Research and Case Center (Ed.), Cases on business and management in the MENA region: New trends and opportunities (pp. 177-203). Hershey, PA: IGI Global. doi:10.4018/978-1-60960-583-4.ch012

Akabawi, M. S. (2013). Ghabbour group ERP deployment: Learning from past technology failures. In *Industrial engineering: Concepts, methodologies, tools, and applications* (pp. 933–958). Hershey, PA: IGI Global. doi:10.4018/978-1-4666-1945-6.ch051

Akbulut, A. Y., & Motwani, J. (2008). Integration and information sharing in e-government. In G. Putnik & M. Cruz-Cunha (Eds.), *Encyclopedia of networked and virtual organizations* (pp. 729–734). Hershey, PA: IGI Global. doi:10.4018/978-1-59904-885-7.ch096

Akers, E. J. (2008). Technology diffusion in public administration. In G. Garson & M. Khosrow-Pour (Eds.), *Handbook of research on public information technology* (pp. 339–348). Hershey, PA: IGI Global. doi:10.4018/978-1-59904-857-4.ch033

Al-Shafi, S. (2008). Free wireless internet park services: An investigation of technology adoption in Qatar from a citizens' perspective. *Journal of Cases on Information Technology, 10*(3), 21–34. doi:10.4018/jcit.2008070103

Al-Shafi, S., & Weerakkody, V. (2009). Implementing free wi-fi in public parks: An empirical study in Qatar. *International Journal of Electronic Government Research, 5*(3), 21–35. doi:10.4018/jegr.2009070102

Aladwani, A. M. (2002). Organizational actions, computer attitudes and end-user satisfaction in public organizations: An empirical study. In C. Snodgrass & E. Szewczak (Eds.), *Human factors in information systems* (pp. 153–168). Hershey, PA: IGI Global. doi:10.4018/978-1-931777-10-0.ch012

Aladwani, A. M. (2002). Organizational actions, computer attitudes, and end-user satisfaction in public organizations: An empirical study. *Journal of Organizational and End User Computing, 14*(1), 42–49. doi:10.4018/joeuc.2002010104

Allen, B., Juillet, L., Paquet, G., & Roy, J. (2005). E-government and private-public partnerships: Relational challenges and strategic directions. In M. Khosrow-Pour (Ed.), *Practicing e-government: A global perspective* (pp. 364–382). Hershey, PA: IGI Global. doi:10.4018/978-1-59140-637-2.ch016

Alshawaf, A., & Knalil, O. E. (2008). IS success factors and IS organizational impact: Does ownership type matter in Kuwait? *International Journal of Enterprise Information Systems, 4*(2), 13–33. doi:10.4018/jeis.2008040102

Ambali, A. R. (2009). Digital divide and its implication on Malaysian e-government: Policy initiatives. In H. Rahman (Ed.), *Social and political implications of data mining: Knowledge management in e-government* (pp. 267–287). Hershey, PA: IGI Global. doi:10.4018/978-1-60566-230-5.ch016

Amoretti, F. (2007). Digital international governance. In A. Anttiroiko & M. Malkia (Eds.), *Encyclopedia of digital government* (pp. 365–370). Hershey, PA: IGI Global. doi:10.4018/978-1-59140-789-8.ch056

Amoretti, F. (2008). Digital international governance. In A. Anttiroiko (Ed.), *Electronic government: Concepts, methodologies, tools, and applications* (pp. 688–696). Hershey, PA: IGI Global. doi:10.4018/978-1-59904-947-2.ch058

Amoretti, F. (2008). E-government at supranational level in the European Union. In A. Anttiroiko (Ed.), *Electronic government: Concepts, methodologies, tools, and applications* (pp. 1047–1055). Hershey, PA: IGI Global. doi:10.4018/978-1-59904-947-2.ch079

Amoretti, F. (2008). E-government regimes. In A. Anttiroiko (Ed.), *Electronic government: Concepts, methodologies, tools, and applications* (pp. 3846–3856). Hershey, PA: IGI Global. doi:10.4018/978-1-59904-947-2.ch280

Amoretti, F. (2009). Electronic constitution: A Braudelian perspective. In F. Amoretti (Ed.), *Electronic constitution: Social, cultural, and political implications* (pp. 1–19). Hershey, PA: IGI Global. doi:10.4018/978-1-60566-254-1.ch001

Amoretti, F., & Musella, F. (2009). Institutional isomorphism and new technologies. In M. Khosrow-Pour (Ed.), *Encyclopedia of information science and technology* (2nd ed.; pp. 2066–2071). Hershey, PA: IGI Global. doi:10.4018/978-1-60566-026-4.ch325

Andersen, K. V., & Henriksen, H. Z. (2007). E-government research: Capabilities, interaction, orientation, and values. In D. Norris (Ed.), *Current issues and trends in e-government research* (pp. 269–288). Hershey, PA: IGI Global. doi:10.4018/978-1-59904-283-1.ch013

Anderson, K. V., & Henriksen, H. Z. (2005). The first leg of e-government research: Domains and application areas 1998-2003. *International Journal of Electronic Government Research, 1*(4), 26–44. doi:10.4018/jegr.2005100102

Anttiroiko, A. (2009). Democratic e-governance. In M. Khosrow-Pour (Ed.), *Encyclopedia of information science and technology* (2nd ed.; pp. 990–995). Hershey, PA: IGI Global. doi:10.4018/978-1-60566-026-4.ch158

Baker, P. M., Bell, A., & Moon, N. W. (2009). Accessibility issues in municipal wireless networks. In C. Reddick (Ed.), *Handbook of research on strategies for local e-government adoption and implementation: Comparative studies* (pp. 569–588). Hershey, PA: IGI Global. doi:10.4018/978-1-60566-282-4.ch030

Becker, S. A., Keimer, R., & Muth, T. (2010). A case on university and community collaboration: The sci-tech entrepreneurial training services (ETS) program. In S. Becker & R. Niebuhr (Eds.), *Cases on technology innovation: Entrepreneurial successes and pitfalls* (pp. 68–90). Hershey, PA: IGI Global. doi:10.4018/978-1-61520-609-4.ch003

Becker, S. A., Keimer, R., & Muth, T. (2012). A case on university and community collaboration: The sci-tech entrepreneurial training services (ETS) program. In Regional development: Concepts, methodologies, tools, and applications (pp. 947-969). Hershey, PA: IGI Global. doi:10.4018/978-1-4666-0882-5.ch507

Bernardi, R. (2012). Information technology and resistance to public sector reforms: A case study in Kenya. In T. Papadopoulos & P. Kanellis (Eds.), *Public sector reform using information technologies: Transforming policy into practice* (pp. 59–78). Hershey, PA: IGI Global. doi:10.4018/978-1-60960-839-2.ch004

Bernardi, R. (2013). Information technology and resistance to public sector reforms: A case study in Kenya. In *User-driven healthcare: Concepts, methodologies, tools, and applications* (pp. 14–33). Hershey, PA: IGI Global. doi:10.4018/978-1-4666-2770-3.ch002

Bolívar, M. P., Pérez, M. D., & Hernández, A. M. (2012). Municipal e-government services in emerging economies: The Latin-American and Caribbean experiences. In Y. Chen & P. Chu (Eds.), *Electronic governance and cross-boundary collaboration: Innovations and advancing tools* (pp. 198–226). Hershey, PA: IGI Global. doi:10.4018/978-1-60960-753-1.ch011

Borycki, E. M., & Kushniruk, A. W. (2010). Use of clinical simulations to evaluate the impact of health information systems and ubiquitous computing devices upon health professional work. In S. Mohammed & J. Fiaidhi (Eds.), *Ubiquitous health and medical informatics: The ubiquity 2.0 trend and beyond* (pp. 552–573). Hershey, PA: IGI Global. doi:10.4018/978-1-61520-777-0.ch026

Borycki, E. M., & Kushniruk, A. W. (2011). Use of clinical simulations to evaluate the impact of health information systems and ubiquitous computing devices upon health professional work. In *Clinical technologies: Concepts, methodologies, tools and applications* (pp. 532–553). Hershey, PA: IGI Global. doi:10.4018/978-1-60960-561-2.ch220

Buchan, J. (2011). Developing a dynamic and responsive online learning environment: A case study of a large Australian university. In B. Czerkawski (Ed.), *Free and open source software for e-learning: Issues, successes and challenges* (pp. 92–109). Hershey, PA: IGI Global. doi:10.4018/978-1-61520-917-0.ch006

Buenger, A. W. (2008). Digital convergence and cybersecurity policy. In G. Garson & M. Khosrow-Pour (Eds.), *Handbook of research on public information technology* (pp. 395–405). Hershey, PA: IGI Global. doi:10.4018/978-1-59904-857-4.ch038

Burn, J. M., & Loch, K. D. (2002). The societal impact of world wide web - Key challenges for the 21st century. In A. Salehnia (Ed.), *Ethical issues of information systems* (pp. 88–106). Hershey, PA: IGI Global. doi:10.4018/978-1-931777-15-5.ch007

Burn, J. M., & Loch, K. D. (2003). The societal impact of the world wide web-Key challenges for the 21st century. In M. Khosrow-Pour (Ed.), *Advanced topics in information resources management* (Vol. 2, pp. 32–51). Hershey, PA: IGI Global. doi:10.4018/978-1-59140-062-2.ch002

Bwalya, K. J., Du Plessis, T., & Rensleigh, C. (2012). The "quicksilver initiatives" as a framework for e-government strategy design in developing economies. In K. Bwalya & S. Zulu (Eds.), *Handbook of research on e-government in emerging economies: Adoption, e-participation, and legal frameworks* (pp. 605–623). Hershey, PA: IGI Global. doi:10.4018/978-1-4666-0324-0.ch031

Cabotaje, C. E., & Alampay, E. A. (2013). Social media and citizen engagement: Two cases from the Philippines. In S. Saeed & C. Reddick (Eds.), *Human-centered system design for electronic governance* (pp. 225–238). Hershey, PA: IGI Global. doi:10.4018/978-1-4666-3640-8.ch013

Camillo, A., Di Pietro, L., Di Virgilio, F., & Franco, M. (2013). Work-groups conflict at PetroTech-Italy, S.R.L.: The influence of culture on conflict dynamics. In B. Christiansen, E. Turkina, & N. Williams (Eds.), *Cultural and technological influences on global business* (pp. 272–289). Hershey, PA: IGI Global. doi:10.4018/978-1-4666-3966-9.ch015

Capra, E., Francalanci, C., & Marinoni, C. (2008). Soft success factors for m-government. In A. Anttiroiko (Ed.), *Electronic government: Concepts, methodologies, tools, and applications* (pp. 1213–1233). Hershey, PA: IGI Global. doi:10.4018/978-1-59904-947-2.ch089

Cartelli, A. (2009). The implementation of practices with ICT as a new teaching-learning paradigm. In A. Cartelli & M. Palma (Eds.), *Encyclopedia of information communication technology* (pp. 413–417). Hershey, PA: IGI Global. doi:10.4018/978-1-59904-845-1.ch055

Charalabidis, Y., Lampathaki, F., & Askounis, D. (2010). Investigating the landscape in national interoperability frameworks. *International Journal of E-Services and Mobile Applications, 2*(4), 28–41. doi:10.4018/jesma.2010100103

Charalabidis, Y., Lampathaki, F., & Askounis, D. (2012). Investigating the landscape in national interoperability frameworks. In A. Scupola (Ed.), *Innovative mobile platform developments for electronic services design and delivery* (pp. 218–231). Hershey, PA: IGI Global. doi:10.4018/978-1-4666-1568-7.ch013

Chen, I. (2005). Distance education associations. In C. Howard, J. Boettcher, L. Justice, K. Schenk, P. Rogers, & G. Berg (Eds.), *Encyclopedia of distance learning* (pp. 599–612). Hershey, PA: IGI Global. doi:10.4018/978-1-59140-555-9.ch087

Chen, I. (2008). Distance education associations. In L. Tomei (Ed.), *Online and distance learning: Concepts, methodologies, tools, and applications* (pp. 562–579). Hershey, PA: IGI Global. doi:10.4018/978-1-59904-935-9.ch048

Chen, Y. (2008). Managing IT outsourcing for digital government. In A. Anttiroiko (Ed.), *Electronic government: Concepts, methodologies, tools, and applications* (pp. 3107–3114). Hershey, PA: IGI Global. doi:10.4018/978-1-59904-947-2.ch229

Chen, Y., & Dimitrova, D. V. (2006). Electronic government and online engagement: Citizen interaction with government via web portals. *International Journal of Electronic Government Research*, *2*(1), 54–76. doi:10.4018/jegr.2006010104

Chen, Y., & Knepper, R. (2005). Digital government development strategies: Lessons for policy makers from a comparative perspective. In W. Huang, K. Siau, & K. Wei (Eds.), *Electronic government strategies and implementation* (pp. 394–420). Hershey, PA: IGI Global. doi:10.4018/978-1-59140-348-7.ch017

Chen, Y., & Knepper, R. (2008). Digital government development strategies: Lessons for policy makers from a comparative perspective. In H. Rahman (Ed.), *Developing successful ICT strategies: Competitive advantages in a global knowledge-driven society* (pp. 334–356). Hershey, PA: IGI Global. doi:10.4018/978-1-59904-654-9.ch017

Cherian, E. J., & Ryan, T. W. (2014). Incongruent needs: Why differences in the iron-triangle of priorities make health information technology adoption and use difficult. In C. El Morr (Ed.), *Research perspectives on the role of informatics in health policy and management* (pp. 209–221). Hershey, PA: IGI Global. doi:10.4018/978-1-4666-4321-5.ch012

Cho, H. J., & Hwang, S. (2010). Government 2.0 in Korea: Focusing on e-participation services. In C. Reddick (Ed.), *Politics, democracy and e-government: Participation and service delivery* (pp. 94–114). Hershey, PA: IGI Global. doi:10.4018/978-1-61520-933-0.ch006

Chorus, C., & Timmermans, H. (2010). Ubiquitous travel environments and travel control strategies: Prospects and challenges. In M. Wachowicz (Ed.), *Movement-aware applications for sustainable mobility: Technologies and approaches* (pp. 30–51). Hershey, PA: IGI Global. doi:10.4018/978-1-61520-769-5.ch003

Chuanshen, R. (2007). E-government construction and China's administrative litigation act. In A. Anttiroiko & M. Malkia (Eds.), *Encyclopedia of digital government* (pp. 507–510). Hershey, PA: IGI Global. doi:10.4018/978-1-59140-789-8.ch077

Ciaghi, A., & Villafiorita, A. (2012). Law modeling and BPR for public administration improvement. In K. Bwalya & S. Zulu (Eds.), *Handbook of research on e-government in emerging economies: Adoption, e-participation, and legal frameworks* (pp. 391–410). Hershey, PA: IGI Global. doi:10.4018/978-1-4666-0324-0.ch019

Ciaramitaro, B. L., & Skrocki, M. (2012). mHealth: Mobile healthcare. In B. Ciaramitaro (Ed.), Mobile technology consumption: Opportunities and challenges (pp. 99-109). Hershey, PA: IGI Global. doi:10.4018/978-1-61350-150-4.ch007

Comite, U. (2012). Innovative processes and managerial effectiveness of e-procurement in healthcare. In A. Manoharan & M. Holzer (Eds.), *Active citizen participation in e-government: A global perspective* (pp. 206–229). Hershey, PA: IGI Global. doi:10.4018/978-1-4666-0116-1.ch011

Cordella, A. (2013). E-government success: How to account for ICT, administrative rationalization, and institutional change. In J. Gil-Garcia (Ed.), *E-government success factors and measures: Theories, concepts, and methodologies* (pp. 40–51). Hershey, PA: IGI Global. doi:10.4018/978-1-4666-4058-0.ch003

Cropf, R. A. (2009). ICT and e-democracy. In M. Khosrow-Pour (Ed.), *Encyclopedia of information science and technology* (2nd ed.; pp. 1789–1793). Hershey, PA: IGI Global. doi:10.4018/978-1-60566-026-4.ch281

Cropf, R. A. (2009). The virtual public sphere. In M. Pagani (Ed.), *Encyclopedia of multimedia technology and networking* (2nd ed.; pp. 1525–1530). Hershey, PA: IGI Global. doi:10.4018/978-1-60566-014-1.ch206

D'Abundo, M. L. (2013). Electronic health record implementation in the United States healthcare industry: Making the process of change manageable. In V. Wang (Ed.), *Handbook of research on technologies for improving the 21st century workforce: Tools for lifelong learning* (pp. 272–286). Hershey, PA: IGI Global. doi:10.4018/978-1-4666-2181-7.ch018

Damurski, L. (2012). E-participation in urban planning: Online tools for citizen engagement in Poland and in Germany. *International Journal of E-Planning Research, 1*(3), 40–67. doi:10.4018/ijepr.2012070103

de Almeida, M. O. (2007). E-government strategy in Brazil: Increasing transparency and efficiency through e-government procurement. In M. Gascó-Hernandez (Ed.), *Latin America online: Cases, successes and pitfalls* (pp. 34–82). Hershey, PA: IGI Global. doi:10.4018/978-1-59140-974-8.ch002

de Juana Espinosa, S. (2008). Empirical study of the municipalitites' motivations for adopting online presence. In A. Anttiroiko (Ed.), *Electronic government: Concepts, methodologies, tools, and applications* (pp. 3593–3608). Hershey, PA: IGI Global. doi:10.4018/978-1-59904-947-2.ch262

de Souza Dias, D. (2002). Motivation for using information technology. In C. Snodgrass & E. Szewczak (Eds.), *Human factors in information systems* (pp. 55–60). Hershey, PA: IGI Global. doi:10.4018/978-1-931777-10-0.ch005

Demediuk, P. (2006). Government procurement ICT's impact on the sustainability of SMEs and regional communities. In S. Marshall, W. Taylor, & X. Yu (Eds.), *Encyclopedia of developing regional communities with information and communication technology* (pp. 321–324). Hershey, PA: IGI Global. doi:10.4018/978-1-59140-575-7.ch056

Devonshire, E., Forsyth, H., Reid, S., & Simpson, J. M. (2013). The challenges and opportunities of online postgraduate coursework programs in a traditional university context. In B. Tynan, J. Willems, & R. James (Eds.), *Outlooks and opportunities in blended and distance learning* (pp. 353–368). Hershey, PA: IGI Global. doi:10.4018/978-1-4666-4205-8.ch026

Di Cerbo, F., Scotto, M., Sillitti, A., Succi, G., & Vernazza, T. (2007). Toward a GNU/Linux distribution for corporate environments. In S. Sowe, I. Stamelos, & I. Samoladas (Eds.), *Emerging free and open source software practices* (pp. 215–236). Hershey, PA: IGI Global. doi:10.4018/978-1-59904-210-7.ch010

Diesner, J., & Carley, K. M. (2005). Revealing social structure from texts: Meta-matrix text analysis as a novel method for network text analysis. In V. Narayanan & D. Armstrong (Eds.), *Causal mapping for research in information technology* (pp. 81–108). Hershey, PA: IGI Global. doi:10.4018/978-1-59140-396-8.ch004

Dologite, D. G., Mockler, R. J., Bai, Q., & Viszhanyo, P. F. (2006). IS change agents in practice in a US-Chinese joint venture. In M. Hunter & F. Tan (Eds.), *Advanced topics in global information management* (Vol. 5, pp. 331–352). Hershey, PA: IGI Global. doi:10.4018/978-1-59140-923-6.ch015

Drnevich, P., Brush, T. H., & Luckock, G. T. (2011). Process and structural implications for IT-enabled outsourcing. *International Journal of Strategic Information Technology and Applications*, *2*(4), 30–43. doi:10.4018/jsita.2011100103

Dwivedi, A. N. (2009). *Handbook of research on information technology management and clinical data administration in healthcare* (Vols. 1–2). Hershey, PA: IGI Global. doi:10.4018/978-1-60566-356-2

Elbeltagi, I., McBride, N., & Hardaker, G. (2006). Evaluating the factors affecting DSS usage by senior managers in local authorities in Egypt. In M. Hunter & F. Tan (Eds.), *Advanced topics in global information management* (Vol. 5, pp. 283–307). Hershey, PA: IGI Global. doi:10.4018/978-1-59140-923-6.ch013

Eom, S., & Fountain, J. E. (2013). Enhancing information services through public-private partnerships: Information technology knowledge transfer underlying structures to develop shared services in the U.S. and Korea. In J. Gil-Garcia (Ed.), *E-government success around the world: Cases, empirical studies, and practical recommendations* (pp. 15–40). Hershey, PA: IGI Global. doi:10.4018/978-1-4666-4173-0.ch002

Esteves, T., Leuenberger, D., & Van Leuven, N. (2012). Reaching citizen 2.0: How government uses social media to send public messages during times of calm and times of crisis. In K. Kloby & M. D'Agostino (Eds.), *Citizen 2.0: Public and governmental interaction through web 2.0 technologies* (pp. 250–268). Hershey, PA: IGI Global. doi:10.4018/978-1-4666-0318-9.ch013

Estevez, E., Fillottrani, P., Janowski, T., & Ojo, A. (2012). Government information sharing: A framework for policy formulation. In Y. Chen & P. Chu (Eds.), *Electronic governance and cross-boundary collaboration: Innovations and advancing tools* (pp. 23–55). Hershey, PA: IGI Global. doi:10.4018/978-1-60960-753-1.ch002

Ezz, I. E. (2008). E-governement emerging trends: Organizational challenges. In A. Anttiroiko (Ed.), *Electronic government: Concepts, methodologies, tools, and applications* (pp. 3721–3737). Hershey, PA: IGI Global. doi:10.4018/978-1-59904-947-2.ch269

Fabri, M. (2009). The Italian style of e-justice in a comparative perspective. In A. Martínez & P. Abat (Eds.), *E-justice: Using information communication technologies in the court system* (pp. 1–19). Hershey, PA: IGI Global. doi:10.4018/978-1-59904-998-4.ch001

Fagbe, T., & Adekola, O. D. (2010). Workplace safety and personnel well-being: The impact of information technology. *International Journal of Green Computing*, *1*(1), 28–33. doi:10.4018/jgc.2010010103

Fagbe, T., & Adekola, O. D. (2011). Workplace safety and personnel well-being: The impact of information technology. In *Global business: Concepts, methodologies, tools and applications* (pp. 1438–1444). Hershey, PA: IGI Global. doi:10.4018/978-1-60960-587-2.ch509

Farmer, L. (2008). Affective collaborative instruction with librarians. In S. Kelsey & K. St.Amant (Eds.), *Handbook of research on computer mediated communication* (pp. 15–24). Hershey, PA: IGI Global. doi:10.4018/978-1-59904-863-5.ch002

Favier, L., & Mekhantar, J. (2007). Use of OSS by local e-administration: The French situation. In K. St.Amant & B. Still (Eds.), *Handbook of research on open source software: Technological, economic, and social perspectives* (pp. 428–444). Hershey, PA: IGI Global. doi:10.4018/978-1-59140-999-1.ch033

Fernando, S. (2009). Issues of e-learning in third world countries. In M. Khosrow-Pour (Ed.), *Encyclopedia of information science and technology* (2nd ed.; pp. 2273–2277). Hershey, PA: IGI Global. doi:10.4018/978-1-60566-026-4.ch360

Filho, J. R., & dos Santos, J. R. Junior. (2009). Local e-government in Brazil: Poor interaction and local politics as usual. In C. Reddick (Ed.), *Handbook of research on strategies for local e-government adoption and implementation: Comparative studies* (pp. 863–878). Hershey, PA: IGI Global. doi:10.4018/978-1-60566-282-4.ch045

Fletcher, P. D. (2004). Portals and policy: Implications of electronic access to U.S. federal government information services. In A. Pavlichev & G. Garson (Eds.), *Digital government: Principles and best practices* (pp. 52–62). Hershey, PA: IGI Global. doi:10.4018/978-1-59140-122-3.ch004

Fletcher, P. D. (2008). Portals and policy: Implications of electronic access to U.S. federal government information services. In A. Anttiroiko (Ed.), *Electronic government: Concepts, methodologies, tools, and applications* (pp. 3970–3979). Hershey, PA: IGI Global. doi:10.4018/978-1-59904-947-2.ch289

Forlano, L. (2004). The emergence of digital government: International perspectives. In A. Pavlichev & G. Garson (Eds.), *Digital government: Principles and best practices* (pp. 34–51). Hershey, PA: IGI Global. doi:10.4018/978-1-59140-122-3.ch003

Franzel, J. M., & Coursey, D. H. (2004). Government web portals: Management issues and the approaches of five states. In A. Pavlichev & G. Garson (Eds.), *Digital government: Principles and best practices* (pp. 63–77). Hershey, PA: IGI Global. doi:10.4018/978-1-59140-122-3.ch005

Gaivéo, J. M. (2013). Security of ICTs supporting healthcare activities. In M. Cruz-Cunha, I. Miranda, & P. Gonçalves (Eds.), *Handbook of research on ICTs for human-centered healthcare and social care services* (pp. 208–228). Hershey, PA: IGI Global. doi:10.4018/978-1-4666-3986-7.ch011

Garson, G. D. (1999). *Information technology and computer applications in public administration: Issues and trends*. Hershey, PA: IGI Global. doi:10.4018/978-1-87828-952-0

Garson, G. D. (2003). Toward an information technology research agenda for public administration. In G. Garson (Ed.), *Public information technology: Policy and management issues* (pp. 331–357). Hershey, PA: IGI Global. doi:10.4018/978-1-59140-060-8.ch014

Garson, G. D. (2004). The promise of digital government. In A. Pavlichev & G. Garson (Eds.), *Digital government: Principles and best practices* (pp. 2–15). Hershey, PA: IGI Global. doi:10.4018/978-1-59140-122-3.ch001

Garson, G. D. (2007). An information technology research agenda for public administration. In G. Garson (Ed.), *Modern public information technology systems: Issues and challenges* (pp. 365–392). Hershey, PA: IGI Global. doi:10.4018/978-1-59904-051-6.ch018

Gasco, M. (2007). Civil servants' resistance towards e-government development. In A. Anttiroiko & M. Malkia (Eds.), *Encyclopedia of digital government* (pp. 190–195). Hershey, PA: IGI Global. doi:10.4018/978-1-59140-789-8.ch028

Gasco, M. (2008). Civil servants' resistance towards e-government development. In A. Anttiroiko (Ed.), *Electronic government: Concepts, methodologies, tools, and applications* (pp. 2580–2588). Hershey, PA: IGI Global. doi:10.4018/978-1-59904-947-2.ch190

Ghere, R. K. (2010). Accountability and information technology enactment: Implications for social empowerment. In E. Ferro, Y. Dwivedi, J. Gil-Garcia, & M. Williams (Eds.), *Handbook of research on overcoming digital divides: Constructing an equitable and competitive information society* (pp. 515–532). Hershey, PA: IGI Global. doi:10.4018/978-1-60566-699-0.ch028

Gibson, I. W. (2012). Simulation modeling of healthcare delivery. In A. Kolker & P. Story (Eds.), *Management engineering for effective healthcare delivery: Principles and applications* (pp. 69–89). Hershey, PA: IGI Global. doi:10.4018/978-1-60960-872-9.ch003

Gil-Garcia, J. R. (2007). Exploring e-government benefits and success factors. In A. Anttiroiko & M. Malkia (Eds.), *Encyclopedia of digital government* (pp. 803–811). Hershey, PA: IGI Global. doi:10.4018/978-1-59140-789-8.ch122

Gil-Garcia, J. R., & González Miranda, F. (2010). E-government and opportunities for participation: The case of the Mexican state web portals. In C. Reddick (Ed.), *Politics, democracy and e-government: Participation and service delivery* (pp. 56–74). Hershey, PA: IGI Global. doi:10.4018/978-1-61520-933-0.ch004

Goldfinch, S. (2012). Public trust in government, trust in e-government, and use of e-government. In Z. Yan (Ed.), *Encyclopedia of cyber behavior* (pp. 987–995). Hershey, PA: IGI Global. doi:10.4018/978-1-4666-0315-8.ch081

Goodyear, M. (2012). Organizational change contributions to e-government project transitions. In S. Aikins (Ed.), *Managing e-government projects: Concepts, issues, and best practices* (pp. 1–21). Hershey, PA: IGI Global. doi:10.4018/978-1-4666-0086-7.ch001

Gordon, S., & Mulligan, P. (2003). Strategic models for the delivery of personal financial services: The role of infocracy. In S. Gordon (Ed.), *Computing information technology: The human side* (pp. 220–232). Hershey, PA: IGI Global. doi:10.4018/978-1-93177-752-0.ch014

Gordon, T. F. (2007). Legal knowledge systems. In A. Anttiroiko & M. Malkia (Eds.), *Encyclopedia of digital government* (pp. 1161–1166). Hershey, PA: IGI Global. doi:10.4018/978-1-59140-789-8.ch175

Graham, J. E., & Semich, G. W. (2008). Integrating technology to transform pedagogy: Revisiting the progress of the three phase TUI model for faculty development. In L. Tomei (Ed.), *Adapting information and communication technologies for effective education* (pp. 1–12). Hershey, PA: IGI Global. doi:10.4018/978-1-59904-922-9.ch001

Grandinetti, L., & Pisacane, O. (2012). Web services for healthcare management. In D. Prakash Vidyarthi (Ed.), *Technologies and protocols for the future of internet design: Reinventing the web* (pp. 60–94). Hershey, PA: IGI Global. doi:10.4018/978-1-4666-0203-8.ch004

Groenewegen, P., & Wagenaar, F. P. (2008). VO as an alternative to hierarchy in the Dutch police sector. In G. Putnik & M. Cruz-Cunha (Eds.), *Encyclopedia of networked and virtual organizations* (pp. 1851–1857). Hershey, PA: IGI Global. doi:10.4018/978-1-59904-885-7.ch245

Gronlund, A. (2001). Building an infrastructure to manage electronic services. In S. Dasgupta (Ed.), *Managing internet and intranet technologies in organizations: Challenges and opportunities* (pp. 71–103). Hershey, PA: IGI Global. doi:10.4018/978-1-878289-95-7.ch006

Gronlund, A. (2002). Introduction to electronic government: Design, applications and management. In Å. Grönlund (Ed.), *Electronic government: Design, applications and management* (pp. 1–21). Hershey, PA: IGI Global. doi:10.4018/978-1-930708-19-8.ch001

Gupta, A., Woosley, R., Crk, I., & Sarnikar, S. (2009). An information technology architecture for drug effectiveness reporting and post-marketing surveillance. In J. Tan (Ed.), *Medical informatics: Concepts, methodologies, tools, and applications* (pp. 631–646). Hershey, PA: IGI Global. doi:10.4018/978-1-60566-050-9.ch047

Hallin, A., & Lundevall, K. (2007). mCity: User focused development of mobile services within the city of Stockholm. In I. Kushchu (Ed.), Mobile government: An emerging direction in e-government (pp. 12-29). Hershey, PA: IGI Global. doi:10.4018/978-1-59140-884-0.ch002

Hallin, A., & Lundevall, K. (2009). mCity: User focused development of mobile services within the city of Stockholm. In S. Clarke (Ed.), Evolutionary concepts in end user productivity and performance: Applications for organizational progress (pp. 268-280). Hershey, PA: IGI Global. doi:10.4018/978-1-60566-136-0.ch017

Hallin, A., & Lundevall, K. (2009). mCity: User focused development of mobile services within the city of Stockholm. In D. Taniar (Ed.), Mobile computing: Concepts, methodologies, tools, and applications (pp. 3455-3467). Hershey, PA: IGI Global. doi:10.4018/978-1-60566-054-7.ch253

Hanson, A. (2005). Overcoming barriers in the planning of a virtual library. In M. Khosrow-Pour (Ed.), *Encyclopedia of information science and technology* (pp. 2255–2259). Hershey, PA: IGI Global. doi:10.4018/978-1-59140-553-5.ch397

Haque, A. (2008). Information technology and surveillance: Implications for public administration in a new word order. In T. Loendorf & G. Garson (Eds.), *Patriotic information systems* (pp. 177–185). Hershey, PA: IGI Global. doi:10.4018/978-1-59904-594-8.ch008

Hauck, R. V., Thatcher, S. M., & Weisband, S. P. (2012). Temporal aspects of information technology use: Increasing shift work effectiveness. In J. Wang (Ed.), *Advancing the service sector with evolving technologies: Techniques and principles* (pp. 87–104). Hershey, PA: IGI Global. doi:10.4018/978-1-4666-0044-7.ch006

Hawk, S., & Witt, T. (2006). Telecommunications courses in information systems programs. *International Journal of Information and Communication Technology Education, 2*(1), 79–92. doi:10.4018/jicte.2006010107

Helms, M. M., Moore, R., & Ahmadi, M. (2009). Information technology (IT) and the healthcare industry: A SWOT analysis. In J. Tan (Ed.), *Medical informatics: Concepts, methodologies, tools, and applications* (pp. 134–152). Hershey, PA: IGI Global. doi:10.4018/978-1-60566-050-9.ch012

Hendrickson, S. M., & Young, M. E. (2014). Electronic records management at a federally funded research and development center. In J. Krueger (Ed.), *Cases on electronic records and resource management implementation in diverse environments* (pp. 334–350). Hershey, PA: IGI Global. doi:10.4018/978-1-4666-4466-3.ch020

Henman, P. (2010). Social policy and information communication technologies. In J. Martin & L. Hawkins (Eds.), *Information communication technologies for human services education and delivery: Concepts and cases* (pp. 215–229). Hershey, PA: IGI Global. doi:10.4018/978-1-60566-735-5.ch014

Hismanoglu, M. (2011). Important issues in online education: E-pedagogy and marketing. In U. Demiray & S. Sever (Eds.), *Marketing online education programs: Frameworks for promotion and communication* (pp. 184–209). Hershey, PA: IGI Global. doi:10.4018/978-1-60960-074-7.ch012

Ho, K. K. (2008). The e-government development, IT strategies, and portals of the Hong Kong SAR government. In A. Anttiroiko (Ed.), *Electronic government: Concepts, methodologies, tools, and applications* (pp. 715–733). Hershey, PA: IGI Global. doi:10.4018/978-1-59904-947-2.ch060

Holden, S. H. (2003). The evolution of information technology management at the federal level: Implications for public administration. In G. Garson (Ed.), *Public information technology: Policy and management issues* (pp. 53–73). Hershey, PA: IGI Global. doi:10.4018/978-1-59140-060-8.ch003

Holden, S. H. (2007). The evolution of federal information technology management literature: Does IT finally matter? In G. Garson (Ed.), *Modern public information technology systems: Issues and challenges* (pp. 17–34). Hershey, PA: IGI Global. doi:10.4018/978-1-59904-051-6.ch002

Holland, J. W. (2009). Automation of American criminal justice. In M. Khosrow-Pour (Ed.), *Encyclopedia of information science and technology* (2nd ed.; pp. 300–302). Hershey, PA: IGI Global. doi:10.4018/978-1-60566-026-4.ch051

Holloway, K. (2013). Fair use, copyright, and academic integrity in an online academic environment. In *Digital rights management: Concepts, methodologies, tools, and applications* (pp. 917–928). Hershey, PA: IGI Global. doi:10.4018/978-1-4666-2136-7.ch044

Horiuchi, C. (2005). E-government databases. In L. Rivero, J. Doorn, & V. Ferraggine (Eds.), *Encyclopedia of database technologies and applications* (pp. 206–210). Hershey, PA: IGI Global. doi:10.4018/978-1-59140-560-3.ch035

Horiuchi, C. (2006). Creating IS quality in government settings. In E. Duggan & J. Reichgelt (Eds.), *Measuring information systems delivery quality* (pp. 311–327). Hershey, PA: IGI Global. doi:10.4018/978-1-59140-857-4.ch014

Hsiao, N., Chu, P., & Lee, C. (2012). Impact of e-governance on businesses: Model development and case study. In *Digital democracy: Concepts, methodologies, tools, and applications* (pp. 1407–1425). Hershey, PA: IGI Global. doi:10.4018/978-1-4666-1740-7.ch070

Huang, T., & Lee, C. (2010). Evaluating the impact of e-government on citizens: Cost-benefit analysis. In C. Reddick (Ed.), *Citizens and e-government: Evaluating policy and management* (pp. 37–52). Hershey, PA: IGI Global. doi:10.4018/978-1-61520-931-6.ch003

Hunter, M. G., Diochon, M., Pugsley, D., & Wright, B. (2002). Unique challenges for small business adoption of information technology: The case of the Nova Scotia ten. In S. Burgess (Ed.), *Managing information technology in small business: Challenges and solutions* (pp. 98–117). Hershey, PA: IGI Global. doi:10.4018/978-1-930708-35-8.ch006

Hurskainen, J. (2003). Integration of business systems and applications in merger and alliance: Case metso automation. In T. Reponen (Ed.), *Information technology enabled global customer service* (pp. 207–225). Hershey, PA: IGI Global. doi:10.4018/978-1-59140-048-6.ch012

Iazzolino, G., & Pietrantonio, R. (2011). The soveria.it project: A best practice of e-government in southern Italy. In D. Piaggesi, K. Sund, & W. Castelnovo (Eds.), *Global strategy and practice of e-governance: Examples from around the world* (pp. 34–56). Hershey, PA: IGI Global. doi:10.4018/978-1-60960-489-9.ch003

Imran, A., & Gregor, S. (2012). A process model for successful e-government adoption in the least developed countries: A case of Bangladesh. In F. Tan (Ed.), *International comparisons of information communication technologies: Advancing applications* (pp. 321–350). Hershey, PA: IGI Global. doi:10.4018/978-1-61350-480-2.ch014

Inoue, Y., & Bell, S. T. (2005). Electronic/digital government innovation, and publishing trends with IT. In M. Khosrow-Pour (Ed.), *Encyclopedia of information science and technology* (pp. 1018–1023). Hershey, PA: IGI Global. doi:10.4018/978-1-59140-553-5.ch180

Islam, M. M., & Ehsan, M. (2013). Understanding e-governance: A theoretical approach. In M. Islam & M. Ehsan (Eds.), *From government to e-governance: Public administration in the digital age* (pp. 38–49). Hershey, PA: IGI Global. doi:10.4018/978-1-4666-1909-8.ch003

Jaeger, B. (2009). E-government and e-democracy in the making. In M. Khosrow-Pour (Ed.), *Encyclopedia of information science and technology* (2nd ed.; pp. 1318–1322). Hershey, PA: IGI Global. doi:10.4018/978-1-60566-026-4.ch208

Jain, R. B. (2007). Revamping the administrative structure and processes in India for online diplomacy. In A. Anttiroiko & M. Malkia (Eds.), *Encyclopedia of digital government* (pp. 1418–1423). Hershey, PA: IGI Global. doi:10.4018/978-1-59140-789-8.ch217

Jain, R. B. (2008). Revamping the administrative structure and processes in India for online diplomacy. In A. Anttiroiko (Ed.), *Electronic government: Concepts, methodologies, tools, and applications* (pp. 3142–3149). Hershey, PA: IGI Global. doi:10.4018/978-1-59904-947-2.ch233

Jauhiainen, J. S., & Inkinen, T. (2009). E-governance and the information society in periphery. In C. Reddick (Ed.), *Handbook of research on strategies for local e-government adoption and implementation: Comparative studies* (pp. 497–514). Hershey, PA: IGI Global. doi:10.4018/978-1-60566-282-4.ch026

Jensen, M. J. (2009). Electronic democracy and citizen influence in government. In C. Reddick (Ed.), *Handbook of research on strategies for local e-government adoption and implementation: Comparative studies* (pp. 288–305). Hershey, PA: IGI Global. doi:10.4018/978-1-60566-282-4.ch015

Jiao, Y., Hurson, A. R., Potok, T. E., & Beckerman, B. G. (2009). Integrating mobile-based systems with healthcare databases. In J. Erickson (Ed.), *Database technologies: Concepts, methodologies, tools, and applications* (pp. 484–504). Hershey, PA: IGI Global. doi:10.4018/978-1-60566-058-5.ch031

Joia, L. A. (2002). A systematic model to integrate information technology into metabusinesses: A case study in the engineering realms. In F. Tan (Ed.), *Advanced topics in global information management* (Vol. 1, pp. 250–267). Hershey, PA: IGI Global. doi:10.4018/978-1-930708-43-3.ch016

Jones, T. H., & Song, I. (2000). Binary equivalents of ternary relationships in entity-relationship modeling: A logical decomposition approach. *Journal of Database Management, 11*(2), 12–19. doi:10.4018/jdm.2000040102

Juana-Espinosa, S. D. (2007). Empirical study of the municipalitites' motivations for adopting online presence. In L. Al-Hakim (Ed.), *Global e-government: Theory, applications and benchmarking* (pp. 261–279). Hershey, PA: IGI Global. doi:10.4018/978-1-59904-027-1.ch015

Jun, K., & Weare, C. (2012). Bridging from e-government practice to e-government research: Past trends and future directions. In K. Bwalya & S. Zulu (Eds.), *Handbook of research on e-government in emerging economies: Adoption, e-participation, and legal frameworks* (pp. 263–289). Hershey, PA: IGI Global. doi:10.4018/978-1-4666-0324-0.ch013

Junqueira, A., Diniz, E. H., & Fernandez, M. (2010). Electronic government implementation projects with multiple agencies: Analysis of the electronic invoice project under PMBOK framework. In J. Cordoba-Pachon & A. Ochoa-Arias (Eds.), *Systems thinking and e-participation: ICT in the governance of society* (pp. 135–153). Hershey, PA: IGI Global. doi:10.4018/978-1-60566-860-4.ch009

Juntunen, A. (2009). Joint service development with the local authorities. In C. Reddick (Ed.), *Handbook of research on strategies for local e-government adoption and implementation: Comparative studies* (pp. 902–920). Hershey, PA: IGI Global. doi:10.4018/978-1-60566-282-4.ch047

Kamel, S. (2001). *Using DSS for crisis management*. Hershey, PA: IGI Global. doi:10.4018/978-1-87828-961-2.ch020

Kamel, S. (2006). DSS for strategic decision making. In M. Khosrow-Pour (Ed.), *Cases on information technology and organizational politics & culture* (pp. 230–246). Hershey, PA: IGI Global. doi:10.4018/978-1-59904-411-8.ch015

Kamel, S. (2009). The software industry in Egypt as a potential contributor to economic growth. In M. Khosrow-Pour (Ed.), *Encyclopedia of information science and technology* (2nd ed.; pp. 3531–3537). Hershey, PA: IGI Global. doi:10.4018/978-1-60566-026-4.ch562

Kamel, S., & Hussein, M. (2008). Xceed: Pioneering the contact center industry in Egypt. *Journal of Cases on Information Technology, 10*(1), 67–91. doi:10.4018/jcit.2008010105

Kamel, S., & Wahba, K. (2003). The use of a hybrid model in web-based education: "The Global campus project. In A. Aggarwal (Ed.), *Web-based education: Learning from experience* (pp. 331–346). Hershey, PA: IGI Global. doi:10.4018/978-1-59140-102-5.ch020

Kardaras, D. K., & Papathanassiou, E. A. (2008). An exploratory study of the e-government services in Greece. In G. Garson & M. Khosrow-Pour (Eds.), *Handbook of research on public information technology* (pp. 162–174). Hershey, PA: IGI Global. doi:10.4018/978-1-59904-857-4.ch016

Kassahun, A. E., Molla, A., & Sarkar, P. (2012). Government process reengineering: What we know and what we need to know. In *Digital democracy: Concepts, methodologies, tools, and applications* (pp. 1730–1752). Hershey, PA: IGI Global. doi:10.4018/978-1-4666-1740-7.ch086

Khan, B. (2005). Technological issues. In B. Khan (Ed.), *Managing e-learning strategies: Design, delivery, implementation and evaluation* (pp. 154–180). Hershey, PA: IGI Global. doi:10.4018/978-1-59140-634-1.ch004

Khasawneh, A., Bsoul, M., Obeidat, I., & Al Azzam, I. (2012). Technology fears: A study of e-commerce loyalty perception by Jordanian customers. In J. Wang (Ed.), *Advancing the service sector with evolving technologies: Techniques and principles* (pp. 158–165). Hershey, PA: IGI Global. doi:10.4018/978-1-4666-0044-7.ch010

Khatibi, V., & Montazer, G. A. (2012). E-research methodology. In A. Juan, T. Daradoumis, M. Roca, S. Grasman, & J. Faulin (Eds.), *Collaborative and distributed e-research: Innovations in technologies, strategies and applications* (pp. 62–81). Hershey, PA: IGI Global. doi:10.4018/978-1-4666-0125-3.ch003

Kidd, T. (2011). The dragon in the school's backyard: A review of literature on the uses of technology in urban schools. In L. Tomei (Ed.), *Online courses and ICT in education: Emerging practices and applications* (pp. 242–257). Hershey, PA: IGI Global. doi:10.4018/978-1-60960-150-8.ch019

Kidd, T. T. (2010). My experience tells the story: Exploring technology adoption from a qualitative perspective - A pilot study. In H. Song & T. Kidd (Eds.), *Handbook of research on human performance and instructional technology* (pp. 247–262). Hershey, PA: IGI Global. doi:10.4018/978-1-60566-782-9.ch015

Kieley, B., Lane, G., Paquet, G., & Roy, J. (2002). e-Government in Canada: Services online or public service renewal? In Å. Grönlund (Ed.), Electronic government: Design, applications and management (pp. 340-355). Hershey, PA: IGI Global. doi:10.4018/978-1-930708-19-8.ch016

Kim, P. (2012). "Stay out of the way! My kid is video blogging through a phone!": A lesson learned from math tutoring social media for children in underserved communities. In *Wireless technologies: Concepts, methodologies, tools and applications* (pp. 1415–1428). Hershey, PA: IGI Global. doi:10.4018/978-1-61350-101-6.ch517

Kirlidog, M. (2010). Financial aspects of national ICT strategies. In S. Kamel (Ed.), *E-strategies for technological diffusion and adoption: National ICT approaches for socioeconomic development* (pp. 277–292). Hershey, PA: IGI Global. doi:10.4018/978-1-60566-388-3.ch016

Kisielnicki, J. (2006). Transfer of information and knowledge in the project management. In E. Coakes & S. Clarke (Eds.), *Encyclopedia of communities of practice in information and knowledge management* (pp. 544–551). Hershey, PA: IGI Global. doi:10.4018/978-1-59140-556-6.ch091

Kittner, M., & Van Slyke, C. (2006). Reorganizing information technology services in an academic environment. In M. Khosrow-Pour (Ed.), *Cases on the human side of information technology* (pp. 49–66). Hershey, PA: IGI Global. doi:10.4018/978-1-59904-405-7.ch004

Knoell, H. D. (2008). Semi virtual workplaces in German financial service enterprises. In P. Zemliansky & K. St.Amant (Eds.), *Handbook of research on virtual workplaces and the new nature of business practices* (pp. 570–581). Hershey, PA: IGI Global. doi:10.4018/978-1-59904-893-2.ch041

Koh, S. L., & Maguire, S. (2009). Competing in the age of information technology in a developing economy: Experiences of an Indian bank. In S. Koh & S. Maguire (Eds.), *Information and communication technologies management in turbulent business environments* (pp. 326–350). Hershey, PA: IGI Global. doi:10.4018/978-1-60566-424-8.ch018

Kollmann, T., & Häsel, M. (2009). Competence of information technology professionals in internet-based ventures. In I. Lee (Ed.), *Electronic business: Concepts, methodologies, tools, and applications* (pp. 1905–1919). Hershey, PA: IGI Global. doi:10.4018/978-1-60566-056-1.ch118

Kollmann, T., & Häsel, M. (2009). Competence of information technology professionals in internet-based ventures. In A. Cater-Steel (Ed.), *Information technology governance and service management: Frameworks and adaptations* (pp. 239–253). Hershey, PA: IGI Global. doi:10.4018/978-1-60566-008-0.ch013

Kollmann, T., & Häsel, M. (2010). Competence of information technology professionals in internet-based ventures. In *Electronic services: Concepts, methodologies, tools and applications* (pp. 1551–1565). Hershey, PA: IGI Global. doi:10.4018/978-1-61520-967-5.ch094

Kraemer, K., & King, J. L. (2006). Information technology and administrative reform: Will e-government be different? *International Journal of Electronic Government Research, 2*(1), 1–20. doi:10.4018/jegr.2006010101

Kraemer, K., & King, J. L. (2008). Information technology and administrative reform: Will e-government be different? In D. Norris (Ed.), *E-government research: Policy and management* (pp. 1–20). Hershey, PA: IGI Global. doi:10.4018/978-1-59904-913-7.ch001

Lampathaki, F., Tsiakaliaris, C., Stasis, A., & Charalabidis, Y. (2011). National interoperability frameworks: The way forward. In Y. Charalabidis (Ed.), *Interoperability in digital public services and administration: Bridging e-government and e-business* (pp. 1–24). Hershey, PA: IGI Global. doi:10.4018/978-1-61520-887-6.ch001

Lan, Z., & Scott, C. R. (1996). The relative importance of computer-mediated information versus conventional non-computer-mediated information in public managerial decision making. *Information Resources Management Journal*, *9*(1), 27–0. doi:10.4018/irmj.1996010103

Law, W. (2004). *Public sector data management in a developing economy*. Hershey, PA: IGI Global. doi:10.4018/978-1-59140-259-6.ch034

Law, W. K. (2005). Information resources development challenges in a cross-cultural environment. In M. Khosrow-Pour (Ed.), *Encyclopedia of information science and technology* (pp. 1476–1481). Hershey, PA: IGI Global. doi:10.4018/978-1-59140-553-5.ch259

Law, W. K. (2009). Cross-cultural challenges for information resources management. In M. Khosrow-Pour (Ed.), *Encyclopedia of information science and technology* (2nd ed.; pp. 840–846). Hershey, PA: IGI Global. doi:10.4018/978-1-60566-026-4.ch136

Law, W. K. (2011). Cross-cultural challenges for information resources management. In *Global business: Concepts, methodologies, tools and applications* (pp. 1924–1932). Hershey, PA: IGI Global. doi:10.4018/978-1-60960-587-2.ch704

Malkia, M., & Savolainen, R. (2004). eTransformation in government, politics and society: Conceptual framework and introduction. In M. Malkia, A. Anttiroiko, & R. Savolainen (Eds.), eTransformation in governance: New directions in government and politics (pp. 1-21). Hershey, PA: IGI Global. doi:10.4018/978-1-59140-130-8.ch001

Mandujano, S. (2011). Network manageability security. In D. Kar & M. Syed (Eds.), *Network security, administration and management: Advancing technology and practice* (pp. 158–181). Hershey, PA: IGI Global. doi:10.4018/978-1-60960-777-7.ch009

Marich, M. J., Schooley, B. L., & Horan, T. A. (2012). A normative enterprise architecture for guiding end-to-end emergency response decision support. In M. Jennex (Ed.), *Managing crises and disasters with emerging technologies: Advancements* (pp. 71–87). Hershey, PA: IGI Global. doi:10.4018/978-1-4666-0167-3.ch006

Markov, R., & Okujava, S. (2008). Costs, benefits, and risks of e-government portals. In G. Putnik & M. Cruz-Cunha (Eds.), *Encyclopedia of networked and virtual organizations* (pp. 354–363). Hershey, PA: IGI Global. doi:10.4018/978-1-59904-885-7.ch047

Martin, N., & Rice, J. (2013). Evaluating and designing electronic government for the future: Observations and insights from Australia. In V. Weerakkody (Ed.), *E-government services design, adoption, and evaluation* (pp. 238–258). Hershey, PA: IGI Global. doi:10.4018/978-1-4666-2458-0.ch014

i. Martinez, A. C. (2008). Accessing administration's information via internet in Spain. In F. Tan (Ed.), *Global information technologies: Concepts, methodologies, tools, and applications* (pp. 2558–2573). Hershey, PA: IGI Global. doi:10.4018/978-1-59904-939-7.ch186

Mbarika, V. W., Meso, P. N., & Musa, P. F. (2006). A disconnect in stakeholders' perceptions from emerging realities of teledensity growth in Africa's least developed countries. In M. Hunter & F. Tan (Eds.), *Advanced topics in global information management* (Vol. 5, pp. 263–282). Hershey, PA: IGI Global. doi:10.4018/978-1-59140-923-6.ch012

Mbarika, V. W., Meso, P. N., & Musa, P. F. (2008). A disconnect in stakeholders' perceptions from emerging realities of teledensity growth in Africa's least developed countries. In F. Tan (Ed.), *Global information technologies: Concepts, methodologies, tools, and applications* (pp. 2948–2962). Hershey, PA: IGI Global. doi:10.4018/978-1-59904-939-7.ch209

Means, T., Olson, E., & Spooner, J. (2013). Discovering ways that don't work on the road to success: Strengths and weaknesses revealed by an active learning studio classroom project. In A. Benson, J. Moore, & S. Williams van Rooij (Eds.), *Cases on educational technology planning, design, and implementation: A project management perspective* (pp. 94–113). Hershey, PA: IGI Global. doi:10.4018/978-1-4666-4237-9.ch006

Melitski, J., Holzer, M., Kim, S., Kim, C., & Rho, S. (2008). Digital government worldwide: An e-government assessment of municipal web sites. In G. Garson & M. Khosrow-Pour (Eds.), *Handbook of research on public information technology* (pp. 790–804). Hershey, PA: IGI Global. doi:10.4018/978-1-59904-857-4.ch069

Memmola, M., Palumbo, G., & Rossini, M. (2009). Web & RFID technology: New frontiers in costing and process management for rehabilitation medicine. In L. Al-Hakim & M. Memmola (Eds.), *Business web strategy: Design, alignment, and application* (pp. 145–169). Hershey, PA: IGI Global. doi:10.4018/978-1-60566-024-0.ch008

Meng, Z., Fahong, Z., & Lei, L. (2008). Information technology and environment. In Y. Kurihara, S. Takaya, H. Harui, & H. Kamae (Eds.), *Information technology and economic development* (pp. 201–212). Hershey, PA: IGI Global. doi:10.4018/978-1-59904-579-5.ch014

Mentzingen de Moraes, A. J., Ferneda, E., Costa, I., & Spinola, M. D. (2011). Practical approach for implementation of governance process in IT: Information technology areas. In N. Shi & G. Silvius (Eds.), *Enterprise IT governance, business value and performance measurement* (pp. 19–40). Hershey, PA: IGI Global. doi:10.4018/978-1-60566-346-3.ch002

Merwin, G. A. Jr, McDonald, J. S., & Odera, L. C. (2008). Economic development: Government's cutting edge in IT. In M. Raisinghani (Ed.), *Handbook of research on global information technology management in the digital economy* (pp. 1–37). Hershey, PA: IGI Global. doi:10.4018/978-1-59904-875-8.ch001

Meso, P., & Duncan, N. (2002). Can national information infrastructures enhance social development in the least developed countries? An empirical investigation. In M. Dadashzadeh (Ed.), *Information technology management in developing countries* (pp. 23–51). Hershey, PA: IGI Global. doi:10.4018/978-1-931777-03-2.ch002

Meso, P. N., & Duncan, N. B. (2002). Can national information infrastructures enhance social development in the least developed countries? In F. Tan (Ed.), *Advanced topics in global information management* (Vol. 1, pp. 207–226). Hershey, PA: IGI Global. doi:10.4018/978-1-930708-43-3.ch014

Middleton, M. (2008). Evaluation of e-government web sites. In G. Garson & M. Khosrow-Pour (Eds.), *Handbook of research on public information technology* (pp. 699–710). Hershey, PA: IGI Global. doi:10.4018/978-1-59904-857-4.ch063

Mingers, J. (2010). Pluralism, realism, and truth: The keys to knowledge in information systems research. In D. Paradice (Ed.), *Emerging systems approaches in information technologies: Concepts, theories, and applications* (pp. 86–98). Hershey, PA: IGI Global. doi:10.4018/978-1-60566-976-2.ch006

Mital, K. M. (2012). ICT, unique identity and inclusive growth: An Indian perspective. In A. Manoharan & M. Holzer (Eds.), *E-governance and civic engagement: Factors and determinants of e-democracy* (pp. 584–612). Hershey, PA: IGI Global. doi:10.4018/978-1-61350-083-5.ch029

Mizell, A. P. (2008). Helping close the digital divide for financially disadvantaged seniors. In F. Tan (Ed.), *Global information technologies: Concepts, methodologies, tools, and applications* (pp. 2396–2402). Hershey, PA: IGI Global. doi:10.4018/978-1-59904-939-7.ch173

Molinari, F., Wills, C., Koumpis, A., & Moumtzi, V. (2011). A citizen-centric platform to support networking in the area of e-democracy. In H. Rahman (Ed.), *Cases on adoption, diffusion and evaluation of global e-governance systems: Impact at the grass roots* (pp. 282–302). Hershey, PA: IGI Global. doi:10.4018/978-1-61692-814-8.ch014

Molinari, F., Wills, C., Koumpis, A., & Moumtzi, V. (2013). A citizen-centric platform to support networking in the area of e-democracy. In H. Rahman (Ed.), *Cases on progressions and challenges in ICT utilization for citizen-centric governance* (pp. 265–297). Hershey, PA: IGI Global. doi:10.4018/978-1-4666-2071-1.ch013

Monteverde, F. (2010). The process of e-government public policy inclusion in the governmental agenda: A framework for assessment and case study. In J. Cordoba-Pachon & A. Ochoa-Arias (Eds.), *Systems thinking and e-participation: ICT in the governance of society* (pp. 233–245). Hershey, PA: IGI Global. doi:10.4018/978-1-60566-860-4.ch015

Moodley, S. (2008). Deconstructing the South African government's ICT for development discourse. In A. Anttiroiko (Ed.), *Electronic government: Concepts, methodologies, tools, and applications* (pp. 622–631). Hershey, PA: IGI Global. doi:10.4018/978-1-59904-947-2.ch053

Moodley, S. (2008). Deconstructing the South African government's ICT for development discourse. In C. Van Slyke (Ed.), *Information communication technologies: Concepts, methodologies, tools, and applications* (pp. 816–825). Hershey, PA: IGI Global. doi:10.4018/978-1-59904-949-6.ch052

Mora, M., Cervantes-Perez, F., Gelman-Muravchik, O., Forgionne, G. A., & Mejia-Olvera, M. (2003). DMSS implementation research: A conceptual analysis of the contributions and limitations of the factor-based and stage-based streams. In G. Forgionne, J. Gupta, & M. Mora (Eds.), *Decision-making support systems: Achievements and challenges for the new decade* (pp. 331–356). Hershey, PA: IGI Global. doi:10.4018/978-1-59140-045-5.ch020

Mörtberg, C., & Elovaara, P. (2010). Attaching people and technology: Between e and government. In S. Booth, S. Goodman, & G. Kirkup (Eds.), *Gender issues in learning and working with information technology: Social constructs and cultural contexts* (pp. 83–98). Hershey, PA: IGI Global. doi:10.4018/978-1-61520-813-5.ch005

Murphy, J., Harper, E., Devine, E. C., Burke, L. J., & Hook, M. L. (2011). Case study: Lessons learned when embedding evidence-based knowledge in a nurse care planning and documentation system. In A. Cashin & R. Cook (Eds.), *Evidence-based practice in nursing informatics: Concepts and applications* (pp. 174–190). Hershey, PA: IGI Global. doi:10.4018/978-1-60960-034-1.ch014

Mutula, S. M. (2013). E-government's role in poverty alleviation: Case study of South Africa. In H. Rahman (Ed.), *Cases on progressions and challenges in ICT utilization for citizen-centric governance* (pp. 44–68). Hershey, PA: IGI Global. doi:10.4018/978-1-4666-2071-1.ch003

Nath, R., & Angeles, R. (2005). Relationships between supply characteristics and buyer-supplier coupling in e-procurement: An empirical analysis. *International Journal of E-Business Research, 1*(2), 40–55. doi:10.4018/jebr.2005040103

Nissen, M. E. (2006). Application cases in government. In M. Nissen (Ed.), *Harnessing knowledge dynamics: Principled organizational knowing & learning* (pp. 152–181). Hershey, PA: IGI Global. doi:10.4018/978-1-59140-773-7.ch008

Norris, D. F. (2003). Leading-edge information technologies and American local governments. In G. Garson (Ed.), *Public information technology: Policy and management issues* (pp. 139–169). Hershey, PA: IGI Global. doi:10.4018/978-1-59140-060-8.ch007

Norris, D. F. (2008). Information technology among U.S. local governments. In G. Garson & M. Khosrow-Pour (Eds.), *Handbook of research on public information technology* (pp. 132–144). Hershey, PA: IGI Global. doi:10.4018/978-1-59904-857-4.ch013

Northrop, A. (1999). The challenge of teaching information technology in public administration graduate programs. In G. Garson (Ed.), *Information technology and computer applications in public administration: Issues and trends* (pp. 1–22). Hershey, PA: IGI Global. doi:10.4018/978-1-87828-952-0.ch001

Northrop, A. (2003). Information technology and public administration: The view from the profession. In G. Garson (Ed.), *Public information technology: Policy and management issues* (pp. 1–19). Hershey, PA: IGI Global. doi:10.4018/978-1-59140-060-8.ch001

Northrop, A. (2007). Lip service? How PA journals and textbooks view information technology. In G. Garson (Ed.), *Modern public information technology systems: Issues and challenges* (pp. 1–16). Hershey, PA: IGI Global. doi:10.4018/978-1-59904-051-6.ch001

Null, E. (2013). Legal and political barriers to municipal networks in the United States. In A. Abdelaal (Ed.), *Social and economic effects of community wireless networks and infrastructures* (pp. 27–56). Hershey, PA: IGI Global. doi:10.4018/978-1-4666-2997-4.ch003

Okunoye, A., Frolick, M., & Crable, E. (2006). ERP implementation in higher education: An account of pre-implementation and implementation phases. *Journal of Cases on Information Technology*, *8*(2), 110–132. doi:10.4018/jcit.2006040106

Olasina, G. (2012). A review of egovernment services in Nigeria. In A. Tella & A. Issa (Eds.), *Library and information science in developing countries: Contemporary issues* (pp. 205–221). Hershey, PA: IGI Global. doi:10.4018/978-1-61350-335-5.ch015

Orgeron, C. P. (2008). A model for reengineering IT job classes in state government. In G. Garson & M. Khosrow-Pour (Eds.), *Handbook of research on public information technology* (pp. 735–746). Hershey, PA: IGI Global. doi:10.4018/978-1-59904-857-4.ch066

Owsinski, J. W., & Pielak, A. M. (2011). Local authority websites in rural areas: Measuring quality and functionality, and assessing the role. In Z. Andreopoulou, B. Manos, N. Polman, & D. Viaggi (Eds.), *Agricultural and environmental informatics, governance and management: Emerging research applications* (pp. 39–60). Hershey, PA: IGI Global. doi:10.4018/978-1-60960-621-3.ch003

Owsiński, J. W., Pielak, A. M., Sęp, K., & Stańczak, J. (2014). Local web-based networks in rural municipalities: Extension, density, and meaning. In Z. Andreopoulou, V. Samathrakis, S. Louca, & M. Vlachopoulou (Eds.), *E-innovation for sustainable development of rural resources during global economic crisis* (pp. 126–151). Hershey, PA: IGI Global. doi:10.4018/978-1-4666-4550-9.ch011

Pagani, M., & Pasinetti, C. (2008). Technical and functional quality in the development of t-government services. In A. Anttiroiko (Ed.), *Electronic government: Concepts, methodologies, tools, and applications* (pp. 2943–2965). Hershey, PA: IGI Global. doi:10.4018/978-1-59904-947-2.ch220

Pani, A. K., & Agrahari, A. (2005). On e-markets in emerging economy: An Indian experience. In M. Khosrow-Pour (Ed.), *Advanced topics in electronic commerce* (Vol. 1, pp. 287–299). Hershey, PA: IGI Global. doi:10.4018/978-1-59140-819-2.ch015

Papadopoulos, T., Angelopoulos, S., & Kitsios, F. (2011). A strategic approach to e-health interoperability using e-government frameworks. In A. Lazakidou, K. Siassiakos, & K. Ioannou (Eds.), *Wireless technologies for ambient assisted living and healthcare: Systems and applications* (pp. 213–229). Hershey, PA: IGI Global. doi:10.4018/978-1-61520-805-0.ch012

Papadopoulos, T., Angelopoulos, S., & Kitsios, F. (2013). A strategic approach to e-health interoperability using e-government frameworks. In *User-driven healthcare: Concepts, methodologies, tools, and applications* (pp. 791–807). Hershey, PA: IGI Global. doi:10.4018/978-1-4666-2770-3.ch039

Papaleo, G., Chiarella, D., Aiello, M., & Caviglione, L. (2012). Analysis, development and deployment of statistical anomaly detection techniques for real e-mail traffic. In T. Chou (Ed.), *Information assurance and security technologies for risk assessment and threat management: Advances* (pp. 47–71). Hershey, PA: IGI Global. doi:10.4018/978-1-61350-507-6.ch003

Papp, R. (2003). Information technology & FDA compliance in the pharmaceutical industry. In M. Khosrow-Pour (Ed.), *Annals of cases on information technology* (Vol. 5, pp. 262–273). Hershey, PA: IGI Global. doi:10.4018/978-1-59140-061-5.ch017

Parsons, T. W. (2007). Developing a knowledge management portal. In A. Tatnall (Ed.), *Encyclopedia of portal technologies and applications* (pp. 223–227). Hershey, PA: IGI Global. doi:10.4018/978-1-59140-989-2.ch039

Passaris, C. E. (2007). Immigration and digital government. In A. Anttiroiko & M. Malkia (Eds.), *Encyclopedia of digital government* (pp. 988–994). Hershey, PA: IGI Global. doi:10.4018/978-1-59140-789-8.ch148

Pavlichev, A. (2004). The e-government challenge for public administration. In A. Pavlichev & G. Garson (Eds.), *Digital government: Principles and best practices* (pp. 276–290). Hershey, PA: IGI Global. doi:10.4018/978-1-59140-122-3.ch018

Penrod, J. I., & Harbor, A. F. (2000). Designing and implementing a learning organization-oriented information technology planning and management process. In L. Petrides (Ed.), *Case studies on information technology in higher education: Implications for policy and practice* (pp. 7–19). Hershey, PA: IGI Global. doi:10.4018/978-1-878289-74-2.ch001

Planas-Silva, M. D., & Joseph, R. C. (2011). Perspectives on the adoption of electronic resources for use in clinical trials. In M. Guah (Ed.), *Healthcare delivery reform and new technologies: Organizational initiatives* (pp. 19–28). Hershey, PA: IGI Global. doi:10.4018/978-1-60960-183-6.ch002

Pomazalová, N., & Rejman, S. (2013). The rationale behind implementation of new electronic tools for electronic public procurement. In N. Pomazalová (Ed.), *Public sector transformation processes and internet public procurement: Decision support systems* (pp. 85–117). Hershey, PA: IGI Global. doi:10.4018/978-1-4666-2665-2.ch006

Postorino, M. N. (2012). City competitiveness and airport: Information science perspective. In M. Bulu (Ed.), *City competitiveness and improving urban subsystems: Technologies and applications* (pp. 61–83). Hershey, PA: IGI Global. doi:10.4018/978-1-61350-174-0.ch004

Poupa, C. (2002). Electronic government in Switzerland: Priorities for 2001-2005 - Electronic voting and federal portal. In Å. Grönlund (Ed.), *Electronic government: Design, applications and management* (pp. 356–369). Hershey, PA: IGI Global. doi:10.4018/978-1-930708-19-8.ch017

Powell, S. R. (2010). Interdisciplinarity in telecommunications and networking. In *Networking and telecommunications: Concepts, methodologies, tools and applications* (pp. 33–40). Hershey, PA: IGI Global. doi:10.4018/978-1-60566-986-1.ch004

Priya, P. S., & Mathiyalagan, N. (2011). A study of the implementation status of two e-governance projects in land revenue administration in India. In M. Shareef, V. Kumar, U. Kumar, & Y. Dwivedi (Eds.), *Stakeholder adoption of e-government services: Driving and resisting factors* (pp. 214–230). Hershey, PA: IGI Global. doi:10.4018/978-1-60960-601-5.ch011

Prysby, C., & Prysby, N. (2000). Electronic mail, employee privacy and the workplace. In L. Janczewski (Ed.), *Internet and intranet security management: Risks and solutions* (pp. 251–270). Hershey, PA: IGI Global. doi:10.4018/978-1-878289-71-1.ch009

Prysby, C. L., & Prysby, N. D. (2003). Electronic mail in the public workplace: Issues of privacy and public disclosure. In G. Garson (Ed.), *Public information technology: Policy and management issues* (pp. 271–298). Hershey, PA: IGI Global. doi:10.4018/978-1-59140-060-8.ch012

Prysby, C. L., & Prysby, N. D. (2007). You have mail, but who is reading it? Issues of e-mail in the public workplace. In G. Garson (Ed.), *Modern public information technology systems: Issues and challenges* (pp. 312–336). Hershey, PA: IGI Global. doi:10.4018/978-1-59904-051-6.ch016

Radl, A., & Chen, Y. (2005). Computer security in electronic government: A state-local education information system. *International Journal of Electronic Government Research*, *1*(1), 79–99. doi:10.4018/jegr.2005010105

Rahman, H. (2008). Information dynamics in developing countries. In C. Van Slyke (Ed.), *Information communication technologies: Concepts, methodologies, tools, and applications* (pp. 104–114). Hershey, PA: IGI Global. doi:10.4018/978-1-59904-949-6.ch008

Ramanathan, J. (2009). Adaptive IT architecture as a catalyst for network capability in government. In P. Saha (Ed.), *Advances in government enterprise architecture* (pp. 149–172). Hershey, PA: IGI Global. doi:10.4018/978-1-60566-068-4.ch007

Ramos, I., & Berry, D. M. (2006). Social construction of information technology supporting work. In M. Khosrow-Pour (Ed.), *Cases on information technology: Lessons learned* (Vol. 7, pp. 36–52). Hershey, PA: IGI Global. doi:10.4018/978-1-59140-673-0.ch003

Ray, D., Gulla, U., Gupta, M. P., & Dash, S. S. (2009). Interoperability and constituents of interoperable systems in public sector. In V. Weerakkody, M. Janssen, & Y. Dwivedi (Eds.), *Handbook of research on ICT-enabled transformational government: A global perspective* (pp. 175–195). Hershey, PA: IGI Global. doi:10.4018/978-1-60566-390-6.ch010

Reddick, C. G. (2007). E-government and creating a citizen-centric government: A study of federal government CIOs. In G. Garson (Ed.), *Modern public information technology systems: Issues and challenges* (pp. 143–165). Hershey, PA: IGI Global. doi:10.4018/978-1-59904-051-6.ch008

Reddick, C. G. (2010). Citizen-centric e-government. In C. Reddick (Ed.), *Homeland security preparedness and information systems: Strategies for managing public policy* (pp. 45–75). Hershey, PA: IGI Global. doi:10.4018/978-1-60566-834-5.ch002

Reddick, C. G. (2010). E-government and creating a citizen-centric government: A study of federal government CIOs. In C. Reddick (Ed.), *Homeland security preparedness and information systems: Strategies for managing public policy* (pp. 230–250). Hershey, PA: IGI Global. doi:10.4018/978-1-60566-834-5.ch012

Reddick, C. G. (2010). Perceived effectiveness of e-government and its usage in city governments: Survey evidence from information technology directors. In C. Reddick (Ed.), *Homeland security preparedness and information systems: Strategies for managing public policy* (pp. 213–229). Hershey, PA: IGI Global. doi:10.4018/978-1-60566-834-5.ch011

Reddick, C. G. (2012). Customer relationship management adoption in local governments in the United States. In S. Chhabra & M. Kumar (Eds.), *Strategic enterprise resource planning models for e-government: Applications and methodologies* (pp. 111–124). Hershey, PA: IGI Global. doi:10.4018/978-1-60960-863-7.ch008

Reeder, F. S., & Pandy, S. M. (2008). Identifying effective funding models for e-government. In A. Anttiroiko (Ed.), *Electronic government: Concepts, methodologies, tools, and applications* (pp. 1108–1138). Hershey, PA: IGI Global. doi:10.4018/978-1-59904-947-2.ch083

Riesco, D., Acosta, E., & Montejano, G. (2003). An extension to a UML activity graph from workflow. In L. Favre (Ed.), *UML and the unified process* (pp. 294–314). Hershey, PA: IGI Global. doi:10.4018/978-1-93177-744-5.ch015

Ritzhaupt, A. D., & Gill, T. G. (2008). A hybrid and novel approach to teaching computer programming in MIS curriculum. In S. Negash, M. Whitman, A. Woszczynski, K. Hoganson, & H. Mattord (Eds.), *Handbook of distance learning for real-time and asynchronous information technology education* (pp. 259–281). Hershey, PA: IGI Global. doi:10.4018/978-1-59904-964-9.ch014

Roche, E. M. (1993). International computing and the international regime. *Journal of Global Information Management, 1*(2), 33–44. doi:10.4018/jgim.1993040103

Rocheleau, B. (2007). Politics, accountability, and information management. In G. Garson (Ed.), *Modern public information technology systems: Issues and challenges* (pp. 35–71). Hershey, PA: IGI Global. doi:10.4018/978-1-59904-051-6.ch003

Rodrigues Filho, J. (2010). E-government in Brazil: Reinforcing dominant institutions or reducing citizenship? In C. Reddick (Ed.), *Politics, democracy and e-government: Participation and service delivery* (pp. 347–362). Hershey, PA: IGI Global. doi:10.4018/978-1-61520-933-0.ch021

Rodriguez, S. R., & Thorp, D. A. (2013). eLearning for industry: A case study of the project management process. In A. Benson, J. Moore, & S. Williams van Rooij (Eds.), Cases on educational technology planning, design, and implementation: A project management perspective (pp. 319-342). Hershey, PA: IGI Global. doi:10.4018/978-1-4666-4237-9.ch017

Roman, A. V. (2013). Delineating three dimensions of e-government success: Security, functionality, and transformation. In J. Gil-Garcia (Ed.), *E-government success factors and measures: Theories, concepts, and methodologies* (pp. 171–192). Hershey, PA: IGI Global. doi:10.4018/978-1-4666-4058-0.ch010

Ross, S. C., Tyran, C. K., & Auer, D. J. (2008). Up in smoke: Rebuilding after an IT disaster. In H. Nemati (Ed.), *Information security and ethics: Concepts, methodologies, tools, and applications* (pp. 3659–3675). Hershey, PA: IGI Global. doi:10.4018/978-1-59904-937-3.ch248

Ross, S. C., Tyran, C. K., Auer, D. J., Junell, J. M., & Williams, T. G. (2005). Up in smoke: Rebuilding after an IT disaster. *Journal of Cases on Information Technology*, *7*(2), 31–49. doi:10.4018/jcit.2005040103

Roy, J. (2008). Security, sovereignty, and continental interoperability: Canada's elusive balance. In T. Loendorf & G. Garson (Eds.), *Patriotic information systems* (pp. 153–176). Hershey, PA: IGI Global. doi:10.4018/978-1-59904-594-8.ch007

Rubeck, R. F., & Miller, G. A. (2009). vGOV: Remote video access to government services. In A. Scupola (Ed.), Cases on managing e-services (pp. 253-268). Hershey, PA: IGI Global. doi:10.4018/978-1-60566-064-6.ch017

Saekow, A., & Boonmee, C. (2011). The challenges of implementing e-government interoperability in Thailand: Case of official electronic correspondence letters exchange across government departments. In Y. Charalabidis (Ed.), *Interoperability in digital public services and administration: Bridging e-government and e-business* (pp. 40–61). Hershey, PA: IGI Global. doi:10.4018/978-1-61520-887-6.ch003

Saekow, A., & Boonmee, C. (2012). The challenges of implementing e-government interoperability in Thailand: Case of official electronic correspondence letters exchange across government departments. In *Digital democracy: Concepts, methodologies, tools, and applications* (pp. 1883–1905). Hershey, PA: IGI Global. doi:10.4018/978-1-4666-1740-7.ch094

Sagsan, M., & Medeni, T. (2012). Understanding "knowledge management (KM) paradigms" from social media perspective: An empirical study on discussion group for KM at professional networking site. In M. Cruz-Cunha, P. Gonçalves, N. Lopes, E. Miranda, & G. Putnik (Eds.), *Handbook of research on business social networking: Organizational, managerial, and technological dimensions* (pp. 738–755). Hershey, PA: IGI Global. doi:10.4018/978-1-61350-168-9.ch039

Sahi, G., & Madan, S. (2013). Information security threats in ERP enabled e-governance: Challenges and solutions. In *Enterprise resource planning: Concepts, methodologies, tools, and applications* (pp. 825–837). Hershey, PA: IGI Global. doi:10.4018/978-1-4666-4153-2.ch048

Sanford, C., & Bhattacherjee, A. (2008). IT implementation in a developing country municipality: A sociocognitive analysis. *International Journal of Technology and Human Interaction*, *4*(3), 68–93. doi:10.4018/jthi.2008070104

Schelin, S. H. (2003). E-government: An overview. In G. Garson (Ed.), *Public information technology: Policy and management issues* (pp. 120–138). Hershey, PA: IGI Global. doi:10.4018/978-1-59140-060-8.ch006

Schelin, S. H. (2004). Training for digital government. In A. Pavlichev & G. Garson (Eds.), *Digital government: Principles and best practices* (pp. 263–275). Hershey, PA: IGI Global. doi:10.4018/978-1-59140-122-3.ch017

Schelin, S. H. (2007). E-government: An overview. In G. Garson (Ed.), *Modern public information technology systems: Issues and challenges* (pp. 110–126). Hershey, PA: IGI Global. doi:10.4018/978-1-59904-051-6.ch006

Schelin, S. H., & Garson, G. (2004). Theoretical justification of critical success factors. In G. Garson & S. Schelin (Eds.), *IT solutions series: Humanizing information technology: Advice from experts* (pp. 4–15). Hershey, PA: IGI Global. doi:10.4018/978-1-59140-245-9.ch002

Scime, A. (2002). Information systems and computer science model curricula: A comparative look. In M. Dadashzadeh, A. Saber, & S. Saber (Eds.), *Information technology education in the new millennium* (pp. 146–158). Hershey, PA: IGI Global. doi:10.4018/978-1-931777-05-6.ch018

Scime, A. (2009). Computing curriculum analysis and development. In M. Khosrow-Pour (Ed.), *Encyclopedia of information science and technology* (2nd ed.; pp. 667–671). Hershey, PA: IGI Global. doi:10.4018/978-1-60566-026-4.ch108

Scime, A., & Wania, C. (2008). Computing curricula: A comparison of models. In C. Van Slyke (Ed.), *Information communication technologies: Concepts, methodologies, tools, and applications* (pp. 1270–1283). Hershey, PA: IGI Global. doi:10.4018/978-1-59904-949-6.ch088

Seidman, S. B. (2009). An international perspective on professional software engineering credentials. In H. Ellis, S. Demurjian, & J. Naveda (Eds.), *Software engineering: Effective teaching and learning approaches and practices* (pp. 351–361). Hershey, PA: IGI Global. doi:10.4018/978-1-60566-102-5.ch018

Seifert, J. W. (2007). E-government act of 2002 in the United States. In A. Anttiroiko & M. Malkia (Eds.), *Encyclopedia of digital government* (pp. 476–481). Hershey, PA: IGI Global. doi:10.4018/978-1-59140-789-8.ch072

Seifert, J. W., & Relyea, H. C. (2008). E-government act of 2002 in the United States. In A. Anttiroiko (Ed.), *Electronic government: Concepts, methodologies, tools, and applications* (pp. 154–161). Hershey, PA: IGI Global. doi:10.4018/978-1-59904-947-2.ch013

Seufert, S. (2002). E-learning business models: Framework and best practice examples. In M. Raisinghani (Ed.), *Cases on worldwide e-commerce: Theory in action* (pp. 70–94). Hershey, PA: IGI Global. doi:10.4018/978-1-930708-27-3.ch004

Shareef, M. A., & Archer, N. (2012). E-government service development. In M. Shareef, N. Archer, & S. Dutta (Eds.), *E-government service maturity and development: Cultural, organizational and technological perspectives* (pp. 1–14). Hershey, PA: IGI Global. doi:10.4018/978-1-60960-848-4.ch001

Shareef, M. A., & Archer, N. (2012). E-government initiatives: Review studies on different countries. In M. Shareef, N. Archer, & S. Dutta (Eds.), *E-government service maturity and development: Cultural, organizational and technological perspectives* (pp. 40–76). Hershey, PA: IGI Global. doi:10.4018/978-1-60960-848-4.ch003

Shareef, M. A., Kumar, U., & Kumar, V. (2011). E-government development: Performance evaluation parameters. In M. Shareef, V. Kumar, U. Kumar, & Y. Dwivedi (Eds.), *Stakeholder adoption of e-government services: Driving and resisting factors* (pp. 197–213). Hershey, PA: IGI Global. doi:10.4018/978-1-60960-601-5.ch010

Shareef, M. A., Kumar, U., Kumar, V., & Niktash, M. (2012). Electronic-government vision: Case studies for objectives, strategies, and initiatives. In M. Shareef, N. Archer, & S. Dutta (Eds.), *E-government service maturity and development: Cultural, organizational and technological perspectives* (pp. 15–39). Hershey, PA: IGI Global. doi:10.4018/978-1-60960-848-4.ch002

Shukla, P., Kumar, A., & Anu Kumar, P. B. (2013). Impact of national culture on business continuity management system implementation. *International Journal of Risk and Contingency Management, 2*(3), 23–36. doi:10.4018/ijrcm.2013070102

Shulman, S. W. (2007). The federal docket management system and the prospect for digital democracy in U S rulemaking. In G. Garson (Ed.), *Modern public information technology systems: Issues and challenges* (pp. 166–184). Hershey, PA: IGI Global. doi:10.4018/978-1-59904-051-6.ch009

Simonovic, S. (2007). Problems of offline government in e-Serbia. In A. Anttiroiko & M. Malkia (Eds.), *Encyclopedia of digital government* (pp. 1342–1351). Hershey, PA: IGI Global. doi:10.4018/978-1-59140-789-8.ch205

Simonovic, S. (2008). Problems of offline government in e-Serbia. In A. Anttiroiko (Ed.), *Electronic government: Concepts, methodologies, tools, and applications* (pp. 2929–2942). Hershey, PA: IGI Global. doi:10.4018/978-1-59904-947-2.ch219

Singh, A. M. (2005). Information systems and technology in South Africa. In M. Khosrow-Pour (Ed.), *Encyclopedia of information science and technology* (pp. 1497–1502). Hershey, PA: IGI Global. doi:10.4018/978-1-59140-553-5.ch263

Singh, S., & Naidoo, G. (2005). Towards an e-government solution: A South African perspective. In W. Huang, K. Siau, & K. Wei (Eds.), *Electronic government strategies and implementation* (pp. 325–353). Hershey, PA: IGI Global. doi:10.4018/978-1-59140-348-7.ch014

Snoke, R., & Underwood, A. (2002). Generic attributes of IS graduates: An analysis of Australian views. In F. Tan (Ed.), *Advanced topics in global information management* (Vol. 1, pp. 370–384). Hershey, PA: IGI Global. doi:10.4018/978-1-930708-43-3.ch023

Sommer, L. (2006). Revealing unseen organizations in higher education: A study framework and application example. In A. Metcalfe (Ed.), *Knowledge management and higher education: A critical analysis* (pp. 115–146). Hershey, PA: IGI Global. doi:10.4018/978-1-59140-509-2.ch007

Song, H., Kidd, T., & Owens, E. (2011). Examining technological disparities and instructional practices in English language arts classroom: Implications for school leadership and teacher training. In L. Tomei (Ed.), *Online courses and ICT in education: Emerging practices and applications* (pp. 258–274). Hershey, PA: IGI Global. doi:10.4018/978-1-60960-150-8.ch020

Speaker, P. J., & Kleist, V. F. (2003). Using information technology to meet electronic commerce and MIS education demands. In A. Aggarwal (Ed.), *Web-based education: Learning from experience* (pp. 280–291). Hershey, PA: IGI Global. doi:10.4018/978-1-59140-102-5.ch017

Spitler, V. K. (2007). Learning to use IT in the workplace: Mechanisms and masters. In M. Mahmood (Ed.), *Contemporary issues in end user computing* (pp. 292–323). Hershey, PA: IGI Global. doi:10.4018/978-1-59140-926-7.ch013

Stellefson, M. (2011). Considerations for marketing distance education courses in health education: Five important questions to examine before development. In U. Demiray & S. Sever (Eds.), *Marketing online education programs: Frameworks for promotion and communication* (pp. 222–234). Hershey, PA: IGI Global. doi:10.4018/978-1-60960-074-7.ch014

Straub, D. W., & Loch, K. D. (2006). Creating and developing a program of global research. *Journal of Global Information Management, 14*(2), 1–28. doi:10.4018/jgim.2006040101

Straub, D. W., Loch, K. D., & Hill, C. E. (2002). Transfer of information technology to the Arab world: A test of cultural influence modeling. In M. Dadashzadeh (Ed.), *Information technology management in developing countries* (pp. 92–134). Hershey, PA: IGI Global. doi:10.4018/978-1-931777-03-2.ch005

Straub, D. W., Loch, K. D., & Hill, C. E. (2003). Transfer of information technology to the Arab world: A test of cultural influence modeling. In F. Tan (Ed.), *Advanced topics in global information management* (Vol. 2, pp. 141–172). Hershey, PA: IGI Global. doi:10.4018/978-1-59140-064-6.ch009

Suki, N. M., Ramayah, T., Ming, M. K., & Suki, N. M. (2013). Factors enhancing employed job seekers intentions to use social networking sites as a job search tool. In A. Mesquita (Ed.), *User perception and influencing factors of technology in everyday life* (pp. 265–281). Hershey, PA: IGI Global. doi:10.4018/978-1-4666-1954-8.ch018

Suomi, R. (2006). Introducing electronic patient records to hospitals: Innovation adoption paths. In T. Spil & R. Schuring (Eds.), *E-health systems diffusion and use: The innovation, the user and the use IT model* (pp. 128–146). Hershey, PA: IGI Global. doi:10.4018/978-1-59140-423-1.ch008

Swim, J., & Barker, L. (2012). Pathways into a gendered occupation: Brazilian women in IT. *International Journal of Social and Organizational Dynamics in IT, 2*(4), 34–51. doi:10.4018/ijsodit.2012100103

Tarafdar, M., & Vaidya, S. D. (2006). Adoption and implementation of IT in developing nations: Experiences from two public sector enterprises in India. In M. Khosrow-Pour (Ed.), *Cases on information technology planning, design and implementation* (pp. 208–233). Hershey, PA: IGI Global. doi:10.4018/978-1-59904-408-8.ch013

Tarafdar, M., & Vaidya, S. D. (2008). Adoption and implementation of IT in developing nations: Experiences from two public sector enterprises in India. In G. Garson & M. Khosrow-Pour (Eds.), *Handbook of research on public information technology* (pp. 905–924). Hershey, PA: IGI Global. doi:10.4018/978-1-59904-857-4.ch076

Thesing, Z. (2007). Zarina thesing, pumpkin patch. In M. Hunter (Ed.), *Contemporary chief information officers: Management experiences* (pp. 83–94). Hershey, PA: IGI Global. doi:10.4018/978-1-59904-078-3.ch007

Thomas, J. C. (2004). Public involvement in public administration in the information age: Speculations on the effects of technology. In M. Malkia, A. Anttiroiko, & R. Savolainen (Eds.), *eTransformation in governance: New directions in government and politics* (pp. 67–84). Hershey, PA: IGI Global. doi:10.4018/978-1-59140-130-8.ch004

Treiblmaier, H., & Chong, S. (2013). Trust and perceived risk of personal information as antecedents of online information disclosure: Results from three countries. In F. Tan (Ed.), *Global diffusion and adoption of technologies for knowledge and information sharing* (pp. 341–361). Hershey, PA: IGI Global. doi:10.4018/978-1-4666-2142-8.ch015

van Grembergen, W., & de Haes, S. (2008). IT governance in practice: Six case studies. In W. van Grembergen & S. De Haes (Eds.), *Implementing information technology governance: Models, practices and cases* (pp. 125–237). Hershey, PA: IGI Global. doi:10.4018/978-1-59904-924-3.ch004

van Os, G., Homburg, V., & Bekkers, V. (2013). Contingencies and convergence in European social security: ICT coordination in the back office of the welfare state. In M. Cruz-Cunha, I. Miranda, & P. Gonçalves (Eds.), *Handbook of research on ICTs and management systems for improving efficiency in healthcare and social care* (pp. 268–287). Hershey, PA: IGI Global. doi:10.4018/978-1-4666-3990-4.ch013

Velloso, A. B., Gassenferth, W., & Machado, M. A. (2012). Evaluating IBMEC-RJ's intranet usability using fuzzy logic. In M. Cruz-Cunha, P. Gonçalves, N. Lopes, E. Miranda, & G. Putnik (Eds.), *Handbook of research on business social networking: Organizational, managerial, and technological dimensions* (pp. 185–205). Hershey, PA: IGI Global. doi:10.4018/978-1-61350-168-9.ch010

Villablanca, A. C., Baxi, H., & Anderson, K. (2009). Novel data interface for evaluating cardiovascular outcomes in women. In A. Dwivedi (Ed.), *Handbook of research on information technology management and clinical data administration in healthcare* (pp. 34–53). Hershey, PA: IGI Global. doi:10.4018/978-1-60566-356-2.ch003

Villablanca, A. C., Baxi, H., & Anderson, K. (2011). Novel data interface for evaluating cardiovascular outcomes in women. In *Clinical technologies: Concepts, methodologies, tools and applications* (pp. 2094–2113). Hershey, PA: IGI Global. doi:10.4018/978-1-60960-561-2.ch806

Virkar, S. (2011). Information and communication technologies in administrative reform for development: Exploring the case of property tax systems in Karnataka, India. In J. Steyn, J. Van Belle, & E. Mansilla (Eds.), *ICTs for global development and sustainability: Practice and applications* (pp. 127–149). Hershey, PA: IGI Global. doi:10.4018/978-1-61520-997-2.ch006

Virkar, S. (2013). Designing and implementing e-government projects: Actors, influences, and fields of play. In S. Saeed & C. Reddick (Eds.), *Human-centered system design for electronic governance* (pp. 88–110). Hershey, PA: IGI Global. doi:10.4018/978-1-4666-3640-8.ch007

Wallace, A. (2009). E-justice: An Australian perspective. In A. Martínez & P. Abat (Eds.), *E-justice: Using information communication technologies in the court system* (pp. 204–228). Hershey, PA: IGI Global. doi:10.4018/978-1-59904-998-4.ch014

Wang, G. (2012). E-democratic administration and bureaucratic responsiveness: A primary study of bureaucrats' perceptions of the civil service e-mail box in Taiwan. In K. Kloby & M. D'Agostino (Eds.), *Citizen 2.0: Public and governmental interaction through web 2.0 technologies* (pp. 146–173). Hershey, PA: IGI Global. doi:10.4018/978-1-4666-0318-9.ch009

Wangpipatwong, S., Chutimaskul, W., & Papasratorn, B. (2011). Quality enhancing the continued use of e-government web sites: Evidence from e-citizens of Thailand. In V. Weerakkody (Ed.), *Applied technology integration in governmental organizations: New e-government research* (pp. 20–36). Hershey, PA: IGI Global. doi:10.4018/978-1-60960-162-1.ch002

Wedemeijer, L. (2006). Long-term evolution of a conceptual schema at a life insurance company. In M. Khosrow-Pour (Ed.), *Cases on database technologies and applications* (pp. 202–226). Hershey, PA: IGI Global. doi:10.4018/978-1-59904-399-9.ch012

Whybrow, E. (2008). Digital access, ICT fluency, and the economically disadvantages: Approaches to minimize the digital divide. In F. Tan (Ed.), *Global information technologies: Concepts, methodologies, tools, and applications* (pp. 1409–1422). Hershey, PA: IGI Global. doi:10.4018/978-1-59904-939-7.ch102

Whybrow, E. (2008). Digital access, ICT fluency, and the economically disadvantages: Approaches to minimize the digital divide. In C. Van Slyke (Ed.), *Information communication technologies: Concepts, methodologies, tools, and applications* (pp. 764–777). Hershey, PA: IGI Global. doi:10.4018/978-1-59904-949-6.ch049

Wickramasinghe, N., & Geisler, E. (2010). Key considerations for the adoption and implementation of knowledge management in healthcare operations. In M. Saito, N. Wickramasinghe, M. Fuji, & E. Geisler (Eds.), *Redesigning innovative healthcare operation and the role of knowledge management* (pp. 125–142). Hershey, PA: IGI Global. doi:10.4018/978-1-60566-284-8.ch009

Wickramasinghe, N., & Geisler, E. (2012). Key considerations for the adoption and implementation of knowledge management in healthcare operations. In *Organizational learning and knowledge: Concepts, methodologies, tools and applications* (pp. 1316–1328). Hershey, PA: IGI Global. doi:10.4018/978-1-60960-783-8.ch405

Wickramasinghe, N., & Goldberg, S. (2007). A framework for delivering m-health excellence. In L. Al-Hakim (Ed.), *Web mobile-based applications for healthcare management* (pp. 36–61). Hershey, PA: IGI Global. doi:10.4018/978-1-59140-658-7.ch002

Wickramasinghe, N., & Goldberg, S. (2008). Critical success factors for delivering m-health excellence. In N. Wickramasinghe & E. Geisler (Eds.), *Encyclopedia of healthcare information systems* (pp. 339–351). Hershey, PA: IGI Global. doi:10.4018/978-1-59904-889-5.ch045

Wyld, D. (2009). Radio frequency identification (RFID) technology. In J. Symonds, J. Ayoade, & D. Parry (Eds.), *Auto-identification and ubiquitous computing applications* (pp. 279–293). Hershey, PA: IGI Global. doi:10.4018/978-1-60566-298-5.ch017

Yaghmaei, F. (2010). Understanding computerised information systems usage in community health. In J. Rodrigues (Ed.), *Health information systems: Concepts, methodologies, tools, and applications* (pp. 1388–1399). Hershey, PA: IGI Global. doi:10.4018/978-1-60566-988-5.ch088

Yee, G., El-Khatib, K., Korba, L., Patrick, A. S., Song, R., & Xu, Y. (2005). Privacy and trust in e-government. In W. Huang, K. Siau, & K. Wei (Eds.), *Electronic government strategies and implementation* (pp. 145–190). Hershey, PA: IGI Global. doi:10.4018/978-1-59140-348-7.ch007

Yeh, S., & Chu, P. (2010). Evaluation of e-government services: A citizen-centric approach to citizen e-complaint services. In C. Reddick (Ed.), *Citizens and e-government: Evaluating policy and management* (pp. 400–417). Hershey, PA: IGI Global. doi:10.4018/978-1-61520-931-6.ch022

Young-Jin, S., & Seang-tae, K. (2008). E-government concepts, measures, and best practices. In A. Anttiroiko (Ed.), *Electronic government: Concepts, methodologies, tools, and applications* (pp. 32–57). Hershey, PA: IGI Global. doi:10.4018/978-1-59904-947-2.ch004

Yun, H. J., & Opheim, C. (2012). New technology communication in American state governments: The impact on citizen participation. In K. Bwalya & S. Zulu (Eds.), *Handbook of research on e-government in emerging economies: Adoption, e-participation, and legal frameworks* (pp. 573–590). Hershey, PA: IGI Global. doi:10.4018/978-1-4666-0324-0.ch029

Zhang, N., Guo, X., Chen, G., & Chau, P. Y. (2011). User evaluation of e-government systems: A Chinese cultural perspective. In F. Tan (Ed.), *International enterprises and global information technologies: Advancing management practices* (pp. 63–84). Hershey, PA: IGI Global. doi:10.4018/978-1-60960-605-3.ch004

Zuo, Y., & Hu, W. (2011). Trust-based information risk management in a supply chain network. In J. Wang (Ed.), *Supply chain optimization, management and integration: Emerging applications* (pp. 181–196). Hershey, PA: IGI Global. doi:10.4018/978-1-60960-135-5.ch013

Compilation of References

Abebrese, J. (2015). *Social Protection in Ghana: An overview of existing programmes and their prospects and challenges*. Fredrich Ebert Stiftung. Retrieved from http//:library.fes.de/pdf-files/bueros/Ghana/10497.pdf

Adebisi, M. A. (2015). The Political Economy of Oil Price Deregulation and the Subsidy Fraud Crisis: A Study of Systematic Bureaucratic Corruption in Nigeria. *Journal of Energy, Technology and Policy*, *5*(9), 2015.

Adhvaryu, A., Chari, A. V., & Sharma, S. (2013). Firing Costs and Flexibility: Evidence from Firms' Employment Responses to Shocks in India. *The Review of Economics and Statistics*, *95*(3), 727–740. doi:10.1162/REST_a_00305 PMID:24357882

Aghion, P., Burgess, R., Redding, S. J., & Zilibotti, F. (2008). The Unequal Effects of Liberalization: Evidence from Dismantling the License Raj in India. *The American Economic Review*, *98*(4), 1397–1412. doi:10.1257/aer.98.4.1397

Aghion, P., Burgess, R., Redding, S., & Zilibotti, F. (2006). *The unequal effects of liberalization: Evidence from dismantling the license raj in india*. St. Louis, MO: Federal Reserve Bank of St Louis. doi:10.3386/w12031

Aghion, P., & Howitt, P. (1998). *Endogenous Growth Theory*. Cambridge, MA: MIT Press.

Aguirre Botello, M. (2017). *Evolución del salario mínimo en México de 1935 a 2017*. Retrieved from http://www.mexicomaxico.org/voto/salmininf.htm

Ahsan, A., & Pagés, C. (2009). Are all labor regulations equal? Evidence from Indian manufacturing. *Journal of Comparative Economics*, *37*(1), 62–75. doi:10.1016/j.jce.2008.09.001

Akerlof, G. A. (1982). Labor Contracts as a Partial Gift Exchange. *The Quarterly Journal of Economics*, *97*(4), 543–569. doi:10.2307/1885099

Alberola, E., Aldeghi, I., & Hoibian, S. (2016). *Les mutations du travail. L'envie du salariat domine sauf chez les jeunes. Document de recherche*. Paris: Crédoc.

Aleksynska, M., & Eberlein, F. (2016). Coverage of employment protection legislation. *IZA Journal of Labor Policy*, *5*(1), 17. doi:10.1186/s40173-016-0073-x

Algan, Y., & Cahuc, P. (2007). *La société de défiance. Comment le modèle social français s'autodétruit*. Paris: Editions Rue d'Ulm.

Almeida, R. K., & Carneiro, P. (2007). *Inequality and employment in a dual economy: Enforcement of labor regulation in brazil*. St. Louis, MO: Federal Reserve Bank of St Louis. doi:10.1596/28270

Almeida, R. K., & Susanlı, Z. B. (2012). Firing Regulations and Firm Size in the Developing World: Evidence from Differential Enforcement. *Review of Development Economics*, *16*(4), 540–558. doi:10.1111/rode.12003

Almeida, R., & Carneiro, P. (2006). *Enforcement of regulation, informal labor, firm size and firm performance*. St. Louis, MO: Federal Reserve Bank of St Louis.

Almeida, R., & Carneiro, P. (2009). Enforcement of labor regulation and firm size. *Journal of Comparative Economics*, *37*(1), 28–46. doi:10.1016/j.jce.2008.09.004

Amin, M. (2009). Labor regulation and employment in India's retail stores. *Journal of Comparative Economics*, *37*(1), 47–61. doi:10.1016/j.jce.2008.07.001

Anant, T. C. A., Hasan, R., Mohapatra, P., Nagaraj, R., & Sasikumar, S. K. (2006). Labor Markets in India: Issues and Perspectives. In J. Felipe & R. Hasan (Eds.), *Labor Markets in Asia: Issues and Perspectives* (pp. 205–300). Basingstoke, UK: Palgrave Macmillan. doi:10.1057/9780230627383_5

Autor, D., Kerr, W., & Kugler, A. (2007). *Do employment protections reduce productivity? evidence from U.S. states*. St. Louis, MO: Federal Reserve Bank of St Louis. doi:10.3386/w12860

Autran, A. (n.d.). *Folha Explica*. Retrieved March 06, 2016 from http://arte.folha.uol.com.br/poder/operacao-lava-jato/

Avato, J., Koettl, J., & Sabates-Wheeler, R. (2009). *Definitions, Good Practices, and Global Estimates on the Status of Social Protection for International Migrants*. Social Protection and Labor: The World Bank; SP Discussion Paper no. 0909. Retrieved from http//:library.fes.de/pdf-files/bueros/Ghana/10497.pdf

Badinter, R., & Lyon-Caen, A. (2015). *Le travail et la loi*. Paris: Editions Fayard.

Bagwasi, T. (2016). *Gov't Changes Approach on Unions*. Retrieved, July 24, 2017, from http://www.weekendpost.co.bw/wp-news-details.php?nid=3184

Baker, D., Glyn, A., Howell, D., & Schmitt, J. (2005). Labor market institutions and unemployment: assessment of the cross-country evidence. In Fighting Unemployment: The Limits of Free Market Orthodoxy. New-York: Oxford University Press.

Baker, D., Glyn, A., Howell, D., & Schmitt, J. (2004). *Unemployment and labor market institutions: The failure of the empirical case for deregulation*. St. Louis, MO: Federal Reserve Bank of St Louis.

Bank of Botswana. (2001). *Bank of Botswana Annual Report 2000*. Gaborone: Bank of Botswana.

Bank of Botswana. (2017). *Bank of Botswana Annual Report 2016*. Gaborone: Bank of Botswana.

Banker, R. D., Byzalov, D., & Chen, L. (2013). Employment protection legislation, adjustment costs and cross-country differences in cost behavior. *Journal of Accounting and Economics*, *55*(1), 111–127. doi:10.1016/j.jacceco.2012.08.003

Barbarosch, E. (2011). *La seguridad jurídica en la decisión judicial. ¿Utopía o realidad?* Buenos Aires, Argentina: La Ley.

Barnard, C. (2013). *EU employment law*. Oxford, UK: Oxford Press.

Barros, R. P., Corseuil, C. H., & Bahia, M. (1999). *Labor Market Regulation and the Duration of Employment in Brazil*. Discussion Paper 676. Rio de Janeiro, Brazil: IPEA.

Barros, R. P., Corseuil, C. H., & Gonzaga, G. (1999). *Labor Market Regulation and the Demand for Labor in Brazil*. Discussion Paper 656. Rio de Janeiro, Brazil: IPEA.

Barros, R. P., Corseuil, C. H., & Foguel, M. (2001). *The Impact of Regulations on Brazilian Labor Market Performance*. Inter-American Development Bank.

Bastagli, F. (2013). *Feasibility of Social Protection Schemes in Developing Countries.* European Parliament: Director-General for External Policies of the Union. EXPO/B/DEVE/FWC/2009-01/Lot5/34, February.

Berdugo, B., & Hadad, S. (2012). How Do Firing Costs Affect Innovation and Growth when Workers' Ability is Unknown? Employment Protection as a Burden on a Firm's Screening Process. *European Journal of Comparative Economics*, *9*(1), 3–30.

Bertola, G. (1991). *Flexibility, investment, and growth.* Cambridge, MA: National Bureau of Economic Research, Inc. doi:10.3386/w3864

Bertola, G. (1994). Flexibility, Investment, and Growth. *Journal of Monetary Economics*, *34*(2), 215–228. doi:10.1016/0304-3932(94)90050-7

Bertola, G., Boeri, T., & Cazes, S. (2000). Employment protection in industrialized countries: The case for new indicators. *International Labour Review*, *139*(1), 57–72. doi:10.1111/j.1564-913X.2000.tb00402.x

Besley, T., & Burgess, R. (2004). Can Labor Regulation Hinder Economic Performance? Evidence from India. *The Quarterly Journal of Economics*, *119*(1), 91–134. doi:10.1162/003355304772839533

Better Work Haiti. (2014). *Garment Industry, 8th Biannual Synthesis Report Under the HOPE II. Legislation. Synthesis Report.* ILO/IFC.

Better Work Haiti. (2016). *Garment Industry, 13th Biannual Synthesis Report Under the HOPE II. Legislation. Synthesis Report.* ILO/IFC.

Bhalotra, S. R. (1998). The Puzzle of Jobless Growth in Indian Manufacturing. *Oxford Bulletin of Economics and Statistics*, *60*(1), 5–32. doi:10.1111/1468-0084.00084

Bhattacharjea, A. (2006). *Labor market regulation and industrial performance in India: A critical review of the empirical evidence.* St. Louis, MO: Federal Reserve Bank of St Louis.

Bhattacharjea, A. (2009). The Effects of Employment Protection Legislation on Indian Manufacturing. *Economic and Political Weekly*, *44*(22), 55–62.

Blackburn, D. (2006). The role, impact and future of labour law. *Labour Education*, *2-3*, 143-144.

Blanchard, O., & Wolfers, J. (2000). The Role of Shocks and Institutions in the Rise of European Unemployment: The Aggregate Evidence. *Economic Journal (London)*, *110*(462), 1–33. doi:10.1111/1468-0297.00518

Boeri, T. (2011). Institutional reforms and dualism in European labor markets. Handbook of Labor Economics, 4.

Boeri, T., & Garibaldi, P. (2007). Two Tier Reforms of Employment Protection: A Honeymoon Effect? *Economic Journal (London)*, *117*(521), F357–F385. doi:10.1111/j.1468-0297.2007.02060.x

Boeri, T., & Jimeno, J. F. (2005). The effects of employment protection: Learning from variable enforcement. *European Economic Review*, *49*(8), 2057–2077. doi:10.1016/j.euroecorev.2004.09.013

Boon, E. K. (2007). Knowledge Systems and Social Security in Africa: A Case Study of Ghana. *Tribes and Tribals*, *1*(Special), 63–76.

Bordieu, P., & Passeron, J. C. (1992). *A reprodução: elementos para uma teoria do sistema de ensino*. Rio de Janeiro, RJ: Francisco Alves.

Botswana Confederation of Commerce Industry and Manpower. (2006). *A Code of Conduct for the Private Sector.* Retrieved July 24, 2017, from http://bb.org.bw/downloads/code_of_conduct-Final.pdf

Botswana Federation of Trade Unions. (2009). *State of Information Technology in the Botswana Federation of Trade Unions: Challenges, Opportunities and Needs.* Author.

Botswana Federation of Trade Unions. (2012). *A Country Report on Botswana Decent Work Country Programme*. Retrieved July 23, 2017, from http://actrav-courses.itcilo.org/en/a105067/country-reports/bftu-botswana/at_download/file

Brown, R. C. (2009). *Understanding labor and employment law in China*. Cambridge, UK: Cambridge University Press. doi:10.1017/CBO9780511642258

Bureau of International Labour Affairs. (2013). *2013 Findings on the Worst Forms of Child Labour*. Retrieved July 24, 2017, from https://www.dol.gov/ilab/reports/child-labor/findings/2013TDA/2013TDA.pdf

Business France. (2016). *International Rankings. Distinguishing between Perception and Reality, 2016 Edition*. Retrieved June 28, 2017, from http://www.businessfrance.fr/Media/Default/discover/livre_blanc_des_classements_internationaux_en_dave_2016-07-05.pdf

Cahuc, P., & Prost, C. (2015). Améliorer l'assurance chômage pour limiter l'instabilité de l'emploi. *Notes d'analyse économique*, *24*, 1-12.

Cairns, D. S. S. (2015). New Formalities for Casual Labor: Addressing Unintended Consequences of China's Labor Contract Law. *Washington International Law Journal, 24*(1), 219–252.

Cao, J. (2006). *Macroeconomics*. Beijing: Tsenghua Press.

Casale, G., & Perulli, A. (2014). *Towards the Single Employment Relationship: Comparative Reflections*. Oxford, UK: ILO.

Central Statistics Office. (2008a). *2005/06 Labour Force Survey Dissemination Seminar Summary Report*. Author.

Central Statistics Office. (2008b). *2005/06 Labour Force Survey Report*. Author.

CEPAL. (2015). *Panorama Social de América Latina 2015*. Retrieved from http://www.cepal.org/es/publicaciones/panorama-social-america-latina-2015-documento-informativo

CEPF (Centro de Estudios de las Finanzas Públicas). (2010). *Inversión Extranjera y Empleo*. Retrieved from http://www.cefp.gob.mx/publicaciones/nota/2010/mayo/notacefp0152010.pdf

Céreq. (2014). *Quand l'école est finie. Premiers pas dans la vie active de la génération 2013*. Paris: Céreq.

Champoux, D., & Brun, J. (2003). Occupational health and safety management in small size enterprises: An overview of the situation and avenues for intervention and research. *Safety Science, 41*(4), 301–318. doi:10.1016/S0925-7535(02)00043-7

Chan, A. (2003). A 'race to the bottom': Globalisation and China's labor standards. *China Perspectives, 46*, 41–49.

Chan, C. K.-C., & Nadvi, K. (2014). Changing labor regulations and labor standards in China: Retrospect and challenges. *International Labour Review, 153*(4), 513–534. doi:10.1111/j.1564-913X.2014.00214.x

Chang, X. (2014). *Society Building: A China Model of Social Development*. Cambridge, UK: Cambridge Scholars Publishing.

Charmettant, H., Juban, J.-Y., Magne, N., & Renou, Y. (2016). La "sécuflexibilité": au-delà des tensions entre flexibilité et sécurité de l'emploi, les sociétés coopératives et participatives (Scop). *Formation emploi, 134*, 107-124.

Chinese Government. (n.d.). *China annual report 2017*. Retrieved June 17, 2017, from https://www.google.nl/url?sa=t&rct=j&q=&esrc=s&source=web&cd=1&cad=rja&uact=8&sqi=2&ved=0ahUKEwicxtm967HKAhXIwA4KHWn7BAUQFggdMAA&url=http%3A%2F%2Fwww.clb.org.hk%2Fschi%2F&usg=AFQjCNFB67hJAZowulv8TTLkdyAYqu5nLQ&bvm=bv.112064104,d.ZWU

Cichon, M., Behrendt, C., & Wodsak, V. (2011). *The UN Social Protection Floor Initiative: Moving Forward with the Extension of Social Security*. Retrieved from library.fes.de/pdf/ipg-files/2011-2/05_a_cichon.pdf

COE. (2014). *L'évolution des formes d'emploi*. Rapport, 8 April. COE.

COE. (2015). *Labour markets reforms in Europe -Executive summary*. Report, 5th November. COE.

COE. (2016). *Labour markets reforms in Europe -Executive summary*. Report, 5th November. COE.

Cohen, T., & Matee, L. (2014). Public Servants' Right to Strike in Lesotho, Botswana and South Africa-A Comparative Study. *Potchefstroom Electronic Law Journal*, (17): 4.

Compensation for Occupational Injuries and Diseases Act, 1993 (Act 130 of 1993)

Cooper, R., Gong, G., & Yan, P. (2015). Dynamic labor demand in China: public and private objectives. *RAND Journal of Economics*, *46*(3), 577-610. doi:10.1111/1756-2171.12098

Cooper, R., Gong, G., & Yan, P. (2013). *Costly labor adjustment: General equilibrium effects of china's employment regulations*. Cambridge, MA: National Bureau of Economic Research, Inc. doi:10.3386/w19324

Cornia, G. A. (2012). *Inequality Trends and their Determinants: Latin America over 1990-2011*. Working Paper Series UNU-WIDER Research Paper (2012/09).

Cornia, G. A., Gomez-Sabaini, J. C., & Martorano, B. (2011). *A new fiscal pact, tax policy changes and income inequality: Latin America during the last decade*. Working Paper Series UNU-WIDER Research Paper (2011/70).

Cornia, G. A. (2014). *Falling Inequality in Latin America: Policy changes and Lessons*. Oxford University Press. doi:10.1093/acprof:oso/9780198701804.001.0001

Cornia, G. A., & Martorano, B. (2011). Democracy, the New Left and Income Distribution: Latin America over the Last Decade. In V. E. Fitzgerald, J. Heyer, & R. Thorpe (Eds.), *Overcoming the Persistence of Inequality and Poverty*. London: Palgrave Macmillan. doi:10.1057/9780230306721_8

Cuñat, A., & Melitz, M. J. (2007). *Volatility, labor market flexibility, and the pattern of comparative advantage*. St. Louis, MO: Federal Reserve Bank of St Louis. doi:10.3386/w13062

D'Souza, E. (2010). The employment effects of labor legislation in India: A critical essay. *Industrial Relations Journal*, *41*(2), 122–135. doi:10.1111/j.1468-2338.2009.00558.x

Davis, S. J., & Henrekson, M. (1995). *Industrial policy, employer size, and economic performance in Sweden*. Cambridge, MA: National Bureau of Economic Research, Inc. doi:10.3386/w5237

De la Vega, B. V. (2013). Occupational health and safety: An EU law perspective. In E. Ales (Ed.), Health and safety at work: European and comparative perspective (pp. 1-32). Alphen aan den Rijn: Kluwer Law International.

Décret du 24 février 1984 actualisant le Code du travail du 12 septembre 1961. Le Moniteur No 18-A du 5 mars 1984. Port-au-Prince.

Décret du 4 novembre 1974 créant le Service des prêts hypothécaires, Le Moniteur No 89 du 14 novembre 1974. Port-au-Prince.

Devereux, S., & Cipryk, R. (2009). *Social Protection in Sub-Saharan Africa: A Regional Review*. Centre for Social Protection Institute of Development Studies. Retrieved from https://www.ids.ac.mc/files/dmfile/SocialProtectioninSubSaharanAfrica.pdf

Devereux, S., & Sabates-Wheeler, R. (2004). *Transformative Social Protection*. IDS Working Paper 232. Institute of Development Studies, University of Sussex, UK. Retrieved from www2.unicef,org/socialpolicy/files/Transformative_Social_Protection.pdf

Diario Oficial de la Federación, D. O. F. (2015a). Ley Federal del Trabajo. Última reforma publicada el 12 de junio de 2015.

Diario Oficial de la Federación, D. O. F. (2015b). Ley del Seguro Social. Última reforma publicada el 12 de noviembre de 2015.

Diario Oficial de la Federación, D. O. F. (2015c). Reglas de operación para el programa de apoyo al empleo. Novena sección.

Dollar, D., Iarossi, G., & Mengistae, T. (2002). *Investment Climate and Economic Performance: Some Firm Level Evidence from India*. Development Research Group, The World Bank, Working Paper No. 143.

Dorn, A. J., & Wang, X. (1990). *Economic reform in China: problems and prospects*. Chicago: University of Chicago Press.

Dostoievski, F. (2011). *Gente Pobre*. São Paulo, SP: Associação Cultural Letra Selvagem.

Dougherty, S., Robles, V. F., & Krishna, K. (2011). Employment protection legislation and plant-level productivity in India. Paris: Organization for Economic Cooperation and Development (OECD). doi:10.1787/18151973

Dougherty, S., Frisancho, V., & Krishna, K. (2013). *State-level labor reform and firm-level productivity in India*. New Delhi, India: Brookings-NCAER India Policy Forum.

Dutta Roy, S. (2004). Employment dynamics in Indian industry: Adjustment lags and the impact of job security regulations. *Journal of Development Economics*, *73*(1), 233–256. doi:10.1016/j.jdeveco.2003.01.003

ECLAC. (2010). *Economic Survey of Latin America and the Caribbean, 2009–2010*. ECLAC, Santiago de Chile.

ECLAC. (2013). *Fiscal Panorama of Latin America and the Caribbean Tax Reform and Renewal of the Fiscal Covenant*. ECLAC.

Elbadawi, I., Mengistae, T., & Zeufack, A. (2006). Market access, supplier access, and Africa's manufactured exports: A firm level analysis. *The Journal of International Trade & Economic Development*, *15*(4), 493–523. doi:10.1080/09638190601037567

Employment Equity Act, 1998 (Act 55 of 1998)

Employment Services Act, 2014 (Act 4 of 2014)

Esping-Andersen, G. (2007). *Les trois mondes de l'Etat-providence; essai sur le capitalisme moderne*. Paris: PUF. doi:10.3917/puf.espin.2007.01

Etala, J. J. (1976). *La política salarial desde mayo de 1976 en adelante.* Buenos Aires Argentina: D.T.

Eurofound. (2015). *Third European Company Survey - Workplace innovation in European companies.* Luxembourg: Publications Office of the European Union.

Eurofound. (2016). *Win-win arrangements: Innovative measures through social dialogue at company level.* Eurofound report. Luxembourg: Publications Office of the European Union.

European Agency for Safety and Health at Work. (2012). *Worker representation and consultation on health and safety: an analysis of the findings of the European survey of enterprises on new and emerging risks.* Retrieved June 17, 2017, from https://osha.europa.eu/en/tools-and-publications/publications/reports/esener_workers-involvement

European Agency for Safety and Health at Work. (2017). *European directives on safety and health at work.* Retrieved June 17, from https://osha.europa.eu/en/safety-and-health-legislation/european-directives

European Commission. (2017). *Council Recommendations on the 2017 National Reform Programme of France and delivering a Council opinion on the 2017 Stability Programme of France.* Retrieved June 28, 2017, from https://ec.europa.eu/info/sites/info/files/2017-european-semester-country-specific-recommendations-commission-recommendations-france.pdf

Eurostat. (2016). *Employment and unemployment data.* Retrieved June 17, 2017, from http://ec.europa.eu/eurostat/web/lfs/data/database

Eurostat. (2017). *Unemployment statistics.* Retrieved June 17, 2017, from http://ec.europa.eu/eurostat/statistics-explained/index.php/Unemployment_statistics

Everaere, C. (2014). *Les emplois atypiques. Quelles réponses au besoin de flexicurité?* Paris: Editions Liaisons sociales, Walters Kluwer.

Ezekwesili, O. (2012). *Corruption, National Development, The Bar and The Judiciary.* Paper presented at the 52nd Annual General Conference of the Nigerian Bar Association.

Fallon, P., & Lucas, R. E. B. (1991). The Impact of Changes in Job Security Legislations in Industrial and Zimbabwe. *The World Bank Economic Review*, *5*(3), 395–413. doi:10.1093/wber/5.3.395

Fallon, P., & Lucas, R. E. B. (1993). Job Security Regulations and the Dynamic Demand for Industrial Labor in India and Zimbabwe. *Journal of Development Economics*, *40*(2), 241–275. doi:10.1016/0304-3878(93)90085-2

Fan, S., Kanbur, R., Wei, S., & Zhang, X. (2014). *The oxford companion to the economics of China*. Oxford, UK: OUP Oxford. doi:10.1093/acprof:oso/9780199678204.001.0001

Fernández-Arias, E., & Montiel, P. (2010). *The Great Recession, 'Rainy Day' Funds, and Countercyclical Fiscal Policy in Latin America*. Department of Economics Working Papers (2010-17). Williams College.

Financial Times. (2017). *Want cheap labour? Head to Mexico, not China*. Retrieved from https://www.ft.com/content/bddc8121-a7a0-3788-a74c-cd2b49cd3230?mhq5j=e1

Flamand, J. (2016). *Les transitions professionnelles, révélatrices d'un marché du travail à deux vitesses*. Paris: France Stratégie.

Fox, L., & Oviedo, A. M. (2013). Institutions and Job Growth in African Manufacturing: Does Employment Protection Regulation Matter? *Journal of African Economies*, *22*(4), 616–650. doi:10.1093/jae/ejt017

Fragale Filho, R. (2015). Brazilian's fissured workplace: David Weil's vignettes in the new world. *Comparative Labor Law & Policy Journal*, *37*(1), 37–53.

France Stratégie. (2016). *2017-2027 - Enjeux pour une décennie*. Paris: La Documentation Française.

Freeman, R. B. (2005). Labor market institutions without blinders: The debate over flexibility and labor market performance. *International Economic Journal*, *19*(2), 129–145. doi:10.1080/1016873050008067 5

Freije, S., López-Acevedo, G., & Rodríguez-Oreggia, E. (2014). Effects of the 2008–09 Economic Crisis on Labor Markets in Mexico. In A. Banerji, D. Newhouse, P. Paci, & D. Robalino (Eds.), *Working through the Crisis: Jobs and Policies in Developing Countries during the Great Recession*. Washington, DC: World Bank.

Friedman, L. M. (1977). *Law and Society: An Introduction*. Prentice Hall.

Friedrich Ebert Stiftung. (2003). *Trade Unions in Botswana: Country Report*. Author.

Friedrich Ebert Stiftung. (2008). *Trade Unions in Botswana: Country Report*. Author.

Gámez, A., Ivanova, A., & Compiranon, K. (2014). Tourism and Economic Crisis Management within APEC. Cases: Phuket (Thailand) and Los Cabos (Mexico). *International Journal of Sustainable Development and Planning*, *9*(2), 143–157. doi:10.2495/SDP-V9-N2-143-157

Garcia, A. B., & Gruat, J. V. (2003). *Social Protection/Social Justice-A life Cycle of Continuum Investment*. Retrieved from http://www.ilo.org/public/english/protection/download/lifecycle/lifecycle.pdf

Garibaldi, P. (1998). Job flow dynamics and firing restrictions. *European Economic Review*, *42*(2), 245–275. doi:10.1016/S0014-2921(97)00062-7

Gazier, B., & Gautie, J. (2011). The "Transitional Labour Markets" Approach: Theory, History and Future Research Agenda. *Journal of Economic and Social Policy*, *14*(1), 6.

Goldin, A. O., Alimenti, J. F., & Caparrós, F. J. (2013). *Curso de Derecho del Trabajo y de la Seguridad Social*. Buenos Aires, Argentina: La Ley.

Gong, G., & Hu, G. (2016). The role of returns to scale in measuring frictions in resource allocation: Revisiting misallocation and manufacturing TFP in China. *Economics Letters*, *138*, 26–29. doi:10.1016/j.econlet.2015.11.014

Govindjee, A., & Dupper, O. (2011). Constitutional perspectives on unemployment security and a right to work in South Africa. *Stellenbosch Law Review*, *22*(3), 775–803.

Greenblot, K. (2008). *Four Types of Social Protection. Protecting Africa's Future: Livelihood-based social protection for orphans and vulnerable children (OVC) in east and southern Africa.* Food and Agriculture Organization of the United Nation (FAO). Regional Emergency Office for Southern *Africa*.

Griffith, R., Harrison, R., & Macartney, G. (2007). Product Market Reforms, Labor Market Institutions and Unemployment. *Economic Journal (London)*, *117*(519), C142–C166. doi:10.1111/j.1468-0297.2007.02039.x

Griffith, R., & Macartney, G. (2014). Employment Protection Legislation, Multinational Firms, and Innovation. *The Review of Economics and Statistics*, *96*(1), 135–150. doi:10.1162/REST_a_00348

Guo, B., & Guo, S. (2008). *China in search of a harmonious society*. Lanham, MD: Lexington Books.

Gupta, P., Hasan, R., & Kumar, U. (2009). *Big reforms but small payoffs: Explaining the Weak Record of Growth and Employment in Indian Manufacturing*. St. Louis, MO: Federal Reserve Bank of St Louis.

Gust, C., & Marquez, J. (2004). International comparisons of productivity growth: The role of information technology and regulatory practices. *Labour Economics*, *11*(1), 33–58. doi:10.1016/S0927-5371(03)00055-1

Gwatidzo, T., & Moyo, B. (2014). Impact of employment protection legislation on employment and exporting in select African countries. *Development Southern Africa*, *31*(2), 299–321. doi:10.1080/0376835X.2014.880877

Habyarimana J. (2008). *The Role of Labor Regulation in Explaining the Low Growth in Employment in South Africa.* Washington, DC: The World Bank.

Hagen-Zander, J., & Holmes, R. (2012). *Social Protection in Nigeria.* Overseas Development Institute (ODI).

Hale, A. R. (1984). Is safety training worthwhile? *Journal of Occupational Accidents*, *6*(1-3), 17–33. doi:10.1016/0376-6349(84)90026-9

Hämäläinen, R. M. (2008). *The Europeanisation of occupational health services: A study of the impact of EU policies*. Retrieved June 17, 2017, from https://helda.helsinki.fi/bitstream/handle/10138/20390/theeurop.pdf?sequence=1iitattu

Hartwell, C. A. (2010). Employment Protection Legislation and Labor Markets in Transition: Assessing the Effects of the Labor Code in Armenia. *European Journal of Comparative Economics*, *7*(2), 413–445.

Hesse, K. (1991). *A força normativa da Constituição*. Porto Alegre, RS: Sergio Antonio Fabris.

Hishida, M., Kojima, K., Ishii, T., & Qiao, J. (2010). *China's trade unions - how autonomous are they?: a survey of 1811 Enterprise Union chairpersons*. London: Routledge.

Hobsbawn, E. J. (2008). *A Era das Revoluções: A Revolução Francesa*. São Paulo, SP: Paz e Terra. Jurídico, C. *Cortes na Justiça do Trabalho preocupam TST e advogados*. Retrieved April 20, 2016. From http://www.conjur.com.br/2016-fev-28/cortes-orcamento-justica-trabalho-preocupam-tst-advogados

Hoek, J. (2002). *Labor Market Institutions and Restructuring: Evidence from Regulated and Unregulated Labor Markets in Brazil.* William Davidson Institute, University of Michigan, Working Paper, 484.

Holmes, R., Akinrimisi, B., Morgan, J., & Buck, R. (2011). *Social Protection in Nigeria: an overview of programmes and their effectiveness*. Overseas Development Institute (ODI); Project Briefing No 59, September.

Holmes, T. J. (1998). The effect of state policies on the location of manufacturing: Evidence from state borders. *Journal of Political Economy, 106*(4), 667–705. doi:10.1086/250026

Hopenhayn, H., & Rogerson, R. (1993). Job turnover and policy evaluation: A general equilibrium analysis. *Journal of Political Economy, 101*(5), 915–938. doi:10.1086/261909

Hornbeck, J. F. (2010). *The Haitian Economy and the HOPE Act. CRS Report for Congress*. Washington, DC: Congressional Research Service.

Howell, D. R., Baker, D., Glyn, A., & Schmitt, J. (2006). Are protective labor market institutions at the root of unemployment? A critical review of the evidence. *Capitalism and Society, 2*(1), 1–71.

Hsieh, C.-T., & Klenow, P. J. (2009). Misallocation and Manufacturing TFP in China and India. *The Quarterly Journal of Economics, 124*(4), 1403–1448. doi:10.1162/qjec.2009.124.4.1403

Huang, Y. (2008). *Capitalism with Chinese characteristics: Entrepreneurship and the state*. Cambridge, UK: Cambridge Press.

IDC on line. (2013). *Permiso de paternidad efectos ante el IMSS*. Retrieved from http://www.idconline.com.mx/seguridad/2013/02/06/permiso-de-paternidad-efectos-ante-el-imss

IGAS. (2016). *Evaluation du contrat à durée déterminée dit d'usage*. Retrieved June 28, 2017, from http://www.igas.gouv.fr/IMG/pdf/2015 049R_Rapport_CDDU_.pdf

IMF. (2010). *Mexico: Arrangement under the Flexible Credit Line and Cancellation of the Current Arrangement. Country Report 10/81*. Washington, DC: International Monetary Fund.

IMSS. (2017). *Puestos de trabajo afiliados al Instituto Mexicano del Seguro Social (IMSS) al mes de diciembre de 2016 No.011/2017*. Retrieved from http://www.imss.gob.mx/prensa/archivo/201701/011

INEGI. (2008). *Encuesta Nacional de Ocupación y Empleo, segundo trimestre de 2008*. Retrieved from http://www3.inegi.org.mx/sistemas/infoenoe/Default_15mas.aspx?s=est&c=26227&p=

INEGI. (2015a). *Estadísticas a propósito del día del niño (30 de abril)*. Retrieved from http://www.inegi.org.mx/saladeprensa/aproposito/2015/ni%C3%B1o0.pdf

INEGI. (2016). *Encuesta Nacional de Educación y Empleo (ENOE)*. Retrieved from http://www.beta.inegi.org.mx/temas/empleo/

INEGI. (2017). *Población ocupada según sector de actividad económica, nacional trimestral*. Retrieved from http://www.inegi.org.mx/sistemas/BIE/CuadrosEstadisticos/GeneraCuadro.aspx?s=est&nc=597&c=25586

International Labour Organisation. (2011). *Social Protection Floors for Social Justice and a Fair Globalisation*. Report ILC. 101/IV/1. ILO.

International Labour Organisation. (2013). *Social Protection Floors and Gender Equality: A brief overview*. ESS Working Paper no 37. ILO.

International Labour Organisation. (2014). *Database of national labour, social security and related human rights legislation*. Retrieved July, 24, 2017 from http://www.ilo.org/dyn/natlex/natlex4.detail?p_lang=en&p_isn=842

International Labour Organization. (2003/04). *Moral harassment: Work organization to blame?* Newcastle upon Tyne, UK: Labour Education.

International Monetary Fund (IMF). (2017). *People's Republic of China and the IMF*. Retrieved June 17, 2017, https://www.imf.org/external/country/chn/

International Monetary Fund. (2015). *Haiti: Selected Issues*. IMF Country Report No 15/158. IMF.

Islam, I., & Nazara, S. (2000). *Minimum Wage and the Welfare of Indonesian Workers. Occasional Discussion Papers Series 3*. Jakarta: ILO.

Jacinto, C., & Aspinwall, E. (2004). A Survey on occupational accidents reporting and registration systems in the European Union. *Safety Science*, *42*(10), 933–960. doi:10.1016/j.ssci.2004.07.002

James, P., & Walters, D. (2002). Worker representation in health and safety: Options for regulatory reform. *Industrial Relations Journal*, *33*(2), 141–156. doi:10.1111/1468-2338.00225

Jaspers, T., & Pennings, F. (2013). Occupational health and safety in The Netherlands: A shift of responsibilities. In E. Ales (Ed.), Health and safety at work: European and comparative perspective (pp. 1-32). Alphen aan den Rijn: Kluwer Law International.

Johnstone, R., Quinlan, M., & Walters, D. (2005). Statutory occupational health and safety workplace arrangements for the modern labour market. *The Journal of Industrial Relations*, *47*(01), 93–116. doi:10.1111/j.1472-9296.2005.00160.x

Jolly, C., Prouet, E., & Wisnia-Weill, V. (2016). *2017-2027: Repenser la protection des actifs. Note d'analyse, décembre*. Paris: France Stratégie.

Kalula, E., Ordor, A. O., & Fenwick, C. (2008). *Labour Law reforms that Support Decent Work: The Case of southern Africa. Issue paper No 28. International Labour organization (ILO)*.

Khanna, G., Newhouse, D., & Paci, P. (2014). Fewer Jobs or Smaller Paychecks? Aggregate Crisis Impacts in Selected Middle-Income Countries. In A. Banerji, D. Newhouse, P. Paci, & D. Robalino (Eds.), *Working through the Crisis: Jobs and Policies in Developing Countries during the Great Recession*. Washington, DC: World Bank.

Kinkel, J., & Hurst, W. (2011). Review essay—access to justice in post-Mao China: Assessing the politics of criminal and administrative law. *Journal of East Asian Studies (Seoul)*, *11*(3), 467–499. doi:10.1017/S1598240800007414

Kolobe, M., Bakwena, M., & Siphambe, H. (2015). Analysis of Gender Wage Differentials: The Case of Botswana's Labour Market. *Asian-African Journal of Economics and Econometrics*, *15*(2), 127–146.

Kucera, D. (2003). Effects of Labor Standards on Labor Costs and FDI Flows. In J. Bhagwati & H. Corbet (Eds.), *Labor Standards in an Integrating World Economy*. Washington, DC: Cordell Hull Institute.

Labour Relations Act, 1995 (Act 66 of 1995)

Larson, L. K., & Larson, A. (2008). *Workers' compensation law: cases, materials, and text*. Leiden: LexisNexis.

Le Goff, J. (2004). *Du silence à la parole. Une histoire du droit du travail des années 1830 à nos jours. Collection: L'Univers des normes*. Rennes: PUR.

LEGOSH Database. (2014). *China – 2013*. Retrieved June 17, 2017, http://www.ilo.org/dyn/legosh/en/f?p=14100:1100:0:NO:1100:P1100_ISO_CODE3,P1100_YEAR:CHN,2013:NO

Li, B. (2013). Research on the occupational health guardian system. *Academic Journal Graduate School Chinese Academy of Social Sciences*, *34*(06), 25–28.

Li, J. (2008). China's New Labor Contract Law and Protection of Workers. *Fordham International Law Journal*, *32*(3), 1083–1131.

Li, L. (2014). It is necessary to break through the status quo that "power is superior to law" in order to build rule of law in China. *The Qiushi Journal*, *14*(5), 33–37.Li, J., & Zhang, L. (2012). Research on health and safety law: From the human rights perspective. *Law and Society*, *22*(03), 87–90.

Lisi, D. (2008). *Analysis of employment protection legislation: A model with endogenous labor productivity*. St. Louis, MO: Federal Reserve Bank of St Louis.

Lithur, N. O. (2013). *Social Protection in Ghana: History, Challenges and Opportunities. Honourable Nana Oye Lithur. Paper presented at the Minister for Gender*, Children, and Social Protection.

Liu, K. (2013). Conundrums in the legal protection of migrant workers' health rights and relative resolutions: Implications from the case of Tseng Hei-tao. *Medicine, Health Care, and Philosophy*, *16*(3), 543–553. doi:10.1007/s11019-012-9445-1 PMID:23073738

Liu, K. (2015). Comparative study of regulating the moral harassment: Lessons for China. *Occupational Medicine & Health Affairs*, *3*(4), 66–72.

Liu, K., & Liu, W. (2015). The development of EU law in the field of occupational health and safety: A new way of thinking. *Management and Labour Studies*, *40*(3&4), 207–238. doi:10.1177/0258042X15624990

Loi du 25 août 1971 créant le Comptoir d'épargne et de prêts, Le Moniteur No 70 du 2 septembre 1971. Port-au-Prince.

Loi organique du Ministère des Affaires Sociale et du Travail (MAST) du 28 août 1967. Le Moniteur No 84-A du 28 septembre 1967. Port-au-Prince.

López-Calva, L. F., & Lustig, N. (2010). *Declining inequality in Latin America: A decade of progress?* Brookings Institution Press.

López, J. (1998). *Derecho Colectivo del Trabajo*. Buenos Aires, Argentina: La Ley.

Lora, E. (2007). *The State of State Reform in Latin America*. Stanford University Press.

Luce, L. (2005). *The Case For International Labour Standards: A "Northern" Perspective.* IDS Working Paper 250. Institute of Development Studies.

Lukács, G. (1982). *Estética 1. La peculiaridad de lo estético*. Barcelona: Grijalbo.

Ma, Y. (2015). *Resolving conflicts between conservation and recreation in protected areas a comparative legal analysis of the United States and China* (PhD Dissertation). Erasmus University Rotterdam.

Majone, G. (1993). The European community between social policy and social regulation. *Journal of Common Market Studies*, *31*(2), 153–170. doi:10.1111/j.1468-5965.1993.tb00455.x

Marangoni, G. (2012). *Anos 1980, década perdida ou ganha?* Retrieved March 12, 2016 from http://www.ipea.gov.br/desafios/index.php?option=com_content&id=2759:catid=28&Itemid=23

Marcolino, A., Horie, L., Serrao, R. S., Peres, C. L., Roberto, D. O., & Oliveira, S. (n.d.). *Terceirização e Desenvolvimento- uma conta que não fecha*. Retrieved June 2, 2016 from http://www.cut.org.br/system/uploads/ck/files/Dossie-Terceirizacao-e-Desenvolvimento.pdf

Martorano, B. (2014a). *From Volatility to Stabilization: Cyclicality of Fiscal Policy in Latin America over the Last Decades*. Working Papers-Economics (WP07/2014), Universita' degli Studi di Firenze, Dipartimento di Scienze per l'Economia e l'Impresa.

Martorano, B. (2014b). *Pre-crisis Conditions and Government Policy Responses: Chile and Mexico during the Great Recession*. Innocenti Working Paper (2014-15), UNICEF Office of Research, Florence.

McGolgan, A. (2004). *Report on sexual harassment in the workplace in EU Member States*. Retrieved June 17, 2017, from http://www.justice.ie/en/JELR/SexualHrrsmtRpt.pdf/Files/SexualHrrsmtRpt.pdf

Messina, J., & Vallanti, G. (2007). Job Flow Dynamics and Firing Restrictions: Evidence from Europe. *Economic Journal (London)*, *117*(521), 279–301. doi:10.1111/j.1468-0297.2007.02057.x

Michelson, E., & Li, K. (2012). *Judicial performance without independence: the delivery of justice and political legitimacy in rural China*. Prepared for Workshop on Works-in-Progress on Chinese Law, Center for Chinese Legal Studies, Columbia Law School.

Millán, A., Millán, J. M., Román, C., & Van Stel, A. (2013). How does employment protection legislation influence hiring and firing decisions by the smallest firms? *Economics Letters*, *121*(3), 444–448. doi:10.1016/j.econlet.2013.09.021

Mirta Griselda and others v Sociedad Italiana de Beneficencia en Buenos Aires – Hospital Italiano s/dismissal. CSJ 1468/2011 (47-C), Recurso de Hecho de 19/02/2015.

Mitra, D., & Ural, B. P. (2008). Indian manufacturing: A slow sector in a rapidly growing economy. *The Journal of International Trade & Economic Development*, *17*(4), 525–559. doi:10.1080/09638190802250282

Mogalakwe, M., & Siphambe, H.K. (2013). *Review of Social Dialogue Status and Relevant Policies in Botswana and Assessment of Effectiveness of Trade Union Engagement in Policy Dialogue: Final Draft.* International Labour Organization (ILO).

Mogapaesi, T. (n.d.). *Sexual Harassment in the Workplace: Lessons for Botswana from a South African Perspective* (Unpublished Master's Dissertation). North-West University, Potchefstroom Campus.

Moreno-Brid, J. C., Garry, S., & Krozer, A. (2016). Minimum Wages and Inequality in Mexico: A Latin American Perspective. *Revista de Economía Mundial.* Retrieved from http://www.redalyc.org/articulo.oa?id=86647324006

Morgan, H. M., Černič, J. L., & Milligan, L. (2010). *Perspectives on power: an inter-disciplinary approach.* Cambridge, UK: Cambridge Scholars Publishing.

Mortensen, D. T., & Pissarides, C. A. (1999). Unemployment Responses to 'Skill-Based' Technology Shocks: The Role of Labor Market Policy. *Economic Journal (London), 109*(455), 242–265. doi:10.1111/1468-0297.00431

Motshegwa, B., & Tshukudu, T. T. (2012). Deep Rooted Conflicts and Industrial Relations Interface in Botswana. *Journal of Public Administration and Governance, 2*(3), 118–133. doi:10.5296/jpag.v2i3.2349

Moyano, D. (1868). *El trabajo.* Buenos Aires, Argentina: D.T.

Mpedi, L. G. (2014). *Understanding Unemployment Insurance Law.* Cape Town, South Africa: Juta.

Muller, L., & Berger, D. P. (2013). The Impact of a Country's Employment Protection Legislation on its Economic Prosperity. *International Journal of Humanities and Social Science, 3*(12), 1–13.

Muqtada, M. (2013). *Botswana: A national Employment policy: Revised draft.* Academic Press.

Mwatcha, M. P. (n.d.). *Botswana Labour Relations System: Lessons from 2011 Public Sector Strike* (Unpublished Master's Thesis). University of Witwatersrand, Johannesburg, South Africa.

Naghavi, A. (2007). Asymmetric Labor Markets, Southern Wages and the Location of Firms. *Review of Development Economics*, *11*(3), 463–481. doi:10.1111/j.1467-9361.2007.00355.x

Nicholas, J. (2012). *21st century China: Does civil society play a role in promoting reform in China?* Center for Democracy, Development and the Rule of Law Thesis.

Nicholson, P. J. (2002). Occupational health in the European Union. *Occupational Medicine*, *52*(2), 80–84. doi:10.1093/occmed/52.2.80 PMID:11967350

Nickell, S., Nunziata, L., & Ochel, W. (2005). Unemployment in the OECD Since the 1960s. What Do We Know? *Economic Journal (London)*, *115*(500), 1–27. doi:10.1111/j.1468-0297.2004.00958.x

Norton, A., Conway, T., & Foster, M. (2000). *Social protection concepts and approaches: implications for policy and practice in international development.* Working Paper 143, London Centre for Aid Public Expenditure, Overseas Development Institute (ODI).

OCDE. (2015). *Employment Outlook 2015.* Paris: Organización para la Cooperación y el Desarrollo Económicos. Retrieved from http://ifuturo.org/documentacion/Employment%20outlook%202015.pdf

OECD. (2006). *OECD Employment Outlook 2006.* OECD Publishing.

OECD. (2009). *OECD Review of Budgeting in Mexico 2009, Supplement 1.* Paris: OECD.

OECD. (2013). *OECD Employment Outlook 2013.* OECD Publishing.

OECD. (2014). *Les indicateurs de l'OCDE sur la protection de l'emploi.* Retrieved from http://www.oecd.org/fr/emploi/emp/lesindicateursdelocdesurlaprotectiondelemploi.htm

OECD. (2015). *OECD Economic Surveys.* OECD Publishing.

OECD. (2016). *Making the most of the minimum: statutory minimum wages, employment and poverty, Chapter 2, Employment Outlook 2016.* Retrieved from https://www.oecd.org/employment/emp/2080222.pdf

OECD. (2016). *OECD Employment Outlook 2016*. OECD Publishing.

Ofori-Ado, L. (n.d.). *Social Protection Landscape in Ghana*. Retrieved from www.interreseaux.org/IMG/pdf/presentation_SOCIAL_PROTECTION_LANDSCAPE_IN_GHANA.pdf

OIT. (2009). *Trabajo decente un mundo mejor comienza aquí. Notas sobre la crisis*. Retrieved from http://www.ilo.org/wcmsp5/groups/public/---americas/---ro-lima/documents/article/wcms_limd2_9_es.pdf

Olivier, M., & Govindjee, A. (2015). A critique of the Unemployment Insurance Amendment Bill, 2015. *Potchefstroom Electronic Law Journal*, *8*(7), 2739–2776.

Olivier, M., & Govindjee, A. (2017). Improving return to work and disability management in the developing world: Pointers emanating from international instruments, standards and guidelines. *Bulletin of Comparative Labour Relations*, *97*, 193–218.

Omilola, B., & Kaniki, S. (2014). *Social Protection in Africa: A Review of Potential Contribution and Impact on Poverty Reduction*. Study Report, UNDP. Retrieved from www.za.undp.org/content/dam/south_africa/docs/mdgs/SocialProtectioninAfrica-A Review of Potential Contribution.pdf

Organisation for Economic Co-operation and Development. (2015). *Labour force participation rate*. Retrieved June 17, 2017, from https://data.oecd.org/emp/labour-force-participation-rate.htm

Örücü, A. E. (2006). Methodology of Comparative Law. In J. M. Smits (Ed.), *Elgar encyclopedia of comparative law* (pp. 446–447). Cheltenham, UK: Edward Elgar Publishing. doi:10.4337/9781847200204.00047

Ostry, S., Alexandroff, A. S., & Gomez, R. (2003). China and the long march to global trade: the accession of China to the World Trade Organization. Psychology Press, 2003, 171-174.

Ourliac, B. (2017). *Comparaisons internationales des régimes d'assurance chômage: quels enseignements? Documents d'études, n°209, mai*. Paris: DARES.

Paes, B., Corseuil, C. H., & Gonzaga, G. (2015). *Labor market regulations and the demand for labor in brazil*. St. Louis, MO: Federal Reserve Bank of St Louis.

Paraire, X. (2015). Plus d'un tiers des CDI sont rompus avant un an. DARES Analyses, janvier, n°05, DARES.

Peerenboom, R. (2010). *Judicial independence in China: Lessons for global rule of law promotion*. Cambridge, UK: Cambridge University Press.

People's Congress. (2017). *The Government Working Report 2017*. Retrieved June 17, 2017, from http://www.gov.cn/zhuanti/2017lhzfgzbg/

Percival, R. V. (2013). The role of civil society in environmental governance in the United States and China. *Duke Environmental Law & Policy Forum*, *24*, 141.

Picart, C. (2014). Une rotation de la main-d'œuvre presque quintuplée en 30 ans: plus qu'un essor des formes particulières d'emploi, un profond changement de leur usage. In INSEE Références (Ed.), *Emplois et salaires, édition 2014* (pp. 29–46). Paris: INSEE.

Piketty, T. (2016). *Loi travail: un effroyable gâchis*. Retrieved June 28, 2017, from http://piketty.blog.lemonde.fr/2016/06/02/loi-travail-un-effroyable-gachis/

Pinheiro, P. S. (1991). *Estratégias da Ilusão: A revolução mundial e o Brasil (1922-1935)*. São Paulo, SP: Companhia das Letras.

Podetti, H. A. (1990). *Cambio social y adaptabilidad del Derecho del Trabajo*. Buenos Aires, Argentina: D.T.

Podetti, H. A., (1990). Cambio Social y Adaptabilidad del Derecho del Trabajo [Social Change and Adaptability from Labour Law]. *DdelT, L, 1990-B*, 2519-2526.

Poschke, M. (2009). Employment protection, firm selection, and growth. *Journal of Monetary Economics*, *56*(8), 1074–1085. doi:10.1016/j.jmoneco.2009.10.013

Powell, A. (2012). *The World of Forking Paths: Latin America and the Caribbean facing global economic risks*. Washington, DC: Inter-American Development Bank.

Pringle, T. E., & Frost, S. D. (2003). The absence of rigor and the failure of implementation: Occupational health and safety in China. *International Journal of Occupational and Environmental Health*, *9*(4), 309–316. doi:10.1179/oeh.2003.9.4.309 PMID:14664482

Priz, E., & Priz, S. M. (2010). *Worker's compensation: a field guide for employers*. Charleston, SC: Book Surge Publishing.

Ramírez Bosco, L., & Rodríguez Mancini, J. (2007). *Ley de Contrato de trabajo*. Buenos Aires, Argentina: La Ley.

Rangel Delgado, J. E., & Ivanova Boncheva, A. (2012). *The Crisis in two Pacific Rim Economies: Higher Eduation and Employment in Mexico and Thailand*. Southampton, UK: Witpress.

Republic of Botswana. (2013). *Mid-Term Review of NDP 10*. Gaborone: Government Printers.

Robalino, D. A., Newhouse, D., & Rother, F. (2014). Labor and Social Protection Policies during the Crisis and the Recovery. In A. Banerji, D. Newhouse, P. Paci, & D. Robalino (Eds.), *Working through the Crisis: Jobs and Policies in Developing Countries during the Great Recession*. Washington, DC: World Bank.

Rodríguez Mancini, J. (1990). *La negociación colectiva*. Buenos Aires, Argentina: Astrea.

Rodrik, D. (1996). Labor Standards in International Trade: Do They Matter and What Do We Do About Them? In R. Lawrence, D. Rodrik, & J. Whalley (Eds.), *Emerging Agenda for Global Trade: High Stakes for Developing Countries*. Washington, DC: Overseas Development Council.

Rohregger, B. (2010). Social Protection and Governance. Discussion Papers on Social Protection. Deutsche Gesellschaft fur Technische Zusammenarbeit (GTZ) GmBH German Technical Cooperation.

Romagnoli, U. (2008). Sobre el despido o la violencia del poder privado. In *Revista de Derecho Social Latino América* (Vol. 4-5, p. 9). Buenos Aires: Editorial Bomarzo.

Ros, J. (2011). The Economic Crisis of 2008–09 and Development Strategy: the Mexican Case. In M. Haddad & B. Shepherd (Eds.), *Managing Openness: Trade and outward-oriented growth after the crisis*. Washington, DC: World Bank. doi:10.1596/9780821386316_CH14

Rousseau, J. J. (1998). *Julie ou La Nouvelle Heloise*. Paris: Preface Dialoguée.

Rubery, J. (2011). Towards a gendering of the labor market regulation debate. *Cambridge Journal of Economics*, *35*(6), 1103–1126. doi:10.1093/cje/ber001

Sabel, C. F., & Zeitlin, J. (2008). Learning from difference: The new architecture of experimentalist governance in the EU. *European Law Journal*, *14*(3), 271–327. doi:10.1111/j.1468-0386.2008.00415.x

Sachs, J. D., & Warner, A. M. (1997). Sources of Slow Growth in African Economies1. *Journal of African Economies*, *6*(3), 335–376. doi:10.1093/oxfordjournals.jae.a020932

Sadurski, W., Czarnota, A., & Krygier, M. (2006). *Spreading democracy and the rule of law?: the impact of EU enlargement for the rule of law, democracy and constitutionalism in post-communist legal orders*. Dordrecht: Springer Science & Business Media. doi:10.1007/1-4020-3842-9

Saint-Paul, G. (1996). *Dual Labor Markets: A Macroeconomic Perspective*. Cambridge, MA: MIT Press.

Saint-Paul, G. (1997). Is labor rigidity harming Europe's competitiveness? The effect of job protection on the pattern of trade and welfare. *European Economic Review*, *41*(3–5), 499–506. doi:10.1016/S0014-2921(97)00017-2

Saint-Paul, G. (2002). Employment protection, international specialization, and innovation. *European Economic Review*, *46*(2), 375–395. doi:10.1016/S0014-2921(01)00093-9

Samaniego, R. M. (2006). Employment protection and high-tech aversion. *Review of Economic Dynamics*, *9*(2), 224–241. doi:10.1016/j.red.2005.10.002

Sandoval Malori, S., & Straulino-Rodríguez, P. (2016). 2017 Increase to Daily Minimum Wage for Mexico. *Ogletree Deakins*. Retrieved from https://ogletree.com/shared-content/content/blog/2016/december/2017-increase-to-daily-minimum-wage-for-mexico?utm_source=Mondaq&utm_medium=syndication&utm_campaign=View-Original

Santiago Reyes, M. (2011). Los salarios en México. *Análisis Político*. Retrieved from http://library.fes.de/pdf-files/bueros/mexiko/08742.pd

Sauze, D. (2005). Stabilité de l'emploi: conquête sociale ou politiques patronales? *Travail et Emploi*, *103*, 113-122.

Schivardi, F. (2000). Labor Market Rigidities, Unemployment and Growth. *Giornale degli Economisti e Annali di Economia*, 115–141.

SDOIA. (2016). *Investment Climate Statement Mexico-Labor. US Embassies Abroad*. Retrieved from https://www.export.gov/article?id=Mexico-Labor

Shapiro, C., & Stiglitz, J. E. (1984). Equilibrium Unemployment as a Worker Discipline Device. *The American Economic Review*, *74*(3), 433.

Sharma, A.N. (2006). Flexibility, Employment and Labor Market Reforms in India. *Economic and Political Weekly, 41*, 2078-86.

Shyam Sundar, K.R. (2005). Labor Flexibility Debate in India: A Comprehensive Review and Some Suggestions. *Economic and Political Weekly, 40*, 2274-85.

Sigot, J.-C., & Vero, J. (2014). Politiques d'entreprise et sécurisation des parcours: un lien à explorer. *Bref du Céreq, 318*.

Siphambe, H. K. (2003). Understanding Unemployment in Botswana. *The South African Journal of Economics*, *71*(3), 480–495. doi:10.1111/j.1813-6982.2003.tb00082.x

Siqueira, G. S. (n.d.). *Anamatra ingress no STF contra cortes no orçamento da Justiça do Trabalho*. Retrieved April 1, 2016 from http://www.trt7.jus.br/index.php?option=com_content&view=article&id=2805:anamatra-ingressa-no-stf-contra-cortes-no-orcamento-da-justica-do-trabalho&catid=152&Itemid=302

Smith, B., Brecher, J., & Costello, T. (2006). Multinationals to China: No New Labor Rights. *Multinational Monitor*, *27*(6), 34–37.

Smith, J. C. (2000). Nominal Wage Rigidity in the United Kingdom. *Economic Journal (London)*, *110*(462), C176–C195. doi:10.1111/1468-0297.00528

Sofi, I. A., & Sharma, P. (2015). Does Employment Protection Legislation Matter in Dualistic Labor Market? Panel Evidence from Indian Manufacturing Sector. *Labor Studies Journal*, *40*(2), 149–168. doi:10.1177/0160449X15587829

Solidar. (2010). *Domestic Workers' Rights- Botswana*. Retrieved July, 24, 2017 from http://www.solidar.all2all.org/IMG/pdf/b5_2010_domestic_workers_report_botswana.pdf

Song, Z., Storesletten, K., & Zilibotti, F. (2011). Growing Like China. *The American Economic Review*, *101*(1), 196–233. doi:10.1257/aer.101.1.196

Sotubo, J. (2015). *$400bn oil money stolen since independence-UK firm*. Retrieved from www.pulse.ng/news/business/in-nigeria-400bn-oil-money-stolen-since-independence-uk-firm-id3745342.html

Statistics Botswana. (2013). *Botswana Core Welfare Indicators Survey 2009/10*. Gaborone: Statistics Botswana.

Statistics Botswana. (2016). *Selected Statistical Indicators 1966-2016*. Gaborone: Statistics Botswana.

Statistics South Africa. (2014). *Survey of Employers and the Self-employed 2013*. Retrieved June 8, 2017 from www.statssa.gov.za/publications/P0276/P02762013.pdf

Statistics South Africa. (2017). *Quarterly Labour Force Survey: Quarter 1*. Retrieved June 8, 2017 from www.statssa.gov.za/publications/{0211/P02111stQuarter2017.pdf

Supiot, A. (2007). *Homo Juridicus, un ensayo sobre la función antropológica del derecho*. Buenos Aires, Argentina: Siglo XXI Editores Argentina S.A.

Su, Z. (2003). Occupational health and safety legislation and implementation in China. *International Journal of Occupational and Environmental Health*, *9*(4), 302–308. doi:10.1179/oeh.2003.9.4.302 PMID:14664481

Taylor, I. (2003). As Good as it gets? Botswana's Democratic Development. *Journal of Contemporary African Studies*, *21*(2), 215–231. doi:10.1080/02589000305446

The Constitution of the Republic of South Africa, 1996

The Economist. (2015). *Yuan for all*. Retrieved June 17, 2017, from http://www.economist.com/news/leaders/21641203-chinas-loans-foundering-governments-may-seem-challenge-imf-biggest-risks-are

The News. (2016). *Buhari formally launches N500b Social Protection Programme*. Retrieved from http://thenewsnigeria.com/2016/05/buhari-formally-lauanches-n500b-social-protection- programme/

Tirole, J. (2016). *Economie du Bien commun*. Paris: PUF.

Tissembaum, M. R. (1958). *La reforma constitucional de 1957. Las disposiciones de Derecho del Trabajo y de la Seguridad Social.* Buenos Aires, Argentina: D.T.

UN. (2015). *Sustainable Development Goals.* Retrieved from https://sustainabledevelopment.un.org/?menu=1300

UNAM. (2009). *Los Sindicatos en México*. UNAM.

Unedic. (2016). La majorité des embauches en contrats courts se font chez un ancien employeur. *Eclairages – Études & Analyses, 14.*

Unemployment Insurance Act, 2001 (Act 63 of 2001)

United States International Trade Administration. (n.d.). Retrieved from https://www.export.gov/article?id=Haiti-Apparel

Valencia Lomelí, E., Foust Rodríguez, D., & Tetreault Weber, D. (2013). *Sistemas de protección social en América Latina y el Caribe*. ECLAC, Santiago de Chile.

van Ginneken, W. (Ed.). (1999). Social Security for the Excluded Majority. Case Studies of Developing Countries. Geneva: International Labour Office (ILO).

van Schaik, T., & van de Klundert, T. (2013). Employment protection legislation and catching-up. *Applied Economics*, *45*(8), 973–981. doi:10.1080/00036846.2011.613784

Vázquez Vialard, A. (1991). *Cincuenta años en la evolución del Derecho del Trabajo Argentino*. Buenos Aires, Argentina: Academia Nacional de Derecho y Ciencias Sociales.

Viana, M. T., Delgado, G. N., & Amorim, H. S. (2011). Terceirização- aspectos gerais. A última decisão do STF e a Súmula 331 do TST. Novos enfoques. Revista TST, 77(1), 54-84.

Villafranco, G. (2014, August). 7 riesgos mortales para la operación de una Pyme. *Forbes.*

Vlagopoulou, M. (2017). *Psychological harassment in the workplace ("mobbing") in Greece and its legal implications*. Retrieved June 17, 2017, from http://www.globalhrlaw.com/resources/psychological-harassment-in-the-workplace-mobbing-in-greece-and-its-legal-implications

Walby, S. (1999). The new regulatory state: The social powers of the European Union. *The British Journal of Sociology*, *50*(1), 118–140. doi:10.1080/000713199358842 PMID:15266677

Wang, G., & Zheng, Y. (2013). *China: development and governance*. Singapore: World Scientific.

Wang, Z. (2007). *Improving the economic growth model*. Beijing: Social Sciences Academic Press.

World Bank Group. (2016). *Doing Business 2017: Equal Opportunity for All*. Washington, DC: World Bank.

World Bank. (2004). Retrieved from http://wbln0018.worldbanl.org/HDNet/hddocs.nsf/c207c7f854bd0a098525660b007a272d/fb93d792069e704e8525681900d7bc?OpenDocument

World Bank. (2007). Armenia – Labor Market Dynamics: Volume 2. Human Development Sector Unit. Europe and Central Asia Region Report, 35361-AM. Washington, DC: World Bank.

World Bank. (2008c). *Enterprise Survey*. Washington, DC: The World Bank.

World Bank. (2016). *Labor force participation rate*. Retrieved June 17, 2017, from http://data.worldbank.org/indicator/SL.TLF.CACT.ZS

World Bank. (2017). *GDP growth*. Retrieved June 17, 2017, http://data.worldbank.org/indicator/NY.GDP.MKTP.KD.ZG

Wu, F., & Chi, Y. (2015). Regulatory system reform of occupational health and safety in China. *Industrial Health*, *53*(3), 300–306. doi:10.2486/indhealth.2014-0119 PMID:25843565

Yan, P. (2015). What did China's labor contract law do to its private manufacturing firms? *China Economic Journal*, *8*(2), 158–171. doi:10.1080/17538963.2015.1070492

Yu, H. (2013). Jiajn Li's argument that "laws are not well executed or strictly executed although they are well enacted" undermines the law's credibility. *China Renda Journal*, *24*(05), 48–52.

Yu, Y. (2007). The role of future of civil society in transitional China. *Polish Perspectives*, *12*(1), 15–18.

Zanini, P. J. (1990). Reflexiones acerca de la necesidad de la modernización integral del Derecho Laboral. Buenos Aires, Argentina: D.T.

Zhang, Z., Zhang, M., & Xie, S. (2010). The research on the possibilities of integrating the occupational safety and health law. *China Information Technology*, *10*(8), 263–264.

Zhao, J., Tu, E. J., McMurray, C., & Sleigh, A. (2012). Rising mortality from injury in urban China: Demographic burden, underlying causes and policy implications. *Bulletin of the World Health Organization*, *90*(06), 461–467. doi:10.2471/BLT.11.093849 PMID:22690036

Zhao, L., & Lim, T. S. (2010). *China's new social policy: initiatives for a harmonious society*. Singapore: World Scientific.

Zhou, J. (2010). *China's peaceful rise in a global context: a domestic aspect of China's road map to democratization*. Lanham, MD: Lexington Books.

Zhou, Y. (2010). *Occupational safety and health law*. Beijing: Higher Education Press.

Zong, L., Zhang, Z., Zhang, M., & Xie, S. (2011). The research on the integration of occupational safety and health law in china. *Journal of Xi'an Shiyou University*, *23*(1), 32–34.

About the Contributors

Samir Amine is a full-professor of economics at the department of labor and industrial relations at the Université du Québec en Outaouais in Canada. He is also director of the Research Center for Public Policy Evaluation and Fellow at The Interuniversity Center of Public Policies (CIRANO). Labor economics specialist, his work focuses on the evaluation of public policies and on the development of income inequalities. His research has been funded by the Quebec Fund for Research on Society and Culture (FQRSC) and by The Social Sciences and Humanities Research Council of Canada (SSHRC).

* * *

Moses Adebisi has been a sociology teacher for around twenty-five years at the University of Ilorin, Ilorin, Nigeria. In 2007, he was a visiting lecturer at the Ibrahim Babangida University, Lapai, Niger State, Nigeria. He has traveled widely in Nigeria, Africa, and Europe for one academic engagement or the order, especially for international conferences. His teaching and research experience are in the field of industrial sociology/industrial relations, development and globalization, social research and psychology (industrial and social) and general sociology, especially sociological theory. He is happily married with children.

Hervé Charmettant works at the Deparment of Economics, University of Grenoble-Alpes, since 2010. He teaches labor economics and theory of organizations up to the postgraduate level. He is responsible for training in first year of economics-management. His research focuses on contemporary developments in the employment relationship. He specialized in the study of Labor-Managed Firms (LMF) and leads an interdisciplinary team of researchers in a research program funded by the French national research agency.

Andrea Franconi is an Argentinean Labour Law Especialist, who graduated with Honors from Law School of Buenos Aires University and has a Diplomature in Individual and Collective Labour Relations. She is currently finishing her final thesis for her Master Degree in International Labour Standards and Relations. Dr. Franconi has been a faculty member at the Law School of Buenos Aires University since 2009, teaching different areas of Labour Law and its general theory. She is the Chief of Labour Regulation in a public agency and is a permanent member of the collective bargaining committee. The author has been a keynote speaker in a number of national and international conferences and seminars, on the subjet of workers rights and labour law legislation. She is a member of the Argentinean Delegation of Young Jurist Section of the International Society for Labour and Social Security Law.

Antonina Ivanova is professor and senior researcher at the Department of Economics of the Autonomous University of Southern Baja California, Mexico and Director of the APEC Studies Center of the State of Southern Baja California. She is member of the National System of Researchers of Mexico (SNI II). Since 2002 she is member of the Intergovernmental Panel on Climate Change (IPCC), and for the period 2008-2015 was part of the IPCC Bureau as Vice-chair of Working Group III "Mitigation of Climate Change". She holds Master in Economic Journalism from the University of International Economics, Bulgaria and the Institute for European Integration, Belgium; PhD in Economics from the National Autonomous University of Mexico (Cum Laude); and Postdoctoral Degree in Peace Studies from the University of Bradford, UK. Her research focuses on international cooperation, climate change and sustainable development, and has appeared in outlets such as Journal of Social Science, Global Economy, Energy Efficiency Journal, Asia-Pacific Business, Current Urban Studies, Modern Economy and International Journal on Sustainable Development and Planning. She participated as Lead Author in the Fourth Assessment Report (AR4) of the IPCC (Peace Nobel Price Award, 2007), and as Review Editor in the Special Report on Renewable Energies and Climate Change Mitigation (SRREN) and in the Fifth Assessment Report (AR5) of the IPCC. Dr. Ivanova is author and/or editor of 23 books, more than 200 peer-reviewed articles, and has been invited as visiting professor at the San Diego State University, the University of Northridge, California, the University of Bradford and University of Leeds, UK, the University of Tottory, Japan and the Institute of Economics of the Bulgarian Academy of Sciences.

Mavis Kolobe is a lecturer in the department of Economics at the University of Botswana, a post she has held for 3 years. She joined the university in 2012, as a Staff Development Fellow (SDF) in the department of economics. Her research mainly focuses in labour issues and public sector economics. Her areas of teaching specialization are public sector economic and quantitative methods. She is currently a co-editor of the Botswana Journal of Economics and the mentor of the University of Botswana Economics Society (UBES). UBES is a student led organisation, whose mandate is to bridge the gap between theory and practice as well as to raise economic and financial literacy in the UB community and beyond.

Kai Liu was born in Xuzhou, China on October 12, 1984. Before studying in the Netherlands, Kai obtained bachelor degree in law and as master in occupational safety and health law in China. For almost two years, Kai studied law in Erasmus University Rotterdam and he has been working in Utrecht University since September 2013, and is under co-supervision by Prof. Frans Pennings and Prof. Teun Jasper. Kai's academic focus is centered on comparative study of the Chinese occupational health and safety law and the European Union legal regime. Meanwhile, he is a member of School of Human Rights Research, an inter-university alliance of universities and research institutes – a joint effort of the School of Law and the Faculty of the Humanities of Utrecht University, and the Faculties of Law of Maastricht University, Erasmus University Rotterdam, Tilburg University and Leiden University. From May 1st to June 15, 2015, he was visiting scholar in Nanjing University, China. In addition, he is contributor to United Nation's LEGOSH database (Global Database On National Occupational Safety And Health Legislation), since September 2015. Frome March 14 to April 12, 2016, he was a visiting scholar in Lund University, Sweden. From 21 November 2016 to 20 May 2017, he is also a visiting researcher in the School of Law of Erasmus University Rotterdam. He is going to defend his dissertation on 1 December 2017.

José Ernesto Rangel Delgado holds a Russian Academy of Science Ph.D in Economics (1991). He is a Mexican Ministry of Education certified professor (Perfil PRODEP, in Spanish words); member of the Researchers National System (SNI I, in Spanish words). He is full time professor and senior researcher of the Faculty of Economics at the University of Colima. Dr. Rangel has been participated in national and international conferences, presenting more than 100 papers, author/coauthored 44 peer-reviewed articles; 15 books, and 32 book chapters related to human resource development and higher education and employment policies in the Pacific Basin region. He was guarded by the Korea Foundation fellowship (2010); was visiting professor at the Autonomous University of Baja California Sur, in the Graduate Program of Sustainable Development and Globalization Economics Department (2013) and was nominated by Mexican and Australian Governments to the APEC Labor Mobility Framework (Vietnam, 2017). Dr. José Ernesto Rangel Delgado is director of the Pacific Basin Studies Center and APEC Studies Center of the University of Colima (2001--). He was president of the Pacific Circle Consortium (2007-2009), getting the Honorary Membership in 2013; was twice Technical Secretary of the Mexican APEC Studies Centers Consortium (2009-2011) (2014-2017); and was Director of the Faculty of Economics (1986-2000), and coordinator of the PhD program degree in Transpacific Relations of the University of Colima, Mexico (2001-2016).

Wilner Predelus is a Ph.D. Candidate in Applied Social Science at the Université du Québec en Outaouais. He holds a diploma in law from the Université d'État d'Haïti and a masters in Economics from the Université du Québec à Montréal. He works as Senior Economist at the Government of Canada and lectures Economics at the Université du Québec en Outaouais.

Happy Siphambe is a Professor of Economics at the University of Botswana. He lectures and researches in the area of labour market, economics of education and economic impact of HIV/AIDS. He has served in the Board of Bank of Botswana (Central Bank) for 10 years, and Public Enterprises Evaluation and Privatisation Agency (PEEPA) for 8 years. He also served as Head of Department and Dean of the faculty of Social Sciences at UB and is currently the Managing Editor of the Botswana Journal of Economics- an international journal under the Botswana Economics Association. He has published more than 20 journal articles, a book and many book chapters covering the areas of labour economics and development economics.

Roberta Sivolella is a Labor Judge at Rio de Janeiro, currently working as auxiliary judge of the Assistant judge of the minister vice president of the Superior Labor Court ; Member of the IPEATRA- Institute for Research and Advanced Studies of the Magistracy and the Labor Public Ministry; Member representing Brazil in Cielo Laboral- Community for research and labor and occupational study (Europe); Collaborator of Adapt-International (Association for International and Comparative Studies in Labor and Industrial relations), representing Latin America; Graduated in Law from the University of the State of Rio de Janeiro - UERJ; Master's degree

/ Doctorate in Social Rights from the Universidad Castilla la Mancha - UCLM / Spain, including obtaining the D.E.A (Diploma of Advanced Studies) in recognition of the investigative sufficiency of the presented thesis; Specialist in Labor and Material Law at Gama Filho University; Director of Press and Communication of the Association of Labor Magistrates of the 1st Region - Amatra-1 in the 2014/2015 biennium and Director of Human Rights of the same Association in the biennium 2015/2016; Professor of Labor Procedure Law and Collective Law of AVM - Faculdades Integradas / Cândido Mendes University; Professor of Judicial Ethics and Judgment Office of the Judicial School of the Regional Labor Court of the 1st Region; Professor of Labor Procedure Law and Training Course for Judge Assistants at "Toga Estudos Jurídico."

Index

Q

R

S

T

U

V

www.ingramcontent.com/pod-product-compliance
Lightning Source LLC
LaVergne TN
LVHW081334300926
849161LV00008B/1969
9781522541349